Collected essays

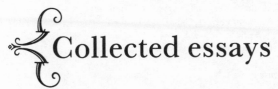

Collected essays

Volume 3
The novel of religious controversy

Q. D. LEAVIS

COLLECTED AND
EDITED BY G. SINGH

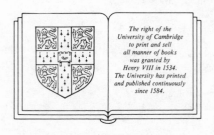

The right of the
University of Cambridge
to print and sell
all manner of books
was granted by
Henry VIII in 1534.
The University has printed
and published continuously
since 1584.

CAMBRIDGE UNIVERSITY PRESS

CAMBRIDGE
NEW YORK   NEW ROCHELLE
MELBOURNE   SYDNEY

Published by the Press Syndicate of the University of Cambridge
The Pitt Building, Trumpington Street, Cambridge CB2 1RP
32 East 57th Street, New York, NY 10022, USA
10 Stamford Road, Oakleigh, Melbourne 3166, Australia

First published 1989

Printed in Great Britain at
the University Press, Cambridge

British Library cataloguing in publication data

Leavis, Q. D. (Queenie Dorothy)
Collected essays.
Vol. 3: The novel of religious controversy.
1. Fiction in European languages, 1800–1900
Forms: Novels – Critical studies
I. Title II. Singh, G. (Ghan), *1926–*
809.3

Library of Congress cataloguing in publication data

Leavis, Q. D. (Queenie Dorothy)
Collected essays.
Includes bibliographical references.
Contents: v. 1. The Englishness of the English
novel – v. 2. The American novel and reflections on the
European novel – v. 3. The novel of religious
controversy.
1. Fiction – History and criticism – Addresses,
essays, lectures. 2. English fiction – History and
criticism – Addresses, essays, lectures. 3. American
fiction – History and criticism – Addresses, essays,
lectures. I. Singh, G. II. Title.
PN3491.L34   1983   823'.009   83–1978

ISBN 0 521 25417 5 hard covers (vol. 1)
ISBN 0 521 27677 2 paperback (vol. 1)

ISBN 0 521 26702 1 hard covers (vol. 2)
ISBN 0 521 31825 4 paperback (vol. 2)

ISBN 0 521 26703 X (vol. 3)

Contents

Sources and acknowledgements   *page* vii

Editor's introduction   1
Mrs Inchbald: *A Simple Story*   5
'That great controversy': the novel of religious
   controversy in the nineteenth century   12
The Anglo-Irish novel   61
Appendix: Notes on some Anglo-Irish novels   82
Women writers of the nineteenth century   99
The development of character in George Eliot's novels   122
Appendix: George Eliot and the novel of religious
   controversy   130
Mrs Oliphant: *Miss Marjoribanks* (Introduction)   135
Mrs Oliphant: *The Autobiography and Letters*
   (Introduction)   159
Trollope and Evangelicalism   182
Howard Sturgis: *Belchamber*   191
Literary values and the novel   196
Leslie Stephen: Cambridge critic   216
Professor Chadwick and English studies   227
Reviews   234
   Charlotte Yonge and 'Christian discrimination'   234
   Hardy and criticism   245
   Lives and works of Richard Jefferies   254
   Gissing and the English novel   264
   George Gissing: *Born in Exile*   272
   E. M. Forster: *Abinger Harvest*   276
   Dorothy Richardson: *Clear Horizon*   281
   The literary life respectable: 1. Edwin Muir;
      2. George Orwell   283

v

Academic case-history   290
Aldous Huxley: *Eyeless in Gaza*   296
The case of Miss Dorothy Sayers   300
'Femina vie-heureuse' please note   307
The background of twentieth-century letters   312
Lady novelists and the lower orders   318

Notes   337

Sources and acknowledgments

Q. D. Leavis's Introductions to Mrs Margaret Oliphant's *Miss Marjoribanks* (Chatto and Windus) and *Autobiography and Letters* (ed. Mrs Harry Coghill, Leicester University Press) appeared in 1969 and 1974 respectively; 'Leslie Stephen: Cambridge critic', 'Professor Chadwick and English studies' and the reviews 'Charlotte Yonge and "Christian discrimination"', 'Hardy and criticism', 'Lives and works of Richard Jefferies', 'Gissing and the English novel', 'Dorothy Richardson: *Clear Horizon*', 'E. M. Forster: *Abinger Harvest*', 'The literary life respectable, 1. Edwin Muir; 2. George Orwell', 'Academic case-history', 'Aldous Huxley: *Eyeless in Gaza*', 'The case of Miss Dorothy Sayers', '"Femina vie-heureuse" please note', 'Lady novelists and the lower orders' and 'The background of twentieth-century letters' all appeared in *Scrutiny* (vols. XIV, VII, XII, XI, VI, VII, IX, V, IX, XI, V, VI, VII, IV and VII respectively).

The remaining material – which it is not possible to date but which was mostly written in the last ten or so years of her life – including the texts of two public lectures ('The Anglo-Irish novel' given at Queen's University, Belfast in 1980 and ' "That great controversy": the novel of religious controversy in the nineteenth century' given in the same year to the theology faculty of Bristol University) is published for the first time.

Editor's introduction

The bulk of this volume – eight out of eleven chapters – consists of essays published for the first time. They are essays that Q. D. Leavis had been working on in the last few years of her life. Many of them had not been completed for publication when she died; some are only drafts. In the last years she was busy tackling a number of themes – themes to which she was drawn by virtue of her absorbing interest in the Victorian novel, and to which, after *Scrutiny* had ceased publication, she could devote more of her time and research. What particularly interested her is what she considered to be the 'neglected aspects' of the Victorian novel – such as the novel of religious controversy (which is the longest chapter in the volume), the Anglo-Irish novel, the women writers of the nineteenth century and certain aspects of George Eliot's work. These themes afforded Q. D. Leavis a wide scope for exercising her powers both as a literary historian and as a critic with a sociological approach to literature. Such an approach brought within the purview of her analytically inquisitive eye such data as 'social attitudes, instinctive behaviour, physical appearance and health, style of speech, way of living, dress, deportment, emotional habits – the whole idiom of life'. Hence on what was, in *Scrutiny* days, a new and pioneering approach to the novel, Q. D. Leavis brought to bear a vast and varied reading, an extraordinary critical acumen, and a vivaciously lucid and vigorous style. This volume is therefore an eloquent testimony to her triple distinction – a critic of the novel, a cultural and sociological historian, and a reviewer, all at their most mature and impressive.

In her essay on the novel of what Mrs Humphry Ward called 'that great controversy', between Protestantism and

Catholicism, Q. D. Leavis cogently demonstrates how practically all Victorian novelists, major and minor, were very much alive to and more or less directly involved in the religious topics and controversies of the day, how they responded to them, and what impact their response and involvement had on their writings. She cites contemporary theologians, divines, politicians and intellectuals as well as the novelists and writers themselves. For instance, she points out how the novels of Mrs Gaskell, Mrs Oliphant and Charlotte Yonge deal with what was regarded in the Victorian age as 'the curious helplessness in the face of Catholicism', the 'deep-down feeling of the pull of Catholicism against all reason and English habit' – a subject Q. D. Leavis considered peculiarly suited for the novelist, for it can only be treated 'outside the field of controversy, by a sympathetic study of feelings and impulses and early environment'.

As to the religious situation in Victorian Ireland, Q. D. Leavis found it 'simpler but certainly not less impassioned, since politics and class were in that unhappy country inevitably mixed up with the Catholic–Protestant dualism'; and the literature of religious controversy was, therefore, 'more clear-cut and so more spirited, and, on the Roman Catholic side, much bitterer than in England'. This accounts for 'livelier, if not better' novels in Ireland, which, she thought, were of considerable interest to the student of social history, and also to the student of literature because of the Anglo-Irish idiom and vocabulary. In fact some of Q. D. Leavis's most penetrating criticism is to be found in the chapter on the Anglo-Irish novel, where her composite interests and approaches (sociological, historical and literary) combine to offer her an ideal context and platform. But underlying and giving direction to all these interests and approaches was Q. D. Leavis's overriding concern – viz. that of critically weighing and assessing the literary and artistic worth of the Anglo-Irish novels and distinguishing a work of art from 'a merely ephemeral novel'.

One of the plans Q. D. Leavis had in mind for some years before her death was to write a book on the women writers of the nineteenth century. The essay included in this volume, 'Women writers of the nineteenth century', outlines, with some illuminating autobiographical glimpses and reflections, what that plan, had it materialized, would have amounted to. The essays on Jane Austen, George Eliot and the Brontë sisters (included in *The Englishness of the English Novel*) were to have been the backbone of the book. In her two essays on Mrs Oliphant included here – *'Miss Marjoribanks'* and *'Autobiography'* – Q. D. Leavis assigns to Mrs Oliphant the role of bridging the gap between Jane Austen and George Eliot; and argues how Lucilla, the protagonist of *Miss Marjoribanks*, is 'a triumphant intermediary between Emma and Dorothea, and, incidentally, more entertaining, more impressive and more likeable than either'.

'The development of character in George Eliot's novels' and 'Literary values and the novel' are both texts of talks Q. D. Leavis gave in the seventies at various grammar schools. Hence they are expository in intention and character. And yet there are valuable critical insights offered in the course of these talks that justify their inclusion in this volume. Tracing George Eliot's interest in religious sects – as elaborated in the appendix 'George Eliot and the novel of religious controversy' – as something deep-rooted in her own religious history, Q. D. Leavis argues how, under Wordsworth's influence, she managed to retain 'religious feelings without a theological orthodoxy', and combined 'the Wordsworthian religion of nature with compassion for all, particularly . . . those ill-used by nature and society'. As to the relation between George Eliot and 'the necessary public taste for and ability to appreciate the serious novel', it was, Q. D. Leavis points out, Dickens who created a serious reading public for the novel which George Eliot, as a late starter, inherited. Another important thing she inherited was Shakespeare's use of an art form in prose which would be the 'equivalent of the great dramatic art in verse'.

In 'Literary values and the novel' Q. D. Leavis distinguishes between a novel that comes direct from the raw material of a novelist's own life, so that it is 'only a piece of autobiography' and has 'no real form, no objectivity, no general application, and cannot offer value judgements'; and a novel that possesses all these qualities. She refers to Wordsworth's view on Burns's less decorous poems, and points out how, even though they have no moral intention, they have a moral effect, and points out how this is true of all good literature, for no artist can create in a moral vacuum or 'shut out from his works the values he lives by'. She quotes with whole-hearted approval Henry James's view that the value of a work of art is determined by the quality of the mind of the writer.

Q. D. Leavis's early essay 'Leslie Stephen: Cambridge critic', more than any other in this volume, while summing up the ethos and quality of Stephen's criticism and critical outlook, sums up also that of Q. D. Leavis's own criticism. In fact, Stephen was an important formative influence on Q. D. Leavis – especially with regard to her notion of literature as 'a product of the interplay between the writer and the reader, a collaboration between them'. The essay therefore embodies not only the ethos of Stephen's criticism and critical outlook, but also that of Q. D. Leavis herself.

One – perhaps the most telling – way through which *Scrutiny* made its immediate impact was in the severity of its reviews, Q. D. Leavis's own reviews, so trenchant and drastic, offered penetrating analyses of and first-hand evaluative judgements on what was under review. Not only was a review by her an exercise in literary criticism of the first order, but it also epitomized the *Scrutiny* ethos as well as the aims and directions of modern criticism. A model of the most exacting kind of critical criteria disinterestedly applied, her best reviews still have an edge, a vitality and a relevance which some of the books and authors she reviewed have lost, and one still goes to them, as she herself said of Jane Austen's novels, 'to be alerted and braced'.

G. SINGH

Mrs Inchbald:
A Simple Story

Mrs Inchbald (born 1753) came of a Catholic family, married a co-religionist, and in later life became devout. Yet her novel (sketched in 1777, written in 1790) is not propaganda, for she holds the balance fairly and evenly between her Protestant heroine, the lovely and vivacious Miss Milner, and her dignified guardian, a Catholic priest, Dorriforth. And though after true love has eventually conquered their religious disparity the marriage breaks down, this is on usual novelistic grounds (years of absence of the husband leading to the wife's seduction by a former suitor) and is not explicitly laid at the door of Protestantism, as it easily might have been. After the consequent separation, the erring cast-off wife is shown repentant and, tended in her loneliness by her husband's director who comforts (but not converts) her before her death, she even compares favourably with Dorriforth, whose domestic disaster has made him now turn to his religion for consolation but rendered him arbitrary, implacable, and tyrannical. *A Simple Story* is thus a powerful novel of considerable merit as a work of art. One cannot help reflecting that if written after the first quarter of the next century it would have been very different, and unlikely to have been a work of art in any case.

The opening sentence of this novel is remarkable in its eighteenth-century version of Roman Catholicism, where even in a priest the religion is subordinated to the eighteenth-century philosophic idea of virtue:

Dorriforth, bred at St Omer's in all the scholastic rigour of that college, was, by education, and the solemn vows of his order, a Roman Catholic priest – but nicely discriminating between the philosophical and the superstitious part of that character, and adopting the former only, he possessed qualities not unworthy of the first professors of Christianity . . . He refused to shelter himself from the temptations of the layman by the walls of a cloister, but sought for, and found that shelter in the centre of London, where he dwelt, in his own prudence, justice, fortitude and temperance.

No doubt the 'superstitious' was in deference to a Protestant readership, this being the eighteenth century, when 'super-stition' was the ground for rejecting Roman Catholicism; and the assurance that it was possible to be a Catholic and more-over a priest, without subscribing to what for Protestants was the objectionable aspect of that religion, was defensive. Mr Milner, an old friend of the younger Dorriforth, was also a Catholic, but 'on his marriage with a lady of Protestant tenets, they mutually agreed their sons should be educated in the religious opinion of their father, and the daughters in that of their mother'. This curious compromise was not invented for fictional purposes; there is a great deal of evidence both in fiction and fact for its being a custom in different countries until the later nineteenth century; and in Germany it was a legal enactment, where, as George Eliot discovered to her surprise, it worked well.

Thus Dorriforth at thirty, when Mr Milner has died leaving him guardian to his daughter, finds himself obliged to receive as inmate into the house where he resides with a Catholic family as housekeeper, a heretic, a rich heiress of eighteen, who having had only a Protestant boarding-school education is impulsive, coquettish, and unquenchably witty in conver-sation, as well as being a beauty. 'Her replies had all the effect of repartee', and she never fails in repartee, even to the Jesuit tutor of the family of the Earl of Elmwood, to which Dorri-forth belongs. Sandford naturally detests her, and achieves a relationship designed to humiliate by slighting her. He openly compares her to her disadvantage with a pattern young Catholic lady, Miss Fenton, whom the young Earl of Elmwood is directed to marry. The running battle between Miss Milner and the Jesuit is both amusing and painful, and our sympathy is generally engaged on her behalf, compared with whom Miss Fenton appears colourless, and merely con-ventionally virtuous, while Miss Milner with all her faults is interesting in her strength of feeling, her honesty and her dauntless refusal to submit to any authority but her guardian's. Her love of gaiety and of keeping suitors about her is distressing to poor Dorriforth; he tries to get her to accept some one of them so as to have her off his hands. He is embarrassed at having constantly to defend her against his friend Sandford, whose harshness and deliberate provocation amount at times to cruelty to his ward, though he has from habit to treat Sandford with respect and deference.

Miss Milner refuses to marry, and confides to her (Catholic) confidante that it is because she has fallen in love with her guardian. The horror of the confidante, the misery of the heroine, the necessity to deceive Dorriforth and to separate from him by a long visit to friends, is managed without a false note. Lord Elmwood dies and Dorriforth, succeeding to the title, is absolved from his vows, so that an ancient Catholic family may not die out. Miss Milner's natural hopes of winning his love are soon dashed by the news that he has been instructed to marry the model beauty Miss Fenton, to whom one Lord Elmwood is as acceptable a match as the other: she has no feelings in that or any other matter inconsistent with the rigorous religious education she has received, while Miss Milner is a prey to feelings of real distress, passion and despair. The Protestant and Catholic characters of the various personages in the novel are consistent, and the drama lies in their inevitable conflict. The author has no recourse to melodrama or sentimentality, working like Jane Austen, her successor, in delicate shades of feeling and slight everyday actions that, though minimal, in their context have significance and convey a whole inner drama. In fact, Mrs Inchbald, having bolder psychological matter to analyse and deeper conflicts to explore, has created a novel superior to *Pride and Prejudice* in interest and not less witty, or rich in memorable scenes. Like *Pride and Prejudice*, *A Simple Story* is written mainly in dramatic form (Mrs Inchbald was an actress and dramatist), interspersed where necessary by brief authorial comment.

The confidante now behaves with unusual sense for a character in a novel: she intimates delicately to the new Lord Elmwood that his ward's alarming state of health is due to her desperate love for himself. Knowing Miss Fenton's disposition he has no hesitation in breaking his engagement, and finds that even this is welcome to her as she would be

able now to retire from the world into a convent – 'Her
brother, on whom her fortune devolved if she took this resolution, was exactly of her opinion.' He then becomes Miss
Milner's professed lover, in spite of his tutor's opposition.
We now have a series of surprises. Miss Milner cannot but
treat the former Dorriforth as a lover, to whom she is exacting, capricious and rebellious. Sandforth sees the possibilities of the situation and exploits them to sunder the
lovers, for Lord Elmwood's character, formed in another convention from society's, will not tolerate such treatment. After
a decisive battle of wills he breaks with her, and arranges to
travel abroad with Sandford. Miss Milner had never for a
moment expected such an issue, confident in her powers of
keeping him at her feet however ill-used, and her agonies of
remorse, though concealed from Lord Elmwood, are visible
to Sandford, who shows slight signs of discomfort at his
achievement, though trying to rejoice. Miss Milner had
always recovered her good humour after each conflict with
him in the past, and at times shown herself to be magnanimous, in contrast to his surly enmity; and to her surprise he
begins to show her small kindnesses and to deny that he
bears her any ill-will, even inviting her to the last breakfast,
finding that neither she nor his pupil have been to bed that
night and are in equal agony. Here, having observed their
wretchedness and aware that it is his responsibility as much
as Miss Milner's, he explains that he thought he was acting
for the best in saving them from 'the worst of misfortunes,
conjugal strife' – 'But though old, and a priest, I can submit
to think I have been in error', and he marries them on the
spot. As no ring had been provided, the bridegroom marries
her with a ring from his own finger. They then perceive it was
a mourning ring. On this ominous note the second volume
closes.

Mrs Inchbald had found a subject that was to be a central
one for the next century's novel of religious controversy, for
in the mixed marriage and the conflicts leading up to it, the
radical contrast between Protestant and Catholic could be
expressed, studied and worked out to its tragic conclusion, or
some plausible compromise found. Essentially a subject not
for the theologian but for the psychologist and sociologist, it
lends itself ideally to the novelist's purposes as radically

serious and important; the psychology and social conditioning of characters in conflict in a typical situation is a subject
which the novelist, with his insight and unbiassed sympathies, is uniquely qualified to represent and explore. And
this sentiment entails exposing basic ideas about the conduct
of life and the formation of character, as well as showing their
results in representative action, with the emotional consequences.

Mrs Inchbald had already discovered the conditions on
which alone the subject could be made into a serious work of
art. She is impartial; she always goes below externals and
appearances to show the causes and the realities; she has
firmly defined characters who respond individually but
according to their natures and religious conditioning; and
though she employs some stylization of speech, yet the
elegance of educated speech at that date, and the prevalently
witty tone it employed, makes it a flexible and entertaining
medium. The novel is full of genuinely moving situations and
the range of characters, where so few are employed, is
remarkable. The eighteenth-century's realism, with its dis-
illusionment as to human character, so noticeable in Fielding, Dr Johnson and Jane Austen (to mention some very
different exponents of this trait) is one of Mrs Inchbald's
assets. Thus, when Sandford mentions a headache after he
has had a snub from his pupil about his abuse of Miss Milner,
she, who never bore malice, good-naturedly fetches him her
own 'specific for the headache' so that 'with all his churlish-
ness, he could not refuse taking it': 'This was but a commonplace civility, such as is paid by one enemy to another every
day; but the *manner* was the material part.' It pleases Dorriforth, who had been provoked previously, and 'Even
Sandford was not insensible to her behaviour, and in return,
when he left the room, "Wished her a good night".' This from
him was a great concession. And on a later occasion, when
she is in distress and he has been profiting by it, he is discon-
certed by being asked innocently by her friend if he has any
of the drops left that Miss Milner gave him for the headache,
Miss Milner being disabled by hers; he is obliged to say he
used them all, but the recollection of her kindness 'somewhat embarrassed him'; and after she has gone to bed and he
is alone with his friend he is inhibited from making unkind

insinuations at her expense, as he had intended. It is with such slight everyday events and actions that this novelist works so successfully, using them as indications of attitudes and changes of feeling and individualities of character, building them up to power the larger events of the novel.

Though the differences in Protestant and Catholic education and values are stressed, there is absolutely no emotion on the novelist's part in treating them, no bias in exhibiting the character of either religion's representatives, and no feeling is aroused in the reader towards either religion as such. This is so unthinkable in any nineteenth-century novel on the same theme, or in this field at all, that we might have supposed, if we had read *only* the nineteenth-century novels of religious controversy, that it represents an unattainable ideal. Yet it is in line, as we have seen, with the attitudes of Catholic and Protestant writers, whether novelist, critic or theologian, in the calmer waters of the century before the Victorians arrived to change all that. It is in fact these latter who are abnormal. The conditions that brought about this abnormality, the inflamed religious attitudes that produced novels of passionate feelings (on the novelist's part) with their denunciations, stock characters and vituperations, will be examined in the following chapter. I shall here mention as the characteristic Victorian opposite of *A Simple Story* the case of the novels of a typical Catholic convert of the Victorian age, Monsignor Hugh Benson. A biographer of his family (Miss Betty Askwith) wrote:

His work was marred by its passionate propaganda element. In his historical novels the martyrs are all on one side. In his contemporary ones all the Protestants, particularly the Anglican vicars, are hidebound, snobbish, reactionary and hypocritical, while the Catholics are spiritual, humble-minded and understanding [and all described in] the flood of somewhat second-hand purplish prose.

It is true that Father Martindale, Monsignor Benson's biographer, had a higher opinion of these novels, and probably their only effect was to bring comfort to Roman Catholics, who suffered a good deal at the hands of Victorian novelists of the opposite persuasion, whose novels were not much better than Hugh Benson's. Neither class can aspire to the condition of art, and I don't propose to waste time on fiction of this order. It is to the novels of religious controversy in the nineteenth century that are of permanent interest, and to non-belligerents, that I shall now turn, bearing in mind that *A Simple Story* has provided a touchstone by which to assess them.

'That great controversy': the novel of religious controversy in the nineteenth century

I

The great controversy that Mrs Humphry Ward was referring to was that of Protestantism and Catholicism; but this,
though the main, was by no means the only religious dispute
going on in the nineteenth century exploited by novelists,
nor the only one arousing deep and bitter feelings. It is odd
that so little notice has been taken of the fact by critics[1] and
students of the novel in the Victorian Age, for not only were
an enormous number of novels in the last century written
about religious controversies, but hardly any novel fails to
touch on some of these religious issues or to refer to them
with maddening obscurity on some controversial point of
detail or of ecclesiastical history of the day; hardly any Victorian novelist could avoid employing religious characters,
either professionals or amateurs who have thrown themselves into the fray. Jane Austen's novels usually contain one
or more clergymen, but they are just like her other young
men – nothing to choose between the Rev. Mr Collins and Mr
John Dashwood, odious in much the same way, or between
the vivacious Rev. Henry Tilney and the dashing Captain
Wentworth; and though ordination she *said* was to be the
subject of *Mansfield Park*, the only controversy there is Miss
Crawford's argument with Edmund against taking holy
orders on social grounds: he hunts and plays cards and
dances, and is otherwise, too, indistinguishable from worthy

Regency young men not about to take orders. In a Victorian novel this would be impossible. Virtually all Victorian novelists are very much alive to and pervaded by religious topics. They responded to the successive waves of controversy in this field compulsively, glad to make use of each well-known theme in turn, or positively feeling it their duty to show their colours, or glad to seize the opportunity. Well-known of course at the time, but now, it seems, mystifying even to the 'Eng. Lit.' student who slides over these references and themes in his reading without a thought to the matter, thus losing part or nearly all of the point of the novel he is supposed to be studying.

A book on Class in Victorian fiction (*Proper Stations* by Richard Faber) recently appeared, presumably to help modern readers living in a classless state to read their own classics, but, except for Americans, the class system in Victorian novels explains itself, or at least it offers no insuperble difficulties to the educated English reader (as yet). It is otherwise with the innumerable references to the changing religious climate of the nineteenth century which infest or even underpin Victorian novels, yet the subject has been virtually ignored by literary critics and university teachers. Can this be because to admit nowadays that religious controversy can have powered creative work of permanent value would be in bad taste? or that sleeping dogs had better be let lie? Perhaps it is rather like pointing out the fallacies and sins of Communism to the intelligentsia between the wars, or since. As one who is not and never has been either a Protestant or an Anglican or a Roman Catholic or a Nonconformist, I would like to try and mitigate the student's ignorance of some of these issues by sketching in these old unhappy far-off things and battles of long ago, in a strictly non-partisan spirit, since they are necessary to an understanding of most Victorian novels. In the general disappearance of belief and religious knowledge (in Dickens's day everyone had read *Pilgrim's Progress*; nowadays scarcely any of one's English Literature students has) and the widespread modern scepticism as to any church's being the true one, it can hardly raise ill-feeling and might even serve as a warning that, as this subject seems to suggest, novels of permanent interest are not produced by impartiality and enlightenment, but by people with strong views based on experience in depth, and who write for a public wanting some substance in their entertainment.

But it was not a matter of cold-blooded choice for a novelist so much as being directed by the common element in which novelists and public equally lived. A nation that even liked to drink its tea in early Victorian times from a Faith-Hope-and-Charity-patterned tea-service was hardly likely to forget religion in its reading. Even George Eliot, who, though she had gone through an Evangelical phase in girlhood, had soon shed that and all other sectarian dogma, even she, when she started to write fiction rather late in life, and as an experienced woman of letters, turned instinctively to a series of tales based on reminiscences of the clergymen of her early days, collected and published as *Scenes of Clerical Life*, hardly a title any publisher would now consider attractive. The last one projected turned into a novel, *Adam Bede*, in which the clergyman, intended originally to be the leading character, is rather displaced from the central role, but only by a Methodist girl preacher. *Silas Marner* is based on the pitiful and amusing contrast between a back-street urban dissenting sect and the traditional religion of 'church' as understood in rural England during and soon after the Napoleonic Wars, the latter shown to be a blend of paganism and simple Christian village habits. In *Felix Holt* Independents and their minister are played off against churchmen and parsons, even though politics is the main subject. Maggie's religious and moral problems dominate *The Mill on the Floss* after her childhood phase; and *Middlemarch* is largely devoted to illustrating Dorothea Brooke's spiritual formation as a girl of the Evangelical period and her rescue from its constrictions by a lover who is a Radical and an artist and of such mixed ancestry as to suggest he must be a freethinker. In the last novel, *Daniel Deronda*, the inescapable Victorian religious interest is diverted into Messianic Judaism. Certainly no one would have supposed from her novels and tales that George Eliot was an emancipated agnostic. Thackeray, writing a historical novel set in the seventeenth and early eighteenth centuries, makes a point in the controversy between the two religions in a variety of ways that would be recognized by his readers as relevant to them. Trollope, with a popular novelist for a mother (whose first great hit was with an anti-Evangelical novel, *The Vicar of Wrexhill*), tried his hand at different kinds of fiction – Irish romances and a historical novel – without any luck until, taking a leaf out of his mother's best-selling book, he set his next novel in the clerical world. Though *The Warden*, he complained, sold only slowly, he must have realized that he had found the right vein and continued with the Barchester circle enlarged to include the Close, with the addition of an Evangelical villain Mr Slope, on the lines laid down by his mother as the vicar of Wrexhill (the original of whom, the Harrow vicar, had insulted Trollope in his boyhood). There is no doubt that the Barchester series is far better than the Palliser series, although a conscienceless travesty of the latter to make a television attraction has given these a factitious popularity; politics, except in the hands of a Disraeli, was never so juicy or meaningful in the nineteenth-century novel as religion, and even Disraeli cannot dissociate politics from religion in his novels nor wished to.

To judge from the nineteenth-century novel, the situation of Protestants and Catholics (at least, among the literary and articulate classes) – perpetually at each other's throats, with a peripheral warfare, equally savage, going on first between Evangelicals and Anglicans, later on between Protestants and Ritualists, and always between Anglicans and Dissenters – was a normal state of free-for-all religious and sectarian warfare. But that this was not a norm in English and Irish history in the past can easily be demonstrated. The eighteenth century, with its deprecation of 'enthusiasm' in religion[2] and its optimistic belief in the ultimate prevalence of reason and goodwill even in religious matters, could look calmly at the existence of a rival religious system because assured that 'superstition', a composite term, would inevitably give way to rationality in the course of intellectual progress and the spread of sober Protestant truth. It is on this assumption that Sydney Smith, though a parson, argued early in the nineteenth century for Catholic Emancipation and the financial support of the Irish priesthood by the English government as both prudent and morally requisite: he confidently expected that this would free the native Irish aristocracy from its subservience to what he could only feel to be religious nonsense by opening general society and public office to them; and thus liberating them from sulking in their country houses under the dominion of their confessors. He believed, and freely wrote to the annoyance of his natural enemies the English bishops, and with wit and humour, that only good could come of Catholic Emancipation because it would tend to diminish Catholicism, while all Church of England members must be too firmly assured of the superiority they enjoyed to be infected by what he assumed everyone else saw to be an archaic theology and absurd ritual. He could not, of course, have been expected to foresee the Oxford Movement and its consequences, much less the religious civil wars in Northern Ireland. He did live to see the Oxford Movement and the subsequent spread of Ritualism, to his surprise and disgust.

Similarly, Harriet Martineau, a strong-minded intellectual woman born in 1802 of Huguenot origins and bred a Unitarian (and subsequently evolving into something that was described by contemporary enemies as 'a female atheist'), felt obliged to correct her friend Charlotte Brontë for her irrational reaction to the Catholic culture of Brussels that precipitated a novel, *Villette*. Reviewing it in the *Daily News* (3 Feb. 1853), Miss Martineau, unaffected by the storms of the Tractarian movement and its consequences, wrote of Miss Brontë (the review, to Harriet's surprise, put an end to the friendship):

She goes out of her way to express a passionate hatred of Romanism. It is not the calm disapproval of a ritual religion, such as we should have expected from her, ensuing upon a presentment of her own better faith . . . the Catholicism on which she enlarges is even virulently reprobated. We do not exactly see the moral necessity of this (there is no artistical necessity) and we are rather sorry for it, occurring as it does at a time when catholics and protestants hate each other quite sufficiently; and in a mode which will not affect conversion. A better advocacy of protestantism would have been to show that it can give rest to the weary and heavy laden; whereas it seems to yield no comfort in return for every variety of sorrowful invocation.

Miss Martineau thus attacked the novelist's attitude to Romanism, without criticizing *Villette* as a novel – that is, what it is, the record of an actual experience of a Catholic society and of a Protestant's reaction to that – and on three grounds: first, that 'there is no moral necessity for it', meaning either that Protestant truth will prevail over superstition in the nature of things or else that all religions have an equal right to exist; and second, that 'there is no artistical necessity', meaning that 'calm disapproval' would have been sufficient, though in fact that – the controversialist's method – was disastrous in a novel, not to mention that no one is ever convinced by argument to give up what was founded in emotion. Her third point is that the novel is 'in a mode which will not effect conversion' – of Catholics, that is – for it could only antagonize them, showing that she had become so accustomed to the novel as a weapon for controversialists that she could not recognize the distinction between that and a work of creative art, which is not of that kind (it would have surprised her to learn that the merely controversial novels have dropped out of esteem while *Villette* remains and will remain, a disturbing classic, even if religious differences become non-existent). One notes with interest Harriet Martineau's avoidance of capital letters in mentioning sects and similarly the dispassionate attitude that lowers the temperature of religious conflicts.

But here is the voice of the 'well-regulated mind' (a term current in her youth and a standard in Jane Austen's novels, but which disappeared with the rise of Evangelicalism), yet except for Sydney Smith's (born 1771), and Queen Victoria's own, it was largely unsupported. And by 1853, when Miss Martineau reviewed *Villette*, it was an untenable position, after the conversion of Newman and the constant stream of clerics and laymen from the intelligentsia and upper classes who followed him – an inconceivable relapse into barbarism from the Protestant point of view, and their loud condemnation was exactly comparable to the stunned horror of English reaction nearly a century later to the fact that Germany, the most highly cultured nation in the world, had succumbed to Nazism with scarcely a struggle. The approach of those bred in the age of reason to differences of religion is typified by Dr Richard Whately's work published in 1830, called *The Errors of Romanism Traced to Their Origins in Human Nature* and dedicated to the Rev. Joseph Blanco White who, 'educated in the Romish Church', 'escaped from that spiritual bondage' and was therefore able to realize not only the *differences* between Romanists and Protestants but also 'the points of *resemblance* in all men', 'to recognize in all the tendency towards each of these Romish errors which you have seen magnified and exaggerated in that Church'. The author, an eminent divine, says he neither wishes to engage in controversy nor to excite it. His object is to reconcile, to 'soften the feelings of the candid among Romanists and Protestants towards each other'. No one after him, certainly not any novelist, seems to have considered such a project practicable. And the eighteenth-century belief in the inevitable triumph of Reason is clearly manifest in this touchingly idealistic passage in Thomas Bewick's *Memoir* (he died in 1828 and wrote it late in life):

To withhold Catholic emancipation from Ireland appears to me to be invidious and unjust; and, if emancipated, it would be found at no very distant period that they would, under the foregoing tuition, individually become enlightened, think for themselves, adopt a rational religious belief, and throw off the bigotry and superstition taught them with such sedulous care from their infancy, and by which they have been long led blindfold. If they could be brought to think, and to muster up so much of the reasoning power as to do all this, they would soon emancipate themselves.

Dr Chalmers also thought that Catholic Emancipation was necessary as the first step towards conversion of Ireland to Protestantism. Sydney Smith's line of argument was rather different, though he shared Bewick's view of the relative rationality of Protestantism compared with Catholicism. In appealing to motives of self-interest in the Irish and the English (on ten different grounds) Smith trusted no less to reason to do away with the Irish problem eventually; and in his series of (anonymous) 'Peter Plymley' letters, addressed supposedly to Peter's brother Abraham, a country parson, he stated these views with irresistible wit. The letters were immensely popular from their beginning in 1807 and had a very large sale in the collected edition. He ridiculed the English 'terror of the Pope' – 'I thought it had been confined to the nursery' – and said boldly that if the argument for shameful treatment of the Irish Catholics was that we must not offend the Orangemen, he would not mind Orange dis-

affection, whereas 'If a rich young Catholic were in Parliament, he would belong to White's and to Brooke's, would
keep race-horses . . . and return home with a supreme contempt for Father O'Leary and Father O'Callaghan[3] . . . The
true receipt for preserving their religion is Mr Percival's
receipt for destroying it: it is to deprive every rich Catholic of
all the objects of secular ambition, to separate him from the
Protestant, and to shut him up in his castle with priests and
relics.' On the same principle Sydney Smith would provide,
he said, adequate government salaries for Catholic parish
priests and prelates and financial support for Catholic
schools and churches, for the Irish priesthood are 'the
religious guides of six millions of people'. He argued that by
emancipating Catholics in the fullest sense we should
redress the Irish grievances and deliver a blow to Irish
agitation; and that this must be done some time, so why put
it off 'till too late to earn us Ireland's goodwill'? Thanks to
Smith and his effect on the public, if not on the bishops,
politicians like Peel were led to change their minds about
Catholic Emancipation, and this finally came about in 1829 in
spite of George IV's dislike of the bill, nearly as strong as his
father's that had made such a measure impossible while
George III reigned. The Catholic population of England at
this time was small, and mainly aristocratic or at least Old
Catholics; known to be patriotic and opposed to ultra-
montane guidance; therefore not a threat in any respect.

But Maria Edgeworth, who lived with the Irish problem,
had no such illusions, though an eighteenth-century intellectual and wit. She had helped run the family estates and turn
Edgeworthstown into a model community with priest and
parson working harmoniously together and the children of
both sects attending the same school. In her old age, in 1843,
she got hold of Sydney Smith and had a talk with him about
the Irish priesthood and the difficulties they caused:

I told him . . . the facts which had actually come within my own
knowledge . . . did not accord at all with his preconceived notion of
their oppressed, depressed state diabolically treated by the
protestant church, protestant landlords and protestant and Tory
Government. He civilly waved aside my evidence . . . [saying] 'The
Catholics should have an established church.' '*An* would turn into
the.' He scoffed at such superstitions but I appealed to his own

knowledge of history regarding the encroachments and predomi-
nating nature or art of Catholics. He asked me whether the
Catholic priests are a moral, sober, well-conducted people. To
moral and sober I gave a good and I trust true testimony – as clergy
formerly, especially ere they took to politics, zealous and excellent
parish priests – as to well-conducted in politics and elections and so
forth and Repeal agitations, vide Bishop O'Higgins – and hear him
– hear him.

Miss Edgeworth, from experience of a Catholic country, was
not so simple-minded as some at home in England, and knew
the difficulties of coping with the actuality of Catholic Emancipation, having no illusions as to a priesthood's allowing its
flock to be eroded by non-Catholic truths, nor of failing to
perform its bounden duty of attempting by fair means or foul
to 'predominate'. The novelists agreed with her, and therefore make lively reading, having a dramatic cast and plenty of
tragic and comical situations at their disposal in Ireland,
without needing stage Irishmen in their cast.

There may have been illusions founded on theory and
ignorance in England, but in Europe Protestants in Catholic
or mixed-population countries had no such optimism. On
the eve of the passing of the Catholic Emancipation Bill 'the
learned Niebuhr', Professor of Roman History at Bonn, who
had negotiated with the Pope the Concordat with Prussia,
wrote a public letter to a Member of Parliament for Northern
Ireland, which was subsequently published as a handsome
book entitled *Letter upon the Roman Catholic Emancipation Question, and the State of Ireland in 1829*. He had had long intercourse
with the papal officials and much experience, as he said, of
'Roman Catholic statesmen', whose principles he had investigated both as a scholar and a practical politician; and he felt
obliged to give the result of his experience to another
Protestant country on the brink of a decision fraught with
perils it evidently did not anticipate. While he had no doubts
about the moral necessity of doing 'complete justice to the
Catholics' and having 'their clergy acknowledged by the laws
of the realm', he insisted that certain realistic steps must be
taken for protection of the Protestant realm: for instance, in
education, not to leave Catholic colleges and educational
establishments uncontrolled; and that the Jesuits should be
expelled from the soil of Britain and Ireland; he also recom-

mended very strongly that a deal should be made with the
Pope to order his clergy in England and France, in return for
Emancipation, to solemnize mixed marriages 'without insist-
ing on a promise that the children should be brought up in
the Catholic religion'. His advice was ignored, and the
English had reason to regret it. On the other hand, if his
advice had been taken, while there would have been more
social and domestic peace, we should not have had many
valuable novels, not least those on the central issue of mixed
marriages and the fate of their children.

Until the effects of the Catholic Emancipation Act were felt
– and of course this was not for some time – the novel of
religious controversy was occupied by the satire of Anglican
or merely unregenerate novelists against the Evangelicals,
who had become socially dominant before Victoria ascended
the throne, and who abounded in targets for literary artists,
by definition opposed to such a repressive form of religion.
The Evangelicals had from early on been the object of some
of Sydney Smith's wittiest shafts. Hannah More, who had
been the friend of the Garricks and a playwright herself, after
conversion retired to the country to spend her life in works of
piety, and held the theatre and novel- and play-reading to be
pernicious. The case-history of William Wilberforce is
equally remarkable, and can be read in sufficient detail in a
very useful book *Before Victoria: Changing Standards and Behaviour
1787–1837* (1967) by Muriel Jaeger. Evangelicals were Mrs
Trollope's targets for satire and indeed denunciation in *The
Vicar of Wrexhill* (1837) and continued to be those of her son,
for they did not cease to be a menace, as Samuel Butler's *The
Way of All Flesh* showed; for Palmerston as prime minister gave
his stepson-in-law Shaftesbury the major appointment in the
English church, which Shaftesbury conscientiously filled
with Evangelicals. And when they had become merely a bore
socially, they were kept alive in such novels as *Barchester
Towers*, Wilkie Collins's *The Moonstone* (1868) and Thackeray's
The Newcomes. The Rev. Obadiah Slope, red-haired, oily-
tongued with unction, amorous and determined to dominate,
and ending up by marrying a rich widow, was the standard
Evangelical monster of many novels before Trollope's; the
two Evangelical clergymen of *Jane Eyre* were quite different

from these except in the characteristic, common to all missionary religions presumably, of striving to overcome resistance to them by strength of will, bullying or moral blackmail. Charlotte Brontë was an artist and was registering something that had made a hated impression on her childhood at the clergy orphan school, whereas Mr Slope is a stock figure Trollope manipulates to provide low comedy, as Dickens does with another version of the type[4] in *Pickwick Papers*, who is the plague of the Weller home. It was in fact a libel on the Evangelicals, who had as much variety of good and indifferent as other sects, no doubt, and did much good as well as harm. A truthful insight into the Evangelical culture, to compare with the novelists' presentation of it, is available in many autobiographies and memoirs of the Victorian age. Leslie Stephen's mother was the daughter of the Evangelical rector of Clapham, but her son described her 'strength absolutely free from harshness'. Lord Frederic Hamilton's *The Vanished Pomps of Yesterday* (1919) gives the tone of the aristocratic Evangelicals, a true piety, and essentially unworldly without being at all opposed to pleasure and amusement of any kind that was not deleterious. He says:

Both my father and mother had an intense horror of gambling in any form whatever, and in some subtle manner they managed to instil this horror into every one of their children . . . My mother's character was a blend of extreme simplicity and great dignity, with a limitless gift of sympathy for others . . . Very early in life she fell under the influence of the Evangelical movement, which was then stirring England to its depths, and she throughout her days remained faithful to its rigid tenets . . . Although deeply religious, her religion had no gloom about it, for her inextinguishable love of a joke and irresistible sense of fun remained with her to the end of her life . . . She continued to the end of her life visiting among her less fortunate neighbours, and finding friends in every house. As she still retained her prejudices against the use of carriages on Sundays, she walked to and from the village church every Sunday up to her ninety-second year.

The Duchess of Abercorn's children had to endure the strict observance of the Sabbath, but it did not seem so dreadful to them as to us: they had *The Pilgrim's Progress* read to them, and on Sunday evenings a popular work of religious instruction, *The Peep of Day*, read out by their nurse, where the account of

Hell was listened to with rapt attention and thoroughly enjoyed by the nursery; and on Sundays as well as these they were allowed to read *The Fairchild Family*, which they took in selectively: 'There was plenty about eating and drinking; one could always skip the prayers, and there were three or four very brightly written accounts of funerals in it.' A similar record by a girl[5] – girls were less resilient – shows a greater impact made by the sombre side of the Evangelical outlook, but testifies equally to the moral dignity, simplicity and unworldliness of the better Evangelical families. Mabell, Countess of Airlie, was born in 1866 and, as her mother died soon after, her early background was dominated by the stern figure of Lady Jocelyn, her grandmother, daughter of the Lady Cooper who later became Lady Palmerston and who was sister to Lord Melbourne. Her grandmother therefore had been formed like the Duchess of Abercorn and Lord Shaftesbury (Lady Jocelyn's brother-in-law) in the first fervent period of the Evangelical movement. The Countess of Airlie wrote:

Our grandmother encouraged no worldly ambition in us. On the contrary, she exhorted us to lives of piety and good works . . . Uncle Ashley [Lord Shaftesbury] was sincerely religious and his philanthropic work sprang from a profoundly pitying heart. He practised what he preached . . . I look back with tender recollections to the laughter in the crowded dining-room and to the happiness of the whole household, family, guests and servants.

Her grandmother's family had an Irish seat, Tullymore Park in Northern Ireland, where the orphaned grandchildren were taken for the holidays, and

Even in the relaxed holiday atmosphere of Tullymore, religion had a prominent place in our daily lives . . . the chapel served in addition to its sacred functions as a centre of practical Christianity. It was always well heated, weekdays and Sundays, and anyone homeless and in need of a night's lodging was given a meal and allowed to sleep there. Sometimes whole families would be seated on the benches (receiving a square meal) . . .

But the preoccupation with religion and preparation for life beyond the grave took very unexpected forms:

Children asked to tea at each other's houses were encouraged to hold prayer meetings and play at Sunday Schools.[6] Death was a favourite topic both in the drawing-room and the nursery. Much of the piety proclaimed was morbid and sentimental, lending itself to hypocrisy, but my grandmother was completely sincere. In her eyes duty to God was represented by church-going, duty to one's neighbour by visiting the sick and caring for the poor . . . Abstinence was enforced on us. We were taught that to waste money on oneself was inexcusable.

There was evidently much more to be said about the Evangelicals than one would have supposed from the portrayal of them by Victorian novelists; though in *Middlemarch* George Eliot, in exposing the elements of her character and outlook that Dorothea Brooke got from her religion, stresses the social conscience that Evangelicalism aroused and the sense of social obligation in good works that it enforced. Dorothea is shown at the beginning of the novel drawing plans for model cottages to rehouse the workers on her uncle's and her suitor's estates, and we are told she has just returned from teaching in the school she had set going. These are at once recognizable as Evangelical characteristics, like her subsequent refusal to wear jewellery, even though inherited from her mother, and her deliberate plainness and economy in dress though she had a handsome private income. To anyone unsympathetic to the Evangelicals they appeared prigs or hypocrites, but George Eliot had known them from the inside and had a lingering tenderness for some of the sect's representatives who had inspired her youth with serious and socially useful interests. But the Evangelicals, though handy enough with the pen in tract and sermon, could not defend themselves in fiction without being charged with inconsistency, since they had declared novel-reading undesirable. And though their tracts and published sermons had incredibly large sales, they did not reach the novel-reading public, and the novel was now the accepted means of influencing public opinion – it was for this reason, as Disraeli wrote in his preface to the fifth edition of *Coningsby*, that he had adopted a form of fiction as little like novels as possible. The Evangelical writers therefore wrote fiction with as little love-interest as possible and weighed down by pages of moralizing and argument. While a great many Evangelicals, male and female, enliven as comedy and satire the pages of early and mid-Victorian novels, they are repetitions of the alleged or actual detrimental qualities of the Evangelicals and by no means tell the whole truth, though they do tell one undoubted truth, that creative minds could not stomach Evangelicalism and desired to make this known.[7] We might otherwise ask why so crude a caricature as Mr Slope destroys the otherwise delicate representation of Barchester Close and the Grantly–Harding clan, or what Lady Emily Sheepshanks and her mother are doing in *Vanity Fair* distributing tracts called *The Washerwoman of Finchley Common*, *A Voice from the Flames*, *The Livery of Sin* to the servants' hall, and proposing to arouse the ailing and wealthy Miss Crawley to the perilous state of her soul; but then agreeing to postpone using their heavy artillery in hopes of acquiring Miss Crawley's fortune. The novelists are fond of representing Evangelicals as designing hypocrites – there are two in *The Moonstone* (1868), one of whom, Miss Clark, probably brings about the death of the heroine's mother by forcing hell-fire tracts on her when she has a bad heart. Serious novelists like George Eliot and Charlotte Brontë do not make such crude reductions of Evangelicals: if the Rev. Mr Brocklehurst is a hypocrite it is unconsciously, as in not applying to the orphans in his school the same rules that he allows his own wife and daughters to live by; but he would argue no doubt that there should be class distinctions.

It is impossible to overrate the contribution of the Evangelical Movement to the Early Victorian and Mid-Victorian novel and even to a fine Edwardian novel, *Belchamber*, by the Anglicized American (Howard Sturgis), a tragic history of an English great house from Regency owners, which has the matriarch as the prime source of the disastrous history of her two sons.

But the stirring events leading up to the Catholic Emancipation Act did little for the novel apart from Disraeli's early novel, *The Young Duke*, which is interesting chiefly as a trial run for his later society novels like *Coningsby* and *Lothair*, as *The Professor* is for *Villette*. This was because the political situation was socially confusing and it is social life that Victorian novels are about; for the national picture with regard to Catholic Emancipation shows a characteristic English muddle. The Whigs were the party of liberal thought and progress, so it was natural that they should have worked to prepare the country for the measure that in fact was passed by the combined efforts of the Duke of Wellington and Peel, in a Tory administration. Even the anti-Catholics Wellington and Peel saw, as Sydney Smith had done before them, that it was impossible to withhold full civic rights from the Catholic members of countries governed by England. But in passing a Whig measure they were considered traitors by the Tories in general – in spite of the fact that the Tories were the party of the High Churchmen who in the previous century had been traditionally Jacobites and sympathetic to the Catholic Stuarts, and even now (1829) were less committed to opposition to Catholicism than Low Churchmen and Dissenters were. Yet these last two classes of anti-Catholic bigots were obliged to look to the Whigs as their only political allies. Each political party was therefore, as has been said,[8] an umbrella sheltering conflicting religious views: as there was no clear-cut opposition it was difficult for a novelist to take a partisan line; and it was too serious a matter for mere all-round ridicule. There was no W. S. Gilbert as yet in being to make farcical capital out of the confusion of divided loyalties and public perplexities, and even he did not dare to make *Patience*, as he had intended, a comic opera about rural curates (presumably one High and the other Low).

Dickens however seems to me to have had the subject in mind when writing *Barnaby Rudge*. Forster says he first discussed it with him as a project in 1838 – though it was a blow struck for the Catholic cause long after the battle for Emancipation was over. He could well have chosen the intrigues that led to the Gordon (anti-Catholic) riots in 1775 and onwards in order to be able to represent the Catholics as innocuous victims of Protestant mania,[9] an unprovoked attack on good citizens by a despicable mob operated, he shows, by a lunatic in the hands of an artful sectary who was a Catholic pervert acting out of malice. The anti-Catholics are seen in this novel as either ridiculous (like the play-acting apprentices) or criminals out for violence, destruction and loot: there is no doubt where the reader's sympathy is to lie. The protagonist is the head of an Old Catholic family, a poor gentleman living with his niece the sequestered life that circumstances at that date obliged Catholics to lead, under unjust suspicion of murdering his brother, whilst his rival is a Protestant sceptic who engineers villainous plots at his former friend's expense. Dickens at this date shows a decent man's sympathy on principle with an ill-used section of his fellow-countrymen, very different from his acceptance of the stock figure of the Jew as villain that he employed without any thought in *Oliver Twist*. In fact he goes out of his way in *Barnaby Rudge* to show such sympathy as Thackeray does in *Henry Esmond*, where he created a Jesuit who is a gentleman, kind-hearted, generous and, though inevitably an intriguer, invariably thwarted; thus challenging the stock figure that had been long in circulation of the Jesuit as underhand and sinister but irresistible in intrigue. Disraeli did similarly in sponsoring, in his early novels *Sybil* and *The Young Duke*, the Old Catholics as admirable, dignified and wronged in having been deprived of the religious buildings they had erected in pre-Tudor ages and in being prevented from playing an active part in the political life of their country. By the time Dickens had travelled in Italy and Disraeli had had some experience of the ecclesiastical politicians of Rome operating in England, they had both had something of a change of mind in this respect. When Dickens was in Italy at the time of the revolution in Geneva (1846) consequent on the Catholic cantons rising against the decree to expel the Jesuits, followed by the dissolution by the Protestants of the Catholic League and establishment of a provisional government, he wrote that his 'sympathy is all with the radicals . . . their horror of the introduction of Catholic priests and emissaries into their town seems to me the most rational feeling in the world'. He did not however put any of these feelings into a novel, for he must have realized it would have been inflammatory, though it would have sold even better than those he did write; in *Pictures from Italy* he gives a detailed account of the papal palace at Avignon and some of the horrors of its Inquisition. Disraeli much later in his life wrote *Lothair*, a wry comedy with many sharp touches at recognizable characters of the time in the world of high society, its Catholic converts and high-ranking ecclesiastics. It is as unlike *The Young Duke* as possible, though treating of the same rank of society over forty years later. Much had happened in between which provided the material and the public for the writers of anti-Catholic novels, so abundant that they constitute a sub-section of Victorian fiction.

In the background of this phenomenon is the series of historical facts which had accumulated as a Protestant history of England – selective rather than a myth – and provided the heated atmosphere in which the novel of Catholic–Protestant controversy flourished so tropically in the Victorian age, both in England and Ireland, and to which history there are frequent references in the novels. In the dim past was the Massacre of St Bartholomew and the Revocation of the Edict of Nantes, which had provided England with a Huguenot element in its population and from which many distinguished Victorian families descended, bringing their traditions with them;[10] the Inquisition; the Spanish Armada blessed for its mission against England by the Pope; Bloody Mary and the Protestant martyrs, kept alive by Foxe's *Book of Martyrs* which was a Victorian popular classic; a long English anti-papal tradition from the reign of King John, and the English dislike of the whole ecclesiastical apparatus of the Roman Church so evident in medieval times (as in *The Canterbury Tales* where the only functionary of the Catholic Church Chaucer respects is the poor parish priest – and Chaucer's *Tales* were a current glory of English literature); Wycliffe and the struggle for the English Bible and the right of every Englishman to read it according to his own lights; the Reformation; the deplorable reigns of the Catholic Stuarts; the Protestant interlude of Cromwell after the Civil War, when the Ironsides had been recruited from Cromwell's native East Anglia, then and for ever after a stronghold of dissent and implacably anti-Catholic; and the Jacobite rebellions of the Fifteen and the Forty-five in the previous century which, like the French Revolution, were a great deal closer to the early Victorians than to us; they might have succeeded and if so would have placed a Catholic monarch on the English throne and undone the work of the Bloodless Revolution. Victorian historical novels often drew on this history to reinforce Protestant feelings – *Westward Ho!* deals with Elizabethan England and the Spanish Inquisition, and *Lorna Doone*, an immensely popular historical Victorian novel, deals with Monmouth's Protestant Rebellion as part of its

plot; ringing in the nation's ears still was the traditional mob
cry: 'No wooden shoes, no black bread, no Popery.' Sydney
Smith tells us that in 1807 'the terror of the Pope' was widespread in England.

This English inherited grudge against the Catholic Church
and the tradition of resistance to Catholicism were
reinforced for the Victorians by a number of contemporary or
very recent factors. Sympathy with the French aristocrats
who fled to England from the atheistic Revolution was
countered by the restoration of the Bourbons after the fall of
Napoleon, which was accompanied by the imposition of a
reactionary regime powered by the repressive Catholic
Church, and France was a country which the English commonly visited. Other Catholic countries known to Victorian
English travellers which were for different reasons not good
advertisements for their religion were Ireland, the Iberian
peninsula and Italy. Southey had accompanied his uncle to
Portugal in his early manhood, and lived there some time,
but, though he delighted in the scenery and climate and was
interested in Portugal's literature and history, he acquired a
great dislike for Roman Catholicism as there in operation,
though it is true that he disliked Methodism still more and
cannot therefore be accused of mere prejudice. Dickens
wrote in Naples that 'the general degradation oppresses me
like foul air', and in Switzerland that

where . . . this Protestant canton ends and a Catholic canton begins,
you might separate two perfectly distinct and different conditions
of humanity by drawing a line with your stick in the dust on the
ground. On the Protestant side, neatness; cheerfulness; industry;
education; continual aspiration, at least, after better things. On the
Catholic side, dirt, disease, ignorance, squalor and misery. I have
so constantly observed the like of this, since I first came abroad,
that I have a sad misgiving that the religion of Ireland lies as deep
at the root of all its sorrows, even as English misgovernment and
Tory villainy.

And Forster adds: 'Almost the counterpart of this remark is
to be found in one of the later writings of Macaulay.' We
could add many more such writers,[11] and far more English
travellers felt and talked to this effect. It was also widely
noted that any Irish farm could at sight be classed as Prot-

estant or Catholic by its neatness, order and prosperity, or their absence. The swarms of Irish immigrants in search of work who turned Glasgow into an Irish city and filled the poorer parts of other cities such as Liverpool and London also seemed to the Victorians an unfavourable testimony to their religion. The poorest peasantry in Europe, coming as they did mostly from cabins with earthen floors where they shared their home with the domestic animals, they inevitably turned wherever they settled in towns into slums; in addition to which their habits of heavy drinking (being used to illicit cheap potheen) made them more noticeably savage, brutal and violent even than their English counterparts. Canon Barnett, who worked with his wife in the East End of London late in the nineteenth century, remarked on this, and their contrast to the immigrant Jews there, who, wherever they settled, though equally poor and used to ghetto life, reclaimed slums, having social traditions that made Irish fighting, drunkenness and shiftless housekeeping and neglect of children unthinkable. A radically anti-Catholic novel, *Ravenshoe* (1862) by Henry Kingsley, very widely read, contains a memorable scene in an East End Irish slum with a battle in progress, and testifies to the Irish making whole areas of London alleys practically inaccessible to the police. This was not well regarded by the law-abiding Victorians, and was one more mark chalked up against Catholicism. The Irish were also disliked by the English working-class as being noted for strike-breaking (see Mrs Gaskell's *North and South* on 'the knobsticks').

The deductions about the state of Catholic countries made from their material degradation were reinforced by the publication in 1842–3 of Borrow's *The Bible in Spain*, a book which immediately made him famous. Here the degradation is shown to be also spiritual blindness, in addition to misrule and poverty. Borrow had previously served the British and Foreign Bible Society in Russia, and the letters he wrote to the Society from Spain when working for them there were coloured to suit his employers' views; these letters were used as the basis for his book, which was eminently suited to the prejudices and preconceptions of the English public of the forties, and also reinforced them. It exposed the degraded and lawless condition of the country – Spain at the time of

Borrow's visits was rent by the Carlist wars and, like Italy under Austrian rule and Turkey, was one of the sick men of Europe. With its virulently anti-papist preface, *The Bible in Spain* forms a remarkable document. Describing as it did, with all the skill of a born writer, the obstructions Borrow received in his good work of putting a copy of the word of God into the hands of every Spaniard in his own tongue, a work which sometimes led to imprisonment or ill-usage, generally at the hands of the priesthood (who often seemed never to have heard of the Good Book), it was immensely successful in fuelling anti-papist opinion. Its readers were comforted, whatever their own troubles, by reflections in it such as 'England, thanks be to the Lord, is not a papist country' and that the Pope 'cannot boast of much success' in England. (Borrow's boast was ill-timed: the announcement of Newman's conversion, and of so many others, followed on its heels.) Borrow is so unreliable in all his books in distinguishing truth from imagination, and in other respects so much a skilful journalist as well as a literary craftsman, that *The Bible in Spain* may most safely be considered a novel contributed to the anti-Catholic controversy rather than a document; it is an artfully artless novel like Defoe's, as are also *Lavengro* and *The Romany Rye* where he continued to cater to Protestant prejudices. Borrow seems genuinely to have had experiences in Spain which made him obsessed with the evils of Catholicism; and in *Lavengro* he produced the incarnation of the popular conception of a Jesuit: the Man in Black with Judas-coloured hair, furtive appearance, clever tongue and sneering smile, 'cat-like and gliding' – the villain of many a nineteenth-century Protestant novel, and frequently there shown to be capable of every crime and enormity, proof of the morbidity of the Protestant imagination in its fear of the Pope and his emissaries, and comparable to the Nazi image of the Jew. No wonder a historian of the Victorian age (G. M. Young) wrote that 'to be misgoverned in this world and damned in the next seemed to many thousands of sober Englishmen the necessary consequence of submission to Rome'.

But behind this exaggerated and even paranoic fear of Roman Catholicism there was among the educated classes and the English clergy in particular a rational objection to the theory of it, and well-founded strictures on the practice. G. M. Young summarized it well: 'Behind the No-Popery uproar there was a great body of ancestral prejudice, no doubt, but also of reasoned conviction.' John Locke, though a Whig theorist, had argued that the Roman Church ought not to be tolerated in England in his century because it was bound by dogma to persecute if in power; being a Church that, while demanding religious liberty for its own members when a minority, would not concede it to non-Catholics when in power, an argument still in force (compare Reinhold Niebuhr, who in 1943, in *The Nature and Destiny of Man*, vol. II, devotes a section on 'Catholicism and toleration' where he concludes that 'The intolerance to which the church is forced by its presuppositions is really dangerous to both civil peace and civil liberty'). The Victorians for this reason could not lay the ghost of the Inquisition, which is featured in travellers' tales like Borrow's *The Bible in Spain* and Dickens's *Pictures from Italy*, and in innumerable horror novels with a pseudo-historical background in the early and mid-Victorian periods. The Counter-Reformation had initiated a strategy and programme for large-scale conversions which further alarmed Protestants – had not one country after another felt obliged to expel the Jesuits? It is not surprising that even educated Englishmen should envisage Rome as a Papal International; what Moscow has been to the western world in the last half-century, a threat to national liberty, employing without scruple every device likely to secure its ends.

There was also the English dislike of Catholic practices which had been soberly listed by Dr Richard Whately[12] in *The Errors of Romanism* and which were always coming up in controversy and richly exploited by novelists: 'sanction given to deceit', 'tending to discountenance the education of the poor', 'Christian ministers exercising the offices of pagan priests', the dangerous Auricular Confession, and so on. And even though the Tractarians tried to domesticate in the Church of England the magical idea of the priest, confession, and other Roman practices, these were felt to be un-English, or, like the celibacy of the clergy, unhealthy, and so repellent. An enormous number of buried or overt references to such practices occur in Victorian novels, as well as some of them figuring as comedy or for direct obloquy. The Tractarian

attempt to indoctrinate young Englishmen with the Roman
Catholic belief that a clergyman should be celibate is treated
by some Victorians with disgust as unnatural (for instance,
Charles Kingsley) and by others such as Trollope as ridiculous. He makes a point in *Doctor Thorne* (1858) of showing 'a
man of family and fortune', young Mr Oriel the rector of
Greshambury, 'who, having gone to Oxford . . . had become
inoculated with very high-church principles'. 'He delighted
in lecterns and credence-tables, in services at dark hours of
winter mornings when no one would attend, in chanted
services and intoned prayers . . . He eschewed matrimony,
imagining that it became him as a priest to do so; he fasted
rigorously on Fridays; and the neighbours declared that he
scourged himself', but he was 'thoroughly a gentleman, 'not
given to the low-church severity of demeanour'. The young
rector presently fell in love very suitably with a daughter of
his squire, and the morning services 'died a natural death'.
Thus religious controversy could be slipped into an ordinary
novel about class, love affairs and property, as incidental
comedy, but was none the less insidious in this form. Even
Charlotte Yonge, an Anglican of unwavering Tractarian
principles, seemed to hold that parsons are better married –
what would parishes be without our clergymen's wives? –
and, hovering on the edge of the 'unhealthy' argument, in
some of her novels, which are all steeped in Anglo-Catholic
propaganda, almost unconsciously shows celibate clergy as
not really satisfactory human beings, and in an innocent way
homosexuals. The eldest daughter of Charles Darwin, Gwen
Raverat's Aunt Etty, who was a strong-minded woman but
'was a very fierce anti-Catholic', offered her niece 'a novel to
hot you up against the Catholics, I've got a most shocking
one here'; she once burst in on her niece at night to say, 'with
eyes burning out from the deep hollows under her shaggy
brows: "I could SWALLOW the Pope of Rome, but what I can
NOT swallow is the Celibacy of the Clergy".'[13]
One of the most resented importations of the Puseyites
into Anglican life was sisterhoods (Pusey himself was held to
be the villain, founding the first and helping to spread the
practice). Nuns were popish, and there was a Protestant
horror of the convent on the intelligible grounds that con-
vents prevented daughters from having a normal life as wives

and mothers and made them indifferent and inaccessible to their natural relations. This could not be dispelled even by Charlotte Yonge's pictures in many of her novels of Anglican nuns being devoted to nursing epidemics and to good works among the poor. Trollope acutely noticed what might lead young ladies to join an Anglican order of nuns, as when, in *The Eustace Diamonds*, Lady Baldock's daughter Augusta suddenly becomes 'Sister Veronica John', thus escaping from her overbearing mother, we are told.

Sydney Smith had said that he had supposed that the terror of the Pope was confined to the nursery, but while it had no doubt begun there it generally remained through life, even if not consciously. We know that this was so from the more articulate section of the public, the writers, and I will quote a sample from a few such later Victorian products, and most of them from clerical homes too, to prove this:

1. Robert Graves, born 1895, whose father's father was the Protestant bishop of Limerick and who therefore presumably inherited his anti-Catholic bias, tells us in his autobiography:

   I was brought up with a horror of Catholicism and this remained with me for a very long time. It was not a case of once a Protestant always a Protestant, but rather that when I ceased to be a Protestant I was further off than ever from being a Catholic. I discarded Protestantism in horror of its Catholic element. (*Goodbye to All That*)

2. Winifred Peck was sister of Wilfrid Knox and Monsignor Ronald Knox, all three being children of the Bishop of Manchester:

   Through our old nurse we became aware of more sinister dangers in religious life. For hers centred almost entirely round an immediate anticipation of the Last Day and the Last Judgement and a bigoted hatred of the Church of Rome. From her I gathered the vivid impression that a demoniacal figure called the Pope in far-off Italy was always laying snares to entrap our nursery in especial, and England in general, into the evil lures of superstition. (*A Little Learning: A Victorian Childhood*)

And their governess, she says, read them aloud the historical romances of Mrs Emily Holt which enforced the Protestant view of English history and the wickedness of Rome.

3. Alison Uttley, a Victorian farmer's daughter, overheard the adults discussing politics in her childhood:

Mr Gladstone wants to give them [the Irish] Home Rule, but what would they do? They'd bring the Pope here in no time! (*The Country Child*)

4. Harry Verrier Holman Elwin was born at the end of Victoria's reign, the son of a bishop of Sierra Leone whose wife was a devoted Evangelical. Verrier Elwin took a First in Theology at Oxford and was ordained. As Vice-Principal of Wycliffe Hall, he was converted to Anglo-Catholic views and felt therefore obliged to resign, since at Wycliffe Hall he was 'expected . . . to give the arguments against the Mass, confession, Mariolatry and other exercises of religion connected with the Church of Rome'. Resigning, he wrote, entailed 'a most unpleasant interview' with the Principal. ' "I have long suspected", he said, "that you have been going to confession", in the tone of voice he might have used had he suspected him of visiting brothels' (*The Tribal World of Verrier Elwin: An Autobiography*, 1964).

5. Hugh (subsequently Monsignor) Benson, son of E. W. Benson, Archbishop of Canterbury in Victoria's reign, wrote that when a young man still in Anglican orders he once asked his father about the creed 'I believe in the Holy Catholic Church' – ' "For instance", I said, "are the Roman Catholics a part of the Church of Christ?" After a pause the Archbishop said "Perhaps the Roman Catholics had so far erred in their doctrinal beliefs as to have forfeited their place in the Body of Christ" ' (*Confessions of a Convert*).

6. Dean Church wrote that when a schoolboy at Bristol he was taught to look on Roman Catholics 'with a kind of awful curiosity and dismay'.

7. At the village level, Flora Thompson, brought up in an Oxfordshire village, tells us that they 'looked on

Catholicism with contemptuous intolerance, for they regarded it as a kind of heathenism, and what excuse for that could there be in a Christian country?' As a child she was told that Roman Catholics were 'folks as pray to images' and that they worshipped the Pope, a bad old man, some said in league with the devil.

8. E. E. Kellett, a child of a nonconformist theological family, wrote that he was brought up 'to look on Roman Catholics with dread'.

One could multiply such examples endlessly. We can take the temperature of Victorian England from them. And it is important to realize that the minds of future novelists were as regards Roman Catholics given such ideas to digest in childhood. It is of significance when we come to read their novels. No doubt in Haworth vicarage the servants, in addition to impressing the minds and sensibilities of the Brontë children with the folklore of northern England, conveyed to them as well the folklore concerning Rome. Nannies and servants in good houses were generally Evangelicals or Methodists, the two sects most opposed to Roman (or any other) Catholicism. We can see from *Villette* that Charlotte Brontë knew what to expect in general about the religion of her Brussels school before she went there, and the experience provided her with detail to support existing ideas. In fairness it must be added that her genuinely Protestant character would have found unacceptable anyway many aspects of Catholic conduct and many Catholic ideas and for this reason she disapproved of the High Church movement.

It was quite possible of course to change one's views about Catholicism when older, but this did not change the odour and temper of the essential self. Cardinal Newman was born in 1801, the son of a Huguenot mother and an Evangelical father, and was brought up on Calvinistic literature (undermined, no doubt, to some extent by his devotion in boyhood to Scott's novels). When he visited Rome as a man he still made the standard English reaction to Catholicism: the religion there struck him as being 'polytheistic, degrading and idolatrous', and 'for many years anti-Christ was for him the Pope', as it was to the end for Archbishop Benson. Yet it was in 1833 that Newman began the 'Tracts for the Times' and his 4 o'clock sermons, starting the Anglo-Catholic movement against liberalism in religion and a Protestant interpretation of the Church of England. By 1841, with Tract 9, he was evidently set on the path to Rome. Evangelicals seem to have been unstable people at this time, for a great many other converts to the Roman Church were made then from those brought up in Evangelical homes. Critics have noted that Newman's religion remained one of 'gloom, denunciation, fear and distrust of human nature', so that in changing one faith for another he did not change his outlook on life or attitude to it. In fact, the animus against Rome he had been brought up in remained in the form of post-conversion bitterness against Evangelical Churchmen all his life, and he seems neither to have been a better nor a happier man after 1845.

In 1850, a zealous convert, he delivered the ill-advised 'Lectures on certain difficulties felt by Anglicans in submitting to the Catholic Church', which Professor Owen Chadwick says 'was the only book by Newman which many Anglicans found it impossible to forgive'. This greatly embittered Catholic–Anglican relations. As Thackeray and Charlotte Brontë are said to have been among his audience, it no doubt gave these novelists (and many others present) food for thought and fiction.

Once the Irish, and English, Catholics had been given emancipation – against the wishes of the majority of the English people, as the government knew – the next crisis in the religious history of the Englishman was the waning of Evangelical influence as it lost its original drive; though there is difference of opinion as to whether they had degenerated by 1830, they had certainly changed – the Wilberforce type was succeeded by Carus Wilson. The vacuum was filled by the Tractarians, who replaced the Evangelicals as material for novels. The Evangelicals had transferred their attention to Ireland in the 1820s as 'the New Reformation' movement, galvanizing the torpid Church of Ireland with dramatic results which will be discussed when considering the Irish novels of religious controversy. Newman's gradual conversion, made spectacular by so many of his friends following their leader, gratified the Evangelicals, who were then in the aggravating position of being able to say 'I told you so'; while it put the Anglicans in a predicament, though Pusey and other strong-minded men found it possible to adopt an English Catholic form of belief and practice satisfactory to many. The term 'Puseyite', however, as generally used was derogatory. Sydney Smith when Canon of St Paul's preached there at the age of 72 'against the Puseyites', on the grounds that 'they lessen the aversion to the Catholic faith and the admiration of Protestantism'. Leslie Stephen's parents were second-generation 'Saints' (Evangelicals of the Clapham sect), who sent him to Cambridge, he wrote, to avoid the contamination of 'Puseyism' at Oxford, for Cambridge had earlier been known to foster Evangelical clergymen as the home of the Simeonites. The Stephens had not foreseen that Cambridge would emancipate Leslie from Evangelicalism too; he found when he arrived, he wrote,[14] that by then 'the epithet "Evangelical" generally connoted contempt. The "Oxford Movement" might be altogether mistaken (this was the orthodox Cambridge attitude to it), but we agreed that the old "Low Church" position had become untenable.'

The disappearance of the Evangelicals from the intellectual scene (if not the political field) as serious rivals to the High Church made the opposition now one between Catholicism, whether Roman or Anglican, and the Broad Church party which sheltered progressive thinkers and liberal-minded churchmen generally, who were utterly opposed to Catholicism since it represented the enemy of all they stood for and worked for. Henceforward the controversy for all serious purposes was between the tolerant and open-minded on the one side and all extremists on the other. English novelists of talent (though not Irish novelists) were, as a matter of course almost, of liberal opinions, whatever their origins; so the Puseyites and the dogmaticals and the bigoted Low Church men did not come off very well in fiction. But the best novelists felt obliged to protect even their opponents against vulgar prejudice. Hence Mrs Gaskell, a Unitarian minister's wife, inserts gratuitously into her novel of industrial Manchester, *North and South* (1855), a piece ridiculing the contemporary horror of the Church of Rome. For this purpose alone (as the visit does not happen) the heroine is made to propose to visit her brother in Spain who is marrying a

Spanish girl, and to take with her the old family servant, who baulks at exposing herself to 'a Popish country', saying: 'I'm afraid I must say that my soul is dearer to me than even Master Frederick. I should be in a perpetual terror, Miss, lest I should be converted.' But Dixon 'had, with all her terror, a lurking curiosity about Spain, the Inquisition, and Popish mysteries' so 'she asked Miss Hale whether she thought, if she took care never to see a priest, or enter into one of their churches, there would be very much danger of her being converted?'

Besides the satire, Mrs Gaskell has also made an important point in exhibiting something characteristic of the Victorian era, the curious helplessness in the face of Catholicism that both Lucy Snowe and Charlotte Yonge's heroines exhibit, as well as those of many Victorian popular novelists. The impression made is that no one is safe; and of course when Lord Ripon, the Grandmaster of the Freemasons, Gladstone's sister Lucy, Coleridge's son Henry, Wilberforce's sons and many other such striking conversions were made from the best families socially or intellectually, no one did seem to be safe. English people seem at this time to have had no confidence in being able to stand by the faith of their fathers, whatever it was. If one reads Charlotte Yonge's novels (and she was a disciple of Keble's) one sees that she assumes that so powerful is the attraction of Rome, like a snake to a rabbit, that once she sets foot in a Catholic chapel, even with the innocent intention of merely enjoying the music, a girl brought up in the English Church will end up behind convent bars, equally lost as regards body and soul. Had they no real convictions, one wonders? Lucy Snowe in *Villette*, having been unable to resist the temptation to relieve her moral isolation in the confessional, feels that only by avoiding the priest in future could she resist the 'arms which could influence me'. This deep-down feeling of the pull of Catholicism against all reason and English habit is probably the real cause of 'the terror of the Pope',[15] and a subject peculiarly suitable for the novelist, since it can only be treated outside the field of controversy, by a sympathetic study of feelings and impulses and early environment. This could be helped by an examination of the nature of those who were impelled to join the Roman Catholic Church, like

Cardinals Newman and Manning, Monsignors Hugh Benson and Ronald Knox, and those of the same family or circle who were not, such as Cardinal Newman's brother Francis (who escaped from Evangelicalism into Unitarianism); Monsignor Knox's brother Wilfrid (who became an Anglo-Catholic); Mark Pattison, who came from an Evangelical home and was attracted by Newman but saw that he stood for obscurantism and eventually left even Anglicanism behind him; and Pusey and Keble and others of the Tractarians who did not 'go over'.

The Oxford Movement brought into High Anglican worship a quantity of Catholic properties, activities and un-Protestant ideas which were rich material for the novelist to work with, and the wrangling about them between Low and High Church advocates provided him with new objects of satire. Lighted candles or even unlighted ones, and flowers on the altar, or whether it should be called an altar at all, became matters of importance about which many people felt very strongly; and feelings ran so high that from the Tractarian period till late in the century legal actions were frequently brought against offenders: as late as 1889 the Church Association brought a test case against the Bishop of Lincoln before the Archbishop of Canterbury for un-Anglican practices, such as lighting candles on the communion table when they were not needed to give light; and the case took three years to decide. The difference between candles on the altar but unlighted, and lighted candles, or candles on the altar at all, might cost a young curate a preferment, and does so in Mrs Oliphant's witty novel *The Perpetual Curate*. A cross was allowable but not a crucifix, which was papistical. Somerville and Ross, the Irish novelists, explain in a sketch called 'Irish Aunts' that being of course Low Church their early Victorian aunts in Ireland always went to church twice on Sundays, but considered any week-day services 'Popish'. These subtle differences were God's gift to novelists, but they are apt to misfire for readers of our time. When Mrs Proudie (in *Framley Parsonage*, 1861) attacks the Rev. Mark Robarts, who had said innocently, 'I am thinking of having morning prayers in the church' and who gets snubbed with the reply, 'That's nonsense, and usually means worse than nonsense. I know what that comes to', she means that it would lead to Rome. Nor is it surprising – though of course novelists had fun with it – that Protestants should wish to defend their Church against Mariolatry, Auricular Confession, the Mass, monks and nuns, celibate clergy and other such un-English ideas that the Oxford Movement had countenanced and which had, through Newman, infected a seat of learning like Oxford, which traditionally produced Anglican divines. Leonard Elliott-Binns, in *Religion in the Victorian Era* (1936), cites the case of 'the unfortunate parish of St Saviour's, Leeds',[16] where 'all the staff save one became Romans' and, to make things worse, refused to retire like gentlemen but stayed on to try and make converts, a really Gilbertian situation too farcical and improbable for any novelist to employ. In view of such defections and on such a scale, no wonder no one seemed safe, and to this we must attribute the loss of nerve shown by so many serious and worthy religious people which is a feature of the age from 1845 onwards. Though Pusey remained in the Church of England and seems not to have been himself a ritualist, he defended ritualists when they were attacked and so made himself even more suspect to Protestants.[17]

Trollope winds up *Barchester Towers* (1857) with a very knowing piece about his heroine's change of views now that she has married a High Church dean – formerly she leant towards sympathy with the Evangelical Mr Slope. Some of the points Trollope supplies to his readers in the passage beginning 'The two sisters do not quite agree on matters of church doctrine', and can assume they will understand, would need footnotes now. For example,

It must not be presumed that she has a taste for candles, or that she is at all astray about the real presence; but she has an inkling that way. She sent a handsome subscription towards certain very heavy ecclesiastical legal expenses which have lately been incurred in Bath, her name of course not appearing; she assumes a smile of gentle ridicule when the Archbishop of Canterbury is named, and she has put up a memorial window in the cathedral.

Such a passage assumes a readership well equipped with up-to-date ecclesiastical knowledge, and a burning interest in such topics. The modern reader guesses that the archbishop

wasn't High enough for Eleanor, but does not need to know
that he was Archbishop Sumner; and will conclude that her
subscription went to help the defendant in a prosecution for
for some un-Protestant belief or practice to pay his lawyer.
But the reader of that date knew that the lawyer was defending a Tractarian, the Archdeacon of Taunton, the Rev. G. A.
Denison, who, owing to Evangelical persecution, was tried
and found guilty in 1856 of teaching about the efficacy of the
Sacrament that was too Roman for the 39 Articles (though he
was supported by Pusey), in the Archbishop of Canterbury's
court at Bath. Deprived of his living as he refused to recant,
he had the case reopened; and the prosecution was finally
declared invalid by the Privy Council, which was largely composed of lay lawyers. His legal expenses for all this must
indeed have been heavy. Such cases gave Victorian novelists
plenty of background and occasion for reference of the kind
Trollope here exemplifies. His readers would understand the
reference to poor Sumner (Archbishop of Canterbury since
1848), for though Sumner endeavoured to be impartial
between the two church parties he must have already
incurred the disgust of the Arabin party by his concurrence in
vindicating Gorham for refusing to believe in baptismal
regeneration. It may be remembered that the vindication of
Gorham was the last straw for some High Churchmen, who
thereupon got themselves received into the Roman Church
in protest.

The Victorian novelists found in Ritualism an inexhaustible source for irony and humour for, while it was felt as a
papistical infection by the ordinary Englishman, it was to the
sophisticated novelists (not of course the Charlotte Yonges)
simply ridiculous. So Trollope goes out of his way in *Framley
Parsonage* (1861) to mention 'a certain terrible prelate in the
Midland counties, who was supposed to favour stoles and
vespers, and to have no proper Protestant hatred for
auricular confession and fish on Fridays'. Trollope shows
what he thinks of this animus by referring ironically to the
guilty party, whom his readers would recognize as Samuel
Wilberforce, Bishop of Oxford, as 'terrible', and by coupling
as equal two Protestant bogies, confession and fasting from
meat on Fridays, the irony being directed at those who
thought this 'terrible'. In *Bleak House* Dickens actually dis-

missed the Ritualist movement as 'dandyism' in an up-to-
date form; and it was regarded in a similar light even by many
devout Anglicans: it was not part of the original programme
of the Tractarian movement. Dean Inge, a Victorian from a
thoroughly clerical family, called the vestments so important
to the Ritualists' 'ecclesiastical millinery', and says they were
ignored in his grandfather the archdeacon's days, when such
props, brought into play by many mid- and late Victorian
novelists, were not yet available. He said that the archdeacon
never wore a cassock; copes were not known then to
Anglicans, and surplices were considered subversive (there
had been surplice riots in the 1840s). It seems that intoning
was seen even by the High-and-Dry Church as an affectation
of young curates that was best laughed out of existence, and
Trollope duly has an episode of this kind in *Barchester Towers*.
This novel is a perfect document for the changes from the
time of the old bishop whose clergy danced, played whist and
hunted, and when 'a liberal clergyman was a person not frequently to be met. Sydney Smith was such, and was looked on
as little better than an infidel' – to the defeat of the succeeding High Church principles in favour of the Whigs' idea of
all-round reconciliation if possible, a new wind with which Dr
Proudie filled his sails: 'He bore with the idolatry of Rome,
tolerated even the infidelity of Socinianism, and was hand in
glove with the Presbyterian Synods of Scotland and Ulster.'

Part of the comedy is that Dr Proudie is not himself an
Evangelical, like his chaplain and his wife, but a latitudi-
narian bishop, as Trollope takes care to establish in the
account of him in his first appearance at the opening of the
novel. Thus he is horrified at the rumpus his chaplain has
caused (with Mrs Proudie's support) in altering the cathedral
music and services in Mr Slope's sermon in the cathedral,
and reluctant to be dragged into Mrs Proudie's and the chaplain's schemes and hostilities.

It includes the subsequent history of Anglo-Catholicism
and its being countenanced by such a High-and-Dry die-hard
as Archdeacon Grantly in order to defeat his enemy the Low
Churchman Mr Slope and Slope's patron the bishop's wife.
Therefore we have a historical summary of this kind:

Hitherto Barchester had escaped the taint of any extreme rigour of church doctrine. The clergymen of the city and neighbourhood, though very well inclined to promote high-church principles, privileges and prerogatives, had never committed themselves to tendencies, which are somewhat too loosely called Puseyite practices. They all preached in their black gowns, as their fathers had done before them; they wore ordinary black cloth waistcoats; they had no candles on their altars, either lighted or unlighted; they made no private genuflexions, and were contented to confine themselves to such ceremonial observances as had been in vogue for the last hundred years.

Barchester Towers registers the climate of ecclesiastical opinion and the various circumstances which go to explain why the Gorham case aroused so much feeling, and no doubt why it came about at all. This and the Hampden case come in for reference in the novels. Newman was the unsuccessful candidate for the Regius Professorship of Divinity at Oxford in 1836, and was held to have resentfully attacked Dr Hampden (who was elected to it) and his Bampton Lectures, in consequence, as unorthodox. Hampden had, among other views objectionable to the Tractarians, courageously taken an enlightened stand in favour of relaxing the enforced subscription to the 39 Articles which was required before entering Oxford or receiving a degree at Cambridge; he became the target of the Tractarians, but their display of animus eventually rebounded on themselves. Similarly with the Gorham case, which concerned the possibly unorthodox views of an able and elderly clergyman of some standing, who in his old age had been invited to change to a country living making less demands on his energies. The pugnacious Bishop Phillpotts of Exeter (satirized in *The Warden* as Archdeacon Grantly's eldest son) refused to institute the Rev. Mr Gorham because he suspected the new vicar held Calvinist ideas about baptism. Gorham brought an action in consequence in 1848, and proved to be a formidable theologian, sustaining a series of court cases which finally resulted in the defeat of the bishop in 1851. The intense national interest in the Gorham case is shown by the fact that more than fifty works treating the subject of baptismal regeneration that was in question were published in consequence (Whateley's alone went through two editions); and more significant, that very large sums of money were raised by public subscription to pay the huge legal expenses incurred by the vicar, now a public hero, showing the wide interest in, and sympathy for, a cleric who would not sanction a Catholic interpretation of the baptismal rite. It must be added to the credit of the Church, and characteristic of its traditional desire, in opposition to Roman Catholic dogmatism, to leave as much freedom as possible for individual interpretation of its theology, that though the case was adjudged to Gorham, the *subject* of it was never settled, and no theological ruling was given.

But though this result was agreeable to Evangelicals and to Broad Church liberals, it was wholly unacceptable to many High Churchmen. It was by them considered so intolerable theologically that an Anglican cleric called Manning, and two of William Wilberforce's sons who were also parsons, felt that if this was the Church of England, they must join the Church of Rome; nor were they alone in this by any means. But it had the opposite effect on others: James Mozley, whose brother married Newman's sister Harriet, found the very High Church position untenable now, though he was the friend of many in the Oxford Movement; he subsequently became Hampden's successor as Regius Professor of Divinity at Oxford. Mrs Oliphant devoted a novel[18] to sketching in the various types of cleric now in being, and showing the indignation of Evangelical aunts and old-style squires at finding they had in the family Anglo-Catholic curates, or even holders of family livings who could not be restrained from going over. The ordinary dress of the clergy even became differentiated, so that Evangelicals or Tractarians were visible at a glance, accentuating the differences within the clerical order as well as the differences in religious garb for preaching and conducting services.

While these evidences of a widening rift in the Church of England were making themselves felt at the expense of domestic harmony, the Pope decided, perhaps on the advice of Wiseman, who had been made a bishop in 1840 and was well known for his prozelytizing zeal, that the time had come to make arrangements of a more systematic kind for the Catholic population's benefit in England. In 1850 therefore he divided England into twelve papal dioceses, at the same time making Wiseman a cardinal. This was tactless, for

Wiseman, a flamboyant character who had been educated in Italy, was naturally seen by the average Englishman as a Jesuit and a foreigner, and there had already been uneasiness here at the great increase in the Catholic population due to the Irish immigration and the flood of new Catholic converts from the intellectuals and the aristocracy. The Church of Rome was now seen as a temporal power with designs on England; the new move was at once declared to be 'papal aggression', and the inflamed Protestants, seeing it as a step towards compelling them to come in, demanded political protection in the form of some declaration by parliament of censure on the Pope. It was a really formidable public storm due to psychological fear and patriotic anger combined. Public meetings were held in vast numbers all over the country, and the Prime Minister, Lord John Russell (a staunch Protestant), was plagued to put through parliament a bill that he knew to be useless and unwise. He wrote to the Queen (also a staunch Protestant) on 25 October 1850, point-ing out that the Pope's action was not alarming, for the change could affect only Catholics, but added that what ought to be found alarming was 'the growth of R.C. doctrines and practices within the bosom of the Church'; he quoted Dr Arnold who had said ('very truly') that he looked upon a Tractarian as an enemy disguised as a spy. He then wrote accordingly to the Bishop of Durham deploring the tendency of some clerics to imitate Roman ideas in ritual crossing, worship of the saints, auricular confession and absolution after penance and who were even trying to claim infallibility for the Church of England! – none of which was acceptable to most English churchgoers. Meanwhile the Queen had also received a letter from the opposite side: the Duchess of Norfolk, wife of the leader of the Catholic laymen of England, was alarmed at the recent spate of proselytizing by the Roman priests in England, understanding that anti-Catholic feeling by this and other actions of the Pope might be roused to a dangerous pitch. The Old Catholics in fact deplored the wave of converts, people who had not stood the trials of the faithful in history and who were mainly middle class – a situ-ation that offered scope for any novelist with a sense of humour. The Queen replied to the Duchess reassuringly. She also replied with her usual good sense to Russell, deploring

'the great abuse of the R.C. religion' at public meetings and
denouncing the Pope's arrogance, abuse which she thought
'un-Christian and unwise'; she was not intolerant but,
'sincerely Protestant as I always have been and always will
be', could not approve of the Puseyites. She did not wish the
Ecclesiastical Titles Bill to be passed, which she thought
would only 'exasperate the Irish', and stated her confidence
in the loyalty of her Catholic subjects. She was right of course
about the Irish. The measure Russell reluctantly introduced
in 1851 as the Ecclesiastical Titles Bill caused a parliamentary crisis owing to the violent reaction of Irish members
(known as 'the Pope's brass band'). Added to this was the
rapid advance in the Catholic hierarchy of the former
Anglican clergyman, soon to succeed Wiseman as Archbishop of Westminster and then as Cardinal Manning, who
let it be known that he confidently anticipated the eventual
extinction of the Protestant religion throughout the world. It
is no wonder that various Protestant societies were formed to
act as watch-dogs; it is they who brought the cases against
Ritualists; and they were also said to go up to lighted candles
on church altars and extinguish them by covering them with
their hats, in protest against this papistical tendency.

All this dramatic warfare and absence of brotherly love,
Christian charity, or even a sense of humour, was the
novelists' bread and butter, but painful to an ecclesiastic like
Archbishop Benson. Having come, like so many Victorian
clerics, from an Evangelical home, he had much sympathy
with Evangelicals and even with Methodists, whom he had
encountered in bulk when Bishop of Truro and had there
learnt to admire their character, while they attended his
preachings with mutual regard. He feared that the Catholic
theology and practices of the new Anglicans would force the
Evangelicals to secede from the Church of England as the
Wesleyans had been forced out; Spurgeon had actually in
1864 urged Evangelicals to leave the Church of England on
account of Baptismal Regeneration. Benson was therefore
impatient of Lord Halifax's self-appointed mission for
reunion with Rome in the 1890s, which he saw as simple-
minded and bound to fail since it could only be, he saw, an
attempt to get the English Church to make concessions without getting anything in return; but first Cardinal Vaughan

and then the Pope finally declared Anglican orders invalid, thus putting an end to all possibility of reunion. Benson illustrates in himself the complex, and illogical, situation of a churchman who was required to be both Catholic and Protestant, like the sovereign. He had wide sympathies and various leanings, and considerable knowledge of early ecclesiastical history: yet his son A. C. Benson, in his life of his father, says that when in 1872 the Archbishop visited a former schoolfellow who had 'gone over' at Oxford and had now become Rector of Stonyhurst, he wrote that 'The Mass is a wonderfully strong statement against Transubstantiation', and that his friend's religious practices and arguments made him 'wonder if we are beings of the same sphere' 'so completely it seems to belong to the world where reasoning is mere sequence of words and the Bible has another gospel in it'. In fact, though Benson had sympathy with Methodists and every branch of Protestants, and with Eastern Christian Churches, he stood by the Reformers and could not but be antagonized by Roman Catholicism – 'The Roman falsification of history angered him' and he thought confession a menace, his son says. He represented a sound Broad Church position and stood for everything in England that made submission to Rome out of the question. It is in this climate and amid such scenes of ecclesiastical history that Disraeli's *Lothair* must be understood to exist; and Disraeli had no qualms about exploiting its factions and absurdities for purposes of ironic comedy. The question, Weren't they all Christians, so why couldn't they stop fighting? does not arise once the irreconcilable traditions of belief and practice are understood as emanating from different temperaments and cultures. And that there was a distinctive Protestant culture both English and Anglo-Irish natives made plain, as distinct from the Catholic ethos as was Hindu from Muslim in India.

Yet peaceful coexistence had been possible before what may be called 'the troubles' arose for the Church of England. Bishop Heber, born in 1783, a man of good and ecclesiastical family with landed property, had, we are told, 'lived on terms of lifelong sympathy and friendship with the local nonconformists'. His successor in Hodnet rectory was his nephew, the father of the novelist Mary Cholmondeley, and she wrote in her family memoir *Under One Roof: A Family Record* (1918):

Father followed in his [Heber's] footsteps. He made no distinctions
between those who attended church and chapel . . . I don't think he
felt any difference. We, as children, never realized the gulf which
later in life we discovered to exist between the Church of England
and the Church of Rome. Father's elder brother Charles had
become a Roman Catholic, and used to appear at intervals at
Hodnet Rectory, a tall imposing figure in his soutane, delighting us
all with his caustic wit. We, as children, accepted Father and Uncle
Charles, and the non-conformist minister, as all working in the
same cause, and, in consequence, belonging in a mysterious way to
each other, like soldiers of different regiments. Like Bishop Heber
before him, Father was closely and personally attached to some of
the leading nonconformists in the parish, and they to him. (They
had played together as children of the same village, we are told.)
Their fine faces rise before me as I write. They were through life his
powerful allies. When he held a mission . . . services always opened
with prayer by the leading nonconformist of the district, in the
presence of the High Church Missioner.

This idyllic state of things before the persecuting Evangelicals destroyed with their zeal the peace of the country
parishes, as well as embroiling urban communities, seems
not to have attracted novelists – presumably because there
was no drama or satirizable conflict to be got out of it, and
because it was so great a tribute to the truly Christian possibilities of human beings when not misguided by bigotry as to
be, in the Victorian age, incredible. Mary Cholmondeley's
father was born in 1827, and was even then old-fashioned,
having been brought up by the good Bishop Heber, as he was
called; and his daughter remarks significantly that her father
resembled the Rev. Mr Irwine in *Adam Bede*. We know George
Eliot drew *him* from life. So we see it was possible to retain the
Rector of Hayslope's eighteenth-century tolerance, general
benevolence and unsparing charitableness well into the nineteenth century. Perhaps George Eliot did wish to register this
happier past of the English Church when she makes a point
of showing a late eighteenth-century rector refusing to allow
the Methodists in his parish to be persecuted (no one wants
to interfere with them but the self-important parish clerk)
and forming a personal and lasting friendship with the
Methodist woman preacher Dinah Morris. Another recognition of the change brought about by the Evangelicals'

narrowness and zeal is recorded by Mrs Gaskell (born 1810) in one of the sharper passages of *North and South*, where the heroine, born in a Hampshire vicarage but transplanted when grown up to Milton in the industrial north, returns after her father's death to her former home and finds the vicarage altered out of all recognition by the new Evangelical parson and his wife, who interfere unpardonably with the villagers and set everyone by the ears in their determination to domineer or repress. Trollope, a liberal-minded man (though a Tory), formed in pre-Victorian England, and whose Christianity was only vindictive in the traditional form of anti-semitism, drew his portrait of the ideal Church of England parson in the *Vicar of Bullhampton* (1870). A thorough gentleman and a good fellow, the Rev. Frank Fenwick insists on always extending the hand of Christian fellowship to the Free Church minister of his parish, to the latter's fury, who would prefer their relationship to be on the basis of a running battle (a situation of comedy that Trollope handles with ability). The vicar is tolerant even to the point of wishing not to have removed his enemy's new chapel, which has been built deliberately opposite the vicarage gate (at the instigation of the squire, a Low Church marquis) to annoy the parson and his household, even though it turns out to have been built on part of the glebe. But this ideal was hardly practicable once Low Church bishops and Anglo-Catholic parsons had been produced – we remember that after calling on Bishop Proudie, the Master of an Oxford college sighed at the passing of 'Greek play bishops', that is, bishops of old who were scholars and gentlemen and kept their energies for editing Greek plays. When Sydney Smith died in 1845, it was felt by Greville that he represented the best kind of eighteenth-century clergyman, and he wrote:

I do not suppose that he had any dogmatical and doctrinal opinions in respect to religion. In his heart of hearts he despised and derided all that the world wrangles and squabbles about; but he had the true religion of benevolence and charity, of peace and goodwill to all mankind.[19]

George Eliot wished to write a novel about such a type, but she could do so (in *Adam Bede*) only by putting him into a subordinate position to parishioners whose lives contained sin

and misery, disasters and tragedy. It was not a character that
lent itself to being a novel's protagonist; Goldsmith had the
same difficulty with the Vicar of Wakefield. But the comba-
tive new clergy could and did provide Victorian novelists
with rich scenes of conflict and drama and innumerable
points for satiric comedy, and they took every advantage of
this. Mary Cholmondeley tells us that her father had been
formed before such questions as apostolic succession, the
authenticity of the gospels, doubt in general, and Trac-
tarianism came in, and that he gave no thought to them when
they did.

But in the Victorian age it was more likely to be laymen
than clergy who could be all-tolerant; we see in *Barchester
Towers* how a new bishop and his too-zealous Evangelical wife
and chaplain rouse a hitherto peaceful diocese into a very
un-Christian state of feeling.[20] (Trollope was perhaps mistaken in setting this anachronistically into the late 1850s and
making it contemporary with post-Oxford Movement times.)
Sir Titus Salt was a self-made man, but when he built near
Bradford a model manufacturing and housing estate for the
benefit of his workmen and their families, he provided in
addition to such amenities as almshouses, schools, communal baths and washhouses, park and hospital, *all* varieties
of chapel including Roman Catholic, and also Sunday
schools. Only public houses were banned at Saltaire, for he
held, from long observation, that drink was the working-
man's greatest enemy, but all forms of religion were ben-
eficial, at any rate from the employer's point of view.

After the Tractarian movement and Newman's defection,
God-fearing Victorian parents with sons to educate were in a
dilemma. If they sent their boy to Oxford he was all too likely,
the evidence showed, to be induced to 'go over', or, if not,
then to pick up a lot of pernicious Catholic nonsense that was
nearly as bad. But if they chose Cambridge, the traditional
home of rationality, where Evangelicalism had waned before
minds formed on mathematical sciences and under the
influence of Mill, the boy might be tempted by something
equally intolerable – scepticism. At Cambridge, still dominated by the great names of Newton and Bentley and Mill,
Pusey and Newman were viewed with contempt; and Leslie
Stephen, who went up in 1850, noted that 'It was one of the

great advantages of Cambridge that there was no such person
in the place'. He tells us that when he could not 'come to
terms with the Thirty-nine Articles' he 'was not cast out by
the orthodox indignation of my colleagues' but 'treated with
all possible kindness'. An Evangelical clergyman, grandson
of William Paley (author of *A View of the Evidence of Christianity*
(1794)), brought his daughter Mary to the newly formed
women's college at Cambridge: she wrote later that her
orthodoxy was there gradually undermined by 'Mill's
Inductive Logic and *Ecce Homo* and Herbert Spencer and the
general tone of thought'. She soon turned to the science of
economics and collaborated with, and then married, the
Cambridge pioneer economist Alfred Marshall.[21]

The choice therefore was between High Church Oxford,
liable to lead to Romanism, and ex-Evangelical but still
Protestant Cambridge, where he might become lukewarm or
lose any faith whatever. Thus the opposition in Victorian
religious beliefs was dramatized in the polarization of the
universities. We note in accordance with this that in
religious-theme novels, such as Charlotte Yonge's, high-
souled young men go to Oxford and may have Roman
temptations, whereas clever young men go to Cambridge
where they have, and generally, then or later, succumb to,
doubts (like Samuel Butler's hero in *The Way of All Flesh*), and
return free-thinkers, or scoffers at orthodoxy. Both situations
are of course full of dramatic possibilities and give plenty of
opportunities for religious controversy; and these were fully
exploited by popular novelists.

II

The religious situation in Victorian Ireland was simpler but
certainly not less impassioned, since politics and class were
in that unhappy country inevitably mixed up with Catholic–
Protestant dualism. The Church of Ireland was traditionally,
fanatically, Low, in natural reaction against the native
Roman Catholicism, so that Tractarians could only be seen
as traitors by the Protestant Ascendancy; and Anglicanism of
a Catholic complexion could never take root. The literature
of controversy was more clear-cut and so more spirited, and,
on the Roman Catholic side, much bitterer than in England,

employing all the resources of Irish wit and of a language rich
in terms of abuse and picturesque exaggeration and vilifi-
cation, often translated by the bilingual Irish to emend the
poverty of English in these respects. This makes for livelier if
not better novels, of considerable interest to the student of
social history, and also to the student of literature because of
the racy Anglo-Irish idiom and vocabulary. The situation was
unusual because religion was as a rule decided by the class
structure – on the upper level, the Protestant Ascendancy as
landowner in the Big House (Irish for Great House), the
government, army and police officials, and with its religious
structure of Low Church clergy, bishops and archbishops;
but below these a Catholic working class of peasants and
farmers and a Catholic middle class of shopkeepers, doctors
and the priesthood. Of course this was only roughly true –
there were also Irish Catholic landed gentry (as well as
Protestant shopkeepers), but not enough to signify; and until
well after the Catholic Emancipation Act the Catholic
farmers and gentry carried no weight.

The earlier period remembered by the Irish novelist
William Carleton in his childhood, when chapels were
proscribed and Masses could only be said at open-air altars
(so that devout congregations had to kneel in the snow or
rain), and when Catholics were deprived of Catholic schooling and resorted to (literally) hedge schools,[22] and when
priests had to slip over to France surreptitiously for seminary
training – this had left a legacy of bitter rancour, especially
where the Orangemen operated to harass lawlessly the
peasantry suspected (frequently with justice) of belonging to
subversive political secret societies. This is the phase of (for
them) almost contemporary Irish history exploited by the
talented group of early nineteenth-century Irish novelists,
Carleton, the Banim brothers, and Gerald Griffin. Persecution died down when Whig opinion saw the necessity of
conciliating Ireland during the Napoleonic Wars and making
some reforms and amends. Inevitably the ill-used people
could neither forget nor forgive the past, though Maynooth
was founded in 1795 and the Maynooth Grant was put
through by the English government in 1845, thus establishing a seminary for priests and the right of a Catholic people
to have sectarian schooling. The rancour was against English

landlords who did not consider the interests of their tenants (though many of course did, and were not absentees), the government, and the Church of English clergy, for whom they had been tithed and whom they were always suspecting of trying to pervert them.[23] To individual Englishmen they were polite and even friendly, which made some Englishmen find the South with its happy-go-lucky countrymen pleasanter than the dour North. Trollope did, for one, who lived, worked and married there; he wrote of himself as 'preferring on the whole papistical to presbyterian tendencies'. The failure of the potato crop in 1845 and for several years after, that led to wide-scale disease, death or emigration to England or America, was the tragic background of many novels (even the irresponsible Anglo-Irish popular novelist Charles Lever recorded its disasters in his novel *The Martins of Cro' Martin* (1856), written about Ireland in the 1830s onwards). It impoverished for ever many landowners (this forms part of the deeply-felt historical background of one of the finest of all Irish novels, Somerville and Ross's *The Big House of Inver* (1925)). The potato famine and its part in Irish social history has been recorded in many memoirs too, which often read like passages from a novel – a first-rate novel. This is one way of saying that Ireland offered situations and material and characters, not to mention an Anglo-Irish speech-idiom more high-spirited, eloquent and expressive than classical English, ready-made for the novelist. The only difficulty was to make such eccentricity of character, such melodramatic happenings, such extremes of social life, seem plausible, and to give them a context in which they should have meaning.

The Potato Famine added to the religious rancour of the peasants because well-intentioned efforts to help them find work and to provide them with soup-kitchens, by the owners of estates and by those new Protestant social workers in towns, gave a fresh turn to Irish suspicions: that these charities were insidious attempts to convert them to Protestantism – hence the worst of all terms of abuse, 'souper'. The clergy, in addition to the Evangelicals' resented activities in giving the peasantry Bibles and tracts, had in the past been suspected of getting mixed up with politics; *agents provocateurs* had certainly been used by the government, and the Irish believed, it seems with some truth, that at times some of these were clergymen, thus stoking up the bitterness induced by tithing.[24] There was the Rev. Caesar Otway, who founded the first Irish magazine, *The Christian Examiner*, who was virulently anti-Catholic and who saw that Carleton, now penniless with a family to feed in Dublin, had talent and could be used. Carleton's change of religion cannot be charged to Otway's account, for Carleton had already joined the Church of Ireland and married a Protestant, with whom he lived happily; but Carleton was thus a 'jumper' and Otway was considered a 'souper'. The literature of Ireland was thus inevitably polemical, and no Irish novel could fail to be controversial, whether written by Protestant or Catholic. In that field the Catholics predictably wielded a wickeder, wittier and more trenchant pen than their duller enemies, who had neither the Catholic training in casuistry nor the Celtic freedom from inhibition as to giving blows below the belt. The Irish Catholic weapon was intellectual contempt, whereas the Protestant's line was horror of Catholic practices and proving the inferiority of the Catholic religion by its degraded social results.

The preface by Patrick Kavanagh to Carleton's *Autobiography* (1856) (a fascinating piece of reminiscence of the Ireland of Carleton's early days) has to account for Carleton's error in changing 'his historical Catholicism for Protestantism': 'naturally', writes Kavanagh, 'I have no prejudice against Protestantism, except that it appears to me to be based on everything that is weak in Christianity'; and he then quotes James Joyce who, on being asked whether, having lost his Catholic faith, he would become a Protestant, replied: 'What kind of liberation would that be to forsake an absurdity which is logical and coherent and to embrace one which is illogical and incoherent?'[25] This is of course mere assertion, and does nothing to account for all Carleton's good work (as well as his later bad novels in his decline) being written after leaving his historical Catholicism; nor for the well-attested fact that he refused to see a priest when dying. Carleton was in fact a talented journalist who, like Defoe, could and did write for both sides, according to whether, in Carleton's case, he had uppermost in his mind the nostalgic memories of his peasant childhood or the later insights of maturity in the larger world of Dublin's men of letters. Religious convictions do not really enter into the question, and his work – like everyone else's – has to be judged on its intrinsic merits and not as propaganda, successful or otherwise, nor as regards which side it may be alleged to be 'on'.

When the new Anglicanism (post-Tractarian) was imported into Ireland, it could only weaken the Church of Ireland, to the enjoyment of its Catholic enemies; but in the end the Church of Ireland remained, as traditionally, Low. The rigidity in its members had partly been created by the new missionary zeal of the Evangelical importation from England known as the New Reformation, whose face was by definition set against Rome. In her reminiscent *Happy Days! Essays of Sorts* (1946), Dame Edith Somerville characterized 'period aunts' (Irish) as looking upon 'weekday or Saints-day extras or by-days' as coming 'into the black category of things that they spoke of as Romish'. She explains the nature of Irish Low Church Protestants in a passage too long to quote (in *Mount Music*, 1919), which says that the Church of Ireland made 'more severe demands upon submission and credulity than any other, and yet more freely arraigns other creeds on those special counts'. This ironic situation was irresistible to a novelist, and *Mount Music* is inferior only to *The Real Charlotte* (1894) and *The Big House of Inver* in its recreation of Irish society, taking in all grades from the Protestant Ascendancy to the peasant cabin, but centring on the religious animosities of late Victorian Ireland.

Yet, in spite of the religious and social feuds and the black historical past, it is possible to recover an earlier nineteenth-century and an eighteenth-century Ireland from memoirs that show that in some places and times there existed even in Ireland a greater tolerance and neighbourly mixture of classes and creeds than the subsequent conditions of bigotry would suggest. Carleton mentions 'a circumstance which is not uncommon in Ireland, and is indicative of a very liberal feeling upon the part of its Catholic population', that one of his godmothers (he was born in 1794 in Northern Ireland) was the daughter of a neighbouring farmer who was a Presbyterian, and remarks that he thinks this 'a great stretch of liberality' on the part of his Catholic family. Nor, he says was this uncommon, but that if there was a Protestant godparent there would also be a Catholic one, 'the real sponsor'. This shows there was at least some degree of inter-denominational neighbourliness and some unexpected liberality on the priests' part in those earlier days. More surprising is the evidence of peaceful coexistence in far more testing circumstances, in the history of the Martin family recorded in the joint family memoirs (*Irish Memories*) by Somerville and Ross, the collaborators in many Irish novels and tales.

Violet Martin, who wrote under the name of Ross, being of the branch of Martins that lived at Ross in Galway, had had a Catholic grandfather who, in a family where traditionally 'each generation provided several priests for the Church', fell in love with a Protestant neighbour and became a Protestant in order to marry her, though in old age he returned to the Church of his fathers; nevertheless his six children were born and bred 'strong Protestants, and Low Church according to the fashion of their time, yet they lived in an entirely Roman Catholic district without religious friction of any kind.' His Protestant eldest son Robert married an Irish Roman Catholic beauty and 'Her four children were brought up as Protestants, but the rites of her Church were celebrated at Ross without let or hindrance, and prayers were held daily by her for all her servants, all of whom, then as now, were Roman Catholics.' Her father, she says, inherited from the Martins of Ross 'the Protestant instinct, and a tolerance for the sister religion, born of sympathy and respect' – a state of affairs no one would have supposed possible from the histories and the novels. The characteristic Irish touch of farcical improbability is added by her statement that the Protestant Rosses (and she was one of twelve children in her generation)

all received secret baptism at the hands of the priest. It was a kindly precaution taken by our foster mothers who were, it is needless to say, RCs; it gave them peace of mind in the matter of the foster children whom they worshipped, and my father and mother made no inquiries! Their Low Church training did not interfere with their common sense, nor did it blind them to the devotion that craved for the safe-guard.

This bears out Trollope's fictional tributes to the existence of

a less embroiled Ireland in time past, as when he wrote of
Phineas Finn's father that his 'religion was not of that bitter
kind in which we in England are apt to suppose that all Irish
Roman Catholics indulge' and who had sent his son to
Trinity College, Dublin (an academically respected university but not a Catholic one, and looked on unfavourably by
priests as a place where young men might be disturbed in
their faith; hence Newman tried to raise funds for an Irish
Catholic university college). Trollope had known Ireland in
his youth and early married life and must have been struck
with the difference between the theory and the actuality from
his own observation.

There is another available evidence of the ease with which,
till the hardening set in some time in the nineteenth century,
the 'sister religions' allowed scope for change without
bigotry. George Moore's family similarly oscillated between
Catholic and Protestant in successive generations, and he
explains in *Hail and Farewell* why he, of a Protestant cast of
mind, was so glad to discover that, in spite of his devout
Catholic father and elder brother, there was only one generation of Catholics behind him in his family.

The Irish Church was not disestablished till 1869, after
which a Ballot Act ultimately had to be passed to prevent
priests from intimidating their parishioners into voting as
the Church commanded, a state of affairs that had been
proved by witnesses after the election of 1872 to have been
the practice. The Ballot Act did not, however, really do much
to prevent the Church's domination of the voters, which after
all only superseded that of the landlords. Somerville and
Ross admit this in *Some Irish Yesterdays* (1906) when they say:
'Till that time the landlords took their tenants to the poll *en
masse*; thenceforward they were to advance under the banner
of the Church.' This situation was full of possibilities for
ironic comedy, and explains the admiring peasant's remark
in *Mount Music* when, describing to a friend the election he
had seen, he says: 'Father Sweeny it was marched in the
Pribawn boys. Faith, he had them well regulated. Very nate
they marched.' The identification of religion with class, and
the identification of the priesthood with the peasantry (from
which class they were so often drawn), made the political
scene in Ireland more dramatically clear-cut than in

England, even having two distinct languages, one for each religion, but with the peasants translating their native language into English and the Protestants speaking an English infected to a varying extent in accent, idiom and sentence-form by the Anglo-Irish of the natives. To capture this and make the maximum use of it for literature required a novelist with a fine ear and an intelligent understanding of how the Anglo-Irish speech came about and how it was socially revealing. This is where the Somerville and Ross partnership scores over Carleton, who has difficulty in controlling his flood – not command – of English, having been brought up in an Irish-speaking family, and acquired his English largely from literature.

Later, when Parnell had become Ireland's hope and then the Parnell case broke, Catholics too became split, either bitter pro- or anti-Parnellites; this Dreyfus-like rift is registered in literature, for example by Joyce in his unhappy memories of his home in boyhood, in *Portrait of the Artist as a Young Man*.

The transfer of power from landlord to priest was comparable to something that happened more gradually in England, for there was no abrupt and dramatic change here. England had a long intermediate stage between the ballot-box's freeing the tenant or labourer from voting on the landlord's instructions, and the twentieth-century situation of the trades unions' considerable success in directing the new industrial masses into voting Labour, a period during which the English masses had to make up their minds for themselves. As usual, Ireland seems to have been more dramatic, more extreme, and far more violent. English tenants, whatever their grievances, did not ambush and shoot dead their landlords, or beat up the rent-collector to death's door, or murder the family of anyone who took lawful measures to protect himself against violence or who reported a murder to the police. Yet these are ordinary features of nineteenth-century Irish novels, as facts of life. The Irish novelist had an *embarras de richesses*; his trouble was the difficulty, in the circumstances, of not writing melodrama. This was something that was achieved only by novelists writing in the classical upper-class eighteenth-century tradition of Maria Edgeworth, who could use the vocabulary and irony of novels deriving from Jane Austen, necessarily therefore belonging to the Protestant Ascendancy. Catholic Irish novelists had to employ either a polemical or a peasant-tradition, too hot and uncontrolled in vocabulary, too violent and stagey in choice of incident, running to caricature and stereotypes as regards characterization, but with the advantage therefore of compelling opinion and imaginative sympathy to side with them.

The Anglo-Irish novel

The novel in Ireland occupies a considerably different field from the novel in England or anywhere else; for the Irish situation was unique. First, of course, because Ireland was governed by a foreign power, as Italy and USA had been, with consequently a long history of repression, resentment and outrages on both sides; because there was a population divided unequally between two uncompromising forms of the Christian religion, the majority of the people holding a religion of a different form from that of the Established Church of the governing power; and because of the stratification of the country socially, with a Protestant Ascendancy of landed gentry speaking English – often absentee landlords – with a Catholic farming and a landless peasant class who, until the mid-nineteenth century, were largely Irish-speaking or at any rate bilingual, and a small but rising urban middle class of both religions speaking in a distinctive Anglo-Irish idiom. Some of the bizarre consequences of these anomalies are suggested in Shaw's preface to his play *John Bull's Other Island* (first produced in 1904; published in 1907), where he wrote:

I am a genuine typical Irishman of the Danish, Norman, Cromwellian, and (of course) Scottish invasions. I am violently and arrogantly Protestant by family tradition; but let no English Government therefore count on my allegiance: I am English enough to be an inveterate Republican and Home Ruler. It is true that one of my grandfathers was an Orangeman; but then his sister was an abbess; and his uncle, I am proud to say, was hanged as a rebel.

But this by no means exhausts the subject of Irish divergences and anomalies. The interest for literature lies in its uniquely varied material and stimulus for the native novelist, with its many social, religious and historical tensions that could power both comedy and tragedy, the linguistic orchestra which the novelist had at his disposal, modulating from the one language into the other; and its handicaps – for there was no native public in the nineteenth century large enough to support a novelist, and so Irish novelists had to write with one eye on the English-speaking public, generally needing to go to London to find an English publisher; a hampering factor, of course, and felt to be humiliating by nationalists such as Gerald Griffin.

This was easy for novelists like Maria Edgeworth (1767–1849) and Edith Œnone Somerville (1858–1949) and 'Martin Ross', Violet Martin (1862–1915), who wrote as members of the Protestant Ascendancy as well as living among their peasant tenants. Even so, *Castle Rackrent* was somewhat esoteric for an obviously intended English reading public and required a glossary and footnotes, which she supplied. But the Catholic products of Gaelic-speaking homes, like Carleton and his contemporaries, who had acquired their education in both English and Latin in a hedge-school or something not much better, were in difficulties as novelists in not having access socially to the gentry, whom they needed as figures in their novels if those novels were to find an English market; and in consequence such characters were taken from books and speak the conventional rhetoric of early nineteenth-century English fiction and drama. So the characters of most Irish Catholic novelists fall into two classes: the improbably speaking and conventionally conceived inhabitants of the Big House who are set apart from the multitudinous realistic world of the farmhouse, the cabin and the roads, whose various idioms are pinned down for us in fiction to illuminate otherwise incomprehensible attitudes and actions.

Ireland had the good fortune to have a number of Irish Catholic novelists, from William Carleton to James Joyce, who embodied in *themselves* and who could express in fictional forms the national tensions and historical divisions. The beginning of the nineteenth century saw the appearance of several such talented Irish writers – William Carleton (1794–1869), the Banim brothers – John (1798–1842) and Michael

(1796–1874) – and Gerald Griffin (1803–40). Carleton came
from the Irish-speaking peasantry, the Banims from the
Catholic lower-middle class, and Griffin from a farming class
whose sons were educated to achieve professional status. But
they were all in another respect ideally suited to their function. The conflict of religious cultures is for the novelist suitably represented by the mixed marriage or, if frustrated, a
love between members of the opposing religions, which
offers itself as a symbol and can be explored in terms of
personal drama. Fortunately for literature, therefore, John
Banim had suffered deeply from having early in life fallen in
love with a Protestant girl whose parents rebuffed him as a
Catholic; Griffin had had the painful experience of falling in
love with a married woman who was a Quaker; and Carleton
actually married a Protestant girl and converted himself
officially, though remaining forever stamped by his identification with the Catholic farming community of his youth.
Thus, while all these novelists instinctively sympathized
with their fellow-Catholics and especially with the downtrodden peasantry, they all attempted, to their credit, some
impartiality in using the novel and the tale as a means of
pleading for an end to Irish violence as well as to oppression
from government and landlords.

The Irish-speaking or Anglo-Irish-speaking novelists had
an immense advantage in being steeped from birth in an
exceptionally poetic folklore originating in pagan times but
now aligned with a religious folklore of a later date. Unlike
Yeats, who never made anything of it as an artist because he
had to acquire it academically, *they* possessed it as a birthright. Carleton, after describing the wealth of oral literature
and folklore he heard in his home, adds:

What rendered this, however, of such peculiar advantage to me as
a literary man was, that I heard them as often, if not oftener, in the
Irish language as in the English; a circumstance which enabled me
in my writings to transfer the genius, the idiomatic peculiarity and
conversational spirit of the one language into the other, precisely as
the people themselves do in their dialogues, whenever the heart or
imagination happens to be moved by the darker or better passions.

We can see in the novels of John and Michael Banim how
important an emotional background such beliefs could pro-

vide for a novel's action, and even how they could determine
it. Identifying with the peasants and small farmers as
Carleton did, he led a tradition of taking the events of that
class seriously and exposing the tragic elements in their situation with sympathy, elements which the Protestant writers
tended to notice with impatience or present humorously as
due to the Irish people's improvidence, dirty habits, recklessness and squalid living, without considering that these
characteristics were the product of their economic history.
And these divisions and characteristics looked very different
from the other side, as the Irish novelists show. The most
striking part of one of the best Irish novels, *The Nowlans*
(1826), is where the Catholic ex-priest, John Nowlan, the son
of a prosperous farmer, is living in Dublin in poverty, lodging
in a poor Protestant household. The landlord and his family
are necessarily penny-pinching, but scrupulously clean and
thrifty and unceasingly industrious; and keep themselves to
themselves in the lower-middle-class Protestant tradition.
Seen by John Nowlan, this respectability is odious: he is used
to the open-handed warm-hearted country habits where
everyone including pedlars, fiddlers and even beggars are
welcome to the fireside and a meal; whereas street-
musicians, pedlars and beggars are turned away by Protestant city landlords. The contrast is actually between a rural
farm-owning society with no economic means and an urban
society in a later stage of development, entirely dependent on
earning money competitively, and where there is only one
step from respectability to beggary; and John Nowlan overlooks the drawbacks of Catholic social promiscuousness and
lavish hospitality while stressing the (for him) unpleasant
Protestant passion for order and economy which he sees as
alien and attributes to a mean morality. Both sides saw that
speech embodied these differences: idiom, vocabulary and
intonation expressing different life-styles; and all the Anglo-
Irish novelists used these divisions with brilliant results,
from Carleton and Maria Edgeworth to the stylish Somerville and Ross at the end of the nineteenth century and later.
Thus to the differences of region, religion, class, politics,
historical traditions, of rich and poor, of good and bad, there
was a further division between feudal countryside and commercial city-dwellers.

These natural differences – of division by linguistic idiom, religion and cultural traditions and even of history – were not unique to Ireland, of course; and there ought to be a study of the literary results of such divided nations. The regional differences of Italian dialects were greater; and I imagine Italy and the conquests over the original Latins by Goths in the north, Greek settlers and Moors in the south, Normans and French and Spanish rulers and so on, must have corresponded to the successive waves of conquerors of the Irish by Norsemen, Normans, Scottish planters, the Elizabethan English and the Cromwellian settlers. If, as Professor Thomas Flanagan in his pioneer work, *The Irish Novelists 1800–1850*, holds, the idea of 'What is an Irishman?' was always and continually a matter of debate, the very idea of an Italian society hardly existed till after the unification of Italy in 1870. We see a worse case for literature than Ireland's in Belgium, where the divisions of two religions are increased by the Walloons being French-speaking and the Flemish speaking Dutch; with Belgian literature necessarily written in two quite different languages, and the country being embittered by an unresolvable language rivalry. In Ireland in the nineteenth century everyone could be placed, regionally and in class, by his tongue; but this was an advantage for the novelist, and everyone spoke their regional and class idiom with verve; the Protestant Ascendancy even speaking an Anglo-Irish of considerable individuality which was a gift to novelists.

So the writers of Ireland had a rich land to work for the novel. No serious Irish novelist, surrounded by such challenges, could produce a novel as morally complacent, as spiritually docile and as confidently moralistic as *I Promessi Sposi*. Nor could a major nineteenth-century Irish novelist write as what George Eliot called a 'meliorist', one confident of there being a state of human improvement visibly brought about by mutual goodwill and enlightened government – a tenable mid-Victorian English position (one sees it also in *David Copperfield* and other mid-century English novels).

Trollope, in addition to taking a Catholic Irishman, Phineas Finn, for the hero of two of his novels, wrote several novels wholly about Ireland (two early ones in the early 1840s and two late in his life; the last, called *The Landleaguers*,

unfinished) which are different from any Irish novelist's,
though he lived and worked and hunted in Ireland for some
years, studied Carleton's, the Banims', Griffin's and Maria
Edgeworth's novels, and, staying at Coole Park with Sir
William Gregory, like Yeats later, absorbed the Coole Park
library of Anglo-Irish literature and politics, and always
retained his interest in Irish life and politics. He even wrote,
while living and travelling in Ireland as an official in the Post
Office service, that he preferred the papist south to the
Protestant north, so may be supposed to have been nearer the
Irish in sympathy than any other nineteenth-century
Englishman. Yet, as I said, his Irish novels are still noticeably
English in technique and idiom of speech, and still more
noticeable in being without the overtones and the imaginative life of the Irish novelists and their understanding of a
people steeped in religious belief and other-world superstitions. Michael Sadleir, in his book *Trollopeian Commentary*,
was right to contrast Trollope's treatment of the tragic
melancholy of the Big House with a collapsing family in *The
MacDermots* (1853–5), and that of Somerville and Ross in
The Big House of Inver (1925). Trollope, he says, ignores the
drama of the Irish past inherent in its present; he has no
sense of the poetry in these luckless people's lives; and
though Trollope was genuinely concerned for Ireland and
saw its grievances must be dealt with by England, society and
politics in his novels are explicit and not dissolved into
dialogue, action and feeling, as they are by Anglo-Irish
novelists. Moreover, Trollope proceeds in all his Irish novels
on the rational plan of consistent chronological progress and
plot and separate comic-relief sub-plot as in his English
novels. He really had not learned anything artistically from
the Irish novelists he had studied; and it is his first novel, on
the moral and social decay of an Irish family, that is nearer to
the Irish than any of those he wrote later. This makes my
point, I think, that there *was* an Anglo-Irish novel tradition
distinct from the English novel.

The Irish tradition, in fact, was the spoken tale; and that
belonged to the Gaelic world of storytellers carrying on an
ancient tradition: an art with its own conventions and literary
forms in a language very different from English. William
Carleton explained how he had the benefit of being brought

up in an Irish-speaking household with parents peculiarly gifted in the Irish traditions of song and poetry. And we see in his best tales how he drew on these inherited sources of folklore, but how difficult it was for him to write a *novel*, a form requiring much greater complexity and sophisticated planning than folktale, legend or saga, and not following a fixed form but needing to find its own unique expression. His novels, however, do express the civilization of the Irish-speaking countrymen, and it is this that makes the Irish Catholic novels of the nineteenth century so valuable, with their adaptation of the folktale, and with a native teller instead of the authorial voice, and in a context as like that of the true folktale as possible – that is, told at the fireside or in the inn, or at the still or the drying-kiln. The Banim brothers and Griffin, like Carleton, devised just such traditional settings to enclose their collections of tales. And Maria Edgeworth in *Castle Rackrent* had the tact to relate the downfall of the Rackrent family through the mouth of the old retainer who had seen it pass before his eyes like an epic. Old Thady inherited an art of conversation and tale-telling, with its conventions and rituals, witty and humorous, rich in metaphors and proverbs. The folktale is meant to be heard, not read; it is necessarily short, and belongs to the realm of the imagination. It has been said that 'no two literary forms could be farther apart than the folktale and the novel'. Therefore to translate the forms of oral literature into the novel, which is basically realistic and written for the entertainment not of a peasantry but of an educated middle class or aristocracy, presents almost insuperable difficulties. So what we see the Irish novelists of the last half of the eighteenth century doing when they undertake a *novel* is necessarily a mongrel product. They were attracted to such non-realistic forms of fiction as then existed – the Gothic novel and melodrama – and combined them with a form of realism that included the picaresque novel, social satire which allowed tales within a loose rambling narrative, as seemed convenient. Thus, parts of the Irish Catholic novels are better than the whole, the whole is *not* more than the sum of the parts, as it is in good novels in other countries and in the novels of Anglo-Irish Protestants. So, as in Italy, the Irish Catholic writers were much more successful with the tale and novella than with the novel.

A further disadvantage is that whereas the speech of their countryfolk (including the special idioms of priest and schoolmaster) is impressively alive, the upper classes, when their novels require them, speak a fatally conventional, insipid English evidently imitated from inferior English fiction. Thus *The Croppy* (1828), Michael Banim's novel about the Wexford uprising in 1798 (the year of John Banim's birth), is apt to put the reader off by its opening chapters and subsequent areas of dead melodrama; but the novel lives in interspersed scenes of revolt, violence and tragic events in the lives of the doomed peasantry as the rebellion, led by their gigantic priest, Father Rourke, comes to a head and is crushed, dying out in the bitter sentence with which the novel ends: 'Father Rourke was hanged upon the bridge of Wexford; the weight of his colossal body having broken the rope, however, before Saunders Smyly saw him pending to his heart's content.'

Both *Heart of Midlothian* and *Old Mortality* were no doubt known to Michael Banim. In his novel, there are striking scenes in the smithy where pikes are being forged for the rebels, and when the villagers see their houses in flames and the cavalry torturing croppies to get 'confessions' out of them. The humane Sir Thomas Hartley, who tells the captain that he is driving the people to 'ferocious revolution', is then accused of 'promising an insurrection'. The inevitable rising of the Wexford peasantry follows, as he predicted. He resists their demand – made with threats – to join them as their general; and their priest Father Rourke, whom nature had intended for a soldier, we are told, becomes their leader. Nevertheless, Sir Thomas is arrested, imprisoned and sentenced to death as a traitor to the King. The powerful and terrifying scenes of insurrection are also splendidly managed, conveying the rebels' cruelty and bigotry as impartially as that of their enemies – for instance, though the insurrection had many Protestants in command, and in principle the rebels were united not by religion but by class, nevertheless once in conflict all Protestants are considered Orangemen 'meriting instant vengeance' – a 'curious inconsistency' which the novelist makes comprehensible. Their banner, 'Liberty or Death', owing to the absence of a breeze to float the flag, now shows only 'Death'. A few other priests

hold command too in the insurgents' forces – 'deriving their
inspiration from the very general belief' that they are
charmed persons whom no bullet or weapon could hurt and
whose sacred powers meant they would ensure victory. Yet
their unanimously chosen 'Commander-in-Chief' was a
Protestant – a fanatic who hoped to make converts to his
religion and protect his own flock: of course both proved to
be delusions. In these respects Michael Banim rivals Scott in
making understandable the psychology and conduct of a
popular uprising.

Gerald Griffin's masterpiece *The Collegians* (1829) suffers
still more from stilted dames in castles and young gentlemen
conversing in set speeches that no one could have actually
spoken; but the force of the book lies in images of action and
conflicts of cultures and classes. The least flawed of the
ambitious works – longer and more complex than tales – are
two short novels, one, *Tracy's Ambition* (1829) by Gerald
Griffin, and the other, *The Nowlans* by the Banim brothers,
which, while wholly Irish, can hold their own with the novels
of any country. The strength of these is the psychological
realism and moral investigation arising from a background of
national tensions, with the overtones of peasant belief and
imagination, that makes them utterly different from any
English nineteenth-century novel except *Wuthering Heights*
(*Wandering Willie's Tale* is only an inset into the novel *Red-
gauntlet*). This tradition is seen later in the century, as in
Emily Lawless's *Hurrish* (1886).

The consistently violent history of Ireland socially and
politically lent itself inevitably to melodrama – one
remembers the exponent from Venezuela in Conrad's novel
Nostromo, who says the history of his country is like a stage
melodrama, only in this case the corpses and blood are real.
As Professor Flanagan says of John Banim's novella *Croohore
of the Billhook* (1825), though it was 'founded on fact yet one
instinctively rejects it as lurid beyond belief. Banim was
faced with the task of writing about a bloody and violent land
. . . But there no longer existed in English fiction conventions
by which such a society could be represented. In default, he
accepted the conventions of the shilling shocker.' This hardly
does the Banims justice, for they found means to actualize
those conventions and make them poetic by drawing on the

inherited superstitions and religious beliefs of the Irish
people, as well as making their savage conduct comprehensible by revealing its causes and the code the people lived by.

The Irish tradition of the novel, then, is a mixture of literary forms with interspersed folklore and folksongs, and an
atmosphere in which, as in *Wuthering Heights*, the rational
world is interpenetrated by the other-world. In the Irish
novels, spiritually Catholic and pre-Christian superstition
combined – a combination that was capable of artistic handling, and that, in the hands of the best Irish novelists, gave
birth to striking successes. Mark Hawthorne in his interesting monograph on John and Michael Banim[1] points out that
The Nowlans is divided between episodes of daylight and those
belonging to the night; he says: 'John Banim associated each
main character with a different degree of darkness. John
Nowlan's darkness is the struggle within his own sexual
desires' (struggle, that is, between the natural man who
desires love and marriage, and the conscience of the trained
priest having been pushed by his family into taking orders
without understanding what it entailed). His sister Peggy's
struggle is that of her environment, which she defeats
because she is faithful to her ideal of religion; 'But the
villain's [a Protestant villain, of course] darkness is Gothic,
and his evil is paralleled and assisted by the creatures of the
night who oppose Peggy's ideal.' Thus, Banim overcomes
through this symbolism of construction, as we may call it, his
artistic difficulties, for, Hawthorne says, 'the darkness arises
from the clash of primitive emotion with the manners of
fashionable society' and also, I think we must add, the clash
between the Catholic ideal of the sexless priest and the
Protestant ideal of a human norm necessary for every man,
one of marriage and of family life.

The night in this novel is where lawlessness, violence and
murder take place, and is also the dark night of the soul when
John Nowlan's wife dies in childbirth in the ditch like a
beggar, and the frantic young husband goes mad for a time.
The daylight is when the truth of this is made apparent and
the everyday life of family, courtship and sociality takes
place. The resolution at the end is in John Nowlan's
repentance, reconciliation with his relatives and his child,

and his hoping to return to his priestly duties – calm after the storm.

Another difficulty the Anglo-Irish novelists had and conquered was that the characters the Irish Catholic novelists wanted to use would not fit into the formula of the fashionable English novel. This was dealt with in various ways. One was to show in operation *simultaneously* the different value-systems, either religious or social, of each: as we see in the mixed marriage which the Nowlans contracted – between a young lady, Letty, and John Nowlan – where we also see how each regarded the marriage, laudable from her innocent Protestant point of view, but damning from his as a renegade priest. Also in *The Half-Sir*, a novella by Gerald Griffin, we see the protagonist's, the semi-gentleman's, social anomaly both through his own sensibility and as the drawing-room society of his mistress sees him. This technique has been called the double focus, and comes naturally to the Anglo-Irish novelists who lived in both worlds. One of the characteristics that most distinguishes the nineteenth-century Anglo-Irish novel from English Regency and Victorian novels is that in the Irish novel courtship is not an end; the marriage often occurs early on in order to focus on personal problems caused by religiously and politically mixed unions and, instead of building suspense from the vicissitudes of courtship, the novel delves into the irrationality of frustrated and disillusioned men or the primitive savagery that had been momentarily repressed by English law. This gives the reader constant shocks of the same kind as *Wuthering Heights* provides. Undoubtedly these Irish novelists were as consciously determined as the classic American novelists not to write *English* novels, but to evolve a novel suited to the character of their country's life, of which they refused to be ashamed, but, on the contrary, felt they were able to show reasons for being proud. This effort was addressed both defiantly to the English reader, and to improve the morals of the urban Anglo-Irish, who at that time generally knew little of their country outside the city. It was also a means of integrating the various strands of Irish society and building up a reading public. Thus these novelists were largely able to avoid novelistic conventions.

And the Anglo-Irish language, with all its wit and humour, was exploited by these novelists as Scott worked with the Scottish dialects, in comparison with which the dialogues of his gentry are so dull and insipid. It is felt to be a real language, more expressive than standard English, and as used in the novels from Carleton to Somerville and Ross is employed with great art to reveal the unique character of a people whose idioms and sentence structures derived from an originally Gaelic-speaking and still often Gaelic-thinking nation. It has implications resulting from a national history, an idiom perfected by speech and not tamed by education or literature. But its characteristic developments are psychological. For instance, the persuasively minimizing effort in describing violence is exploited by Griffin in *The Half-Sir*, where someone explains the shooting of a gentleman thus: 'He's a magisthru, and not over and above quite, for which raison one o' the lads comes down to have a crack at him from the rock, as if he was a saagull'. On the one hand, shooting a seagull is an innocent thing to do, and on the other a zealous magistrate is naturally a target and asking for trouble; so attempted murder is passed off as a form of sport. Similarly, consider the euphemisms, as in the same novel where 'A couple had a son that used to get his living *soft* enough by stalen' an' doen' everything that was endefferent'; Griffin in a footnote explains that 'endefferent' equals 'wicked'. Or a girl in Griffin's novel *The Collegians* mentions 'a man that was servin' a process in the mountains, an' a poor man that was in the place had the misfortune of killing him'. This deprecating way of describing the murder of an official is possible, the novelist makes us believe, because of the consensus of opinion among the peasantry that anyone who served writs or a summons is as a servant of the law a wicked enemy. The details of the incident show that it was not in fact an accident but a horribly deliberate murderous assault. 'He was a very foolish man', continues the woman – 'it was only this mornin' he took up two boys for night-walkin', and nothin' could do after him but to go into the mountain to serve a process upon one Naughtin, a first cousin of their own. 'M sure what could he expect? They gathered about him, and one of 'em knocked him down, and another made him go upon his knees, and ate the process, an swally it, an after that he got a blow of a stone from somebody or another, that destroyed his head, an' indeed I'm ferd he never'll do.' He is found to be surrounded by a crowd whose faces expose 'grim satisfaction' at the murder. It is mentioned moreover that 'he's one o' them that *turned*', that is, converted to the Protestant faith; which of course makes him more to be execrated than any mere criminal, the author conveys to us. The Irish novelists write with a sociologist's appreciation of the situation and, as creative writers, a vision of it as black *comedy*, and a profound feeling for the tragic social situation. And they show how attitudes had produced forms of language that euphemized and so almost justified barbarous crime, in order to make it acceptable to a people professedly Christian and dutifully religious.

Compare 'Tubber Berg' or 'The Red Well' in Carleton's stories[2] – where all the widow's children have fallen on the bailiff and having wedged him into a corner, and filled a large tub with water, are trying 'conscientiously' to immerse him into it and drown him, kicking and beating him; meanwhile, the eldest, laid up in bed with a sore back, regrets that he can't assist them, declaring, 'It would be no disgrace to hang for the like of him.' When the bailiff is rescued by a neighbour the children shriek with laughter. Carleton is perfectly aware of the barbarity, but he goes on to make apparent the social and economic conditions that had produced the savagery as morally justified. Somerville and Ross's novels offer many similar examples of insight into the reasons for euphemistic guile of expression as well as the Irish instinct for elegant phrases comparable to French.

This tradition of elegant understatement, of humour and callous glee in cruelty, is seen to be a hallmark of the Irish mentality, and is a trait noted by all Irish novelists – for example Emily Lawless's interesting novel *Hurrish* of the 1880s, Somerville and Ross's novels and Joyce's *Ulysses*.

Griffin later in life told his Religious Brethren that he had deliberately associated with neighbouring farmers and labourers, men and women, living in their homes and listening at their firesides and talking freely with servant boys and girls, making mental note of their flashes of wit and humour. Walking about the countryside, he talked with everyone he met. Somerville and Ross similarly treasured the conversations they heard in court-room and street, at the hunt and in the kitchen, and from their tenants – for use in their fictions. Such novelists lived *with* the people and comprehended them. This is their strength as creative writers. They were not cut off, as were modern French intellectual novelists like Sartre (who, we learn, had never met any peasants or working-men until the German occupation, when he was in a French internment camp for three months and had to meet them, an experience he noted with surprise), or like Italian well-off writers such as Moravia, for whom the war seems to have meant merely some months of discomfort living in the mountains in a peasant hut, an experience from which he learnt nothing as a novelist, to judge by *Two Women*, the novel in which he uses this episode in his own life.

The Irish novelists constantly use speech-forms also to nail down characteristics of the people's code. In Griffin's impressive short novel, *Suil Dhuv* (1857), an elder brother is shattered not because his younger brother has been gaoled for breaking into a house and stealing property, but because he also stole a sheep – in consequence, 'disgrace was fixed upon his reputation'; of someone else who had committed a crime, he says 'Heaven be praised that it wasn't a cow or a sheep he stole'. Those are real crimes, because committed against other members of the farming community. Thus the novelists were revealing an archaic and partly savage society to the outsider and making a work of art from it because they sympathized with individual members.

The Gaelic poetic imagery which was in the people's mouths is therefore recorded as witty or ironic, but never as sentimental or affected, as poetic imagery in English mouths would be. Thus Somerville and Ross in *Irish Memories* (1917) record a countryman's description of a priest who, he said, had been such a good man that when he died 'he went through Purgatory like a flash of lightning. There wasn't a singe on him' – an image at once poetic and Catholic, and Irish in its exaggeration and immediacy. Such gifted speech is a goldmine for a novelist, and in it lies the strength of the Irish novel. Or a lay image, when Griffin's herdsman says darkly, telling of his youth, 'In them days a man couldn't go a lonesome road at night without meetin' things that would make the hair of his head stiffen equal to bristles.' Griffin, though a devout Catholic who gave up writing in his prime in order to join a religious order, was still an Irish writer and unlike Dante, who excluded all folk-elements from his *Divine Comedy* as pagan and therefore unacceptable. No nineteenth-century Irish novelist could truthfully render the experience of the Irish people without admitting their folklore (which includes rituals, superstitious beliefs, dreams and visions, and the oral literature of song and story). Thus Griffin's tales, *Holland Tide* or *Munster Popular Tales* (1827) contain several international folktales translated into the racy Anglo-Irish idiom he no doubt had heard them in, and he used them in an Irish fictional context. So we are not surprised when, in his masterpiece *Tracy's Ambition*, the young man who writes elegant lyrics to sing to the traditional Irish melodies is told by his father that they are unsuitable; what is wanted for such tunes is, he argues, 'a national song-writer, a Burns of the sheelings and pellices'. He rejects Tom Moore's lyrics as 'too cultivated in style'; they are not, he asserts, 'spontaneous and natural'; 'They have not enough of the *bog* in their composition'. Here the author speaks in his own person and most intelligently too.

The advantage of the Irish novelist lay in being spontaneous and natural and, like Burns, in combining high art with native idiom to express national character and embody a traditional way of life seen as being eroded by changing social forms (notably, the emergence of an Irish urban middle class). Through their art they opened up for their own nation what Carlo Levi, living in the archaic peasant society of southern Italy, described as 'that closed world, shrouded in black veils, bloody and earthy, the other world where the peasants live and which no-one can enter without a magic key.' The magic key can only be the informed imagination of a creative writer. But having entered it, the problem is how to use it in the novel – which is not the archaic form the epic or folktale was – in order to appeal to and touch the imagination of a modern public like the nineteenth-century middle class.

This problem seems to me to have been best solved in Griffin's novel *Tracy's Ambition*. It is told through his narrator, whose limitations as a Protestant middle-class trader and farmer with aspirations towards gentility are thus recorded and are the mainspring of the drama. These have been practically solved by his runaway marriage with a young lady of superior Catholic family, resulting in a happy family life, though the daughter is brought up in her mother's religion and the two boys in their father's (the usual compromise following a mixed marriage in Ireland, England and Europe until the hardening folly due to the Vatican Council late in the nineteenth century). Tracy's satisfactory relationship with the peasants is due to his well-born wife's good offices as mediator between the two parties; but this is destroyed when Tracy makes friends with Dalton, the new magistrate who takes a hard line with the peasants and holds out to Tracy the bait of a government appointment. As a result, in a peasant outbreak Tracy, in self-defence, shoots one of the ring-leaders, and thus becomes the object of a vendetta, also losing his noble wife who is killed by accident in the struggle. So Tracy is now isolated and obliged to follow Dalton's lead into social and financial disaster, for Dalton forces a big loan from Tracy to pay the debts of his gay and dashing son whom the country people admire as 'an arch boy', a characteristic euphemism. (Somerville and Ross also make great moral use of this disastrous ideal in the fine novel *The Big House of Inver* (1925)). The money that was put aside for the dowry of Tracy's beloved daughter, the image of his dead wife, in her imminent marriage to her sweetheart, son of a prosperous Catholic farmer, is thus jeopardized, for Dalton neither can nor intends to repay the money, to Tracy's agony. Tracy is also in danger of being murdered by the surviving twin brother of the malefactor he was obliged to shoot. And here a further new dimension enters to darken the social, religious and moral drama. The twins were the offspring in tragic cases of a Romeo and Juliet marriage between two very poor peasant families, the Shanahans and the O'Sheas, living on terms of mutual hatred in the mountains in the Hog's Valley. The married couple had to live with the husband's father, whom the husband loves but who resents his daughter-in-law as the child of his enemies. She, for her part, taunts her father-in-law in true Irish fashion with the inferiority of his family's origin, to her husband's misery. Shortly the old man disappears, his murder is suspected though impossible to prove, but the son becomes moody and finally also disappears – it turns out later that he has not committed suicide as supposed, from a guilty conscience, but has joined the army to serve overseas. His wife shortly, as a widow, gives birth to twin sons whom she brings up in great hardship to hopeful manhood when her favourite – about to be married and restore the family fortunes, she hopes – is shot by Tracy, whom the bereaved mother formally curses. The Shanahans and O'Sheas are simply representatives, in the three social strata of the world of the novel, of 'that other world, shrouded in black veils, bloody and earthy, where the peasants live'.

The world of Tracy's family and the well-to-do farmers exists on a plane between the peasants and the world of the rulers – Dalton the magistrate, his tools the informers and agents and petty gentry, and his son Henry who is a drawing-room favourite. Caught between the English administration of law, the peasants' archaic code, and his own bourgeois ambitious impulses, Tracy is driven to disaster, a pregnant theme impeccably handled without either melodrama or sentimental moralisms, the author avoiding identifying with any party, as the narrator is Tracy himself. Dalton's cruel and callous usage of the peasants brings about its inevitable nemesis when the surviving Shanahan twin, driven to madness and barbarous revenge, strangles Henry Dalton as the only means of punishing the father, who has seduced his sister and beggared him and his wife. This scene, the dreadful suspense leading up to it, and Dalton's surprising reaction, are the most astonishing of all this novel's successes. An ironic run-down ends the novel: Tracy's wife's brother returns to restore the fortunes of his niece, so that Tracy can continue with his ambition to rise into government service, though Dalton has now collapsed into senility. A final end in a dramatic return, which is not ironic, is that of the older Shanahan, the presumed suicide, who had disappeared before his twin sons' birth and is now an aged ex-soldier, devoting himself to religious repentance in his native countryside. The co-presence, the interlocking and organic intersection in the novel of all these worlds is a great achievement, it seems to me. Such an artistic integration of a complex world is something Scott never succeeded in achieving, even in his best novel *The Heart of Midlothian*, where the 'primitive' elements in its eighteenth-century society are represented only by the town mob, smugglers and hung robbers, the Scottish peasant being long tamed by Calvinism.

The Irish tradition, triumphantly created by the efforts of the Banims and Griffin, can be seen to continue more or less successfully through the nineteenth century, to as late as Somerville and Ross's *The Big House of Inver* (published in 1925, though set back in time to before the First World War). Here the social and economic grievances of the Irish peasant are paralleled in their social aspirations, their moral degeneration and financial disasters by the tragedy of the inhabitants of the Big House, whose history over two centuries is recorded, like that of *Castle Rackrent*, with the same result in that the unscrupulous agent, a solicitor, lays hold of the property more or less illegally and usurps the social position of the former owners – a characteristic Irish irony. In this novel, just as much as in its Catholic predecessors, Protestantism is seen to be what the Irish called 'the genteel religion' – meaning only the religion of the gentry, no doubt, but in practice, in the novels, shown as having merely a morality of respectability and determined social superiority as its ideal. To the Protestant it must seem equally odd that the ideals of Catholicism, in a country where it was the religion of the majority, did not exclude violence, systematic murder and revenge, no doubt a heritage from its pagan past. It is curious that we do not get in the Irish novels any such scenes as occur in *I Promessi Sposi*, where evil-doing characters are seen having dramatic changes of heart due to a religious upbringing, and thereafter practising humility and the other Catholic virtues. Where an Irish Catholic writer, George Moore, tried to show in a novel the repentance of a free-living Catholic singer, and her retreat into conventional life, it is quite unconvincing. Yet in his Irish-based novel *A Drama in Muslin* (1886), which takes place about 1880 in Galway and Dublin, Moore was successful in treating the traditional Irish themes – the conflict of religions, and the class and economic tensions (revealed in the peasants' comments on the gentry, and the hungry faces staring in at the ballroom windows, and the heroine Alice who 'had begun to see something wrong in each big house being surrounded by a hundred cabins all working to keep it in sloth and luxury') showing a hidebound society in its death-throes. It is in this tradition that Joyce's hero says 'History is a nightmare from which I am trying to awake'; which might serve as the motto of the Irish novelists generally. But when the nightmare was over, and the tensions got rid of, for Southern Ireland at least, the novelist, it appears, had lost his themes. A Dublin critic who corresponded with me wrote to me recently in this connection: 'It is as if there had been a great failure of creativity in modern Ireland; that once having got rid of the English there was nothing in particular we wanted to do with our country. Or one might reflect that the art of literary criticism (which keeps the classics alive) had hardly ever been practised in Ireland.'

The characteristics of the Irish novel are therefore responses to national feeling, and produced recognizable patterns such as:

1. The decay, morally, financially and socially, of the old gentry, ending in the Big House and estate being taken over by an odiously usurping middle-class figure (generally a lawyer or money-lender). This survives into twentieth-century novels – a tragic theme lending itself to ironic and poetic treatment. This is a Protestant pattern, for such a result, the downfall of a Protestant Ascendancy family, will presumably be viewed with pleasure by the native population, rather than as tragic.

2. The destruction by feuds, poverty, famine or injustice of the Irish peasant family: a theme of Catholic writers, who sympathize with the characters and their culture, and identify with the nationalist cause. Both these patterns had the advantage of being rooted in real life.

3. However, a third pattern is a romance of wish-fulfilment, and produces a happy ending in the return of the absentee landlord (generally incognito) to administer justice, to expose his scoundrelly agent, settle with his family in the Big House and make his estate a model of prosperity. This is the pattern of Maria Edgeworth's *The Absentee* (1812).

4. A Catholic pattern is the fantasy of the poor, proud Catholic gentleman with a beautiful and devoted daughter who turns out to be the real heiress to great estates. A Catholic sympathizer like Disraeli (in his earlier days as a novelist) used this pattern in *Sybil* (early 1840s) translated into an English context. Maria Edgeworth's involved novel *Ormond* (1817) combined several of these patterns.

5. A fifth pattern is that centring on the mixed marriage, or a love between members of the opposed religions, in which the natural religious conflicts could be treated individually in terms of a family's life and, for fictional purposes, could end in a reconciliation or the harmony achieved by a compromise. But it is inevitably tragic, and tragedy is made inevitable by making the Catholic lover a member of an order or at least educated by Jesuits, or the Protestant a girl either from a bigoted Protestant family or (like Lucy Snowe, in *Villette*) an extreme Puritan in her attitudes and beliefs.

All these patterns were experimented by the Anglo-Irish novelists, since no other pattern suited, in the early nineteenth century, to what they wanted to do. They had a tremendous scope in a unique subject-matter – the history of Anglo-Irish relations, their peculiarly stratified society, its economic grievances, their social abuses from the Penal Laws onwards, the religious conflict, institutions such as the hedge-school, and characters peculiar to Ireland – and a unique language, not a dialect but a national language evolved in the stage of speaking in English but thinking in Gaelic, a picturesque idiom which spread from the peasantry through the middle-class to the Protestant Ascendancy, who differed from the English in many respects. The Irish novelists had also the Irish oral traditions of verse, song and folktale and folklore, myth and religious superstitions and practices originally pagan. They were powered by genuine grievances and made the most of them, of course. The difficulty was to find forms to express them without being sidetracked by novelistic conventions. The one trap they most often fell into was that of melodramatic fiction, almost

inevitably since Irish social and political history was melodrama in actuality, almost beyond belief – the extreme
opposite of Jane Austen's world. Conrad noted the same
difficulty with using the history and society of Venezuela in
his great novel *Nostromo*, where one of the characters, a native
son who was brought up in France and is now returned,
writes home to describe his society to his friends: 'Imagine an
atmosphere of opera-bouffe in which all the comic business
of stage statesmen, brigands etc., and all their farcical stealing, intriguing and stabbing is done in dead earnest . . . the
blood flows all the time'. Melodrama is a temptation that
must be resisted by novelists if they want to be taken
seriously, and the Irish novelists were often unable to resist
it. But the devices by which they evaded melodrama are
interesting.

(1) Language of understatement and evasion. It arose
naturally from the Irish genius for ignoring or deprecating
reality and the real necessity of avoiding admission of crime
in a truce when the law imposed by Englishmen was rejected.
The technique of witnesses (in Banim's *The Croppy*, Griffin's
The Collegians and other novels) is an example novelists drew
attention to.

(2) As in the Banim brothers there is a division into what
happens in daylight (rational and logical) and what happens
by night (violence, lawlessness, murder etc.). This is acceptable because the secret societies, conspiracies and crimes of
all kinds really did take place mostly under cover of darkness.
To the night also was relegated the supernatural which was
still active in folk belief and religious superstition.

(3) In a country and time where the mass of the population
were at odds with the law of the land and ready therefore to
sympathize with the law-breakers by shielding criminals,
rogues and political conspirators, deception, and double-
faced character and conduct were common practice, so that
unmaskings and surprises were plausible or realistic.

(4) Institutions peculiar to Ireland made vendetta and the
practice of barbarous revenge and cold-blooded political
murder normal, which in nineteenth-century England could
take place only on the stage. To avoid melodramatic
presentation of this kind of action, as in *Tracy's Ambition*, the
novelist used a narrator who was a commonplace person with

no imagination – the events are filtered through his statements and his reactions given, while the novelist is not felt to
be responsible.

APPENDIX:

Notes on some Anglo-Irish novels

To a non-Irishman who wishes to acquire a dispassionate knowledge of Irish history, it seems necessary as an essential preliminary
to correct such acceptance as the unwary may be led into, in any
attempt to grapple with Anglo-Irish fiction, of the Irish interpretation of their past, persuasive as it is. This interpretation is
advanced with fervour or, as in Yeats's poetry, with the rhetoric and
mystique that Irishmen of Protestant origin who identified themselves with the Nationalist movement have brought to the cause,
with even more ardour and skill at self-deception and ignoring of
recalcitrant facts than their Catholic fellow-countrymen. Instead,
he should read some more sober, factual and disenchanted history
of the Irish people, such as Professor Morley Ayearst's *The Republic
of Ireland: Its Government and Politics* (1971), or, for Northern Ireland,
John Biggs-Davison's *The Hand is Red*. (Biggs-Davison is a Catholic
Unionist whose grandfather was a Presbyterian minister from
County Down and a liberal Home Ruler.)

Thus, we learn from N. D. Palmer, *The Irish Land League Crisis*, that
the literary and political deployment of absentee landlordism was
a myth – 'Among proprietors of more than one hundred acres, residents outnumbered absentees by seven to two.' A typical working
of the Irish mind, which proceeds with its own logic hardly comprehensible to non-Irish, is exhibited in the cherishing of Gaelic as
a totem (it has not existed as a national language since the Potato
Famine of the 1840s, and in spite of state encouragement is dying
out among the working class), as in the conversation quoted by Professor Ayearst with an Irish youth at Limerick who said to him
'rather belligerently' (in English), 'You have no language of your
own in your country. I wouldn't belong to a country that didn't have
its own language.' (The myth of a unique Irish race was sustained
by being able to point to the old Irish language, no doubt.)

Ayearst's chapters on 'Irish Political History to the Civil War'
and 'The Irish Society' are useful preliminary reading to Anglo-
Irish fiction of the nineteenth century. In fact, the more one
observes Irish history (if one is non-Irish and non-Catholic), the

less do the facts seem to suit the mythical history promoted by the
Nationalists, the novelists and the poets, when all the facts are
taken into consideration. The situation was always too complicated
and involved to be simplified thus.

In few countries, Ayearst remarks, 'is the sense of history so
strong and all-pervading as in Ireland. No study of Irish politics is
comprehensible without reference to this history and to the selective memory of it that often motivated Irish political behaviour.'
This applies to the study of Irish literature, Anglo-Irish literature
(that is, what was written by Irishmen in English, though no doubt
it applies also to what they wrote in Gaelic) of the eighteenth, nineteenth and twentieth centuries. No study of this literature is possible without some knowledge of the political as well as the social
history of Ireland since Elizabethan times (if not earlier), and in
Ireland politics identifies with religion. Perhaps this is why literary
criticism of this Anglo-Irish literature is so hard to find; for the
most part it has been replaced by partisan or chauvinistic pro-
motion of Catholic and 'peasant' artifacts in words, based on a
wholly one-eyed view of Irish history. This applies even to the
classic pioneer work by Professor Flanagan, *The Irish Novel 1800–
1850*, where the literature is expounded in the light of a conventionally Irish Nationalist view of Ireland in this period, not the less
simple-mindedly Nationalist, because the author is Irish-
American. So much so that a recent attempt at a thoroughly literary
criticism of one of the early nineteenth-century Anglo-Irish
achievements, the novels and tales of the Banim brothers, after a
prefatory tribute to Flanagan, adds: 'while Professor Flanagan fully
discusses and elucidates the political background of the Banims'
novels, I have concentrated on their artistry'. He does not actually
say that Flanagan uses the novels of the Banims and their contemporaries to propagand Nationalism, as he does.

For instance, even in his unusually perceptive and fair (biassed
neither by the Somerville and Ross idolatry of belletrists nor the
animus of Irish nationalists) article in *The Kenyon Review* (January,
1966) Flanagan writes as to the Irish world of middle-class,
Catholic, scheming, small-town bourgeoisie: 'Somerville and Ross
did not know that world, or, rather, they did not know it with love.'
That they knew it *Mount Music* proves, but how could they be
expected to 'love it'? – how could anyone? Flanagan explains:
'Their [the small-town dwellers'] Catholicism is not touching or
amusing, but alien and somehow sinister.' They (Somerville and
Ross) *do* see its amusing side, but this *is* also sinister and they
rightly saw as sinister the conscienceless exploitation of the poor
by the Irish priesthood, exerted solely for the purpose of maintain-

ing and extending the power of their Church and order, as Maria Edgeworth had seen a century earlier.

Griffin's and the Banim brothers' dealings with history were rather different from Sir Walter Scott's. Scott as a humane eighteenth-century gentleman of Conservative views had, apart from a weakness for romantic figures of the Scottish past, like Montrose, tried for a balanced view of the history of his country. He noted the errors of theory and practical mistakes which had led to disaster, and, as we see in *Old Mortality* and *Waverley*, worked for a fair impartial judgement, and the protagonists of such novels, even if sometimes partisans, are not enthusiasts for either side. Scott's aim was to exhibit the manners and language of all Scottish classes and types, and to show what factors in their history had made these people what they were and why they believed and behaved as they did. This is the best form of historical novel, the only one that can rate as high-level literature.

The Irish way of dealing with history in novel form is different. As Hawthorne says in his study of the Banims, they strove to alter the existing literary portrait of the Irishman (a stereotype) and 'to do this, they had to reinterpret history so that an Irishman could see exactly how he had been betrayed by England'. They were creating a new self-image for Irishmen, showing that their history was not merely that of a defeated and subjugated race. They showed, as Carleton had done, the struggle of the Irish to preserve their faith and its practices; and like him they study, but with more sympathy, the rebellions and local resistances of a seething populace against a sombre background of secret societies, private vengeances and treacheries. They bring into play as thrilling witness the superstitious beliefs and folklore of their people; often showing these as operative in tragic outcomes. This implied an Irish and not an English readership, but the Irish readership was not large enough to support a writer. Like Griffin, they had to seek publishers in London, and so they also had to undertake the task of explaining Ireland to the English reading public. Heartening the Irish and showing them where their national identity lay and in what it consisted was important culturally as well as for political purposes; the various layers of Anglo-Irish culture had to be fused and the novel was the appropriate mode of doing it. (Disraeli, a politician primarily, in his introduction to *Coningsby* (1844), wrote that he had adopted the form of fiction because it offered the best chance of influencing opinion.)

John Banim's *The Nowlans* is one of the best treatments of the religious conflict and is very well thought out. The author, travel-

ling in the country, is writing of his adventures to his brother;
weather-bound, he is taken in by a small farmer's family, the
Nowlans, who impress him by their generosity and good feelings
even before he finds out from the two daughters that they are nursing their brother through a serious illness. The narrator, winning
their confidence, gets the brother's story, which is then told
dramatically, the narrator disappearing from it till the end. It is
the story of 'Father' John, a spoiled priest. His family is pressing
him into the priesthood, for which he has no vocation except an
aptitude for study. But the cousin episode shows he is normally
sensual though he escapes the trap set for him, and he falls later to
a good girl (Protestant). Banim's 'everlasting fair-mindedness' is
not, as Professor Flanagan thinks, a disadvantage; quite the contrary. The tragedy of 'Father' John gains dignity and moral stature
from not showing an automatic moral – there are no moral clichés
in it. The bond between husband and wife holds, even in the
desperate poverty that they suffer (due to organized Catholic persecution, of which Banim evidently disapproves), neither
reproaches or taunts the other for the disaster the elopement has
entailed, and when his wife dies in childbirth by the roadside
(appropriately at night, in a storm) the poor young husband goes
mad with grief and horror, returning to his home intending to
murder his parish priest, and only after a spell in the army in
America is returned to the Nowlans, where the book begins. The
narrator reappears, to tell in a final letter that the invalid has
repented and been allowed to return to his duties as a priest.

It is an extremely sensitive and compassionate study of a case-
history – not of an ordinary man whose conscience is callous, but of
one who is the victim of a system of pressures (a priest in every
family) and a dogmatic education.

Carleton is essentially a folktale teller, from a bilingual family with
a tradition of folksong, tale-telling and folklore practices and
beliefs. As his *Autobiography* shows, he had acquired, through reading and schooling, a command of classical English, as distinct from
his much more sensitive and living use of the Anglo-Irish in
dialogue and characterization; and though he became and married
a Protestant and never reconverted, his imagination was fed from
his roots in peasant family life and Catholic habits of mind and
worship. He never really evolved from folktale to the sophisticated
novel, not even one as episodic and wholly Irish in outlook and
idiom as *Castle Rackrent – The Black Prophet* (1847) being the nearest
to a novel he ever managed. Therefore his novels are better represented by extracts, which lose nothing by being taken out of the

novel itself – this would be impossible with Banim or Griffin or any of the three major novels of Somerville and Ross. The problem with any folk-artist is to achieve the insights, co-ordination and compelling theme that the novelist must. Carleton liked to be compared to Scott, but nothing he wrote is comparable with *Old Mortality* or *The Heart of Midlothian* or even *Rob Roy* (Carleton felt for and with the Irish peasantry but he could not grasp the whole natural problem as Scott did); nor are the historical novels by Irish writers (dead historical fiction), even the over-praised but waxwork *The Boyne Water* (1826) by the Banims. The best by non-Ascendency novelists are short novels like *The Nowlans* and *Tracy's Ambition*, but only the last is fully integrated.

Carleton's parents, though uneducated, were in full possession of Irish oral traditions in prose, poetry and song. His father had an amazing memory, and his mother sang notably – a rich environment for a creative writer.

My native place was a spot rife with old legends, tales, traditions, customs and superstitions, so that in my early youth, even beyond the walls of my own humble roof, they met me in every direction. It was at home, however, and from my father's lips in particular, that they were perpetually sounding in my ears. In fact, his memory was a perfect storehouse, and a rich one, of all that the social antiquary, the man of letters, the poet, or the musician would consider valuable. As a narrator of old tales, legends, and historical anecdotes he was unrivalled, and his stock of them inexhaustible. He spoke the Irish and English languages with equal fluency. With all kinds of charms, old ranns, or poems, old prophecies, religious superstitions, tales of pilgrims, miracles and pilgrimages, anecdotes of blessed priests and friars, revelations from ghosts and fairies, he was thoroughly acquainted. And so strongly were all these impressed upon my mind by frequent repetition on his part . . . What rendered this, however, of such peculiar advantage to me as a literary man, was that I heard them as often, if not oftener, in the Irish language as in the English; a circumstance which enabled me in my writings to transfer the genius, the idiomatic peculiarity and conversational spirit of the one language into the other, precisely as the people themselves do in their dialogues, whenever the heart of imagination happens to be moved by the darker or better passions . . . My mother . . . possessed the sweetest and most exquisite of human voices. In her early life . . . any previous intimation of her presence at a wake, dance, or other festive occasion, was sure to attract crowds of persons, many from a distance of several miles, in order to hear from her lips the touching old airs of the country . . . She was not so well acquainted with the English tongue as my father . . . and . . . she generally gave the old Irish versions of the songs . . . Independently of this, she had a prejudice against singing the Irish airs to English words, [saying] 'The Irish melts into the tune but the English doesn't' – she spoke the words in Irish. Her family, how-

ever, had all been imbued with a poetical spirit, and some of her immediate
ancestors composed in the Irish tongue several fine old songs and airs.

His mother sang touching and tender Irish songs, he says, seated at
her spinning-wheel of a winter night, in his childhood. She was also
a memorable performer of the Irish cry or *keen*, 'pouring into its wild
notes a spirit of invincible pathos and sorrow'. These advantages
moulded his being completely into 'that spirit and those feelings
which characterize' the Irish people, and his 'position in life as the
son of a man who was one of the people'. But he also studied literature in hedge-schools.

Yeats, in a percipient introduction to his selection of Carleton's
stories, says that with Carleton's *Traits and Stories* modern Irish
literature began, and that with them he had started the prose literature of Ireland. When Yeats's selection of Carleton's stories
appeared, the Dublin review, *The Nation*, attacked Carlton as a slan-
derer of Catholicism, and demanded that he should be pilloried by
Irish critics; Yeats responded in an admirable letter a fortnight
later (14 Jan. 1890), defending Carleton against Catholic bigotry
and explaining Carleton's religious history plausibly and fairly:

Carleton came up to Dublin a young man, at the age when opinions
change. What literature Ireland then had was Protestant; proselytism and
letters, too, had just come together in a most unnatural marriage . . . He
changed his creed. There is not one fragment of evidence to prove he did
so other than honestly, or that 'he wrote for the market', as your critic puts
it. For a few, a very few years, he was full of zeal for his new opinions – an
ever-lessening zeal.

And Yeats notes that Carleton excised anti-Catholic passages
when reprinting his early stories and dropped 'the more wrong-
headed' altogether from his reprinted works. In his maturity as an
artist, he showed himself 'fierce against proselytising of all kinds'
and 'showed by book after book that his heart was wholly with the
faith of his childhood'. This seems to need some qualification. It
looks to me as if Carleton, while retaining a natural, even sentimental, tenderness for the Catholic culture that surrounded him in
childhood and boyhood, developed after his conversion to Protestantism a tepid and disenchanted attitude to both forms of
religion as to belief and practice. Certainly he had no regrets for his
lost Catholicism, for he refused to see a priest when on his death-
bed, the time when any regrets as to a lost faith are generally made
good. One sees this disenchantment with religious fervour,
whether Catholic or Protestant, in all his later works; and his choice
of the popular ballad 'Willy Reilly' for the subject of a novel, a

ballad celebrating the attempted elopement, in the days of the
Penal Laws, of a Protestant heiress and a Catholic, with his
dramatic trial and deportation and their eventual marriage, in
which Carleton took the opportunity to deprecate the bigots on
both sides, proves this. In fact, those passages which do justice to
the decent Irish non-Catholics who deplored the anti-Catholic laws
and ignored them or helped to mitigate their injustices towards
their Catholic neighbours take the whole question out of the realm
of bigotry and partisanship and into the psychological and social
realities of the age. Apart from these elements, the novel *Willy Reilly*
is, as Yeats declared the whole to be, 'rubbish', though it went
through 'forty editions', Yeats says. Yeats declared in his letter that
Carleton is Ireland's 'great prose Burns' and backed as his masterpieces two novels, *Fardorougha the Miser* and *The Black Prophet*. He
looked on folklore tales and myths as an antidote to the moralistic
literary mode which he held to be the enemy of great literature. He
felt that it was by returning to folklore as a model that Ireland
would produce a literature worthy of its people and its traditions.
He asks: 'Is not the evangel of folklore needed in England also? For
is not England likewise unduly fond of the story and the poem
which have a moral in their scorpion tail?' Carleton, he says, 'was
not an artist, but he was what only a few men have ever been or can
be, the creator of a new imaginative world, the demiurge of a new
tradition. He had no predecessors.'

Carleton says of his professional storyteller Tom Greissey that

His language, when he spoke Irish, was fluent, clear, and sometimes
eloquent; but when he had recourse to English, although his fluency
remained, yet it was the fluency of a man who made an indiscriminate use
of a vocabulary which he did not understand ... His pride was to speak as
learnedly as possible.

Carleton wrote of his attempting 'to transfer the genius, the
idiomatic peculiarity and conversational spirit of the one language
into the other, precisely as the people themselves do in their
dialogue', and says his lifetime was marked by what he called 'a
transition state' in which Irish was retreating before English and
the traditional culture before modernity. This resulted in the juxta-
position of spirited and idiomatic Irish-English as spoken, and
attempted educated English derived from literary sources – they
make very uneasy bedfellows. One sees the same difference in
Scott's Scottish novels, between the living speech of his Scotch
countryfolk and townsfolk and the insipid and stilted dialogues
between his genteel heroes and heroines (though the Scottish

gentry in fact would have spoken not English but Scotch, although of a more refined form than the lower classes).

The Protestant Ascendancy novelists from Maria Edgeworth and Somerville and Ross did not of course suffer in this way, being masters of a supple and exact classical English, and the form of their novels – from *The Absentee* to *The Big House of Inver* and *The Real Charlotte* – is classical too. They concern themselves with the same Irish themes – the conflicting religious and social cultures and the suicidal history of the families in the Big House being a prey to riotous living, debt and recklessness. With the freeing of Ireland from English government, the new prosperity of the countryside, and the Big Houses burnt down during the Troubles, the national themes have disappeared for the novelist.

Edith Œnone Somerville herself wrote in 1944 (then aged 86) that both of them (she and Violet Martin) 'were daughters of old Irish families that had struck roots deep into Irish soil'. Violet Martin was born at Ross House in 1862 (the youngest of eleven daughters), and Edith L. Somerville in 1858, the eldest of seven.

The first formative years of both writers were spent in comfortable old-fashioned Irish country houses, where the atmosphere was surely enriched and mellowed by the pervading spirit of many generations of kindly ancestors. The children (eighteen!) of the two old houses, Ross and Drishane, had happy lives, full of dogs and horses and boating on sea and lake. The atmosphere of their homes was full of good talk, of books and music, of pictures and politics, and they learned from their fathers' tenants, in a mutual friendship as sincere as it was unselfconscious, the idiom of that delightful way of speech that among the Irish country-people has sprung, like a wild flower, from the stiffer soil of the language of English. This was the life in which 'Martin Ross and E. E. Somerville' (to use their literary signatures) absorbed the spirit of the Ireland that they loved, which has saturated all that they have ever written. Their first full-length 3-volume novel, *The Real Charlotte*, was published in May 1894.

Somerville and Ross cannot be written off as 'Big House mentality' and (as Protestants and landowners) Anglo-Irish and not really Irish. Their novels and tales show considerable subtlety in representing a range of attitudes to all shades of Irish society, and these collaborators show themselves to be hospitable to the more reputable of Irish beliefs. Thus, in the *Irish R.M.* stories Major Yeates is appropriately tough-minded, as in the tale 'The Holy Island', where he utterly rejects the suggestion that inexplicable sounds can be attributed to Irish fairies:

'That's the fairies, ma'am', said Slipper with complete certainty; 'sure I know them that seen fairies in that island as thick as the grass, and every one of them with little caps on them . . . there was a man was a night on that island one time, watching duck, and them people cot him, and dragged him through Hell and through Death, and threw him in the tide – '
    'Shove off the boat,' I said.

He turns out to be justified, for the mysterious sounds on the little island are a drunken man's snores, and Slipper is employing superstition or alleged folklore to keep the R.M. from picnicking on the island lest he discover that it is being used as a hiding place for illegally obtained spirits. But in the novel *The Silver Fox*, which has two centres of Irish life, the Big House and the peasant farm, with their totally different outlook and mentality as well as different social and emotional life, the heroine, though cousin to the owner of French's Court and given to hunting, is also a sensitive reader and the friend and ally of the country people; and her sympathy for their ways of feeling and their belief in the occult is founded on her own awareness of irrational forces in the world in which she has a private existence outside the scope of her cousins. When they reject the local superstitions – never explained in the novel, though they determine the action in the main – and are indignant when these take the form of refusing to draw the covert that is the haunt of a silver fox and of obstructing the engineer who is making a railway through those parts, Slaney Morris courageously comes out on the side of the folk:

'Such rot!'
    Slaney did not answer at once. There are some people for whom the limits of the possible seem to be set farther out than for the rest of the world. They see and hear things inexplicable; for them the darkened glass is less dark, to them all things are possible. It cannot be called superstition – being neither ignorant dread nor self-interested faith; it seems like the possession of another sense – imperfect, yet distinct from all others. Slaney had seen and heard – between the sunset and the dawn – things not easily accounted for; she herself accepted them without fear; but she knew – as any one who knows well a half-civilized people must know – how often a superstition is justified of its works.
    'I often think', she said slowly, 'that it isn't much good to go against the country people in these things.'

It is conveyed with tact that Slaney, who feels with and for 'the country people', whom she doctors and advises, has been to some extent penetrated by their beliefs, over and above having learnt from experience that there often *is* some foundation for such superstitions, though the folk give the wrong explanation of them. In this case, the ground in dispute is unsuitable to lay a railway on and

through, and the foolhardy engineer has to stand the losses he
incurs, after having caused two deaths in the family of the old
farmer who was persuaded to sell him the land and who himself
dies of remorse, while his half-mad son drowns himself in consequence, leaving the Quin women without a man. The daughter
Maria, a strong and uninhibited character, then takes the lead in
the confrontation with the arrogant hunting gentry who have
desolated her home, she feels, and cannot even respect their grief
and mourning over the drowned corpse but take the hunt past the
door. Yet when Lady Susan (an Englishwoman of peculiar insensitiveness who has married the Anglo-Irish owner of the Big House)
rides into a hidden ravine, it is Maria Quin who rescues her at considerable risk to herself. But seeing Lady Susan's real grief at
having killed her horse is the last straw for Maria: ' "Little ye cried
yestherday whin ye seen my brother thrown out on the ground by
the pool," said Maria with irrepressible savageness, "You that's
breakin' yer heart afther yer horse." '

But Maria recovers herself, realizing that nothing better can be
expected of a Lady Susan – 'I thought every one in the counthry
knew this place. But sure what are you but a sthranger!' She said it
more kindly, and as if explaining the position to herself. Lady
Susan tries to apologize (having given up the idea of a money
reward to her rescuer) and asks Maria to 'accept my regret for anything I have done to annoy you, and my sympathy about your
brother. I didn't understand how things were – '

'Oh, God help ye!' broke out Maria, 'what does the likes o' ye understand
about the likes of us? It wasn't wanting to desthroy us ye were, I know that
well – and faith! I think ye have nature that'd make ye sorry if ye seen my
brother this day where he's lying beyond. I know well the one that have no
pity; maybe he'll be in the want of it yet.'

'The one that have no pity' refers to the callous engineer, an
Etonian, a philanderer of heartless irresponsibility, and a type of
Englishman even more detestable in the author's eyes than Lady
Susan, who is thoughtless and stupid but not base, as Maria Quin
saw. When Maria encounters Mr Glasgow in the wood where her
brother's corpse has just been dredged from the pond she therefore
has no hesitation in cursing him – the murderer of her father and
brother, as she believes, ending

'That yersel may be lookin' for a place to die and be threw in a grave that
won't be blessed!' There was a general stifled exclamation, and a man said
audibly – 'The Cross of Christ be between us and harm!' One of the
French's Court-workmen caught at Maria Quin's arm as if to silence her;

another pulled him away, telling him in Irish that the curse might fall on anyone who interfered with her.

This seems to be a good deal finer than the equivalents in Carleton and his contemporaries, and one does not doubt that the writer had witnessed such scenes and noted the very words and ritual in which the half-civilized people expressed their deepest feelings. The superstitions are neither provided as amusing nor as folklore interest to superior minds. The dignity of passion, religious conviction and sense of outrage are all there, admirably registered, with the various reactions of Maria's community given equal respect. Though there are many more violent and noisy scenes of resentment at wrongs and outrages in the novels of Carleton and the Banim brothers, for instance, there are none so sensitively controlled in the interest of a total effectiveness in a novel. The imaginative effort made by these lady novelists (Somerville and Ross) goes a good deal further than that of the Irish Nationalist novelists who are limited by being unable to enter into the lives of any above their own degree and who are not good even at presenting convincingly the others that they knew to some extent in daily life, such as their priests, who tend to fall into mere types. In *Mount Music* not only do we see the awe of the peasants and the respectful fear and discomfort of the town middle-class Irish that contact with their priests entails; the motives and intrigues of this ruling caste are also laid bare, the sinister still present under the humour, as when the fateful election is described by one countryman to another. Somerville's knowledge of and sensitiveness to dialects show in her review of Carleton, where she comments on his use of the Anglo-Irish language as one underprivileged in it.

Mount Music starts in the 80s and 90s of the last century when the Talbot-Lowry children were little. Mount Music House was large, intensely solid, practical, sensible, of that special type of old Irish country-house that is entirely remote from the character of the men that originated it, and can only be explained as the expiring cry of the English blood.

Chapter 3 sets out the religious situation: 'Religion, or rather, difference of religion, is a factor in everyday Irish life of infinitely more potency than it is, perhaps, in any other Christian country.' So Major Talbot-Lowry's first cousin Thomas, of the adjoining estate, living at Coppinger's Court, had while in the Indian Army met and married a young lady from an ancient English Catholic family who had first insisted, as her religion demanded, on bringing up their son in her faith, and then, before she died, had converted her husband. He, before he followed her into the next world had

arranged a Jesuit education for his son but left the guardianship
and mothering, however, to his maiden sister, a lady who was a
zealous Irish churchwoman but with a Protestant conscience that
obliged her to carry out her brother's intentions with painful
scrupulousness. Hence social agonies – from the Major: 'you don't
mean to tell me that the boy has to go to Mass with the servants . . .
Good Heavens!' and Miss Coppinger's 'as I believe it to be my Duty
to send Larry to his chapel, to his chapel he shall go!', for

> she had a sense of fair play that was proof against her zeal as an Irish
> Church woman. It is true that she mentioned what she regarded as the
> disaster of Larry's religion in her prayers, but she did so without heat,
> leaving the matter, without irreverence, to the common sense of Larry's
> Creator who, she felt, must surely recognize the disadvantages of the
> position as it stood.

It is obvious that Forster's *A Passage to India* had at least one distinguished predecessor in subject-matter and kind of irony. The
comedy and the painfulness thicken as Miss Coppinger's sense of
fair play hounds her on to logical steps; 'as soon as we are a little
more settled down I shall ask the priest to lunch'. This is painful for
everyone concerned, for the priest is not of the class used to lunch-
ing at the Big House and the servants utterly disapprove of the
social upheaval this causes. Miss Coppinger 'was entirely and
implacably Protestant . . . and it was a master-stroke that
Frederica's sense of duty should compel her to enforce her nephew
to compliance with its [the other Church's] demands'. The last
touch of wry comedy is Lady Isabel's attempt to console her
husband's cousin, Lady Isabel being English and too insentient
even after fifteen years as mistress of Mount Music to have grasped
the realities of the Irish situation: 'I don't suppose his religion will
interfere in *any* way. It seldom does, does it?' (To which Miss
Coppinger grimly retorts: 'Not, I admit, unless he wanted a job in
this country'.)

  Larry turns out not only to be of the wrong religion but also of the
wrong politics, being converted through poetry to Irish Nationalism and standing for election as such, though he doesn't get in
because 'the Clergy is agin him'. The Mount Music servants, or the
Protestant upper section (for Lady Isabel had no more sense of
propriety than to outrage the butler Evans by 'a culpable setting of
attainments, or of convenience, above creed, in the administration
of the household') are scandalized by 'the children of this house
consorting with a Papist' – but how is a neighbour's cousin to be
kept out in the circumstances? The children are also thoroughly
muddled by the social and religious anomalies. Others are con-

cerned to make use of the opportunities for intrigue that the unique situation provides, such as the Big Doctor, who, though hampered by having married (for love) below him, has ambitions for his children that nearly secure Larry for his daughter and Christian, Larry's ex-fiancée and cousin, for his son Barty, as well as the title-deeds of Mount Music by judicious loans and systematic intrigue over the years to the helpless Major Talbot-Lowry. Dr Mangan ends up drowned in the torrent while heroically 'out on a case'; washed up on the bounds of the estate he is found by the butler: 'He stared down at the man whom he hated, with something of pity, more of cynicism. "Well, ye wanted Mount Music!" he said, at last. "How d'ye like it now ye've got it?"'

The interplay of class and religion is impartially and intelligently investigated. Miss Coppinger

was brought up in that school of Irish Low Church Protestantism that makes more severe demands upon submission and credulity than any other, and yet more fiercely arraigns other creeds on those special counts . . . her religious beliefs were only comparable, in their sincerity and simplicity, with those of the Roman Catholic poor people, whose spiritual prospects were to her no less black (theoretically) than were hers to them. Those who know Ireland will have no difficulty in believing that Miss Coppinger had no warmer sympathizers in her feelings concerning Larry and the Mangan household than the Coppinger's Court retainers, despite the fact that none of them were of her communion, nor did they share her political views.

This makes the point neatly that class can in some fields of life blot out religion and politics equally, and that the attitudes of the dominant section of a community (the Ascendancy class here) can infect the rest of it in spite of incompatible religious and political beliefs. The Ascendancy class here being Protestant, the Catholic servants and peasants accept it as right and proper that all members of the governing class should be Protestant; and that Catholicism, their own religion, is the mark of social inferiority, so that they are scandalized by the results of Thomas Coppinger's *mésalliance* (a marriage which was all right in India or England, as Miss Coppinger says). The situation is explored at a much more serious level than the comedy it so abundantly provides, and the problem set by Thomas's having become 'a jumper' is not resolved, for it is insoluble. The mixed marriage with which the novel ends (Larry having been freed by Tishy Mangan's elopement on the eve of their marriage), that of Larry reunited with his true love Christian Talbot-Lowry, only carries the problem on to the next generation. That the Protestant bride is named 'Christian' and has qualities of tolerance and mysticism allegedly bearing out the

allegorical implications of her name is all the hope provided –
vague enough! The theme of the novel is that 'the spirit of the Irish
Nation' is intolerance and separation.

Even the servants feel 'that Larry's parents had, socially, been ill-
advised when they "made a Roman of him" ', for no more than Miss
Coppinger could they 'subdue the feeling of incongruity imparted
by the fact of Master Larry and themselves worshipping together'.
And the author reports the maid who 'indignantly repudiated the
idea of taking service with one of her own church. "No! Thank God!
I never sank to that!" There was no question of religion in it. Merely
of fitness.' On the rector's advice Miss Coppinger sends Larry to
Oxford, but 'it has only the effect of making him take his religion
more seriously', Miss Coppinger complains. The situation is rich in
sociological interest as well as in the ironies that make for novelistic
felicity and Austenian comedy.

In the novel an odious priest is balanced by others who though
undesirable in their activities and influence (from a Protestant
point of view) are to be respected and even liked, while the Protestant clergy are represented by a couldn't-care-less aristocratic
Rector and an insufferable married couple. Larry is ill-regarded
even by the priesthood of his own persuasion: 'He may call himself
a Catholic, but them English Catholics – !'

The Major completes the downfall of his family that extravagance had started by his refusal to sell his lands to his land-hungry
tenants, and not wholly without the author's sympathy (or the
reader's); because 'he still held fast and refused to sell the property
that had come down to him from the men whose portraits had
looked down on him from the old walls of Mount Music all the days
of his life'. He cannot grasp that the tenants 'whose fathers had
loved him had renounced the old allegiance' and instead 'held
indignation meetings against the landlord who refused to resign to
them what they believed to be theirs, and he equally believed to be
his'. ' "English!" ' shouts the Major in a fury. ' "I've got Brian
Boroihme in my pedigree, and that's more than they [the
Nationalists] can say! A pack of half-bred descendants of Cromwell's soldiers!" '

The Ascendancy spirit and code even if dense and blind is to be
admired: 'It's an intolerable nuisance being boycotted, if it's
nothing else' says Christian's elder sister the buccaneer, 'and most
expensive. I was with the O'Donnells that time when they were
boycotted – up at five every morning to milk the cows and light the
kitchen fire, and having to get every earthly thing by post from
London!' (Cf. Nancy Mitford and contrast Forster and Bloomsbury
on patriotism and the English governing class.)

The novel is rich in Edwardian elements: the author's detachment, compared with Jane Austen's or even Dickens's, from the
society she depicts (the element in it she is unable not to identify
herself with is the life of sport – the fox-hunting and its mystique,
the cult of dogs and horses and love of them with which the heroine
is endowed as one of her marks of *being* the heroine – she is adept at
managing dogs practically from birth). But there is also the
Edwardian aestheticism – Christian and Larry are both deeply sus-
ceptible to poetry, or perhaps one should say Poetry, and Larry
goes to Paris to study painting (as the author did) and comes back
a connoisseur and practitioner of merit. The drawing-room of
Mount Music is seen in a historico-anthropological way that is
alien to Jane Austen or George Eliot even:

The long and lofty drawing-room of Mount Music was a pleasant place
enough . . . Some five or six generations of Talbot-Lowrys had lived in it,
and left their marks on it, and though the indelible hand of Victoria, in
youthful vigour, had had, perhaps, the most perceptible influence on it as
a whole, the fancies and fashions of Major Dick's great-grandmother still
held their places.

The complicated fireplace with its 'Nelson ropes' and 'deep hobs,
in whose construction the needs of a punch-kettle had not been forgotten' and the

high, delicately-inlaid marble mantlepiece, brought from Italy by Dick's
great-grandfather, was surmounted by a narrow ledge of marble, just wide
enough to support the base of a Georgian mirror of flamboyant design, in
whose dulled and bluish depths were reflected the row of old white china
birds, that were seated, each on its own rock, on the shelf in front of it.
Family portraits in frames whose charm of design and colour made atone-
ment for the indifference of the painting . . . flotillas of miniatures had
settled, like groups of flies, wherever on the crowded walls footholds could
be found . . . There were long and implacable sofas . . . Empire *consoles*, with
pieces of china incredibly diverse in style, beauty, and value, jostling each
other on the marble slabs . . . chairs of every known breed, and tables,
tables everywhere, and not a corner on one of them on which anything
more could be deposited.

The inventory culminates in, or rather works up to, the really
placing, culturally speaking, account of the claims of literature in
this society whose culture is being investigated and whose conception of the arts of painting, sculpture and furniture has just been
shown:

A tall, glass-fronted cupboard, inaccessibly placed behind the elongated
tail of an early grand piano, was filled with ornate miniature editions of the
classics, that would have defied an effort – had such ever been made – to

remove them from their shelves, whereon they had apparently been
bedded in cement, like mosaic. It was a room that, in its bewildering diver-
sity, might have broken the hearts of housemaids or decorators; untidy,
without plan, with rubbish contending successfully with museum-pieces,
with the past and present struggling in their eternal rivalry; yet, a human
place . . . a place full of the magnetism that is born of past happiness . . .

(Women novelists are eminently successful in saying what they
mean through interiors – compare Jane Austen on Sotherton and
the Musgrove drawing-room, and George Eliot's account of
Dorothea's boudoir and Mrs Wharton's of the showpiece home of
Undine Spragg in her third marital phase. It was a method, however, invented by the fertile critical and Regency-creative mind of
Humphrey Repton. Note Dickens's comparative heavy-handed-
ness in trying to give symbolic significance to the desolate existence of poor Miss Wade with Harriet, and how happy he is to
escape into the jaunty journalistic description of the room itself
when he gets to it, wrenching himself back to his real object in
describing it at the end of *Little Dorrit*. *Belchamber* is more Victorian
in not giving more than indications, for example, of Cissy's bad
taste in the Edwardian style with which she does up the
Belchambers' London house. Note Henry James's feminine sensibility, like Richardson's, with the same felicity in catching the
feminine point of view – Fleda Vetch and Mrs Gereth in *The Spoils*
and the hideous interior of the tasteless family, which successfully
defines their whole outlook and *modus vivendi*.)
    In his book *Writers and Politics* (1965) Conor Cruise O'Brien calls
Somerville and Ross snobs *because* they belonged to the Irish landed
gentry –

They had to look down on other people in order to see them. Or so they
sincerely felt. And they wanted to see them clearly, to place them socially
. . . They wrote on these matters with an almost pedantic care for accuracy,
within social conventions which they thoroughly understood and
thoroughly approved. Their approval is, to profane ears, often excessive,
and one cannot help feeling that the ability to detach themselves from the
conventional values of their class would have enriched their work.

'But,' he continues, 'their snobbery, as I think we must call it, was
at least a live and intelligent system of social apprehension, strictly
contemporary and even brisk.' And he rightly adds that it was not
the same as 'the vicarious nostalgia of Mr Evelyn Waugh' – which
some of us would prefer to describe as true and mere snobbery, and
so odious.
    What Somerville and Ross show is the desire to anatomize, with
a view to judging their own society, and making value-judgments

about its types and modes of life, which is characteristically Edwardian, I believe.

Mr O'Brien thinks *Mount Music*, a classical treatment of the 'spirit of the Nation' theme (Irish religious intolerance), is of antiquarian interest only. But surely its interest, like *Passage to India*, is that it gives classical treatment to an eternal subject by exposing it in a whole context, historical, sociological and psychological – but by a master of the subject, whereas *Passage to India* is too plainly biassed (anti-British) and by an outsider who has succumbed sentimentally to the charms of the picturesqueness of his subject-matter. The Somerville and Ross pair are of sterner stuff being natives, they had no illusions.

The attraction of the Somerville and Ross novels and tales is not merely that they incarnate for the English reader an unimaginable but perfectly convincing world with a unique society speaking in a piquant idiom and an irresistible humour. There is a serious value beyond amusement. *Mount Music*, like *The Real Charlotte* and *Big House of Inver*, exemplifies this. And they create a world in literature that has a close relation (though not an exhaustive one) to the real Irish world of their time. Somerville and Ross's Ireland, like Dostoevsky's Russia (very different from Tolstoy's, though contemporary, and who is to say which was nearer to the reality?), Dickens's England, Scott's Scotland, Stendhal's France, Thomas Mann's Germany, exists as literature, a representation of the reality as recreated by an artist, whose sensibility and insight must be finer and more powerful than the average man's, who lives in his world like a fish in water, taking it for granted as normal and therefore incapable of understanding it.

Women writers of the nineteenth century

Well, I'm very glad to be back in a school with boys again. Addressing St Paul's School for Girls recently on the same subject, I had to admit that I had never been in a good girls' school before. For I have to confess that I was co-educated, from the cradle to the grave, so to speak. For after following through school closely on my brother, a mathematical genius and like so many gifted men an intellectual highflier all round, I followed him to Cambridge, where I enjoyed the society of his mathematician friends of like intellectual calibre. I must add that I was deeply disappointed in the coevals Girton College provided for me (girls from the best girls' public schools for the most part), though not in the women of the High Table of those days. It is true that my Girton tutor, Miss Murray, daughter of the editor of the great Oxford Dictionary, wanted me to go and teach at Cheltenham Ladies' College for a while, after graduating and before becoming a Fellow of Girton, so that I might acquire the stamp of a real lady, but I refused and immediately got married to my director of research instead, and the higher education that I acquired from my brother and his friends quite as much as that from schoolteachers and dons has been continued for the last forty-four years by my husband, and sometimes by his best old pupils too, as well as by my two sons.

On reflection I can't feel sorry that I was deprived of the benefits of a good girls' school education, for so were the women whom I most respected, the elderly women dons of my young days of the mid 1920s who had been the earlier students at the Oxford and Cambridge women's colleges. They had all been educated – except sometimes for the temporary attentions of a governess (generally a French or German one

99

at that) – they had all been educated by men too: by brothers and fathers and uncles often supplemented by visiting masters to teach them art and music, because of course there hadn't been any high schools for them to go to or any qualified women teachers to teach them. And I was immensely impressed by these women: by their remarkable conversational powers (quiet, not brilliant, but quietly devastating when necessary); by their very considerable learning; their incredibly wide general culture; their distinguished manners and appearance, which was not in the least supported by the arts of dress or beauticianry; by their knowledge of foreign languages, ancient and modern, and all those literatures, which these ladies read in the originals naturally, and kept up with by reading the learned international journals; by the impression each gave of being unique and yet not eccentric or self-conscious; and by the stamp of character on all they did and said. It was the character of disinterested, high-minded, unselfish women devoted to the intellectual life, who were plainly the products of good society but quite free from worldliness. They were thoroughly rational and calm: the between-wars women dons who succeeded them seemed to me in comparison to be hysterical and immature (compare Dorothy Sayers's schoolgirl dedication to *Gaudy Night* and *Busman's Honeymoon*) and I found their conversation unrewarding. These were in fact less and not more emancipated than their predecessors, as my husband noted when he was a young don teaching at Girton and Newnham.

It gradually dawned on me that these women whom I so admired and who permanently influenced my own outlook were of the same breed as those other but long-dead women I also admired, the great women writers of the nineteenth century. One of those women writers who made a career for herself by the pen was Harriet Martineau.

Let me read you an extract from her review of Charlotte Brontë's anti-Catholic novel *Villette*, when it appeared in 1853. Harriet herself, I should say, was described by a contemporary as 'a female atheist of European reputation'. She wrote:

The author goes out of her way to express a passionate hatred of

Romanism. It is not the calm disapproval of a ritual religion, such as we should have expected from her, ensuing upon a presentment of her own better faith . . . the Catholicism on which she enlarges is even virulently reprobated. We do not exactly see the moral necessity for this (there is no artistical necessity) and we are rather sorry for it, occurring as it does at a time when catholics and protestants hate each' other quite sufficiently; and in a mode which will not affect conversion.

There is the voice and style I remember of the educated Victorian women, whom I encountered as distinguished old ladies in the Cambridge drawing-rooms of my youth and, near to retiring age, then at the High Tables of the women's colleges. Could anything be further removed from the voice of Women's Lib., for instance?

Harriet Martineau's own character was like this all the way through. Though she supported herself entirely by her pen and was handicapped by extreme deafness since girlhood, she refused a pension from three successive prime ministers (one of these was Gladstone and another Disraeli) who, in spite of disagreeing entirely with her political and religious views, wished to show how they honoured her: she refused a pension on principle. When she undertook to translate, explain and abridge the works of the French philosopher Comte, an invaluable service for the English public, she did it so well (it was a tremendous undertaking) that the French wanted her abridgement re-translated into French as an improvement on the originals! She kept from the proceeds only enough to cover her expenses in doing the work, and sent the rest to the needy philosopher, although at that date she was under no legal obligation to do so. Her very distinguished Victorian male biographer said that in his opinion she had 'a mind of really almost unrivalled innate powers'.

Yes, they were nearly all like that. Jane Austen, Charlotte and Emily Brontë, Mrs Gaskell, Mrs Oliphant, George Eliot, Mrs Gatty and her daughter, Mrs Ewing, whose tales for children you may not, like me, have rejoiced in when young (I mean *really* young); and at the end of that century near to us, Mrs Humphry Ward and the nearest thing to an American Jane Austen, Mrs Wharton – Edith Wharton, the friend of Henry James and other great novelists, English and American, and admired by so many men of letters and intel-

lect. They were all women of letters, literary critics and
novelists of merit in varying degrees; but the breed seems to
have dried up. Most, or nearly all, of these women of letters
– for women novelists are only a sub-division of this general
category – were enterprising translators, dauntless readers,
wrote solid books and contributed shoals of articles to the
serious reviews of the day, did now and then reliable reviewing over wide fields, and wrote good literary and other
criticism, while all of them carried out household duties,
made pleasant homes with much hospitality and were
renowned for their conversation.

And it seems only to be in literature that women have
shown undeniable creative powers – equal to those of men
beyond any argument. In my home the arts, poetry and literature, music, and mathematics and philosophy were recognized as *the* things that mattered most, the things of the mind
and spirit. And it was humiliating to me when my brother and
his friends occasionally pointed out – not maliciously but
with perturbation, for they wished to believe in the equality
of the sexes – that there are no major women poets
(Sappho?), no great women philosophers, composers, play-
wrights, mathematicians; no female painters of the first rank.
Actresses of immense ability, yes, but no women dramatists;
in music, talented performers but no estimable composers,
gifted opera-singers but no composers of opera; in art,
accomplished painters of considerable sensibility like, for
example, Berthe Morisot but no outstanding women artists;
women of outstanding musical endowment like Nadia
Boulanger have limited their creative instincts, if they had
any, to inspiring, training and launching male composers, as
the recent BBC radio programme, a tribute to Boulanger by
many of her famous pupils, made clear. The general truth
here illustrated is undeniable. But there *is* one field in which
women can and certainly did compete with men on equal
terms creatively; that is, in prose fiction and literary criticism
– the highest manifestations of humanity (the two being, as I
shall suggest, closely connected). I don't know why this situation should be so, for women had equal access to music-
paper and painting materials, and teaching and encouragement in both fields, from the eighteenth century onwards and
earlier (and poetry takes even less time to write down than

fiction). And granting women's achievement in literature in
the nineteenth century, why is it that in a span of a century or
little more the achievement of women as writers in the Anglo-
American hemisphere was established and then fell away?
While the supply of women anxious to earn a living and reputation from literature has been even greater than before,
women have failed to rise to their potentialities, it seems to
me, and paradoxically just when they have had such emancipation from drudgery and the benefits of organized higher
education. As both a woman and a literary critic, concerned,
that is, both for women's status and for literature, I feel
impelled to ask: what conditions produced the success of our
predecessors; have we failed to maintain those conditions;
have we perhaps even destroyed the conditions necessary to
produce major women novelists and literary critics, the only
field in which women's claims to equality can be confidently
made where creativity is concerned, as George Eliot implied
when after visiting an exhibition of the paintings of Rosa
Bonheur she wrote: 'What power! *That* is the way women
should assert their rights.'

   Now these women didn't go to school except sometimes
for a couple of years to a boarding-school, where education
was not the primary concern. George Eliot was exceptional in
getting some good intellectual teaching at her Coventry
boarding-school, but it also nearly ruined her for life by
Evangelical indoctrination, from which she was only freed
after much misery by her love of poetry and romantic literature, and she was actually impelled in middle life to attempt
fiction by the encouragement of her husband, the critic G. H.
Lewes. Mrs H. Ward, among other nineteenth-century
women writers and intellectuals, was utterly miserable in her
short stay at school and learnt nothing there. None of these
women went to college either. But these 'underprivileged'
women, paradoxically, were very highly educated indeed and
make the average woman specialist in humane studies at the
High Table nowadays seem an ignorant schoolgirl in comparison, it strikes me.

   They were highly educated largely by their own untram-
melled efforts, of course, for all education ultimately
depends on personal exertion and enterprise; but other factors equally essential were operative then which don't oper-

ate any longer. For equally of course when we say someone is self-educated we really imply, I think, that he or she isn't truly educated, because education is very largely something we can only get by associating with educated people; it has to be transmitted and acquired by other ways than from books alone. Well, what did these nineteenth-century women have to supplement books, to take the place of high-school teaching and college courses and working for examinations with text-books, and to supplement unaided effort? They must have had some alternatives which were perhaps better for fostering creative minds?

In the first place, they had the family libraries, which until the First World War were part of every educated household, however poor. We all know what Dr Johnson thought of the benefits of turning the young loose in a library, to find and nourish their own personal bents. Again and again we find the gentleman's library the primary and indispensable factor in the lives of our young women. You can see that this was so in Jane Austen's novels. Take a few extreme cases: in the poor parsonage in the remote Yorkshire parish of Haworth, the Brontë sisters had the run of their father's library of standard works, which included the new poets and novelists like Scott and Byron and Burns and Wordsworth as well as the classics of our and the old literatures, and he also took in the leading newspapers and magazines (nineteenth-century magazines were mainly solid articles on intellectual subjects and literary reviews). In one of Trollope's best novels, *The Last Chronicle of Barset*, the wretchedly poor perpetual curate in a village without even a square, the Reverend Mr Crawley, always in debt to the butcher and baker, was able to give his daughters at home a real education in literature. We are very convincingly shown his girls reading the Greek dramatists and Italian poetry with him (in the original, of course) to comfort him in his worst hours, as well as knowing Shakespeare and Milton and, what is of even more importance, having been brought up to feel that literature is not an ornament but a necessity of life. Look at another very poor parsonage: Eliza Lynn, later Mrs Lynn Linton the novelist and critic, very well known and esteemed in her day, was the youngest of twelve in a country parson's family where the mother had died in her daughter's infancy. The boys mostly managed to get to school, but Eliza had to make do with the free run of her father's library – a 'typical Church of England clergyman's library', her Victorian biographer wrote, wherein she acquired, with her father's and brother's help no doubt, French, some Italian, German and Spanish, and tried Latin, Greek and Hebrew. The library included of course Goethe's *Faust*, *Don Quixote*, Ovid and other European classics (all these in the original, naturally) and a great range of English books which included philosophy and theology as well as all the English classics up to date. Having prepared herself on these, she persuaded her father to finance her for a year in London to study in the British Museum reading-room, after which she produced an erudite novel and settled in London as a successful novelist and literary journalist, two years before George Eliot did likewise. Dickens, who as magazine editor rewrote his contributors' fiction and articles wherever he thought desirable, made a note on Mrs Lynn Linton as a contributor; it says: 'Good for anything and thoroughly reliable', and Dickens had no use for amateurs in the literary profession.

At the later end of the nineteenth century consider the case of Edith Wharton, born into a rich fashionable family of the New York aristocracy. Daughters of this class didn't get sent to school even at that date. She endured a German governess and French governess at home, from whom as was usual she acquired languages fluently, but otherwise she educated herself in the family libraries, where, for instance, she and her little cousins enjoyed, she wrote, 'a superb unexpurgated Hogarth', in which they delighted, complete editions of the eighteenth-century classics of our language, Shakespeare and Milton of course and all the later poets; the great historians and divines and letter-writers of the past, the Elizabethan dramatists, Goethe and the Bible. I need not go on, but she writes: 'By the time I was seventeen, though I had not read every book in my father's library, I had looked into them all.' The only thing she hadn't read were modern novels, her mother having forbidden them, as to which she says: 'By denying me the opportunity of wasting my time over ephemeral rubbish my mother threw me back on the great classics.' So she naturally started as a child by writing poetry and drama. The invincible female tendency to express herself in fiction burst out in due course. If anyone is interested in the form this took and why, I can refer them to a pioneer article I wrote for *Scrutiny* on Edith Wharton's novels. She didn't write for money or reputation, at first at any rate, but to express, examine and justify her dismay at the disintegrating society she found herself obliged to live in, just as Jane Austen did similarly for the changing society of her own age, and it is interesting that their novels have so much in common, even to their techniques and kind of ironic wit.

Well, we have changed all that, I mean as regards the family libraries and the wide free range of serious reading, English and European, for our girls. I'll leave you to think out the reasons. I will only report that as regards the standard of Church of England libraries, I have for a number of years rented for summer holidays vicarages and parsonages in pleasant country spots or cultivated (one would have thought) towns like Cheltenham and Lewes and always found that there were *no real books* therein. As regards general reading habits in the class aspiring to the professions, I not infrequently discover that my pupils (of both sexes), having chosen to read Honours English and themselves chosen by a university at which it is understood selection is highly competitive, have read almost no works of literature except the set texts for their 'O' and 'A' levels and generally own few books themselves. If I ask: 'How, having read one or two of Shakespeare's tragedies or comedies, can you have failed to go on and acquaint yourself with the rest?', or: 'How, having read *Pride and Prejudice*, did you stop yourself from reading all the rest of Jane Austen's novels?' – the answer always is that there were so many subjects and activities at school that they didn't have time. You see, they were so busy being educated that they weren't able to get an education or even the minimal materials of an education. But lack of time can't be the whole story. When I ask if they've read *Wuthering Heights* or *Jane Eyre* they will say, 'No, but I saw the film of it', or 'I saw it on television', and no one ever seems to have told them, until I make myself disagreeable by doing so, that there is no relation whatever, except a highly undesirable one, between dramatic arrangements, and commercial ones at that, of these novels and the experience of reading the actual words in which they were composed and from those words recovering the work of art for oneself. As to a knowledge of foreign literature in the original among undergraduates, that is expecting too much of them. In the USA even French and Latin tags have to be translated in footnotes to their texts.

The family library provided self-education, but of course was supplemented, as I've incidentally given evidence, by family discussion and guidance. Conversation in the home and the corresponding society open to the gentry, however poor, was recognized as the justification of social life. The theory is explained in Lord Chesterfield's letters to his son, in accordance with which Jane Austen makes her heroine Anne Elliot tell her cousin: 'My idea of good company is the company of clever, well-informed people, who have a great deal of conversation'; and though we don't think of Jane Austen as being a great intellectual or even highly educated, she takes pains to show her heroines as great readers: Anne Elliot, we are told, could translate difficult old Italian poetry into elegant English at sight, as a normal accomplishment. Mrs Humphry Ward (who wrote the best novel of religious controversy) said that the boarding-school she attended for a short time did nothing for her, and 'After sixteen, except in music, I had no definite teaching, everything I learnt came to me from persons – and books – sporadically, without any general guidance or plan. It was all a great voyage of discovery, organized mainly by myself, on the advice of a few men and women very much older, who took an interest in me.' As her father was then an Oxford tutor she was able to read in the Bodleian Library. Mrs Oliphant had no schooling but though poor she had clever brothers as well as a remarkable mother. She wrote: 'We lived in the most singularly secluded way, I never went out, our pleasures were books of all and every kind, newspapers and magazines [magazines were intellectual quarterlies and monthlies], which formed the staple of our conversation, as well as all our amusement.' She wrote her first novel at sixteen and then never stopped writing till her death.

'Conversation' was understood to be a real intellectual activity as well as performing an important social function. It included a mode of discussing character (in which everyone was a connoisseur) and analysing motive, which was obviously of the greatest benefit to a budding novelist (here

again we need only adduce Jane Austen's novels). Second
only to this came the practice of writing long, detailed letters
meant to be read aloud to the section of the family to which
they were addressed. In the novels of Charlotte Yonge and in
the real-life history of Jane Austen such letter- writing is seen
to be recognized as one of the duties of the daughters of the
household, communicating all the family news, reporting as
to visitors and friends, their conversation and their affairs
and adventures, again discussing character and motivation
and passing judgement on all these matters. Thus a mental
habit and a writing practice formed a half-way stage between
conversation and novel-writing; and under this head I would
include the feminine practice, invaluable for a novelist, of
keeping a journal, not the same thing as a diary. In George
Eliot's journals, for instance, we not only get accounts of her
activities but, more important, of her reading, intellectual
and religious evolution, and with carefully considered criticism of what she read, felt and thought, which fostered a
critical habit of mind and the expression of ideas. Of course
no one has time to write letters nowadays and when the tele-
phone is so handy there is no need, while conversation has
been killed by the habit of passive activities and mute watching in the age of radio, cinema and television, which has also
destroyed the habit of solid reading and even, I think, the
ability to do so! I have also touched on the fact that these girls
disciplined themselves to acquire the modern languages,
Latin and often Greek and even Hebrew, which was
accompanied by the practice of translating widely, another
kind of training in the use of language and in sensibility as to
shades of meaning. The characteristic nineteenth-century
professional woman of letters, like Mary Howitt, Harriet
Martineau, Eliza Lynn Linton, George Eliot, Mrs Oliphant,
Mrs Humphry Ward, who were all novelists, was to undertake translation as a sideline, very enterprising translation
too, even from the Scandinavian languages – Mary Howitt,
for instance, learnt Danish in order to translate Hans
Christian Andersen, his novels as well as his fairy-tales.

So what with their unfettered opportunities for free reading in the well-stocked libraries of their homes and family
friends, their opportunities for listening from childhood and
participating in truly adult, elegantly expressed conversation

which included discussion of past and present literature, their protection from debasing and anti-intellectual amusements to which their privileged successors are fatally exposed, their proclivities were actualized to the highest degree and they were even encouraged by their domestic duties, such as correspondence, to become novelists. Study thus became a pleasure and self-cultivation truly satisfying. Let me read you a piece from a letter of Harriet Martineau's about how she spent the years between the ages of sixteen and twenty, which are for us the years when we get intensive teaching in the Sixth Form and are prepared by devoted teachers for college as a full-time activity and are then sent up to study with high academic specialists at college or similar training centres. Harriet, confined to the home and her own resources at that phase, wrote of it:

I liked cooking very well and ironing better. I used to get up at 5 . . . to try whether I cd. not write stories and scraps of verse. My Latin prospered then, and I read much French, and taught myself Italian. Translation was a good exercise, I found, and I translated Tacitus into prose and Petrarch into verse, and used to read to my mother from French books. Then I learnt Wordsworth by heart by the bushel . . . and puzzled out metaphysical questions in my own mind all day long . . . and music burst out at all odd times, besides my daily practice. Oh, those were glorious days! and I wish you joy, dear, that they are coming to you!

This letter was to a young friend of fourteen – and you see Miss Martineau has no doubt that the girl will do, or would be able to do, likewise.

But they, as you can see even from this letter, were not living in an artificially (for women) separate world of study or professional training. Their studies were not only of choice, following a bent encouraged by their natural environment, but pursued along with and indeed inseparable from the ordinary domestic round, the activities of real life and those peculiarly suited to a woman as home-maker, wife and mother. Consider the case of George Eliot, the most famous and probably the greatest blue-stocking who ever lived. When Henry James the great novelist first met her, he wrote home to his father the American philosopher to tell him of the striking impression George Eliot's personality had made

on him, saying that it gave him 'a broad hint of a great underlying world of reserve, knowledge, pride and power – a great
feminine dignity and character in those massively plain
features.' Feminine strength in these women writers had
nothing to do with meretricious charms or sex appeal; it was
something profound, and, we may deduce, the source of their
creative strength. In the *Life* of George Eliot written by her
widower John Cross, a very useful book containing valuable
excerpts from her letters and journals, he wrote:

With a complete library and scholarly knowledge of French,
German, Italian and Spanish, she *spoke* all four languages with difficulty, though accurately and grammatically . . . Greek and Latin
she could read with thorough delight to herself, and Hebrew was a
favourite study to the end of her life.

Mathematics and astronomy it seems were also subjects she
was drawn to. He says:

She had great hope, for the future, in the improvement of human
nature by the gradual development of the affections and the sympathetic emotions . . . rather than by means of legislative enact-
ments . . . She was keenly anxious to redress injustices to women,
and to raise their general status in the community. This, she
thought, could best be effected by women improving their work –
ceasing to be amateurs. But it was one of the most distinctly
marked traits in her character, that she particularly disliked anything generally associated with the idea of a 'masculine woman'.
She was, and as a woman she wished to be, above all things
feminine – 'so delicate with her needle, and an admirable
musician'. She was proud, too, of being an excellent housekeeper –
an excellence attained from knowing how things ought to be done,
and from her early training, and from an inborn habit of extreme
orderliness. Nothing offended her more than the idea that because
a woman had exceptional intellectual powers, therefore it was right
that she should absolve herself, or be absolved, from her ordinary
household duties . . . George Eliot was deeply interested in the
higher education of women [Girton, Newnham, but] . . . The danger
she was alive to in the system of collegiate education, was the possible weakening of the bonds of family affection and family duties. In
her view, the family life holds the roots of all that is best in our
mortal lot; and she always felt that it is far too ruthlessly sacrificed
in the case of English *men* by their public school and university education, and that much more is such a result to be deprecated in the
case of women.

He ends his pen-portrait of his wife with: 'She had the distinctively feminine qualities which lend a rhythm to the movement of life' along with 'the crowning gift of genius'.

I will follow this with an account of the formation of another major woman writer of the nineteenth century, Mrs Oliphant, whose life-span almost coincided with that of Queen Victoria.

In Mrs Oliphant's upbringing, the absence of distractions in the way of amusements other than from literature and conversation, and the fact that conversation was intellectual discussion as well as being part of family life, were formative, just as Mrs Oliphant derived her pattern of wit from her mother's Scotch tongue; also that the centre of her life was in domestic duties, ties and affections. Very similar is the case of Jane Austen, and of the Brontë sisters, as also, as we've heard, of George Eliot. There is plenty of other evidence of the kind. I think the point has now been reached when we can make some generalizations. But as I don't want to be misunderstood, or to encourage what Mrs Oliphant described as 'the inherent contempt for women which is a settled principle in the minds of so many men', let me say first that in comparing men's and women's capabilities I do so only with respect to their creative abilities. I see no reason for thinking women inferior or limited (except by physical strength) in any other field, and no reason why, except for indefensible masculine prejudice, they shouldn't be, for instance, engineers, if they wish, any more than doctors, lawyers or research scientists, except that men don't like women in the engineering sheds, just as medical students formerly didn't like women in the dissecting room – and you can't be a good engineer without having been through the engineering shops (in spite of which I believe there is now at least one woman ship's engineer; whether there are women inventors or ever will be is another story). Women are at least as good as men in routine and administrative work because they are more industrious and conscientious, and they do very well indeed at Classics, because what's chiefly needed in a good Classic seems to be memory and industry. But what I am concerned with is *creativity*.

For the question of what constitutes true creativeness in literature and what fosters or produces it is of the utmost importance, not only to those of us who love literature and the arts in general, and who understand their important function in our own lives. It matters deeply and urgently to the whole race, to humanity. Progress, even the maintenance and not retrogressing, both of society and the human spirit, depends on creative minds. George Eliot was an intellectual but she was *also* a major novelist, that is, something much more than merely a learned person, and late in life she wrote to her friend Lady Ponsonby:

Consider what the human mind *en masse* would have been if there had been no such combination of elements in it as has produced poets. All the philosophers and *savants* would not have sufficed to supply that deficiency. And how can the life of nations be understood without the inward life of poetry, that is, of emotion blending with thought?

In fact, 'the life of nations', to use her term, can only be apprehended and understood through the work of poets and novelists. So that the contribution of women to this essential work for humanity is so important that it clearly ought to be protected and encouraged.

Let us first see how these women regarded their work. There is a surprising consensus of opinion about the sources of creative writing. Charlotte Brontë wanted to write as 'a complete woman', and correlated with this is the heroine of *Villette*'s assertion that she 'felt life at life's sources' and the description of another heroine, Diana Rivers (a symbolic name), who in *Jane Eyre* represents Emily Brontë: 'In her there was an affluence of life and certainty of flow, such as excited my wonder, while it baffled my comprehension'.

We even have a piece of evidence to similar effect from Jane Austen, otherwise a thoroughly impersonal novelist, it would seem. But note what she wrote to her sister, when away enjoying herself in London while *Sense and Sensibility* was in the press. Cassandra wrote suggesting she will have forgotten the novel: 'No, no', she replied, 'I am never too busy to think of *Sense and Sensibility*. I can no more forget it than a mother can forget her sucking child.' Is it not surprising that a spinster, a clergyman's daughter should produce such a simile to enforce her assertion of unceasing preoccupation with her novel in preparation? Surprising at any rate for us now. But it came instinctively even to a middle-class spinster because she shared a full natural family life. Her favourite sister-in-law bore eleven children, and Jane Austen had not only obviously seen them fed naturally as a matter of course, as you can see Dickens had in the use he makes of the wet-nurse Polly Toodles in *Dombey and Son*, but she had perceived what the relation between mother and infant is, that profound and mysterious tie that psychologists now recognize as a fact of primary importance to the child without being able to account for it. And she understood also that a similar link must exist between the creative artist and the work created (as we have seen George Eliot and Charlotte Brontë did), otherwise novels, to stick to this form of creation, will be merely superficial, written to a formula like Iris Murdoch's, Compton-Burnett's, Snow's and such, of no permanent value and little intrinsic interest. But the ambience and the assumptions in which educated women have been reared since the movement for female emancipation (or whatever it has been called at different times since) are visibly anti-humane as well as anti-domestic.

I remember a clever girl student who called on me at Cambridge for some help in her work and whom I took into my nursery as it was my baby daughter's feeding time. Seeing me starting to breastfeed the baby she exclaimed with horror: 'How can an intellectual woman like you turn your-self into a cow?' Then, perceiving no doubt that my horror was even greater than hers she added: 'Besides, don't you know that it is *better* for babies to be fed on dried milk?' She knew no better, she had been indoctrinated with such assumptions without questioning. This is only one instance of indoctrination that has largely cut educated women off from the first-hand sources of experience, sympathetic human experience, and the attitudes to the springs of life behind everyday living that fed the woman novelist of the past with insight, sympathy and understanding.

The end-product of this alienation from full living is beautifully illustrated in the case of the typical contemporary female writer, so entirely the sophisticated product of a deprived life in the city flat; of course it manifested itself first as a diseased form of novelist in the USA, and in Randell Jarrell's masterly university novel *Pictures from an Institution*, which appeared twenty years ago, the diagnosis had already been made. Gertrude Johnson teaches Creative Writing at American universities in the intervals of writing her novels; she has had three husbands but no children and is shown as incapable of home-making and is impatient of housekeeping (her husband is forced into the woman's role here), unable to make any contact with children, or with adults except as satiric material for her novels. She loses all her current friends every time she brings out a novel; her favourite author is Swift, for like him she doesn't *see*, she *sees through* people and life, and her novels, we are told, appeal to the eternal Le Rochefoucauld in everyone. By examining the portrait of Gertrude you can see more clearly what is required in a real novelist, for she is the antithesis of creative, and the awful fact is that Gertrude is drawn from life and had several close originals. We can see the type evolving here too, inevitably, with the decay of natural sensibility, and the contempt for and disgust with the traditional role of woman, the absence of respect for the function of wife and mother, and the rejection of a sense of responsibility which is something required even more of women than of men.

As to the last point, I remember how surprised I was about ten years ago when I had my drawing-room full of third-year pupils and postgraduates, mainly girls, to meet an academic from Nottingham University who was to lecture to the English Society that night. The conversation turned on Lawrence, and I made some comment of an adverse kind on Frieda, who as the wife of Professor Weekley at Nottingham had walked out of their home without even preparing her three children for her non-return to live with D. H. Lawrence, a comment that was warmly supported by the Nottingham academic who knew of the effects this had had on Frieda's children, particularly the boy. My surprise was due to the fact that none of the students, even a postgraduate girl who was about to be married, had any reaction to my criticism of Frieda as a criminally irresponsible mother and a heartless wife, except instinctive defence of her behaviour. When challenged by me about this they said things like: 'Oh well, plenty of others have done the same' or, 'Why shouldn't she?' It is not really surprising that ordinary girls from decent middle-class and working-class homes should reveal such a

complete absence of imaginative sympathy and sense of obligation, when you think of the vaguely Women's Lib. assumptions in the air, and in particular how the last phase of literary
intellectuals' culture, represented by such figures and their
works as Lytton Strachey, Bertrand Russell, Virginia Woolf,
Clive Bell, Maynard Keynes, Harold Nicolson and his wife
Vita Sackville-West and the rest, lived and had their being.
Their lives (recently revealed in biographies) of self-
indulgence and emancipation didn't produce an estimable
literature in spite of the talent many of them undoubtedly
had; their sexual high jinks simply disqualified them as
creative minds. Vita Sackville-West's novels, for instance,
are the feeblest women's-magazine fictions, though nastier
and snobbier than the commercial variety normally was.
Virginia Woolf's very real talent was simply ruined, not
merely impoverished, by the society she was part of and
which petted, flattered and protected her, as it did E. M.
Forster, with disastrous results for them both. It is significant
that the only good novel she wrote (for *Mrs Dalloway* is an
interestingly diagnosable failure) is *To the Lighthouse*, the only
one of her novels likely to last, I think, and that is rooted in
her own childhood; the sensitive exploration of the family life
of the Stephens has considerable insight, enough to make it
more than personal reminiscence, an exemplary model of the
Victorian family and its tensions. Yet set it alongside a comparable novel such as *Portrait of the Artist as a Young Man*, or *Jane
Eyre* or even *The Mill on the Floss* and one can't help seeing how
slight, how unsatisfactory Virginia Woolf is.

For what is a major novelist as distinct from a merely
efficient fiction-writer or a novelist who makes a temporary
hit but no lasting impression, the novelist who is not merely
of modish interest? We can distinguish between a superficial
and a deeply serious representation of social life because that
is shown not in an external manipulation but in a critical
interpretation of the hidden elements and factors that make
up social life. It is meaningful because it contains the
novelist's first-hand experience and because that experience
projects true insight into the essentials of the life of the
novelist's age; to do that a novelist must have special qualifications and for a woman they must be a woman's.

What I have described about Mrs Humphry Ward's case

seems to me to apply to Virginia Woolf also. Only once did she have a subject rooted in her experience which she had assimilated – in *To the Lighthouse*, plus possibly *Mrs Dalloway* as of related interest but as a proof of her otherwise uncoordinated public social life and private life of mania. *To the Lighthouse* is rooted in her childhood awareness of the difficulties of a family life where the parents (obviously her own, or rather representations of them for her purposes in this novel), the loved and admired parents, are temperamentally so alien that the children sense it and suffer from it permanently. While individualizing the characters Mrs Woolf has soared beyond mere novelistic characterization, and the scene of *To the Lighthouse* becomes that of the Victorian family in general and, further, archetypal in its understanding of the traditional family and its psychological structure.

I can bring this point home even better perhaps by adducing the case of Mrs Humphry Ward. Learned, clever, industrious, the niece of Matthew Arnold, the friend of Henry James, reared in Oxford where her father was a tutor and early married to a talented Oxford don who took her to London to a prosperous social and intellectual life, she had an immense reputation in her time for her controversial novels, but she seemed to have no real creative ability. Edmund Gosse, the literary critic, wrote of her:

She was so immensely clever, so clear-brained . . . so resolute and intelligent, that she wrote novels as, if she had chosen to do so, she could undoubtedly have painted landscapes or conducted a business . . . after experiment upon experiment, she had learned every trick of the trade, and the effort, having become mechanical, appeared to be crowned with success.

There you have the difference between a merely successful novelist and a major novelist. We can all supply the names of more modern counterparts to Mrs Ward. Her successful novels have sunk without a trace. But even Mrs Ward managed to write one real novel, that those who have read it and have judgement agree in thinking quite different from all her other novels, and that deserves to be kept current. Though it in some ways is suggestive of *Wuthering Heights*, and it can't of course compete with that, it has its own justification and a quite different interest. The reason seems to be that *Helbeck of*

Bannisdale is both rooted in the countryside (the Lake District) that meant so much to her, where the Arnolds' family house was, where parts of her childhood had been spent so blissfully, and also rooted as regards the theme in the fundamental problems of her own family life, that she had to grow up with and find how to bear with and bear up against, by understanding and sympathizing with conflicting beliefs.

Her father had of course been brought up in Dr Arnold's Broad Church variety of Victorian Christianity, and he married very happily a girl of Huguenot descent. They had three girls and three boys. All was well till Thomas Arnold followed Newman into Roman Catholicism, the characteristic spiritual problem of the age, something that split English families as bitterly as the Dreyfus affair did the French, and explains the other side of Victorian spiritual attitudes, the horror of Catholicism felt by the Protestant side of the Church of England and by all the Nonconformist sects, an instinctive dread of the fascination of Romanism and its rites clearly shown by many Victorian writers – such as Charlotte Brontë, Kingsley, Charlotte Yonge and Ruskin among many others. Mary Arnold, the daughter, never felt any impulse to desert the enlightened form of Protestantism in which she had been reared, though she deeply loved her father as well as her mother, who remained Protestant. The children were brought up on the Continental system in such cases, whereby the daughters took the mother's religion and the sons the father's. This does not seem to have divided Thomas Arnold's family, but the strain on Mary with regard to her parents must have been terrific, feeling sympathy and love for both parents as she did. She wrote of this in her autobiography late in life:

My poor mother felt as though the earth had crumbled under her. Her passionate affection for my father endured till her latest hour, but she never reconciled herself to what he had done. There was in her an instinctive dread of Catholicism . . . It never abated. Many years afterwards, in writing *Helbeck of Bannisdale*, I drew upon what I had remembered of it in describing some traits in Laura Fountain's inbred, and finally indomitable resistance to the Catholic claim upon the will and intellect of men . . . [and she describes this] great controversy in which from my youth up I had been able to follow my father without in the smallest degree chilling the strong affection between us which grew up with my life, and knew no forced silences.

She was evidently a girl of strong feelings and deep sympathies, and in this one novel, instead of writing a rationally argued, fashionably intellectual, merely descriptive piece of fiction, she found a situation in which she could dramatize a subject – 'that great controversy' in which she had been a participator from her youth up – a subject that lived in her and had become part of her emotional life. This was made inescapably harrowing for her not only because of her mother's anguished devotion to her husband but because her father kept the drama alive by wobbling in his convictions. His original conversion meant he lost his comfortable post in education and had to get translating and teaching work at Birmingham Oratory, and his family suffered hardships in consequence. After years of this he returned to the Anglican fold and so was able to become a tutor at Oxford, and this meant also that his boys had to be deconverted from Catholicism too. After some years more he again became a Roman Catholic (for life this time), with further distresses and upsets to his family. No wonder *Helbeck of Bannisdale* is so charged with feeling, though in fact the leading characters are not portraits from life, and the situation she invents for them is considerably removed from her mother's. As author, though her own sympathies with modernism are evident, she held the scales so fairly that while Catholics didn't much like the novel, Protestants alleged that she had given far too favourable a picture of the hero, head of an old Catholic family. Here for once, and once only, in Mrs Ward's prosperous career did she produce a novel which was not got up from mere knowledge but results from knowledge that is experience and assimilated. The novel, like a similar novel, Charlotte Brontë's *Villette*, incarnates a Protestant–Catholic deadlock and ends tragically, for the situation is inevitably tragic. In it Mrs Ward maintains the impartiality and wide understanding through natural sympathies that she had achieved in life, as a girl in a difficult but not unhappy home. The situation, the conflict, and the insoluble deadlock have stature from being representative, not modish, and so transcend the merely personal feelings of the author, as Mrs

Gaskell's sympathy with the factory girls' misery expressed her own suffering but transcended it.

Well, to sum up: perhaps you see what I've been getting at. The conditions from the late eighteenth century to the early nineteenth century seem to have been successful in providing for women of the middle classes the conditions needed in women to create literature. It seems that in rejecting and destroying what George Eliot's husband described 'the feminine rhythm of life' they have brought this development of women as serious creative artists to a close. The two most ambitious novels of the Irish novelists Somerville and Ross (*The Big House of Inver* and *The Real Charlotte*) are both tragic novels though full of wit and humour; and there are not very many truly tragic novels in English (I don't consider *Jude the Obscure* or *Tess* genuinely tragic). In these novels the personal tragedies are inseparable from the disastrous social history of Ireland in the nineteenth century, though the social history is entirely implicit in the dramatic detailing of the lives of the characters of all classes and both religions. Somerville and Ross were of the old Anglo-Irish Ascendancy but entirely committed to the life of the landowner and the Big House society, neither English nor Catholic-Irish in their sympathies and outlook. Mrs Wharton's best novels – and there are a number of these – convey, like Jane Austen's, a reasoned but also deeply felt criticism, as well as appreciation, of the successive phases of the social class she belonged to and was thus able to emancipate herself from to a considerable degree. This demands a witty and ironic mode of writing a novel, which we can see equally in George Eliot, Jane Austen, Edith Wharton, Mrs Oliphant and Somerville and Ross, and is by no means absent from the apparently less sophisticated and much gentler Mrs Gaskell; in fact, it seems to be the authentic feminine note often visible even earlier in the comparatively artless Fanny Burney. Mrs Wharton indeed said that she felt it safest to write only for the ironic critic who dwells within the human breast (as more likely to produce good work than praise and flattery). It seems to me in fact that, in the century or more I've specified, women were not only truly creative but, without forfeiting their feminine advantages had also some of the qualities of mind that we value in men: they were not only equal but different, they had

positive advantages because they had something that men
have and also what men can't have.

Perhaps this is why all these women were either actively or
passively opposed to the women's suffrage movement and its
associated claims. An anti-suffrage movement was actually
set in motion by Mrs Ward and supported by an impressive
list of distinguished women, including Miss Gertrude Bell,
the authority on the Middle East. Their objections, like Mrs
Oliphant's to John Stuart Mill on the enfranchisement of
women, was that political measures and power could not
affect the real questions of the relations between the sexes
and was therefore more likely to do harm than good.
Charlotte Yonge and George Eliot, both highly cultivated
women and successful novelists, agreed in fearing that
colleges for women were to be deplored if (as might well be
the case, they saw) college life unfitted women for natural
duties. They saw, that is, that one can't have one's cake and
eat it, a phrase that reminds me of hearing Frieda Lawrence's
son in a broadcast explain his mother by saying that 'Mamma
was a great one for wanting to have her cake and eat it'. I
remember also much correspondence in the pages of our
leading papers showing that an immense number of the
married women with university degrees are complaining of
the boredom and frustration entailed in rearing their children, the *hardship* of being wives and mothers, and that at a
time when no one need have a child who doesn't want one, or
get married either if it comes to that. You'll find the earliest
novel produced by this childish mentality in Olive
Schreiner's once famous novel *The Story of an African Farm*
(1883).

Now there is no doubt who is responsible for this state of
affairs. Women are produced in response to what men
demand at any given time. Women like Jane Austen and
George Eliot were domestic products just as much as the
Dora Copperfields, who were the attempt to produce a play-
thing and distraction from working life for the new
bourgeoisie of the mid-Victorian age. (Mrs Gaskell shows the
family life of such women in *Mary Barton*.) Fabian Society
woman was the product of a later cultural demand. Women
like Beatrice Webb wouldn't have children because they
wanted to be free to sit on committees, which is anyway

better than having them and neglecting them for a career, as is now so common. Bloomsbury woman was the co-mate of Bloomsbury man, who wanted a partner in irresponsibility. Women's Lib. woman can hardly be the answer to any man's needs, but is more in the nature of a nemesis. Whatever its merits there is one thing we can be sure of – it will never produce a major woman novelist.

The development of character in George Eliot's novels

George Eliot came comparatively late to fiction, so she was exceptionally well qualified as an intellectual who had done much expert reviewing and writing articles for solid periodicals. Though a pre-Victorian by birth, like the other Early Victorian novelists, she did not have, like them, to start from scratch and discover, by trial and error, how to find novelistic forms, conventions, myths and images suitable for conveying the new insights into society, and criticism of a new kind of society that other Early Victorian novelists had to struggle to achieve. She thus had the work not only of predecessors such as Scott and Jane Austen, but also of her contemporaries such as the Brontës, Disraeli, Mrs Gaskell and Dickens, to go no further, who were already well-known 'new' novelists, critics of every aspect of Early Victorian England, by the time she decided to try her hand at fiction.

But she did not at first heed the new lights. Working to try if she could write a story she turned to the memories and experiences of her own early life (as she was still doing later in *Adam Bede*, *Silas Marner*, *Mill on the Floss* and even *Middlemarch*). What is more, in writing that, she turned to memories of clergymen of previous phases of church history and, as she later admitted, she transferred the characters remembered from real life into her tales without transfiguring them for aesthetic purposes. Hence, like the characters who are a blot on Charlotte Brontë's *Shirley*, but unlike the 'black marble clergyman' in *Jane Eyre*, they stick out as lifelike excrescences, so that the tales are very small beer artistically. But why did George Eliot make her first appearance in fiction by a series of tales about clergymen? Maybe her instinct for the market was in fact sound, for these first sketches were so successful in magazine stories that they were published together in book form as *Scenes of Clerical Life* – a title which publishers today would hardly consider attractive. But the book was a hit, and she proceeded to a more ambitious attempt on fiction by a fourth clerical portrait of an eighteenth-century rector of her parents' day (and no doubt the type survived into her own childhood) – and nicely balanced him by a Methodist female.

This interest in religious sects, Church history, ecclesiastical scandals and so on, so characteristic of Early Victorian England and its novelists, was in George Eliot deep-seated in her own religious history, which was not untypical – her imprinting by Calvinist and Evangelical schoolteachers and the influence of the beloved Methodist aunt, the conflicts with her anti-Evangelical brother, the clergymen of her childhood ranging from the High Church aristocratic Mr Irwine to the Evangelical new-light preacher of *Janet's Repentance* and the assorted clerics of *Amos Barton*. It was followed in her case by painful emancipation via German criticism of the Bible and English literature: reading Shakespeare and Scott she cites as liberating influences; and Wordsworth's poetry, which affected her as peculiarly congenial, gave her a guide to the desired effect of retaining religious feelings without a theological orthodoxy by combining the Wordsworthian religion of nature with compassion for all, particularly, as she adopted political Radicalism, with the underdogs, those ill-used by nature and society.

It seems to me that it was the need to channel into fiction these phases of her moral past, in order to examine them dispassionately, that soon turned the George Eliot of *Scenes of Clerical Life* from an amateur storyteller into an important novelist. And she found that to do so the reproduction from life of individual people as portraits, without transforming them to be of representative status, was not satisfactory. Her next phase as artist is seen in her recognition that external characteristics are meaningless without a deep investigation into character, which must be a 'psychological conception'. 'But I am', she says, 'unable to alter anything in relation to the delineation or development of character, as my stories always grow out of my psychological conception of the dramatis personae.' So Maggie Tulliver, who in childhood is shown as reproducing the author's own frustrations and

sense of injustice as a girl-child, and in her teens going
through the novelist's own spiritual troubles, eventually has
to be cut free of her creator and shown as acting in accordance with the circumstances in which she finds herself, circumstances which are so different from George Eliot's own
that unlike her author Maggie renounces the possibility of
fulfilment through a lover, and comes to a tragic end.

Meanwhile, in her first novel, we see George Eliot discovering separately and almost independently the various
growth-points of the budding novelist who is hardly conscious of how she arrives at her goal. *Adam Bede* started as
another clerical or religious controversy novel, where the
Established Church is contrasted with Methodism, but both
are seen as cultural–social phenomena. Methodism, she
says, was a primitive culture, a spiritual movement belonging
to the working class, while the Church of England was a
religious establishment administered by the upper class for
the moral welfare of the rest of the people; so Mr Irwine and
Dinah become representatives of ideas rather than characters as such. This mode of composition naturally arouses in
George Eliot her Radical political views – I was going to say,
but they are feelings rather than views, for they were deeply
felt and based on her loyalty and sympathy with the village
and farmhouse culture in which she was reared, and as late as
Silas Marner still predominant.

I find a source of delicious sympathy in these faithful [Dutch] pictures of a monotonous homely existence . . . Let us love that other
beauty too, which lies . . . in the secret of deep human sympathy . . .
do not impose on us any aesthetic rules which shall banish from the
region of Art those old women scraping carrots with their work-
worn hands . . . those rounded backs and stupid, weather-beaten
faces that have bent over the spade and done the rough work of the
world . . . In this world there are so many of these common coarse
people, who have no picturesque sentimental wretchedness!
Therefore let Art always remind us of them; therefore let us always
have men ready to give the loving pains of a life to the faithful representing of commonplace things . . . I can't afford to give all my
love and reverence to such rarities [as heroes and beauties]: I want
a great deal of those feelings for my everyday fellow-men . . .
Neither are picturesque lazzaroni or romantic criminals half so frequent as your common labourer, who gets his own bread, and eats
it vulgarly but creditably with his own pocket-knife.

Here George Eliot is first seen reacting against the conventional cult of beauty in the novel and in art, and justifying an interest in the life of the lowly by finding a different kind of beauty there, one that the Dutch artists show in the paintings which appealed to George Eliot on aesthetic as well as ideological grounds; and in this opening paragraph we can find *Silas Marner* prefigured. For her 'that other beauty which lies in the secret of deep human sympathy' is paramount. Those ignorant of the aesthetic assumptions of the early nineteenth century may wonder why George Eliot goes out of her way here, and holds up the story, in order to make such obvious points. But at that time they were not obvious but controversial, for art was judged by its subject-matter and we must remember such writers as Ruskin complaining that Constable showed a low taste in choosing such parts of the rural scene to paint as mills and cottages, ruined weirs and so forth. He even suggested that a painter ought to choose whole subjects such as fine architecture, and if ruins then classical ones. George Eliot had to defend her intuitive preference in subject-matter by an argument based on aesthetic principle, but she eventually falls back on an emotional appeal to right feeling, one of moral obligation to those 'who have done the rough work of the world', and she refuses therefore to take as subject-matter Bulwer-Lytton's and Ainsworth's 'romantic criminals' and 'picturesque lazzaroni'. The Wordsworthian theory that the life and feelings of the poor and humble, living the life of peasants in close contact with nature is the richest and truest material for art, is endorsed, and it is supplemented by the socialist belief in the claims of the worker to a moral superiority since he 'gets his own bread, and eats it vulgarly but creditably with his own pocket-knife'. And the masses shall count for more than the 'few sublimely beautiful women' and 'few heroes', who have been commonly considered the true heroes for novelists to concern themselves with in accordance with the aesthetic theory expressed by Ruskin.

Of course George Eliot had already been anticipated by Mrs Gaskell's *Mary Barton*, a novel steeped in sympathy for the working class and their hard life in the new society of class conflict in the industrial city, which had deeply impressed George Eliot and which she read constantly while composing *Adam Bede*. Its influence can be easily seen in *Adam Bede*, particularly in the structure of class-conflict, rife in the countryside, and the loose construction of separate centres of lives (the cottage, the farmhouse, the village, the rectory, the Great House and the factory where Dinah works), which are shown as inevitably drawn together through the seduction of the farmer's niece by 'the young squire' and its tragic outcome, in which everyone is involved and human sympathies burst through the class barriers uniting all in suffering.

So George Eliot found that something more is involved in writing fiction than telling a story and drawing portraits, once she had got her hand well in. 'My books are deeply serious things to me, and come out of all the painful discipline, all the most hardly learnt lessons of my past life.' This was because she was an intellectual *and* a very intelligent person (not by any means the same thing). She had realized by 1859, we see, that a self-respecting novelist must be 'deeply serious' about her fictional publications, which means putting into them the novelist's own experience of life and understanding of that hardly acquired experience. This implied a public that could appreciate a serious art such as this, and she believed this public existed. 'My books are written out of my deepest belief, and as well as I can, for the great public – and every sincere strong word will find its mark in that public.' She had reason to, for by writing only to suit her own high standards concerning this posited public she was able to make a fortune out of her novels. It is only fair to point out that the necessary public taste for and ability to appreciate the serious novel, the novel which is entertaining only in the highest sense, had been formed by Dickens, who had taken that amorphous public with him from the exuberant amusing fiction of his earlier writing days through his own development to the superb 'black novels' of his later period, creating a serious reading public for the novel which George Eliot, as a late starter, inherited. Other contributions to this process had been by Charlotte Brontë, Mrs Gaskell and many minor writers of novels of religious controversy (a tradition which when followed by Trollope gave him his first success – *Barchester Towers* – after unsuccessful attempts in other genres). We should also acknowledge the cumulative effect of the serious reviewing of current fiction by very many responsible writers, often novelists themselves – Harriet Martineau, Mrs Oliphant and George Eliot herself in her earlier days. The public was accustomed to reviews and articles on the novel, equally in the solid quarterlies and monthlies, the periodicals and newspapers catering for different religious sects, and even the ordinary press such as the *Daily News*, in which Harriet Martineau regularly reviewed and in which her striking review of *Villette* appeared. In such reviews standards of criticism were upheld, the aesthetics of the novel discussed, the role of character debated, and often with pungency, wit and intelligent discrimination. George Eliot of course read the periodicals as well as contributing to them.

Another sign of George Eliot's gradual maturing as a practitioner of the novel is shown by comparing the openings of her novels. In *Adam Bede* she relied initially on memories of her childhood – the memories of her father and mother and aunt (inevitably idealized, since she had loved them very greatly as a child) – so the book opens with the carpenter's shop and cottage home of her father as a young man which she had been told of, followed by her own memories of the farmhouse she was born into with Mrs Poyser based on her mother; and then she introduces the Methodist circle of her admired aunt, the only confidante of her early spiritual difficulties. The only link between these is her own nostalgia for this idyllic past, but she could then bring into play what had so strongly impressed her in her favourite reading, Greek drama, the concept of an operative law in the universe, Nemesis. This accorded with the moral rigidity of the theologizing of Calvinism which she had acquired not at home, where the religion of Mr Irwine the rector of *Adam Bede* held, but at her country boarding-school, where teachers converted her to Evangelicalism. The theme – so common in early and mid-Victorian fiction, of the seduction of a working-class girl by a governing-class gentleman – provided the illustration of inevitable punishment for transgression of the moral order which the classical world equally with modern Evangelical society held by. She thus found the value of an operative idea for organizing the desired unified structure, which made the difference between the collection of portraits with dialogue and a slight story which was all she had used in the *Scenes of Clerical Life*. *Adam Bede* is therefore a much better novel than its inspiration, Mrs Gaskell's *Mary Barton*, which has no such organizing ideas, only a pervasive firm ethic.

When we consider *The Mill on the Floss* critically, we see that she was more ambitious as an artist. In spite of the nostalgic reminiscent first chapter, there is nothing nostalgic about the childhood and adolescent memories she draws on for Maggie's earlier phases. Instead a pervasive sociological type of insight is at work and no one, not even the child Maggie, is spared this kind of examination. And along with this sign of greater maturity goes her attempt as a novelist to cope with the most intractable and painful element in her own life – her relations with her very difficult and conventional brother. This attempt at a psychological explanation of human disasters takes the place of applying the classical and theo-logical idea of Nemesis that underpins *Adam Bede*. This part of George Eliot's life did not lend itself to nostalgia, so the novel that results is much more sensitive and personal. Unfortu-nately *The Mill on the Floss* collapses in the last chapters because the novelist cannot in the end bring herself to deal candidly with the sore in her own life which time never healed. Until these last chapters *The Mill* is an equally tragic but a more interesting novel than *Adam Bede*, though without the first novel's charm. But the author weakened *The Mill on the Floss* because she seems unable to believe that her new subject was sufficiently meaningful in itself; we see her trying to magnify it, to give it weight and an extra dimension, by creating a factitious significance: the sentimental, insincere language in which the imitation legend of St Ogg is related to imply some religious association with the river; such things as a piece of alleged folklore (surely a literary invention?) that 'there's a story as when the mill changes hands, the river's angry', as Luke says (though it doesn't flood when Mr Tulliver loses it to Wakem, only when Wakem sells it back to the Tulliver family); and Mrs Tulliver's ominous prediction at the beginning of the novel that little Maggie's fascinated interest in the mill-stream will be the death of her. The con-stant cropping up of water imagery and action taking place on the river is meant to keep these things alive in the reader's mind and suggest a dramatic sequence which simply doesn't exist, and an expectation of tragic outcome which is bogus. Maggie is indeed drowned, but by the debris brought down by the flood – entirely by accident for she has only taken a boat from a noble motive, to rescue her relatives trapped in their homes. The flood is a too convenient means of solving the impasse between Maggie and her brother, but it is unworthy of an artist, merely a melodramatic device, as Henry James complained. For the review of *The Mill on the Floss* (in *The National Review*) too it was a 'failure in unity and as a work of art'. And we can see in a late statement George Eliot made in a letter to Frederick Harrison what difficulty she had from this desire to be a major novelist, to create a great work of art which, though a novel, should be the equivalent in prose of a Shakespearean or Greek tragedy. How convey through prose what poetry had enabled the dramatist to do? How give tragic structure to modern characters in their daily life whether rural or urban? One of her perceptions was that what must be used in the novel is the diction of real life, as spoken by individual characters who are thus characterized by their personal whim, and not the artificial language of the dialogue in genteel fiction. 'The Greeks were not taking an artificial, entirely erroneous standpoint in their art – a standpoint which disappeared altogether with their religion and their art. They had the same essential elements of life presented to them as we have, and their art symbolised these in grand schematic forms.' She saw that this was so in Shakespeare as well as in the novels of the past she admired.

Shakespeare is assumed to be a novelist for her purposes – as indeed he was the model for other ambitious novelists of the first half of the nineteenth century, such as the Brontës, who saw that they must break with the eighteenth-century novel and the polite Regency novel and its language if they aimed at an art-form in prose which would be the equivalent of great dramatic art in verse. (In New England Herman Melville made at this time a similar discovery, and this inaugurated the great American tradition of the novel.)

George Eliot differentiates between genteel Scott, writing of ladies and gentlemen in eighteenth-century English, and the naturalist and Doric-speaking Scott, writing of 'the popular life with which he is familiar', and she rightly feels that the second Scott is the great writer. She herself was familiar in her youth with the speakers of several midland and northern dialects, cherished them for their unique qualities and the impressive characters who spoke them, and insisted on retaining the dialect in *Adam Bede* in spite of the objections of her publishers and friends.

APPENDIX:

George Eliot and the novel of religious controversy

The Puseyite novels show tamed, submissive, selfless creatures as the desirable human product; Kingsley and Charlotte Brontë and Dickens, all thoroughly Protestant in feeling and instinct, represent a healthy protest, and so does Disraeli, who added a wilful representation of Christian ideas to suit his Jewish nature and traditions. George Eliot's early training was in Evangelicalism and her youthful sympathies were secured by her Methodist Aunt Samuel (in general the original of Dinah Morris). Her consistent leaning towards a Nonconformist culture was by the time she wrote *Adam Bede* and *Silas Marner* a tenderness modified by her mature sense of humour and her enfranchisement from all doctrinal religious responsibility. She had therefore no weakness for or fear of Roman Catholicism. By the time she came to write *Felix Holt* she had shed even her tenderness for Dissenters and is seen analysing the defects of their culture in the style of Mrs Oliphant; in *Middlemarch* she even shows herself able to dissect her youthful self: not, as in *The Mill on the Floss*, in pity for her emotional starvation in that phase, but as representative of the early nineteenth-century English disease (compare John Stuart Mill's *Autobiography* and Dombey's case as diagnosed by Dickens). Dorothea is shown in an emotional crisis in her life as helpless in Rome before the terrifying accumulation of man's aesthetic history that seems to her to have culminated in the celebration in St Peter's. But her conversion is not from Evangelicalism to Romanism. It is from a deprived Puritanism to an understanding of the necessity of art: there was an art-shaped blank in her life that marriage to a Casaubon – or to a Lydgate either – could not fill.

However, though emancipated, George Eliot could not avoid the fashionable subject of religious controversy. Indeed, when making her first attempt at fiction she started with scenes of clerical life. It was only natural that she should have wished to pay tribute to the

Evangelicals who represented the religious environment of her schooldays, to examine it subsequently (in *Middlemarch*) and to pay a debt of family; and in *Silas Marner* to pay tribute to the old English rural religion of her childhood (Mr Irwine's eighteenth-century religion of benevolence, good morality and neighbourliness).

All three tales of *Scenes of Clerical Life* belong with the fiction dealing with the religious controversy. *Janet's Repentance* starts off with a scene where the ignorance and religious prejudices of a small town are exhibited with humour and irony (*Adam Bede* carried on this Dissenting preacher versus Church of England parson theme). In *Janet's Repentance* George Eliot is obviously paying a debt she felt she owed to the Evangelical moral and spiritual education she had in her schooldays, an adolescent feeling that resulted in social conscience. The remembered history of the original of Mr Tryan is useful for this, as at the time of her attempting fiction first, in the apprenticeship of *Scenes of Clerical Life*, she was not truly creative (as she later admitted and deplored). Through the Rev. Mr Irwine, who is also evidently a portrait – he has an essential part to play in the plot of *Adam Bede* and is subordinate to it, more so than Bertie Massey or Mrs Poyser even – the novelist has come into her own. By *Middlemarch* we get a wholly novelistic treatment of the Evangelical culture – unsentimental, without illusions, but also without animus (contrast *Jane Eyre*), presented with respect as well as humour (unlike Trollope's in *Barchester Towers*, where social distaste for the vulgarity of a Slope and a Mrs Proudie, though the niece of an earl, is the chief part of his distaste for the religious manifestation of the Evangelical culture). George Eliot was capable by now, in her maturity as an artist, of dissociating herself from her past sufficiently to examine herself in her Evangelical phase through a persona who is herself in sensibility and ideas at that time but in position is her friend Mrs Mark Pattison.

There is some rather laborious irony at the absurd bigotries of Evangelicals. The religious lending library Mr Tryan had founded contains the story of 'Father Clement' – 'a library itself on the errors of Romanism', Mrs Pratt (herself an authoress) says. George Eliot no doubt felt she must show that *she* wasn't vulgarly prejudiced against Roman Catholicism because she was paying a tribute to an Evangelical clergyman. The Evangelical Mr Tryan preaches 'the great doctrine of justification by faith', distributes the publications of the Religious Tractarian Society and introduces Dissenting hymns into the church. Mr Tryan is of 'a race of Dissenters extinct in these days', his 'dissent being of this simple non-polemical kind'.

The ground that was instinctively chosen for her first attempt at fiction returned in the later novels. *Adam Bede* grew out of a 'Clerical Life' scene about Mr Irwine, as the disproportionate space allotted to him shows – for example, Adam's comparison of him with his more spiritual successor; the Methodist parts are even more disproportionate. The novel is really a religious controversy novel. *Silas Marner* also grew out of the problem of the Calvinist-sect culture. *Felix Holt* has the Nonconformist ministry and congregation and a Church of England Dissent controversy (though it in fact never comes off owing to the curate's shrinking from the battlefield). In *Middlemarch* we have the Bulstrode circle and the Church of England parsons. In *Deronda* the Jewish culture is played off against the English establishment, the worldly rector, and so on.

Middlemarch is George Eliot's more mature study of English religious culture than the tribute to Methodism ('a rudimentary culture') that produced *Adam Bede* and the questioning of the Calvinist sectarianism of city masses as opposed to the traditional Christian religion (a blend of Christian practices and pagan superstitious beliefs) of the English countryfolk. The motivation of *Middlemarch* is to examine the effects of an English Puritanical upbringing, in the early nineteenth-century form of Evangelicalism, on a young girl; in fact, a novelistic exploration of George Eliot's own youth after the *Mill on the Floss* stages of childhood and adolescence shown as Maggie Tulliver's. It is shown as unfitting Dorothea Brooke for fending for herself in the real world. The worldly Mrs Cadwallader's shrewd criticisms are not successfully refuted by Dorothea and even her sister Celia's idealistic commonsense emerges triumphantly as sound in practice. The other characters are also defined in relation to the religious positions of the period of George IV.

Miss Brooke is the product of English Puritanism. Her emancipation (like George Eliot's) is achieved through the arts and union with a lover who understands them. George Eliot was notably above the warfare on the Catholic–Protestant front. Though she showed in *Scenes* that she sympathized with the fresh religious current brought into provincial life by the early Evangelicals, and in *Adam Bede* in the eighteenth century by the Methodists, she also showed, in Maynard Oldfield, as later in the Rev. Mr Irwine, that she appreciated the eighteenth-century type of parson who without zeal or fervour functioned as a good Christian in his parish and doubled socially as an ornament to the governing class. Painstakingly accurate as to social and economic history, George Eliot could not in *Middlemarch*, which occurs just after the Catholic Emancipation Act (1829), ignore the feeling this had engendered in the country gentry, and that, like the Dreyfus affair in France, it was

eventually to cause a national split greater even than the Civil War
had brought about in the seventeenth century; for that had been
healed by the Augustans, whereas the other became fundamental
in the nineteenth century and has not by any means petered out yet.
We gather in *Middlemarch* as the stage is set that Mr Brooke, the
Radical landowner, who intends to stand for parliament in the
Radical interest and prides himself on being enlightened and progressive, is told off by his parson's wife for selling 'a bit of land to
the Papists at Middlemarch' (presumably as a site for a chapel, a
Roman Catholic school, or a convent) and is assured he will
be burnt in effigy on Guy Fawkes' Day. Dorothea's suitor Mr
Casaubon is apparently a Whig, and a writer of pamphlets on contemporary religious matters as well as on comparative mythology –
Mr Brooke says 'He is pretty certain to be a bishop. That was a very
seasonable pamphlet of his on the Catholic Question – a deanery at
least. They owe him a deanery.' We should remember that this was
the age of the Rev. Sydney Smith, who was a gifted controversialist
in the Whig interest and a witty fighter for Catholic Emancipation
and the disestablishment of the Irish Church, and whose party
admitted it owed him a bishopric but never paid him with more
than a deanery.

Will Ladislaw is a totally different type of character-creation from
the psychologically and sociologically logical Dorothea. He is constructed, not developed; the result of writing down desired
qualities and drawing a circle round to contain them. His pedigree
is carefully given – pawnbroker grandparents with a hint of Jewish
blood, their daughter, Will's mother, an actress. On the paternal
side, his grandfather was a Polish émigré for political reasons (a
revolutionary patriot), married to a lady of good family and their
son was a violinist. Thus the arts and foreign blood and revolutionary spirit combine in Will, who also paints, cultivates musical
tastes, has had a European education as well as background (non-
insular though now English) and is a man of letters who can be a
practising journalist in the Radical interest. To the sum of these
necessary qualities, necessary for satisfying Dorothea's Evangeli-
cally developed social conscience and personal needs (the necessity of art), George Eliot tries to give the breath of life by a few distinctive traits borrowed from G. H. Lewes – the habit of lying on the
hearth-rug in people's drawing-rooms, for instance. Lewes *was* in
fact an amalgam of artistic and literary tastes and enlightened
politics and scientific interest. Will nevertheless and not surprisingly affects one as a second-year undergraduate (not yet broken in,

as he would be a year later by the necessity of self-discipline to get his degree).

Dorothea is firmly placed as the typical product of a Puritanical education and culture and conforms in every respect to the Evangelical tradition of her age (pre-Reform Act). She has started a school for the children of the locality and draws plans for rehousing the inhabitants in model cottages; she visits the sick poor and prays fervently by their bedsides, she rejects personal ornaments (even her mother's jewellery) and tries to live consistently with her religious views, which makes her an incompatible house-mate for her sister and uncle, and shocks her admirers. She thinks of marriage not as 'personal ease' but as a pious duty and an opportunity for doing good (George Eliot draws comedy out of her disappointment at finding her future husband's villagers don't need her patronage, as also subtle psychological insight into the self-deception Evangelicalism imposes in the distribution-of-the-jewels scene); and in this spirit she welcomes the opportunity of marrying an elderly scholar and cleric (more like a father). She is glad there is no music or art in his home and looks forward to learning Hebrew and Greek from him and a life of dutiful assistance to her husband.

The honeymoon is in Rome, contrived to set up the obligatory Catholic–Protestant opposition. Dorothea, as a strong-minded young lady of the age, is an ardent Evangelical and as the product of a narrow Puritanical education (in Switzerland) is profoundly shocked by Rome, with its sordid present, sunk in the 'deep degeneracy of a superstition divorced from reverence'. But this is all, for Roman Catholics were not felt to be a menace to the Church of England at this date and criticism was directed at Evangelicals. For while the Catholics were pitied for their superstitious religion, and Dissenters were socially contemptible and their religion ridiculous, the Evangelicals were the real threat. It is characteristic of George Eliot's large-minded intellect that she shows the historic Rome, even of 'a degenerate present', able to impress Dorothea with this spectacle of human achievement as exhibited in art and religious history, which seems to culminate in St Peter's and to make her realize the inadequacy of her narrow Protestant conception of life and man; and the rest of the novel works this out.

Mrs Oliphant:
Miss Marjoribanks
(Introduction)

I think most of us have felt at some time that there must have
been somebody who bridged the gap between Jane Austen
and George Eliot – the aspect of course of George Eliot that
had grown out of Jane Austen – and not been satisfied by such
inward reminders as that Trollope in the Barchester series
has frequently the air of being a Victorianized, minor Jane
Austen, or that most of *Coningsby* would surely have delighted
Jane Austen, or that in *Little Dorrit* Dickens presents a serious
comedy of manners in the scenes between the Meagleses and
Mrs Gowan that is decidedly in the Austen tradition. By way
of the novel here reprinted,[1] *Miss Marjoribanks* (pronounced
'Marchbanks'), which first appeared in *Blackwood's Magazine*
in 1865–6, I suggest it and its author, Mrs Oliphant, for that
missing link. Her Lucilla has long seemed to me a triumphant intermediary between their Emma and Dorothea,
and, incidentally, more entertaining, more impressive and
more likeable than either.

That this novel is, in its consistent ironic comedy, probably
unique in Mrs Oliphant's *oeuvre* (I do not claim to have read
the lot, nor does anyone else, I imagine) does not mean that
she hasn't a continuous 'Miss Marjoribanks' vein running
through most of her work, a vein which constantly surfaces
and which the connoisseur will soon learn to recognize and
look out for; in her short stories it is more frequently dominant. Tough-mindedness did not disappear for the rest of the
century with Jane Austen and *Coningsby*. The ironic eye that
Jane Austen turned on Georgian middle-class country life
extends its gaze in *Coningsby* to areas she would have had no
knowledge of, but she would, we can feel sure, have appreciated Rigby and Lord Monmouth, Lord Eskdale and the
ladies of that world, and the manner of their presentation;

whereas her appreciation of *Middlemarch* would, one suspects, have been limited by lack of sympathy with the idealization and apotheosis of Mrs Casaubon. *Miss Marjoribanks* however is something that Jane Austen might almost have created and written herself (though it would have been in fewer words) if she had not died prematurely, for it brings to bear on Victorian provincial-town and county society the same acute and unsentimental critical mind that had produced *Emma* in the Regency period: the technique and style as well as the language of the novel are essentially witty from start to finish. The opening is as anti-sentimental as the author of *Northanger Abbey* could have desired, though of course not directed at her targets but at Victorian conventional sentiment – for example in the course of the novel Rose Lake says of her sister: 'But I am sorry to say she has not a strong sense of duty' and ' "I have always been brought up to believe that duty was happiness," said Miss Marjoribanks with some severity' – authorial jokes inconceivable in *Middlemarch*. Lucilla is a Victorian anti-heroine, large, strong, unsentimental, insubordinate to men and with a hearty appetite.

Who else in 1865 could habitually write thus?

Lucilla had a great deal too much sense to upbraid anyone with ingratitude, or even to make any claim upon that slippery quality.

'He will never learn that he is old', she said in Lucilla's ear; and thus the two old people kept watch upon each other, and noted, with a curious mixture of vexation and sympathy, each other's declining strength.

. . . nor had she the ordinary amount of indifference to other people, or confidence in herself, which stands in the place of self-control with many people.

. . . hurriedly clasping together a pair of helpless hands as if they could find a little strength in union.

'We must leave that to Providence,' said Miss Marjoribanks, with a sense of paying a compliment to Providence in entrusting it with such responsibility.

. . . as Mrs Chiley just remarked, Mrs Woodburn was a woman who would take off the Archbishop of Canterbury or the Virgin Mary if she had the opportunity.

The Archdeacon was one of those men who are very strong for

the masculine side of Christianity; and when he was with the ladies, he had a sense that he ought to be paid attention to, instead of taking that trouble in his own person. Miss Marjoribanks was not a woman to be blind to the advantages of this situation, but still, as was to be expected, it took her a little time to get used to it, and to make all the use of it which was practicable under the circumstances.

He was a worldly man himself, and he thought his daughter a worldly woman; and yet, though he thoroughly approved of it, he still despised Lucilla a little for her prudence, which is a paradoxical state of mind not very unusual in the world.

Her eyes were blacker and more brilliant in a way, but they were eyes which owned an indescribable amount of usage ... and though she looked worn, and like a creature much buffeted about by wind and waves, she was still what connoisseurs in that article call a fine woman.

Of course, in the Victorian Age only Scotland could have fostered such a phenomenon. Mrs Oliphant, born near Edinburgh in 1828, nine years after George Eliot (but publishing novels long before her), spent the first ten years of her life in Scotland and only an intervening period, till her marriage to an Edinburgh cousin, in Liverpool. Through her mother, born an Oliphant – who had the sarcastic tongue and keen wit that she later recognized appreciatively in Mrs Carlyle – she traced her good, even romantic Scotch lineage, with a castle far back. And she was her mother's daughter, the Wilson father seeming to have been a shadowy figure; once married she signed herself 'Mrs Oliphant W. Oliphant'. There is a curious family history of weak, dependent men and spirited women over several generations that Mrs Oliphant herself bore the brunt of, brothers, husbands and sons placing themselves and, where they had children, the children too, on her hands to be supported in every sense. The outcome for her was tragic, since her sons died still in her charge and a more hopeful nephew as soon as she educated and launched him. This history was inevitably reflected in her writings in a preponderance of male characters who disappoint or let down their womenfolk, and in the alcoholics, wastrels or physically ailing characters who ruin them – a general disillusionment with that sex that is too realistic to run to cynical generalizations but has a saddening effect. Perhaps it was this as much as the Scotch traits that saved her from the Victorian weaknesses to which her literary contemporaries so often succumbed. In *Miss Marjoribanks*, where the mode is social comedy, Mrs Oliphant can be seen to be aware of her tendency to extend to men in general her experience with the men of her own family: it is here made fun of as one aspect of her heroine's massive conviction of superiority. Yet in Lucilla's mild and patient contempt for Them there is also some endorsement from the novelist. Edith Wharton, in another age and country, shows a similar feeling about men in relation to women, and for similar personal reasons, and her best novel too, *The Custom of the Country*, is a consistently ironic masterpiece with a dominant heroine, though an odious one.

Yet Mrs Oliphant had reason, as we may see from her autobiography, to conclude that men outside her family also were inherently unreliable and morally contemptible. Over and above the hardships, which she bore cheerfully, of supporting all her life so many by her pen alone, she had had the shock of finding, first that her artist husband could not make a living by his stained-glass work but required her to write steadily though a young family was soon in being, and then that he had tuberculosis and must be taken to Italy (where he died six weeks before yet another child was born to her). It was not this but a moral shock that proved seismic, as recorded in her fragmentary autobiography:

He never was well after. I thought, and perhaps he too thought, that it was the worry of the work, which began to get too much for him, and the difficulty of managing the men, who were of the art-workmen class, and highly paid, and untrustworthy to the last degree. However important it might be to get the work done they were never to be relied upon, not even when they saw him – always most kind and friendly to them, incapable of treating them otherwise than if they had been gentlemen – ill, worn-out, dying by inches; not even when it became a matter of life and death for him to get free. They were well-paid, educated in their way, thinking themselves a kind of artists – and I had always been brought up with a high idea of the honour and virtue of working men. I was very indignant at this behaviour, of course, and cruelly undeceived, – and I do not think I have ever got over the impression made upon

me by their callousness and want of honour and feeling. I
remember most wrathfully contrasting their behaviour with that of
my maids, who stood by me to the last moment; knowing we were
breaking up our home and going away, and that they would be in no
respect advantaged by us, yet who were as loyal and true as the
others were selfish and cruel. My husband did not like it to be said
– but it was so.

First-hand experience of the realities of human nature is
always useful to a novelist, but no wonder that in her novels
it is women who are generally the admirable or at worst the
efficient characters, while the men, unsatisfactory in all
sorts of ways, have to be managed for their own good and to
avert domestic and social disaster. In her novels loyal men-
servants always seem to be Scotch, worthy landowners tend
to be.

Though over-production and also over-extension (into the
necessary three volumes) prevented any other of her novels
than *Miss Marjoribanks* from being outstanding, a number of
them are worth looking at twice and especially some of the
Scottish ones, such as *Kirsteen*, which help to fill the chronological gap in the tradition of the Scottish novel between
Heart of Midlothian and *The Entail* on the one side and *Weir of
Hermiston* and *The House with the Green Shutters* on the other. In
these, and in the many admirable short stories with a Scotch
setting, we find her continuing Sir Walter Scott's investigation into what it meant to be Scottish. She plays the
English off against the natives to the constant disadvantage
of the former while registering the grimmer characteristics of
her fellow-countrymen; she must have been the first novelist
to notice and pay attention to the disconcerting results of
educating young Scots of the landowning class at English
public schools. She herself, it is significant, was always
noticed by those who met her as being 'herself the fine Scots
gentlewoman she drew so incomparably in her book'
(J. M. Barrie) and 'speaking definitely and to the point in her
pretty, racy Scotch accent . . . a little cold in manner and tart
in speech' (Lady Ritchie). In her London life she found most
congenial such compatriots as Mrs Carlyle and Mrs Duncan
Stewart – *grandes dames* of the Scottish kind who held salons.
Henry James, at the end of *Notes on Novelists*, pays Mrs
Oliphant an obituary tribute in which he chiefly complains

that, with so many gifts as a novelist, she did not have more art, specifying *Kirsteen* in illustration. Yet what one remembers about *Kirsteen* is the powerful picture of an unimaginable form of life it imprints – the poor proud violent Douglas laird, his weak wife with a 'bairntime' of fourteen children, the sons each in turn launched early on the world with only an outfit, the daughters with no future unless they fight for it or break with their fearsome father. There is no softening with humour or sentiment as so often in Scott, for even where her Scottishness is concerned Mrs Oliphant is hard-headed; her interest there is chiefly of the sociological and psychological kind, leaving the art of the novel to take care of itself.

It will be noticed that *Miss Marjoribanks* is also part of this inquiry, an illustration of the impact of Scottish capacity on English provincial life in its contemporary (mid-Victorian) phase of civilization, the limitations and ridiculous aspects of which she thus dexterously shows up. Dr Marjoribanks with 'the well-worn cordage of his countenance', who 'had a respect for "talent" in every development, as is natural to his nation', with his complete absence of tenderness or conventional sentiment in the relation of husband and father and his grim enjoyment of his daughter's difficulties as well as his appreciation of her 'capabilities', is yet another of Mrs Oliphant's studies of her own nation. Lucilla, with her large Scotch bones and her moral solidity, her literal-mindedness, and that characteristic Scotch complacency, based on the consciousness of undeniable superiority, which makes her able to ignore other people's so-called sense of humour – thus disabling the mimic Mrs Woodburn – while yet having all her wits about her and a canny tongue of her own, is evidently of a different make from the Carlingford folk who naturally have no chance against her. By the end of the book her father has passed through the successive phases of fearing she will be a nuisance, thinking her a joke, and resenting her dominance, to, finally, unwilling respect and something like affection for her; he dies regretting she could not have been a boy to succeed him in his practice in which, he admits, she might well have done even better than himself – yet without ever understanding her or doing her justice. It is an earlier *Washington Square* written by a woman, whose heroine vindicates herself.

Though for some time it seems that it is Lucilla who is to be the subject for ironic examination, it is in fact the nature of the society she operates in that becomes the main object of irony. The progress of the novel is to take the reader through the father's phases too, and though we may start with the fear that Lucilla is so limited that she will bore us, this is presently seen to be far from being so, since it is soon apparent that she hands out her stock phrases, the acceptable clichés of the age, as passwords, camouflaging herself in conventional clothing to conceal her originality and get her own way. Nor is the joke, as at first seems probable, a matter of repeating a pattern, for though Lucilla's suitors, with one exception, really never come up to scratch, they are all very different cases and are never predictable. In fact, a series of surprises is sprung on us right up to the end, with Lucilla able always to rise to each fresh occasion, and each is increasingly a challenge to her ingenuity and powers. With the death of the old doctor and the advent of the new one (who has, of course, once been one of the gentlemen expected to marry Lucilla), she soars away into county society with an unlimited sphere of usefulness in view. Imperceptibly Lucilla grows ever more interesting and endeared to us as ten years pass before our eyes. Her realization that the man whom she is 'fond of' is, socially speaking, fraudulent (though no one else at Carlingford knows this), and must therefore be permitted to aspire no higher in marriage than the drawing-master's daughter – whom in fact he has always preferred – may be comedy, but with her father's death, and the jolt this gives her, deeper and more complex feelings come into sight, as well as more admirable ones, and Lucilla faces poverty with dignity and fortitude. We are therefore not surprised, nor incredulous, as her father would have been, at her volunteering to the lawyer with regard to the new doctor who had slighted her, that she had never been deceived, having perceived (as so often had been the case with the gentlemen who had 'paid her attentions') that he was in love elsewhere: 'And I am rather fond of men that are in love – it shows they have some good in them.' Which prepares us for the grand and exciting scene of Lucilla's being unable to bring herself to accept the one eligible suitor who actually makes her an offer and of her succumbing instead to the only genuine lover she has ever had and who – though always snubbed – turns out to be the right man for the demanding position of husband to a Lucilla. And this, though still comedy, is yet genuinely moving, a convincing love-scene. (Mrs Oliphant is rare among Victorian novelists in being one who accepts and can establish the existence of passion and the miseries of the thwarted.) Lucilla's future happiness is shown to be at least as likely as Emma Knightley's and a great deal more convincing than Mrs Ladislaw's. At last Lucilla will have adequate scope for 'that delightful sense of power and abundant resources' which she has never as Miss Marjoribanks been able to satisfy.

Mrs Oliphant's irony is maintained to the end, when it is seen that, as Miss Bury's Evangelical faith assured her, everything is for the best; Lucilla's trust in Providence was justified; everyone benefits, even Barbara gets her dream-husband (though both of them are by now much the worse for wear) – except poor Rose Lake who, having to give up her career for a daughter's duties, has even lost her belief in the value of art (except, of course, High Art). That her brother Willie 'who afterwards became so celebrated' as an artist was of the more fortunate sex underlines the plight of a gifted girl in this kind of society. The mode of the novel has not proved restrictive. The range from the broadly comic opening and such irresistibly funny scenes as Miss Bury being outraged by the irreverence of the young barristers at Lucilla's table, to Lucilla's surrender to 'honest love', and the moving history of Dr Marjoribanks's death (than which I know nothing finer of its kind in all Victorian fiction), is really greater than in an Austen novel or many more pretentious Victorian novels. Mrs Oliphant had had rougher experience of life than George Eliot (who, she remarked, had been kept in 'a mental green-house') and knew what men were like when not in the presence of ladies. Her gentlemen are particularly good – though 'good' does not perhaps convey the right idea. *Miss Marjoribanks* is really nearer in sensibility and tone to *Coningsby* than to either *Emma* or *Middlemarch*, and connoisseurs of Disraeli's brilliant novel will appreciate the sly reference to its Lord Monmouth in chapter 18 here. The death of the old doctor is an outstanding artistic achievement: full of feeling as that is, it is kept successfully within the mode of the novel (anti-sentimental and ironic) by her treatment of Carlingford's reaction to it, and by the author's unresentful acceptance of the lack of idealism in real life – a very un-Victorian trait. A more than technical triumph is the inclusion of a systematic humourist whose line is 'taking off' her acquaintances but who is seen to be a weak woman without resources or morale when trouble looms, thus justifying Lucilla's contempt for mere humour as an end in itself.

One can go on frequenting *Miss Marjoribanks*, noticing fresh subtleties and getting ever more enjoyment. As Henry James said in another connection, all novelists of manners 'are historians, even when they least don the uniform', and one aspect of the value of this novel is as social history – the kind that, in default of the novelist, no historian could supply. Mrs Oliphant shows us what it would have felt like to be living then and there. One example is her charting the position of the arts in mid-Victorian society, documenting what Taine noted in general terms, and confirming Du Maurier's later pictorial anecdotes in *Punch* that Henry James found so instructive. As an artist's widow, Mrs Oliphant's observations on the treatment of the arts and their practitioners have authority: the snobbery in privileged Grange Lane, and the real animus of the tradesman class in a Philistine bourgeois society against people like the Lakes with claims to deference not supported in the eyes of the former by birth or in the experience of the latter by spending powers, are more revealing than the treatment of the place of Art in a Puritan society in *Middlemarch*. Rose Lake's real superiority and integrity stand out, even if the way she expresses them is sometimes absurd. Lucilla's discrimination against *professional* singing further illustrates the reactions of a bourgeois culture against the existence of artists.

II

Miss Marjoribanks is one of the chronicles of Carlingford which, first appearing in serial form in *Blackwood's Magazine*, were duly published as books and subsequently issued exactly a century ago by Blackwood's as a set: lucky indeed is he who now possesses one. In 1860 Mrs Oliphant returned, a widow with children and other dependants, from Italy where her husband had died leaving her in debt and unprovided for. An experienced writer now desperate for money, she hit on 'Carlingford' as the scene for a story, I imagine because she had recollected the success novelists had had in the previous decade with Cranford (whose name Carlingford recalls), Barchester, and Milby (the scene of the last of George Eliot's Clerical Lives). The first, a short story, appeared in May 1861, 'The Executor', dealing with two men who figure briefly in the novel: John Brown the lawyer and young Dr Rider. Other characters in *Miss Marjoribanks* who appeared in earlier Carlingford Chronicles are Mr Tufton, the old minister of Salem Chapel, who belongs to the novel of that name (which got wrecked on the rocks of a melodramatic plot half-way through after a promising first half'), and Mr Wentworth the High Church curate of St Roque's who moves in and out of the earlier stories and figures largely in the novel *The Perpetual Curate*. This novel was published in 1864, though Trollope's Perpetual Curate, Mr Crawley, did not see the light till the very end of 1866, [2] when Trollope began to publish *The Last Chronicle of Barset*. Dr Rider, who in our novel is seen as a recently married man, had had his troubles and the story of his courtship of 'that little Australian girl' (with an interlude of 'paying attentions' to Miss Marjoribanks under pressure from the old doctor who would have liked him for partner and son-in-law) told in 'The Doctor's Family' of 1861–2. The series, which had also included *The Rector*, ended with a tired novel, *Phoebe Junior*, in 1876.

Our novel began to appear in 'Maga' (*Blackwood's Magazine*) in February 1865, the first instalment stopping very intriguingly at the point where Lucilla knocks on the door in Grove Street, with such momentous consequences. Other inevitable ends of instalments may be deduced by the reader of the book – they were skilfully contrived and show that, like Dickens, Mrs Oliphant had at any rate mastered the craft of writing to publish in parts. At the same time she was able to think also in terms of the three-decker and contrive suitable volume division – vol. I closes with a mystery introduced by the archdeacon (chapter 18) and vol. II with the Christmas approaching 'amid universal demolition' that 'ended the first portion of Miss Marjoribanks's eventful career'. The use of ecclesiastical types both for comic notes and for indicating a serious criticism of the Victorian ethos she no doubt owed to Trollope, but we should recognize, while admitting the debt, that she is more sensitive and also wittier in this field than he, though she never achieved such success on the serious side as he did with his Mr Harding and Mr Crawley. Her Broad Church Archdeacon is more amusing and more cutting a study than his High-and-Dry Archdeacon Grantly; the Rector of Carlingford, Mr Bury, and his sister are refined and thoroughly contemporary figures of the Evangelical movement in mid-Victorian good provincial society, unlike that coarse hypocrite Mr Slope and the caricature that is Mrs Proudie. Mrs Oliphant had the advantage as a Scot of being able to see the Church of England from the outside, critically, and yet without the resentment of an English sectarian.

But it is in the possible influence of *Miss Marjoribanks* on the production of *Middlemarch* in the form we know it that I would like to dwell, a possibility that I have never seen recognized elsewhere. This would have justified reprinting the novel even if its intrinsic merits hadn't – though of course I think they do. George Eliot and Mrs Oliphant had the same publisher and both wrote for his 'Maga', they moved in overlapping circles, and Mrs Oliphant was known as a novelist before 'George Eliot' existed, both women were critics and intellectuals and middlemen of letters, and worked in similar fields as creative writers; yet though Mrs Oliphant admired the other's novels, they were not friends and George Eliot's references to the Carlingford Chronicles are distinctly sour. She strongly objected to being considered their author – they were published anonymously and even *Miss Marjoribanks* as a book bore only 'By the Author of *Salem Chapel*' on its title page – ostensibly because she disapproved of Mrs Oliphant's presentation of Dissenters. We know that George Eliot, like everyone else then, read 'Maga' in general, even if she didn't much care for reading other people's novels, though I think it evident that she read them a great deal more than she cared to admit. *Middlemarch* appeared in parts from December 1871 and, however long before some of it may have been conceived, the notebook its author called The Quarry for *Middlemarch* was not, it seems, begun before September 1868, whereas the last instalment of *Miss Marjoribanks* had appeared in 'Maga' in May 1866, having run for a year and a quarter there. It is inconceivable that George Eliot did not look through at least some of the instalments in all that time, even if she never read the novel in book form, more especially as Blackwood, her own publisher, had initially the highest opinion of *Miss Marjoribanks* and great hopes for it, as she may well have heard.

There is nothing in George Eliot's notebook to show that she intended to take an unusual tone with her new novel or towards its heroine – who was anyway not part of the original conception; it was not till December 1870 that she notes in her journal: 'I am experimenting in a story ["Miss Brooke"] which I began without any very serious intention of carrying it out lengthily. It is a subject which has been recorded among my possible themes ever since I began to write fiction, but will probably take new shapes in the development. I am today at p. 44' (subsequently she states she began it 'about the opening of November' 1870). She was dissatisfied with the other story, *Middlemarch*, that she had started planning, until the idea occurred to her to combine it with 'Miss Brooke' – they were never really fused, the original Lydgate–Featherstone–Garth elements running parallel to, but hardly ever touching, the history of Miss Brooke, Mrs Casaubon and Mrs Ladislaw. The attempt to present her new heroine Dorothea ironically, with its new tone and attitude, does not come natural to George Eliot, and is uncertainly maintained till it breaks down and is abandoned after Dorothea's marriage; the same thing happens with Gwendolen Harleth in her next and last novel. Yet the attempt at ironical treatment and unsentimental appraisal of these two heroines is what distinguishes Dorothea and Gwendolen from all George Eliot's previous heroines, even from Esther in *Felix Holt*, who might have been supposed to have been a more suitable subject for such treatment – but she began *Felix Holt* about the same time as Mrs Oliphant began *Miss Marjoribanks*, so had no such model as Lucilla then. Nowhere earlier than the 'Miss Brooke' or book I of *Middlemarch* does George Eliot adopt an aloof, ironic view of a heroine and invite the reader to see her as amusing, constantly stressing the contrast between how she conceives herself and how she appears to others. This is of course how Lucilla Marjoribanks is presented to us for the most part. And this aspect of each of these heroines is cleverly underlined by a satirical critic, in the one case Mrs Woodburn who is understood to be by birth 'one of the Cavendishes', and in the other Mrs Cadwallader, who really is of aristocratic origin. Dorothea and Lucilla are alike in suffering from lack of scope in a narrow, provincial society at a time when what a lady – young, married or widowed – might do, feel and say, was extremely restricted and indeed largely dictated by convention, though while Dorothea fights against this naïvely, Lucilla fights by cleverly making use of it. ' "As for *honour*, you know you gentlemen say we have no sense of honour", said Lucilla airily; "and to think that two women could be together and not talk of what might perhaps be a marriage – !" ' or again ' "I am sure I wish I had a vote", said Lucilla; "but I have no vote, and what can a girl do? I am sorry I don't understand about politics. If we were going in for that sort of thing, I don't know what there might be left for the gentlemen to do." ' Neither girl has 'a mamma to keep her right' (in Lucilla's words), so is at liberty to strike out for herself, the busy doctor father of the one being no more of a restraint than the incompetent guardian of the other. Hence the field for the comedy.

But George Eliot cannot maintain the uncongenial attitudes that, I suggest, she absorbed unconsciously or tried to emulate, but which came from Mrs Oliphant's creative centre. George Eliot settles down, with the excuse of Dorothea's being unhappily married, into a more congenial compassion for her heroine and is weak enough to spoil her book by making Mrs Casaubon out to be a pathetic figure – though it is her own obstinacy that has brought about the fatal marriage. Dorothea is thus sentimentalized and at times nauseatingly so. Like Lucilla she eventually solves her problems by marrying a man who has long adored her and will be able to make her a Member of Parliament's wife, thus satisfying her need to feel widely useful by assisting in social reform. The dramatic scene of Lucilla's capture by and surrender to an overwhelmingly masculine lover in her dead father's library is very poorly emulated in the feeble, unintentionally ridiculous scene in the dead husband's library at Lowick, where it takes a thunder-and-lightning storm to bring Will and Dorothea together.

I feel justified in concluding that *Miss Marjoribanks* contributed quite considerably to *Middlemarch*. For example, we can't read such passages as Dorothea's disappointment on visiting her future home at finding that Lowick, with its good cottages, well-found villagers and neither vice, dirt nor poverty – that Lowick has no need of her attentions, for 'her mind had glanced over the possibility, which she would have preferred, of finding that her home would be in a parish which had a larger share of the world's misery, so that she might have had more active duties in it' – without remembering Lucilla's satisfaction on visiting Marchbank before *her* marriage to find that

There was a village not far from the gates of Marchbank, where every kind of village nuisance was to be found . . . It gave her the liveliest satisfaction to think of all the disorder and disarray of the Marchbank village. Her fingers itched to be at it . . . If it had been a model village, with prize flower-gardens and clean as Arcadia, the thought of it would not have given Miss Marjoribanks half so much pleasure. The recollection of all the wretched hovels and miserable cottages exhilarated her heart. The state of the village . . . justified her to herself for her choice which, but for this chance of doing good, might perhaps have had the air of a merely selfish preference. Now she could regard it in a loftier light, and the thought was sweet to Lucilla . . . the sight of the village was sweet to her eyes. That it was not sweet to any other sense did but enhance Miss Marjoribanks's satisfaction. 'A year after this!' she said to herself, and her bosom swelled . . . Lucilla's eyes went over the moral wilderness with the practical glance of a statesman, and at the same time the sanguine enthusiasm of a philanthropist. She saw of what it was capable, and already, in imagination, the desert blossomed like a rose before her beneficent steps, and the sweet sense of well-doing rose in her breast . . . a vision of a parish saved, a village reformed, a county re-organised, and a triumphant election at the end, the recompense and crown of all, which should put the government of the country itself, to a certain extent, into competent hands.

The sphere of usefulness Dorothea finds for herself as Mrs Ladislaw is not protected from our looking at it like this by George Eliot's tenderness for Dorothea, since we can't help reflecting that there is a considerable egoistic impulse in her yearning to do good to others, a yearning which yet never achieved definition and which we are never given any reason to suppose her to have qualifications for actualizing. Far from this essential egoism being exposed for what it is, it is offered for our admiration: ' "I am feeling something which is perhaps foolish and wrong," answered Dorothea with her usual openness – "almost wishing that the people wanted more to be done for them here. I have known so few ways of making my life good for anything." '

Lucilla is always seen in action, getting things well done and acting successfully on others; the humour lies in the precautions she has to take to make this possible. She is not a Mrs Pardiggle even if she isn't, like Mrs Casaubon, an ineffectual angel; she is always seen doing for others – those incompetent or misguided persons – not only what is in their best interests but actually what they really wanted too. She is too amiable and magnanimous ever to turn into a Lady Catherine de Burgh or a Lady Bracknell, and though majestic when necessary is no dragon. Without ever idealizing Lucilla or denaturing her, and without playing tricks on us like Dorothea's creator, Mrs Oliphant manages with great skill to gradually induce sympathy and admiration for Lucilla. Our sense of probability revolts against an unhappy marriage's immediately changing a girl from the Dorothea who is short-sighted in both senses, is given to self-dramatization, and has a ludicrous misapprehension of the nature of things, to someone who is always noble and pathetic. George Eliot has to suffer the consequences of her dishonesty as an artist in this matter: Dorothea's inability to recognize that Will Ladislaw is in love with her, which saves her as Mrs Casaubon from having to face a moral conflict, is not divine innocence as we are given to understand but, the coarser reader must feel, stupidly blind; Lucilla's realization that her cousin is going to make a nuisance of himself and must be suppressed and sent out to India for his own good is entirely in character and the suppression a comic feat. Similarly, Dorothea's exchanges with Rosamond are never memorable and are ultimately implausible, therefore distastefully sentimental, whereas Lucilla's dealings with Barbara Lake (like Rosamond a siren and also one whose strong line is music, with which she too beguiles the heroine's admirer) are human as well as masterly. Mrs Oliphant as a mid-Victorian novelist is unique in not deploying the values conveyed in that uplifting set of words, then so popular, 'sweet' ('a sweet woman' is a term George Eliot even favours), 'pure' and 'noble'; a related term, 'maidenly', is frequently used for ironic purposes in *Miss Marjoribanks*. We have reason to conclude that Mrs Oliphant's purpose in writing this novel was to campaign against false Victorian values where women are concerned. Not that she was at all in favour of the kind of emancipation of women that John Stuart Mill stood for, being, like Miss Gertrude Bell and other outstanding Victorian ladies, opposed to the Women's Rights movement. An expression of this feeling, that enfranchisement for women was irrelevant to the real problems, can be seen in Lucilla's role in the election, when she gets her own hand-picked candidate chosen and elected on a slogan invented by herself which she artfully fathers on influential gentlemen – though she has (as she points out when it suits her) no vote, and doesn't understand politics (that is, pays no attention to party politics because she had perceived they meant nothing). She does it, not because she wants to marry her candidate (as Carlingford naturally supposes, misunderstanding her as always), but simply for the pleasure of 'having a piece of work in hand' and using her talents. I suspect that it is an illusion that Miss Brooke is larger in stature and more intelligent than Miss Marjoribanks, who has a better claim to be the nineteenth-century representative of the eternal St Theresa missionary drive than one who has no qualifications for the part but vague dissatisfactions.

The form George Eliot's comedy takes in Dorothea's maiden days is to show her running her head against everyone and getting into holes because she doesn't admit the necessity for a young lady of practising what Jane Austen's prudent heroine Elinor Dashwood calls 'address'. Lucilla, with her refreshing Scotch freedom from nonsense, and no illusions, has an acute perception of the nature of social life and is therefore able to turn even the limitations of her position to advantage as well as to exercise the privileges of her status as a young lady. This is best shown in the conscious expertise of her handling of the Archdeacon on several delicate occasions. The corresponding drawbacks of being a Victorian gentleman are also understood by Mrs Oliphant – Mr Knightley in Regency society enjoyed much more freedom, we note – and this is only one example:

He was speechless with rage and mortification. He took it for an insult inflicted upon him in cold blood, doing Lucilla as much injustice as the other people who took the candid expression of her sentiments for a piece of acting. He was a gentleman, notwithstanding his doubtful origin, and civilised down to his very fingertips; but he would have liked to have knocked Miss Marjoribanks down, though she was a woman. And yet, as she was a woman, he dared not for his life make any demonstration of his fury . . . He rushed home furious; but she went to a little worsted-work with a mind at peace with itself and all men.

No doubt Mrs Oliphant had studied Jane Austen and more particularly *Emma*, but whereas Emma is the victim of illusions based on vanity and snobbishness, Lucilla is more interesting in that she really has insight, power, capacities and tactical skills. She remains a spinster till thirty because her kind of superiority, like her kind of physique in an age of the 'little woman', does not allure Victorian Man. Here is one of the many aspects of the comedy, that all the gentlemen who go through the routine of paying attentions to Lucilla are then seen running away after other women, women whom Lucilla rightly feels to be inferior to herself in everything but the one quality she despises. The passionate Barbara, the soft, dependent Mrs Mortimer, the 'little Australian girl' are the gentlemen's natural complements, and even the General overlooks his hostess altogether in the presence of 'little' Rose Lake. Lucilla is daunting to the men by her unflattering self-sufficiency. She is quick to catch the signs that they aren't in love with her (she isn't a self-deceiver like Emma) but is irresistibly amusing because she does not therefore think the less of herself (why should she?) but – naturally – even less of men, thus disqualifying herself still further, for of course They sense this. And perhaps Mrs Oliphant symthizes with Them too: the scene where Mr Ashburton tries to decide to propose and goes over his bachelor house in an attempt to summon Lucilla's image into it, without conviction or success, then giving it up goes sadly to bed, is not only comedy.

Emma is a straightforward case of a basically conventional girl, but spoilt and therefore with a disastrous ambition to

meddle; we leave her in the confidence that she will be controlled by a forthright husband she must respect. Lucilla is
very different: with 'a mind made to rule', in her later stage of
Carlingford life 'Lucilla had become conscious that her
capabilities were greater than her work', and left alone and
poor she envies her servant who can take on 'a little business'
(inn-keeping): 'Lucilla cheered up a little in ready interest,
and would have been very glad if she could have taken a little
business too.' That a Lucilla, with all the abilities needed for
success as an ambassador, a lawyer, a principal of a women's
college or a Higher Civil Servant, should have nothing better
to do than organizing the social life of Carlingford is pathetic
as well as ridiculous. Mrs Oliphant evidently felt quite as
strongly as George Eliot did later in *Middlemarch* the waste
Victorian society caused by assuming that a lady was
incapable outside domestic duties. Mrs Oliphant delights in
setting Lucilla free at the end to exercise her talents in a lawful way through marriage to a well-trained helpmate. If Mrs
Oliphant had not been artist enough (*pace* Henry James) to
maintain the tone and mode of *Miss Marjoribanks* unfailingly,
the considerable quantity of seriousness below the surface
would have taken over from the Comic Muse and got out of
hand. But not at all. A final irony is that the only man whom
Lucilla can marry, who wins her by force of 'honest love',
loves her under a misapprehension of her character. Seeing
her as the perfect woman of Victorian theory, he ardently
looks forward to freeing her from having to do anything, even
though she has told him: 'The thing we both want is something to do.'

Miss Marjoribanks regarded her betrothed with mild and affectionate contempt as he thus delivered himself of his foolish sentiments.
'It is of no use trying to make him understand,' she said, with an air
of resignation.

None indeed, for he replies:

'Now you are in my hands I mean to take care of you, Lucilla; you
shall have no more anxiety or trouble. What is the good of a man if
he can't save the woman he is fond of from all that?' cried the honest
fellow – and Lucilla could not but cast a despairing glance round

her, as if appealing to heaven and earth. What was to be done with
a man who had so little understanding of her, and of himself, and
of the eternal fitness of things?

But she knows exactly what to do; she has him buy an estate
– 'You could improve the land, you know,' she says, 'and do
all that sort of thing, and the people you could leave to me.'
No use his arguing that land 'doesn't pay' – ' "*We* could make
it pay," said Miss Marjoribanks, with a benevolent smile,
"and besides there are estates and estates." ' She has the
right one in her eye, confident in her knowledge of the principles of political economy which she had studied in the most
up-to-date form at school (Mount Pleasant, where 'they were
all Cambridge in their way of thinking' – Lucilla must be the
first loyal Old Girl in fiction), and as to which principles Mrs
Oliphant is appropriately ironical.

The seriousness I have called attention to as always below
the surface is what makes this novel as much a valuable
criticism of mid-nineteenth-century provincial society as
George Eliot's. Unlike George Eliot Mrs Oliphant really has
grasped the nettle – created a girl who is a real test for showing its cruel shortcomings (such as led Florence Nightingale
to make her well-known complaint against it). We have
shown us here plenty of its victims and not altogether as
entertainment. There is one kind of married woman, the
banker's wife, the mother of many children, obsessed with
the problems of looking after them and so many servants,
while the Colonel's wife, though happily married, being
childless has no other interest in life but matchmaking for
other people's children; there is the self-pitying, helpless
widow and the Doctor's wife who had taken to an invalid
existence on the sofa because she couldn't keep her husband's affection; there is the recent bride whose trousseau is
the only thing about marriage she isn't disappointed with;
the Rector's spinster sister who has devoted her existence to
'parish work' of the Low Church cast and other spinsters who
are victimized by their parents; above all, there is clever Mrs
Woodburn, prosperous but secretly insecure, who works off
her anxieties by 'taking off' society; that this is a symptom
Mrs Oliphant makes plain in a passage more outspoken than
anything in *Middlemarch*:

But when Lucilla, serenely smiling, was gone, the mimic, with her nerves strung to desperation, burst into the wildest comic travesty of Miss Marjoribanks's looks and manners and sent her unsuspicious husband into convulsions of laughter. He laughed until the tears ran down his cheeks – the unconscious simpleton; and all the time his wife would have liked to throw him down and trample on him, or put pins into him, or scratch his beaming, jovial countenance. Perhaps she would have gone into hysterics instead if she had not possessed that other safety-valve, for Mrs Woodburn had not that supreme composure and self-command which belonged to Lucilla's higher organisation.

There is another revealing passage when she meets Lucilla in the snow and envies her her freedom, for not having to ask a husband for money and not having anybody 'to go on at her'. For Mr Woodburn is 'the master to whom she belonged and for whom she had, with some affection, a great deal of not unnatural contempt'.

Lucilla is perhaps an unexpected development in such a society, though not more so than Dorothea, and unlike her in being explicable (as her father's daughter); she seems to me a much more reliable means of exploring that culture than the Protean Dorothea. One most telling feature in the relegation of this society is that the intelligent Doctor has no use for the drawing-room or his daughter's Evenings but slips away to his library after dinner to write up his cases for *The Lancet* and further the science of medicine, in which life for him centres. Was Dr Marjoribanks the cause of Dr Lydgate's being in Middlemarch to underline the heroine's frustrations? Both, incidentally, are very conscious of being gentlemen of good family.

It seems to me, to sum up, that creative writers generally and George Eliot in particular (as I have noted before) tend to borrow what, more or less unconsciously, they have been impressed by, not as a matter of miscellaneous items, but as a complex whose value or pregnancy inheres in a unique whole; so that whereas one character in common might be a coincidence and even a couple of no significance, such a manifold likeness between *Miss Marjoribanks* and *Middlemarch* as I have demonstrated is good evidence of the use of the former by the author of the latter.

III

As we may see from this novel, Mrs Oliphant was considerably more of an artist than Henry James could perceive, and
with so much against her it is surprising that in one novel at
least she managed to be wholly artist. The correspondence
she had with Blackwood about *Miss Marjoribanks* is worth
citing in illustration of what she had to contend with. In the
first letter she voices anxiety lest he should think that the
first two 'numbers' don't make enough progress and that
'over-minuteness' (what she rightly felt to be the necessary
scale for this novel) is objectionable. Later she writes:

Don't frighten me, please, about *Miss Marjoribanks*. I will do the very
best I can to content you, but you make me nervous when you talk
about the first rank of novelists, etc: nobody in the world cares
whether I am in the first or sixth. I mean I have no one left who
cares, and the world can do absolutely nothing for me, except give
me a little more money. But all the same I will do my best . . .

Later still:

How can I possibly tell whether *Miss Marjoribanks* will be a great
success or not? I am working at her with all my might and power;
but you know yourself that if I happen to have a favourite bit for
which I have a kind of natural weakness, it is always precisely on
that bit that you snub me, so that I am the worst judge in the world
as far as that goes [judging what will succeed – one understands
why George Eliot, being in a position to do so, always took a high-
handed line with her – the same – publisher].

And eventually, which tells its own sad story:

I send you with this the next number of *Miss Marjoribanks* . . . As for
what you say of hardness of tone, I am afraid it was scarcely to be
avoided. [Blackwood had obviously missed the whole point of the
novel, though he had had a good deal of it to go on by now] . . . But
. . . I have a weakness for Lucilla, and to bring a sudden change
upon her character and break her down into tenderness would be
like one of Dickens's maudlin repentances, when he makes Mr
Dombey *trinquer* with Captain Cuttle. Miss M. must be one and
indivisible, and I am pretty sure that my plan is right.

That is, she wanted to be allowed to be an artist instead of a
popular novelist (much as she needed the money a popular

success would have brought her). Evidently she had to contend not only with what the public thought it wanted but also with the magazine publisher's idea of what was attractive to print there; this meant that the public would hardly get the chance to form a better taste in fiction. No wonder she writes later in the following year, of *Felix Holt*: 'I am mightily disappointed in the book . . . One feels as if a great contempt had seized her for the public and her critics (quite legitimate in some respects, I think), and she had concluded that it was not worth her while to put forth her strength.'

In the same defensive or self-deprecating tone Mrs Oliphant described the way she herself wrote: 'ever more really satisfied by some little conscious felicity of words than by anything else. I have always had my sing-song, guided by no sort of law, but by my ear, which was in its way fastidious to the cadence and measure that pleased me.' Another interesting point I noted in the letters printed along with her autobiography is that, though believing that the judgement of her day demanded the opposite, she found she preferred Richardson's novels to Fielding's and 'actually Lovelace to Tom Jones!'

Though *Miss Marjoribanks* enjoyed some success as entertainment and subsequently got into Collins's cheap pocket edition accordingly (in which I myself first made its acquaintance), it was the inferior *Salem Chapel* that made a hit and got taken into 'Everyman' as Mrs Oliphant's classic. It was *Miss Marjoribanks* that, she wrote, 'cost me an infinite deal of trouble', but neither Barrie nor Henry James mentions it in his obituary, nor is it selected for praise in the D.N.B. article on her. Mrs Oliphant had reason to be exasperated at being relegated to inferior status even in her own heyday. Considering how much money as well as esteem her contemporaries earned by fictions like *Cranford* and *John Halifax, Gentleman*, she was entitled to expect to have earned time to enable her to write at leisure and at her own best level, instead of having to turn out two or three novels a year. Her disadvantage was that what I have described as the Oliphant tone was calculated to grate on Victorian sensibility. If the public of the mid-sixties had signified enthusiasm for *Miss Marjoribanks*, no doubt she might have continued to produce interesting fiction that satisfied her own critical judgement.

In her short stories we can see she was able to experiment without attracting adverse comment, and is thoroughly professional. In the volume of them, *A Widow's Tale*, that Barrie edited after her death with an introductory essay as a memorial tribute, I noticed that 'The Story of a Wedding Tour' and another tale called 'John' are really the same condensed novel told from two different points of view separately, the mother's and the son's, and would have constituted an interesting novel if it had been worth her while financially to work at it, as Henry James would have done with such a subject. As it is, *Miss Marjoribanks* stands alone as a *tour de force*. The reading public then had become accustomed to take its domestic fiction straight and in an infusion of warm feeling. Mrs Oliphant had plenty of feeling, but is not simple-minded or self-indulgent, and she had neither the Victorian sentimentality nor even the necessary reticence and sense of propriety. Her very un-Victorian story 'Queen Eleanor and Fair Rosamund' is a surprisingly unconventional piece of realism for its time.

Miss Marjoribanks obliges adjustment to an individual scale as well as tone. The scale of *Emma* and *Cranford* is too minute for it, that of *Middlemarch* and *Barchester Towers* too large. One has also to get into step with the movement and be prepared for its being very slow at first and highly repetitive in phrasing (to get into the mentality of Carlingford). Then it gets brisker and gathers speed with the death of the member for Carlingford, slows down again as if to grind to a halt with the old Doctor's death, and then picks up pace to gallop home with the lover whose return in the nick of time – perhaps a satirical cliché – is heralded by Lucilla's panic at the peal of her dead father's disused night-bell which decides her fate at last. The plotting is faultless and, on top of everything else, we have one of the best elections in Victorian fiction, rich in them as that is.

This novel is full of wit, surprises and intrigue, its heroine a classic addition to the English Comic Characters, subdivision female. Lucilla belongs in the company of Lady Catherine de Burgh, Lady Bracknell, Mrs Proudie, Mrs Poyser, Emma Woodhouse and the rest – all women of ability and presence. One would have expected it to have been kept in print with a loyal following over the years, seeing that its insipid contemporary, *Wives and Daughters*, has. Perhaps our age will at last do justice to this wise and witty novel in which every sentence is exactly right and every word apt and adroitly placed. Barrie wrote of Mrs Oliphant: 'In talk she was tremendously witty without trying to be so . . . and, more noticeable perhaps than anything else, she was of an intellect so alert that one wondered she ever fell asleep.' This is the impression of a daunted male, but Lady Ritchie, Thackeray's daughter and her dear friend, wrote more perceptively: 'She was one of those people whose presence is even more than a *pleasure*, it was a stimulus; she was kindly, sympathetic, and yet answering with that chord of intelligent antagonism which is so suggestive and makes for such good talk.' I think this most accurately indicates the quality that stamps her work. We can imagine Jane Austen reading *Miss Marjoribanks* with enjoyment and approval in the Elysian Fields.

Mrs Oliphant: *The Autobiography and Letters* (Introduction)

Henry James in his 'London Notes' for August 1897 declared that 'the world of books has suffered no small shrinkage by the recent death of Mrs Oliphant', adding that even if 'some study of her remarkable life, and still more of her remarkable character be in preparation', yet 'she was a figure that would on many sides still lend itself to vivid portraiture'. He was a personal friend. The more substantial study he hinted at is provided by the volume of her own autobiographical fragments and accompanying letters, prepared by her cousin Mrs Coghill and here reprinted.[3] There is only besides V. and R. A. Colby's biography, *The Equivocal Virtue* (Archon Books, 1966), which, indispensable for supplementary data, is, as its title implies, a deprecatory account of a writer represented as mainly a pot-boiler and does no justice to Mrs Oliphant as the considerable and original novelist, the intelligent literary critic and the exemplary woman of letters that she needs to be recognized as having been, if our chart of the Victorian literary scene is to be well-informed.[4] James indeed noted that though she had had 'success in her day as great as her activity' yet 'her singular gift was less recognized, less reported on, than it deserved', venturing to guess that this was because 'criticism has come to the pass of being shy of difficult cases'. As regards Mrs Oliphant, criticism has been so ever since.

The *Autobiography and Letters*, though thrice printed in the year of publication (1899), has since been unavailable, suggesting that the immediate public interest having been exhausted Mrs Oliphant then passed into oblivion. *Salem Chapel*, unfortunately her most popular (for it is by no means her best) novel got into 'Everyman', and her undoubtedly best novel, *Miss Marjoribanks*, a brilliant *tour de force*, is now available in Chatto and Windus's Zodiac Library. Otherwise her work can be read only in libraries.

Henry James spoke of Mrs Oliphant's 'heroic production'; of a woman who more than any other writer had had for half a century a public utterance. He writes of her as one who 'understood life itself in a fine free-handed manner' and says 'her capacity for labour was infinite'. She was a massive contributor to the novel of several kinds, the short story, the biography, to the reviewing and the critical essays in many Victorian periodicals, as well as a maker of solid books of non-fiction. She compiled literary histories, did translating, was an eminent figure in intellectual society – in sum important as a case-history of the woman of letters in the nineteenth century. This is a category that included Charlotte Brontë, George Sand and George Eliot, with all of whom she may be profitably compared, and with whom she does compare herself in the moments of greatest depression in her autobiography. Like George Sand, Mrs Oliphant has slipped out of general knowledge and academic esteem, but on her contemporaries and juniors she made a tremendous impression. James noted 'her sharp and handsome physiognomy, that of a person whose eggs are not all in one basket'. The Master of Magdalene, A. C. Benson, who was at Eton with her sons, devoted a whole chapter to her in his book *Memories and Friends*. Kinglake wrote: 'To read her is like being with a delightful woman – a woman of powerful intellect . . . and then her style seems so perfect.' The Carlyles, both difficult people, admired her, and she them. Thackeray's daughter Lady Ritchie wrote: 'She was one of those people whose presence is even more than a *pleasure*, it was a stimulus; she was kindly, sympathetic, and yet answering with that chord of intelligent antagonism which is so suggestive and makes for such good talk.' J. M. Barrie, describing her in the selection of her short stories he edited as a memorial, says: 'In talk she was tremendously witty without trying to be so . . . and . . . she was of an intellect so alert that one wondered she ever fell asleep.' While there is a consensus of opinion as to her charm, dignity, womanliness, witty conversation and brilliant intelligence, there is also a feeling that her distinction was based on a painful fortitude. Benson justly says of this autobiography: 'it seems to me one of the most pathetic and heart-breaking revelations I have ever read . . . the diary is very specific as to the strange, and in many ways rather dreadful, life led by this passionately affectionate, dutiful and industrious woman'.

The autobiography is fragmentary as well as incomplete, but supplemented by the selection of letters made for the book by Mrs Oliphant's cousin – though as so often in the nineteenth century the really personal letters had been destroyed in the interest of privacy – we can get a clear and full enough picture of the literary woman as well as its being in addition a moving human document. 'This shining, noble book', Howard Sturgis called it, and it is indeed the record of a truly tragic life both in its personal and its professional aspects. Briefly happy but then early widowhood, left in debt to support a young family by her pen alone, bereft successively of babies, husband, a beloved daughter, then of a hopeful nephew she had educated, disappointed in her adored sons whom she survived, beset with helpless relatives of two generations and other parasites constantly attaching themselves to her, uncomplaining and selfless, struggling on into old age and actually wearing a hole in her finger with her indefatigable pen which she could never afford to lay aside, dying barely solvent and correcting proofs on her death-bed – this private tragedy was paralleled by the curve of her literary career. She achieved reputation early but never affluence, was conscious of having outlived the attractions she had had for the mid-Victorian reading public though some of her best work was produced in the later period, and knew that her novels had never been valued on their merits nor brought her the acclaim she had deserved. It will be more useful to examine these aspects of her working life separately, so that after considering her as a representative freelance woman of letters – an aristocrat of the new Grub Street, and as a leading contributor to *Blackwood's* and other nineteenth-century periodicals – I will end by discussing Mrs Oliphant's unique achievement as a novelist, as to which there seems to me there can be no doubt.

The woman of letters

Born in 1828 and dying in 1897, Mrs Oliphant's life almost exactly covers the Victorian Age. Like Fanny Burney and Jane Austen a scribbler from girlhood, she was luckier in one

sense than them in having in this new era of numerous outlets
for writing the possibility of a career as a professional woman
of letters, like George Eliot her contemporary. But whereas
George Eliot ended as a novelist after launching herself as a
translator, reviewer, intellectual journalist and editor, Mrs
Oliphant began as a novelist early and then supplemented
perforce by the other kinds of letters. The all-round professional woman of letters could not have emerged before the
Victorian period provided the necessary wide and large reading public, but, we must note, Victorian conventions made
difficulties.

Though Mrs Oliphant launched herself with Scottish
novels – for she was Scottish to the core and retained the
speech all her life – at least as early as 1849, she soon became
a pet of the House of Blackwood and a support to their
'Maga', though she found it necessary to find other publishers to place all her novels, not to mention her non-
fictional works. She retained to the end a special relation with
Blackwood's and wrote two of the three volumes of *Annals of
a Publishing House*[5] (theirs) at the end of her life. It was her
Scottish lineage and upbringing that formed her character
and shaped her outlook, that and her mother, whose tongue
gave her a pattern of caustic wit. Henry James said that her
'easy flow' of writing was 'fed by an immensity of reading', as
is evident; her modern languages seem to have been acquired
mainly during her travels after marriage and during her
widowhood.

As with so many of these talented Victorian girls, we don't
know where or how she got her education, unless from her
brothers (George Eliot, however, was of course excellently
taught at schools); but study seems to have come to all such
girls as naturally as writing and criticism. Mrs Oliphant
never gives the impression of labouring and in her criticism
of George Eliot as she was represented in Cross's *Life* –
'always on duty, never relaxing, her letters ponderous
beyond description' – we see she had a different ideal, claiming for herself to have 'loved the easy swing of life'. She says:
'I have written because it gave me pleasure, because it came
natural to me, because it was like talking or breathing, beside
the big fact that it was necessary for me to work for my children. That however was not my first motive.' The conditions

of her early life excluded all social amusement or entertainment, but 'our pleasures were books of all and every kind,
newspapers and magazines, which formed the staple of our
conversation', and she tells us that at seven or eight she was
already a confirmed novel reader. This seems to be a reliable
formula for turning a clever girl into an authoress (as in the
case of the Brontë sisters), given the necessary incentive in
the need for earning money, though that, as she said, was a
secondary motive.

We may well ask why so prolific a novelist should have
always needed to take on hack work, since the three-decker
novel (and she sometimes published two or three a year)
brought in a good lump sum often in addition to serial rights.
In the first place, she started her widowhood with three children and a thousand pounds in debt, and though her novels
brought in enough to have supported herself and the children
thriftily they could not support all her dependants too and in
the style of living, entertaining and travelling she found
essential to her working life, nor enable her to put her sons
and nephew through Eton and college. So she turned her
hand to all branches of the literary trade and, as she admits, 'I
made on the whole a large income'. And in her life-style she
upheld thus the dignity of her profession, as her pride and
generous nature demanded. Moreover, it seems clear,
writing two or three novels a year could not satisfy such an
indefatigable, or perhaps, rather, compulsive writer. Her
insatiable intellectual needs obliged her to read or sample
everything likely to be of interest that came out in fiction,
non-fiction and periodicals, in poetry and drama, not only in
England but on the Continent and in America. Reporting on
what she had read, and evaluating it, came easy to her, being
used to serious and lively conversation. But we note that still,
as in Jane Austen's family and age, one of the conditions
imposed by her world, an assumption about the position of
even a talented women – which indeed outlasted the Victorian era – was that she could not claim or be granted
professional status. This was equally true, for instance, of
Mrs Gaskell, and only George Eliot who had cut herself off
from her family and society and was put on a pedestal by
Lewes is an exception. Mrs Oliphant could not claim special
consideration, exemption from home duties, and the

privilege of privacy, which were accorded automatically to a man in the same position. How revealing is her acquiescence:

My mother, I believe, would have felt her pride and rapture much checked, almost humiliated, if she had conceived that I stood in need of any artificial aids of that or any other description ['any special facilities or retirement']. That would at once have made the work unnatural to her eyes, and also to mine. I think the first time I ever secluded myself for my work was years after it had become my profession and sole dependence . . . and withdrew with my book and my inkstand from the family drawing-room out of a little conscious ill-temper which made me feel guilty, notwithstanding that the retirement was so very justifiable! But I did not feel it to be so, neither did the companions from whom I withdrew.

How much this attitude explains as to the circumscription of female talents and how it illuminates such cries as her 'How I have been handicapped in life!' (But lest it be thought that Mrs Oliphant could be enlisted in the female emancipation movement, note that in 1866 she had 'just finished [writing] a little paper about Stuart Mill and his mad notion of the franchise of women'.) Her writing, which during her marriage was as essential for the family's support as during her widowhood, had to be done at night for the most part even when, as she says, she worked thirteen hours a day at it. In the day she was occupied with her children and received visitors who found her apparently at leisure with fine sewing or knitting in hand. She writes: 'I had always a lightly flowing stream of magazine articles etc., and refused no work that was offered to me.' But to keep her solvent this needed to be supplemented by 'a large sum at brief intervals', which she naturally expected to get from fiction. When she could not sell her current novel at a good enough price she had to turn to bookmaking, as the list of her published books shows. We note that she could never decide whether she would have been a better novelist if she had not had to drudge – 'driving, ploughing on' – and suit her work to the demands of the three-decker and the libraries. Mrs Oliphant had facility, vitality, self-confidence and abundant material to write about, which gave her unique powers of survival and even of enjoyment of her labours. She felt on the whole that she could not have done much better if she had had less compulsion to earn, if she had got as much for each of her best novels as George Eliot and Trollope did for any of theirs (as to which difference she is bitter, remarking after reading Trollope's *Autobiography* that 'his worst book was better paid than my best'). What she really resented was that she was under-valued by publishers as a novelist and had no status as editor, no salaried post in the literary world.

Already at the age of twenty-eight she notes, 'I suppose I must have become by this time a sort of general utility woman in the Magazine' (*Annals*, vol. ii, p. 475), and she duly acted as publisher's reader, editor of series of books, intro-ducer of new authors, translator as well as critic of European literature, and a biographer over a wide field; in fact a high-level middleman of letters allowed great freedom of choice in reviewing. And, too, her conversational powers were acknowledged to be outstanding. John Blackwood wrote on 10 June 1870: 'The scene was like a drama. Mrs Oliphant up here, Col. Lockhart and Lewes both talking first class with her, and I for some time downstairs speaking with George Eliot . . . ' Evidently a woman capable of filling a high literary position. Yet when, after her greatest achievement as a novelist (with the *Chronicles of Carlingford*), and having been a valued writer for the heavy journals for a quarter of a century, we find her striving for a regular income instead of the uncer-tainties of a freelance now she had turned fifty, no appoint-ment was made available for her, though she suggested some herself. We first note her asking Macmillan's (about 1877) to start a children's magazine and let her edit it. A year later she suggested a weekly magazine to be called 'The Three King-doms', with special sections on Irish and Scottish subjects, embracing literature, history and science, to include reviews, biography and fiction, which she was prepared to edit. Two years later she wrote again to her friend Craik at Macmillan's begging for any editorship or similar source of a regular income. In 1883 she wrote again asking to be provided with, what she had surely earned, 'something like an editorship where there would be steady income without perpetual strain – such as his friends have found more than once for Leslie Stephen – but then he is man' (quoted by V. and R. A. Colby from the Macmillan MSS.). Nothing came of any of these appeals, which to a woman of such proud spirit must have been a great humiliation.

At the beginning of her career she was hailed by Jeffrey of the *Edinburgh Review*, at the end she was hailing Barrie and Kipling (with qualifications): in herself she bridges the gap.

The literary critic

Seeing that she wrote over two hundred articles for 'Maga' alone, it is impossible to give in a short space a fair idea of the extent and originality of her contributions as a literary critic and reviewer, but she has certainly a better record in this department of letters than George Eliot for instance, or some other well-known names. The obituary notice 'Maga' published claimed for Mrs Oliphant 'the proud title of the most accomplished periodical writer of her day' and records that 'She was already an old contributor when she wrote for the memorable number in which George Eliot began the "Scenes of Clerical Life".' I can only give some random examples to show that her perceptions were acute and first-hand, her ideas suggestive and vigorously expressed and her conclusions mostly sound.

Writing on 'Miss Austen and Miss Mitford' in 1870, when Jane Austen was not properly understood and so underrated, she gives us a characteristic series of discriminations. She says incidentally of Miss Austen: 'her character is not the simple character it appears at first glance, but one full of subtle power, keenness, finesse and self-restraint – a type not at all unusual in women of high cultivation'; she remarks 'the fine vein of feminine cynicism which pervades Miss Austen's mind', adding, 'It is something altogether different from the rude and brutal male quality that bears the same name'. But she also notices some limitations: 'Miss Mitford's world is a world twice as full as Miss Austen's', and congenial as she evidently found the Austen novels and though herself a witty writer, a critic of men and women, and a thoroughly unsentimental Scotswoman, she still cannot endorse the remorseless spinster outlook that she felt to be a failure in humanity in a woman. Ripened by love and marriage and softened by maternity, she cannot accept Elizabeth Bennet as the truly superior heroine Jane Austen thinks her, and the callous

picture of Mr Collins's married life (though 'we accept him
gladly as a real contribution to our knowledge of human
kind') is too uncharitable for her sense of justice. She quotes
Elizabeth Bennet's observation of the bride's manoeuvres to
keep her husband out of the way and comments:

This is rather diabolical, it must be owned, and there is a calmness
of acquiescence in the excellent Charlotte's arrangements which it
takes all the reader's fortitude to stomach. It is possible that the
very youth of the author may have produced this final stroke of
unexampled consistency; for youth is always more or less cruel,
and is slow to acknowledge that even the most stupid and arrogant
of mortals has his rights.

Finally, she is highly serious in arguing that the great public
is not what makes a classic, as Jane Austen's case proves.
'Her works have become classic' in spite of the fact that

it is scarcely to be expected that books so calm and cold and keen
. . . would ever be popular. They are rather of the class which
attracts the connoisseur, which charms the critical and literary
mind, and which, by dint of persistency and iteration, is carried by
the superior rank of readers into a half-real, half-fictitious
unanimity of applause . . . Authority was never better employed.

The best judges 'have here, for once done the office of an
Academy, and laureated a writer whom the populace would
not have been likely to laureate, but whom it has learnt to
recognize'.

To point to something quite different, we may note how in
April 1897, two months before her death, the opening article
in 'Maga' ('Recent Books – French and English') is hers, and
that she has taken on Huysmans, Anatole France, Olive
Schreiner, Barrie's *Margaret Ogilvy* (among others) with authority, and defends Burns against Henley's *The Centenary Burns*.
In the number for January 1879 she takes eighteen double-
columned pages for 'The Novels of A. Daudet', where she
gives incidentally a sound judgement on Balzac, and makes it
clear that what she saw as valuable in Daudet's novels was
their moral realism, however painful, and a lesson much
needed for Victorian novelists, as she found in Balzac similar
merit (unlike Charlotte Brontë, George Eliot and other Victorians, who found him merely repellent). She notes as well
that it was his imitation of Dickens which made Daudet

more acceptable to the English than Balzac, and that that was really his weakness. Henry James she admired and read from the start, and had no hesitation in diagnosing 'the complex fate' of being an American novelist in the nineteenth century.

Mr F. Marion Crawford belongs to that curious sept of the Continental American which has become a feature of our time . . . For a full understanding of it, we refer the curious reader to the works of Mr Henry James, who has made various studies, very subtle and delicate after his peculiar manner, of this singular and hybrid people, which is greatly distinguished, among other things, by its love of rank, by its devotion to the old regime, and by a horror and hatred of all modern improvements, national developments, and other falling offs from the models of the past, humorously traversed by the underlying consciousness – half shame, half disgust, half pride – of belonging to the newest and least historical of all nations. The race, however, are not humorous in themselves; their self-consciousness is too strong, and a little angry – feelings which rob the ludicrous of its charms. They have this privilege, however, that they understand foreign life with almost the completeness of native understanding, quickened by that subtle sense of spectatorship which is never wholly absent from the mind of the dwellers, however familiar and accustomed, in a country which is not their own. And as in a great many cases art is the reason or excuse for their expatriation, they know about art thoroughly or at least familiarly, with that acquaintance of habit and jargon which simulates real knowledge in those cases where knowledge does not really exist. There is in Mr Crawford's books a certain cosmopolitanism which serves to make this explanation necessary, and a something which is perhaps the real result of cosmopolitanism though not what is generally understood by it – a slight embarrassing and confusing sense that he 'does not belong' anywhere . . . only a man without a country, so to speak, could, we think, have done this; and so much understanding mingled with an obtusity so remarkable is one of the most curious features of the hybrid American . . . his own nationality is so far from genuine that it does not help him to define what there is in national character which is inalienable. A man cannot gain so much without losing something.

In an article, 'French Periodical Literature', in November 1865 she protests against the popular English idea of the French mind, 'which we in our ignorance call light', arguing that their periodicals (she read them all regularly) 'show an extraordinary capacity for serious exertion' in reader as well as writer, and that 'everything in the *Revue des Deux Mondes*, for example, is scrupulously well done'. She remarks that the lighter reading with which the general mass in France contents itself is represented by *causeries* – 'no contemptible satisfaction, certainly when the *causeries* happen to be those of M. Sainte-Beuve'. She protests with spirit against the current English objection (December 1866) that Balzac and Victor Hugo etc. are 'unEnglish': 'Of course they are French. It is their greatest glory . . . it is the greatest possible advantage that the French writer should be French and the German truly German, as well as that the English should be English', though she does not disguise that Victor Hugo's novels (the subject of the article) are 'in some parts disfigured by false sentiment'. She points out as early as 1855 that Hawthorne's novels and their reputation belong as much to this side of the Atlantic as to the other. She thoroughly appreciated the character and abilities of Lord Chesterfield in spite of her repugnance for his cynicism, and preferred Richardson's Lovelace to Tom Jones. One could go on to any extent with impressive illustration of her powers and scope as a high-class middleman of letters, and literary critic. But she also reviewed the drama and theatrical performances of the age of Irving, and was a connoisseur, and severe critic, of acting. I will end this section by an illustration of the difficulties she (like all Victorian journalists) worked under. In the third volume of Mrs Oliphant's history of the House of Blackwood, which was written by Blackwood's daughter, we find Mrs Porter writing of her father:

There was a very admirable paper by Mrs Oliphant, which he was longing and had settled to publish for its literary excellence, when suddenly something in the tone of it struck him when he saw it in type – something so terrible that 'the whole Kirk of Scotland would be furious, and the Church of England not pleased'; it could not be deleted, 'or the whole spirit of the paper would disappear'. So there was no help for it – it could not be used.

This suggests how ticklish a matter writing for Victorian periodicals was and how difficult for us, and presumably for a too independent-minded contributor like Mrs Oliphant, to understand precisely where the line between the acceptable and the impossible was drawn. Perhaps this accounts for her failure – unlike Leslie Stephen, or Thackeray and other novelists – to be held suitable to edit a magazine.

The novelist

Mrs Oliphant's output as a novelist can best be considered as three phases, overlapping but distinct. The first starts even before her early marriage, the regional novels of Scottish setting and characters; but they are inferior to her later Scottish novels, and the short stories she wrote when more mature, and are not of much account. The shock of losing her husband and the necessity of supporting a destitute family precipitated a better idea for interesting Blackwood, to whom she was in debt, and she launched a series, the Carlingford Chronicles, with a short story in 'Maga' for May 1861, 'The Executor'. No doubt the success of novelists in the previous decade with Cranford, Barchester and Milby had suggested to her an English provincial setting with its opportunities for satiric insights into contemporary social and religious institutions, but her wit and analysis are her own and in no way parasitic. Two excellent *nouvelles*, 'The Rector' and 'The Doctor's Family', followed, then, rapidly, *Salem Chapel*, *The Perpetual Curate* and – the high-water mark – *Miss Marjoribanks*, altogether an amazing flood of creative power while she was also producing an incessant flow of periodical essays, literary criticism, inferior novels of other kinds, and biographical works. In 1876 with *Phoebe, Junior: A Last Chronicle of Carlingford* she ended an impressive series – *Miss Marjoribanks* has claims to be considered the wisest and wittiest of Victorian novels. It is so beautifully 'done' that its ironic comedy is unique outside Jane Austen's works for consistency of tone and maturity of criticism of a closed society. The third phase is miscellaneous, containing more and better Scottish-based fiction that is thoroughly realistic, anti-romantic novels and tales of English social life which are essentially studies of a changing society, and, as a literary curiosity, beginning with *A Beleaguered City* in 1880, a group of tales of supernatural experiences with a *frisson* of a spiritual or professedly mystical nature, which seem to me to have been overrated then and since. Though Mrs Oliphant valued them highly herself and some have Dantean overtones, they represent a self-indulgence, the complement of her hard-headed professional self which required some non-dogmatic vaguely religious sustenance. Yet they are not so much literary curiosities as specimen of that special variety of thriller, the supernatural, of which there are so many examples by respectable writers in the Late Victorian and Edwardian periods – a genre containing 'The Turn of the Screw'. Mrs Oliphant in fact tried her hand, deliberately or instinctively, at every literary form known to her, even verse and drama.

In the interests of economy I must confine myself to examining only cursorily the Carlingford series and the novels and tales of English society, on which I believe Mrs Oliphant's claims to status as a novelist must rest. *The Chronicles of Carlingford* were once published entire as a set and should be again made available for posterity, since they can rival Trollope's Barchester series in several respects and contain material much more valuable as sociology and social criticism than anything in his. Owing to the popularity of *Salem Chapel*, Mrs Oliphant has the reputation of being a novelist who was merely an authority on Dissent, but even so *Salem Chapel* must be supplemented by *Phoebe, Junior*, a sort of sequel and far better. It is true that Mrs Oliphant thoroughly understood the dissidence of Dissent, though George Eliot wrote tartly in 1862: 'I have not read The Chronicles of Carlingford [but] from what Mr Lewes tells me, they must represent Dissenters in a very different spirit from anything that has appeared in my books.' True enough, for her own pictures of them had hitherto been idealizing and nostalgic (in *Adam Bede* and *Silas Marner*, both greatly backward-looking in time), and it is rather remarkable that when George Eliot again handled the subject of a Dissenting community, in *Felix Holt* (1866), she could not have made the same claim, for Mr Lyon's flock is very similar to Mr Vincent's in *Salem Chapel* (and to Mr Northcote's later in *Phoebe, Junior*), the minister in each case being so superior intellectually and spiritually to his arrogant and vulgar congregation as to be in a situation at once comic and painful, and which ends with the minister's retiring from the field. George Eliot's change from the tender-minded to the realistic and ironic treatment of Dissenters is inexplicable other than as the irresistible influence of Mrs Oliphant's wit and validity. In fact, the truth to life of Mrs Oliphant's rendition of provincial Dissent is borne out by the experiences of it recorded by 'Mark Rutherford' and others later in the century as well as by Crabb Robinson, a contemporary Dissenter.

That Mrs Oliphant does not merely make easy play with irony is proved by her sympathetic appreciation of the difficulties, even sufferings, of the rising generation of the better educated Nonconformists and of the really superior members of the old-established Dissenting communities of northern cities, who were still socially non-existent. The masterly charting of the rise of the Beechams, from Salem Chapel in Carlingford to a 'final apotheosis in a handsome chapel near Regent's Park', with a corresponding change in their attitude to the Established Church as 'social elevation modified their sectarian zeal', is not unkind, even though we are told of Phoebe's father: 'He had not, perhaps, much power of thought, but it is easy to make up for such a secondary want when the gift of expression is so strong.' But we are also shown types more worth attention:

Horace Northcote was not of Mr Beecham's class. He was not well-to-do and genial, bent upon keeping up his congregation and his popularity, and trying to ignore as much as he could the social superiority of the Church without making himself in any way offensive to her. He was a political Non-conformist, a vigorous champion of the Dis-establishment Society, more successful on the platform than in the pulpit, and strenuously of opinion in his heart of hearts that the Church was the great drawback to all progress in England, an incubus of which the nation would gladly be rid.

Phoebe Beecham, lovely, clever and unshakably sensible, is the granddaughter of the prosperous but socially impossible Carlingford grocer. She cannot reconcile her superior education and social life in London with the vulgarity of her parents' origins; and though she is heroic in her determination to act rightly by her grandparents, her position when at Carlingford is shown to be painful. She says thoughtfully to Northcote:

Which is best; for everyone to continue in the position he was born in, or for an honest shopkeeper to educate his children and push them up higher, until they come to feel themselves members of a different class, and to be ashamed of him? Either way, you know, it is hard.

Northcote himself is a minister with no sense of perplexity, being well-off, well educated abroad ('2 or 3 years at Jena studying philosophy'), and whose relatives are all 'Manchester people with two or three generations of wealth behind them, relatives of whom nobody need be ashamed'. Mrs Oliphant as a Scot was free of Victorian class-feeling but she thoroughly comprehended its nature and was interested in the problems of social change that were affected by it. Where she saw it to be based on something genuine she did not treat it ironically, as where the really superior children suffer from the narrow outlook, the meanness of mind and the blatant money-values of the Salem congregation. But she was equally appreciative of the Church as a comic spectacle, and more inclined to treat ironically (as richer and worthier material for her satiric powers) the Victorian ecclesiastical establishment – Low, High-and-Dry, Anglo-Catholic, Broad, and Catholic conversion – even than the Nonconformists.

Here are some brief excerpts to show the individuality of her critical insights as well as the liveliness of her mind and style, from *The Perpetual Curate* (1863–4). The protagonist is a young cleric who 'was as near Rome as a strong and lofty conviction of the really superior catholicity of the Anglican Church would permit him to be'. He is to fall out with the new Rector, who with his wife has come to inspect their church. They 'went in to gaze at it with a disgust which only an unhappy priest of high culture and aesthetic taste, doomed to officiate in a building of the 18th century, of the church-warden period of architecture, could fully enter into', whereas the Perpetual Curate of St Roque's was 'happy in the consciousness of possessing a church which, though not old, had been built by Gilbert Scott'. He says he wonders 'where the people expected to go to' who built the parish church, 'such an unhallowed type of construction', 'to think of bestowing *consecration* upon anything so hideous. What a pass the world must have come to, when this erection was counted worthy to be the house of God! No wonder it was an unchristian age.'

Here something more than the idiom of the Victorian Anglican movement is being satirized. The author's irony is distributed equally between a confident aestheticism, which is disgusted by a fine eighteenth-century parish church but gratified by a Victorian Gothic *pastiche*, and the confusion between aesthetic taste (shown to be merely fashionable cant) and religion.

In *Miss Marjoribanks* we meet a totally ironic dissection of the mid-Victorian culture. The Carlingford doctor and his daughter are Scots, their environment being English is unworthy of them; though they both daunt it and elicit respectful admiration, the society is inadequate to Lucilla's needs and provides little scope for her 'capabilities', which are immense, so powerful indeed that the comedy consists largely in the camouflage she must give them in order to operate without alarming her friends and neighbours. The novel is witty and high-spirited yet on a serious basis. I have given the reasons for holding it to be a decisive influence on *Middlemarch* in the introductory essay I wrote for the reprint of it by Chatto and Windus (1969) [see above].

Howard Sturgis, himself the author of a witty and considerable novel, seems to me to be right when he challenged the judgement which still holds the field, by writing (in a moving obituary tribute in *Temple Bar* for September 1899):

One mistake which many of her critics make is the supposition that her work at its best was injured by her immense productiveness. Her best work was of a very high order of merit. The harm that she did to her literary reputation seems rather the surrounding of her best with so much which she knew to be of inferior quality, that her high peaks of achievement, instead of rising out of the plain, as it were, suffer diminution by the neighbourhood of so many foothills.

But these foothills, he argues, are not in themselves contemptible.

She never pandered to the public by consciously bad work, in exchange for popularity or wealth. She never wrote a word she did not believe to be 'true' in the best sense, nor gave her readers anything but honest work for their money, and as good of its kind as she could spare the time to make it.

There is something of interest and much worth reading in most of her works of fiction, and nothing to apologize for.

And there is about all her work a real distinction, an

identifiable Oliphant manner and attitude and tone, more suited to a later age than the ones she lived through. It inheres in her honesty and unflinching realism and her recognition – without cynicism or resentment – of the lack of idealism in ordinary life (a very un-Victorian trait). This did not in that age make for popularity, of course. A characteristic observation in her novels is that 'Next to happiness, perhaps enmity is the most healthful stimulant of the human mind.' There is something disturbing in even her liveliest fictions; just as Trollope's novels always contain unhappy people and that is where his real strength lies, so Mrs Oliphant's concentrate on painful situations of all kinds. She wrote about life as she knew it and made her characters – often faulty or unattractive people – face and cope with, or come to terms with, the dilemmas, the disillusions, the mental sufferings, she herself had survived. But there is no self-pity in her work, as in Hardy's tragic novels, nor any idealization or self-transfiguration, as in George Eliot's. She was the opposite, too, of the bestseller novel-writer who peddles day-dreams and wish-fulfilment. It is typical of her that she wrote that 'a "happy ending" is simply a contemptible expedient' and this no doubt explains her inability to obtain from Victorian publishers, those shrewd judges of the market values, high enough prices for even her best novels.

She investigates by dramatizing the relations of husband and wife and parent and child, and the position of women in a man-dominated society; and here she is genuinely original. She was making studies of masculine arrogance and insensitiveness to the capacities and legitimate claims of wives and daughters and sisters before George Eliot and Meredith, illustrating what she had noted as the 'inherent contempt for women which is a settled principle in the minds of so many men'. Her novels don't end characteristically with happy marriages, sometimes they end with the tragic breakdown of a marriage, or with no marriage at all for the heroine, for her gaze was fixed on the nature of marriage itself – its shortcomings and disasters, the clash of wills, the inability to preserve a balance or make a lasting compromise, and the difficulty of facing and then either cutting losses or accepting them. *A Country Gentleman and his Family* shows a marriage of love hastily contracted between a young widow and a younger man and then breaking down because of the man's obstinate self-assertion in demands for masterhood, and his jealousy of her boy to whom she is more attached than to himself. The consequences of the separation that ensues, for husband, wife and children, are fully investigated in a sequel, *A House Divided Against Itself*, published in the same year (1886). A repeated theme throughout all the phases of her fiction is that of the wife who suffers disillusionment as to her husband or whose apparently happy married life has actually been a bondage or imprisonment; though there is no reason to suppose that her own marriage was unsatisfactory in spite of material difficulties and the incompatibility between her husband and her mother, from which she had suffered.

She had had a great deal of experience of life as a struggle and an exposure to all kinds of hardship and disenchantment, and she seems to have realized that this was an asset to a creative writer for she doubts that she would have done better if, like George Eliot, she 'had been kept in a mental greenhouse and taken care of'. The conception of a heroine in her novels is correspondingly original for a Victorian. Her admirable women are clever, efficient, vital, highly articulate, practical-minded, superior and managing – but magnanimous and tolerant enough of the shortcomings and failings natural to men, whom they often see mainly as means to an end. And most original of all, the Oliphant heroine *works*, a condition otherwise almost unknown in Victorian novels outside *Jane Eyre* and *Villette*. Lucilla, Phoebe, Patty Hewatt, Maisie Rowland, Kirsteen and the rest see what needs doing or saying undaunted by the obstacles men and circumstances set up against them. Lucilla, having reorganized the social life of Carlingford and got her chosen candidate elected for Parliament on a slogan invented by herself, tells her betrothed: 'What we both want is something to do' and has him buy a run-down estate in a squalid village so that 'You can improve the land, you know, and the people you could leave to me. *We* could make it pay.' *Hester* shows women in banking; Kirsteen, a laird's daughter, runs away from an intolerable home to make a career for herself as a Court dressmaker; Patty, the socially ambitious daughter of a village innkeeper, succeeds in eloping with the feeble-minded son of the Great House and by her vulgar arts and unscrupulous tactics ousts and supersedes the well-bred but helpless heirs-at-law in *The Cuckoo in the Nest*. The daughters of *The Curate in Charge*, left penniless on the death of their high-minded father, refuse to fall back on relatives or charity: one resigns herself to the loss of caste by becoming the village schoolmistress (Mrs Oliphant explores the situation with relish, showing that the gentry are embarrassed and drop the girl), the other, who is artistically gifted, trains to become a book illustrator. These are only a few specimens of a rich crop. Her girls paint seriously, play Bach and Beethoven 'scientifically', study the Classics, despise their mothers' merely social lives and insist on working in Whitechapel and the London hospitals; young widows manage their sons' estates and wives like Phoebe and Lucilla write their husbands' speeches. But most remarkable is the working out of the theme in *The Railway Man and His Children*, where the Ruskinian theory about woman's place and the Victorian gospel of work are both logically examined and routed, and 'the new girl' of the age voices her creed (less than twenty years after Dorothea Brooke).

The Railway Man is a Scottish engineer, now very wealthy, the typical self-made industrial man, but thoroughly admirable, and with two children by his first (working-class) marriage. He has now made a happy second marriage to a poor lady of good family. The adjustments of all parties to each other, and their misunderstandings, provide difficulties and humour, but are not the crux of the novel. This comes when the daughter wants to marry a ne'er-do-well and set him up on his dilapidated family estate with her dowry to lead the life of a country gentleman, the only thing he is fit for, while her father insists on principle that Eddy must first make good in the colonies or on a ranch, though Eddy points out that this would only drive him to the bad. Maisie disputes her father's theory of justification by work and vindication by making money, calling in her friend, Eddy's sister, a society girl of remarkable character, to support her. Rosamund tells the Railway Man calmly:

What did I say about work? it is the thing I wish for most. As soon as ever I am of age I am going in for it. Mabel Leighton, who is my dearest friend, is going in for medicine, but I have no distinct turn,

I am sorry to say. But we think that something is certain to turn up
. . . There is always as much work as one can set one's face to in the
East End.

'Women's work is but poorly paid', the Railway Man tells
her, but she replies:

Money! oh, we never thought of money, so long as we could get on
and work . . . lodgings are not dear, and as we shouldn't care for
meat, or anything expensive in the way of living . . . I know people
in society – well, perhaps not quite in society – who have gone on
working for a whole lifetime, gentlemen, yes and women too, working from morning till night, and even have been successful, yet
never made money. So it is clear that work is not the thing to make
a fortune by. But I am of opinion it is the first thing in the world.

She finally knocks him out by arguing that his pride in his
own achievement of a great fortune is fallacious – 'getting
other people to work for you and directing them, and planning everything, and making money – like you, Mr Rowland
. . . is not WORK'. Rowland is angry but helpless:

He felt sure there were arguments somewhere with which he could
confound this silly girl, and show her that to work was to rise in the
world, and make a fortune, and surround yourself with luxury, with
the certainty of a mathematical axiom. But he could not find them.
And the result was that he contented himself with that snort and a
strong expression of his opinion that girls should marry, and look
after men's houses, and not trouble their heads about what was
never intended for them.

He is caught between Rosamund's argument, that work is
essential, real work not organization, but that the money
made by it is not a measure of its value or any proof of
achievement; and his daughter's, that people who can't earn
money but have a talent for living and can fill a useful role in
society ought not to be condemned and thrown to the dogs.
Rowland is indignant at having to rescue Eddy and support
him as Maisie's husband so that they can 'play the fool all the
year round – on my money, that I've worked hard for, every
penny', but even his wife comes in on the girls' side, saying,
'James! she had you there', and collapses in laughter.

'He began to laugh too, though he could hardly have told
why.' He assures his wife that his becoming a millionaire is
indeed proof of his hard work, but she thinks: ' "You might

have been, with a great deal harder work, a respectable fore-
man in the foundry, as good a man, and as admirable an
example of what labour and honest zeal can do." – She did
not say it, but her historian does for her. Mrs Rowland only
pressed her husband's arm, and said, "The young ones,
perhaps, are not without reason too." ' The novel ends after
Maisie's marriage to Eddy, but we are also told: 'Rosamund
has not yet married, and has had full opportunities of testing
the power of work and its results.'

Another example of Mrs Oliphant's insight into the
arbitrary nature of conventional moral assumptions can be
illustrated by the psychology of Phoebe in a situation where
what she knows to be legally right conflicts with her sense of
real justice, when she determines to rescue the wretched
clergyman driven to forge her grandfather's name to an
accommodation bill. This she does by unscrupulously filching the bill and standing up to her grandfather's rage, finally
balking him of his revenge – 'by an unjustifiable expedient
which in itself was a kind of crime. This, however, brought a
slight smile on her face.' The whole episode (chapters 40 to
93) is remarkable.

How did she arrive at this degree of originality? We have
seen one of her assets – her experience of life. It would be
untrue to say that she deliberately drew on this for her novels,
but what we see was the truly creative process of her feeding
the problems she had encountered and the sufferings she had
endured into dramatic arrangements of life where these
could be analysed and discussed and seen in a true light. One
of the nearest to her own experience but translated is the late
story 'Mr Sandford', republished with a similarly painful tale
in *The Ways of Life* (a revealing title). A hitherto successful
artist who suddenly finds that taste has changed and his
pictures have become unsaleable, who has an affectionate
but spoilt family used to opulent living, and nothing put by,
he is grateful when death by an accident releases him from
his insoluble problems and mental anguish. *The Ways of Life*
appeared in the year of her death, and if not an appropriate
epitaph is a characteristic self-judgement, and characteristically impersonal.

Her honesty and disenchanted insight into human
relations are assets, then, and this maturity was what made

her write that though Charlotte and Emily Brontë's novels 'are vivid, original and striking in the highest degree', 'Their philosophy of life is that of a school girl, their knowledge of the world is almost *nil*, their conclusions confused by the haste and passion of a mind self-centred and working in the narrowest orbit.' Comparing herself with Charlotte Brontë she writes: 'I have had far more experience and, I think, a fuller conception of life. I have learned to take perhaps more a man's view of mortal affairs . . . ' Another such asset as her Scottish conditioning was that she had been an artist's wife and lived both in London and in Italy in a mildly Bohemian atmosphere. This certainly emancipated her for ever from the drawing-room point of view and from social conformism; Victorian conventions of feeling and behaviour are always a subject for ironic exposure in her novels. We can see that her knowledge of the artist's life gave her a positive position from which to criticize the snobbery and stupidities of Victorian good society. Before du Maurier and Henry James had made their separate but not unrelated attacks on it from the studio point of view, Mrs Oliphant had, for instance in *Miss Marjoribanks*, used that as a standard of judgement as well as to provide ironic jokes. It must have given her pleasure to make the Colonel's wife say: 'For my part I never like to have anything to do with those artist kind of people – they are all adventurers,' and to give Lucilla's objection to *professional* singing, and to show Carlingford's relegation to social obscurity of a poor but talented family of professional artists. Her style is the natural expression of such a character. It is witty, but the apt epithet, the adroit sentence, the telling phrase, the lively conversational manner, are never sought after or strained, as she herself puts it: 'I have always had my sing-song, guided by no sort of law, but by my ear, which was in its way fastidious to the cadence and measure that pleased me; but it is bewildering to me in my perfectly artless art, if I may use the word at all, to hear of the elaborate ways of forming and enhancing style, and all the studies for that end.' And though intellectually an ostrich she had no intellectual snobbery. Residing in Jowett's Oxford in 1879 and being flatteringly received, she was unimpressed: 'Intellectualism, like every other *ism*, is monotonous, and the timidity and mutual alarm of the younger potentates strikes me a good deal. They are so

much afraid of committing themselves or risking anything
that may be found wanting in any minutiae of correctness.
Scholarship is a sort of poison tree, and kills everything.'

How central Mrs Oliphant's case is as not merely the
Victorian woman of letters but as a more general type of the
nineteenth-century literary woman, perhaps the type of literary woman of all ages, I will prove by a quotation from Henry
James:

She found that she could write, and she took up her pen never to lay
it down . . . Very remarkable, indeed, was the immediate development of the literary faculty in this needy young woman . . . During
the five and forty years of her literary career, she had something to
say about most things in the universe . . . She found she could write
for an extraordinary length of time without weariness and this is as
far as she goes in the way of analysis of her inspiration. From the
time she made the discovery to the day of her death her life was an
extremely laborious one. She had evidently an extraordinary
physical robustness. It was her constant practice to write at night,
beginning after the rest of the world had gone to sleep . . . The history of her mind is of course closely connected with her personal
history . . . Her disposition was the reverse of sceptical. Her
religious feeling, like all her feelings, was powerful and volumin-
ous, and she had an ideal of a sort etherealized and liberated
Christianity . . .

With some further specifications, different of course for
each, this would apply equally to George Eliot and Mrs
Oliphant. But in fact the 'she' of Henry James's piece was
George Sand, who was born and who died a generation
earlier than Mrs Oliphant, and was not even an Englishwoman.

Trollope and Evangelicalism

In 1863 occurred Trollope's bout with the Evangelicals. One
of Queen Victoria's chaplains, the Rev. Norman Macleod,
was editor of *Good Words*, a periodical designed for Sunday
reading. He had what seemed to him a good idea, to enlarge
its appeal and subscribers by adding a serial novel regularly
to the otherwise religiously improving articles. He therefore
contracted with Trollope, as a famous and respectable
novelist, to write him a novel. With characteristic insensitiveness to his market Trollope wrote the obviously unsuitable
(one would have thought) novel *Rachel Ray*; apart from the
fact that it was one of his poorer novels, it is mainly about the
demerits of the Evangelical type of Christianity. The heroine
is made wretched and persecuted in consequence of her elder
sister's falling under the sway of a clergyman who is yet
another example of the Evangelical monster. Rachel's
mother and her friends succumb also, Rachel is forbidden
the company of her eligible but worldly minded sweetheart
(the son of a brewer), her sister marries the monster and is
stripped of her possessions and driven to despair by his
bullying, and in the end Rachel triumphs, her mother and
sister are undeceived, and *savoir-vivre* is vindicated. Trollope
thought it was the heroine's going to a ball that was the cause
of the objection to his novel raised by the editor of *Good Words*,
but obviously from Macleod's point of view *Rachel Ray* was
nothing but Bad Words. The adverse criticism that the
advance advertisement of this attraction aroused in the
hyper-Evangelical journal *The Record* (which objected on principle to novel-reading for good Christians) probably caused
the editor of *Good Words* to read *Rachel Ray*, when Trollope submitted it to him, with a more critical eye; but even without
such a thorn in his side as *The Record* he could see that this

novel was unsuitable for a Sunday magazine edited by a Scottish divine. He complained to Trollope that *Rachel Ray* 'cast a gloom over Dorcas Societies, a glory over balls at 4 a.m.', and 'described and magnified' the 'weaknesses – shams – hypocrisies – gloom – of some species of professing Christians'. He was pained that Trollope had not, as he had requested, apparently, 'brought out more fully the positive good side of the Christian life than you had hitherto done, or avoid at least saying anything to pinch, fret, annoy, or pain those Evangelicals who are *not* Recordites'.

One feels for him, and rather less for Trollope who had no difficulty in finding another publisher for his novel, which rapidly went through seven editions, besides which he extracted £500 compensation from the publisher of *Good Words* for breach of contract. Macleod's letter to Trollope rejecting *Rachel Ray* sounds to me pathetic as well as sincere. He explained:

I know well that my position is difficult, and too because I do *not* wish to please both parties, but simply because I wish to produce a Magazine which, though too wide for the Evangelicals and too narrow for the anti-Evangelicals, and therefore disliked by both cliques, may nevertheless rally round it in the long run the sympathies of all who occupy the middle ground of a decided, sincere and manly Evangelical Christianity.

This suggests the immense difficulties of a publisher of the Victorian age, with its general public so radically and bitterly split into religious sects of such narrow outlook and such vast prejudices. Only Dickens managed to make himself universally acceptable on the basis of undifferentiated Christian feeling, though even he could not make his work acceptable to severe Anglicans like Charlotte Yonge.

As *Rachel Ray* was successful financially far beyond its merits, this suggests that by 1863 there was a large public eager for anti-Evangelical fiction, and also that, contrary to popular belief, the Evangelicals were still in a position of power. It is ironical that *The Warden*, Trollope's first success, was considered to have an appeal for the anti-High Church public. The rejection of *Rachel Ray* by the editor of one religious body's reading matter and the same novel's immense success with another part of the public show that the divisiveness was on sectarian and not, as now, on intellectual or social grounds.

Trollope had tried unsuccessfully, and when no longer in his first youth, to launch himself as a novelist, with uninspired novels of Irish life and its social problems, having read up the early nineteenth-century Irish novelists and especially studied Carleton's books. His own equipment was the belief that *Pride and Prejudice* was the greatest of novels, and he clearly formed his habits of composition, natural dialogue and use of the correct, refined and educated language of the speech coming down from the eighteenth century by his admiration for, and sympathy with, the objects and techniques of Jane Austen. He thus avoided the enveloping melodramatic mode and style of the early nineteenth-century Irish novelists who were not in the English Ascendancy tradition that was continuous from Maria Edgeworth to Somerville and Ross; but his Irish novels are flat because he could not emulate their uninhibited use, at least for lower-class characters, of the racy Irish idiom and its rich vocabulary. His attempt at a historical novel of the French Revolution was a failure. But he *had* a real equipment in his now mature experience of rural and educated England; and a professional life in public service (highly creditable to him in its execution, he was even a success in Ireland) gave him, one feels, his interest in organizations and professions, an interest that he turned on the Established Church, where he no doubt felt that the intrigues, clashes of personalities and wills, the tragedies and comedies, were translatable from those of the postal service he knew from the inside.

The Warden was at first, we see, an attempt to write a story, to make a human story, of a characteristic public scandal of misadministration of charitable funds; in fact he had another in addition to the St Cross affair to draw on. Without needing to know much about the Church as a worldly man, he understood how such things come about and the kinds of situations they give rise to. This at first seems to have been enough for him, and even with its subsequent expansions and proliferations it is still the slightest of his novels. However, it is well worth analysing, like *Joseph Andrews*. Unlike Fielding, Trollope developed a novel of a kind that suited him as he went along, hardly by intention, and it seems to me that he had *Joseph Andrews* somewhere in the back of his mind as an inspiration of the kind of thing he could achieve, starting out as Fielding must have done with not much more than high spirits and a good idea, a tradition of skit and caricature, and a loosely-held-together story made up by fits and starts, drawing in new characters as required to fill it out, constantly changing its tone and object and direction, and finding by accident a moral, justifying theme. Like *Joseph Andrews*, *The Warden* becomes a criticism of the life of the age, and its mode of satire modified by the forthright feelings of an honourable man who must offer positives, so taking the occasion to stand up for what he believes to be of value in life. Trollope started writing it in 1852, when he was thirty-seven; during the writing he returned to Ireland where he finished it in Belfast, and got it out in 1855. It was a success of esteem and went off slowly, though talked about of course; but he must have known he had found his own vein and the Barsetshire sequence followed, intermingled with others on English life of a similar kind, just as Fielding realized that *Joseph Andrews* was the type of his individuality as a novelist.

Trollope *did* have an idea behind the scandal story, that of using it to criticize the state of religion as practised in the Established Church of his time, and that the novel opened with a study of the cathedral precentor Mr Harding proves this. The Rev. Septimus Harding is defined as poor, merely a minor canon until the age of forty, whose life has been devoted to the performance in perfection of the cathedral services and to the resurrection, editing and publication of a 'collection of our ancient church music'; and he is a devoted performer on the viola and cello. He had been rescued, with his two daughters, from indigence by being made Warden, twenty years back, of Hiram's Hospital, where he draws a comfortable income and enjoys a handsome house, tending a dozen bedesmen of the ancient and well-endowed charitable trust, owing to his friendship with his Bishop, whose only son had married Mr Harding's eldest daughter. The aged Bishop is also carefully delineated as the kind unzealous Bishop of the pre-Tractarian and even pre-Evangelical eras, wealthy from his profession without any sense of guilt; having appointed (as was quite usual then) his son to hold rich livings and content to let him run the diocese, which the son,

Archdeacon Grantly, does thoroughly well in the way of efficiency, practical morality and gentlemanly treatment of the clergy. It is also stressed that Archdeacon Grantly though rich, works hard, and keeps at Plumstead Episcopi a useful if unspiritual household and is himself a warm-hearted, well-meaning, if prejudiced and conventional, clergyman of the old High-and-Dry school. It is evident that the terms of the scandal are not going to be laid out with partisan or simple-minded reductions of the complexity of life where the rights and wrongs of a case are at issue. The problems facing Mr Harding, of resigning once the fact is apparent to him that he *is* being made a cause of scandal, are not simply that he will be pauperized if he loses the wardenship. (He is already in debt long since for his public-spirited work on cathedral music, for which in fact his rich son-in-law is paying. Grantly becomes generous as to money but ungenerous in using it to force his own will on his father-in-law, whom he thoroughly loves and only fails to respect because of impatience with unworldliness.) Harding is told by his son-in-law that it is his duty to keep his position in order to support the interests of the Church of England against Radicals and other of its enemies. Mr Harding's delicacy of conscience and humility, which so exasperate the Archdeacon, make him unable to face the opprobrium of an unpopular martyr. Moreover he is painfully aware that his beloved younger daughter is in love with and being courted by the excellent match but misguided agitator who is instigating the public outcry against the over-paid Warden who spends on himself the money that, it is alleged, the founder's will destined for the poor of his alms-houses. Mr Harding is conscious that though he supports his daughter and himself comfortably, he does as well as possible by his old pensioners' love and sympathy and has given his life to the service of the cathedral and sacred music, which he feels to be something that the Church needs if its function is to be fulfilled. Without being a Tractarian he is a musician – both scholar (he specializes in Purcell) and performer with voice and instrument, in contrast to the Archdeacon's idea of religion which is party politics and running a machine. The worldly loud-voiced ecclesiastic is defined in his spiritual deficiencies not only by his father-in-law's delicacies of feeling but in the silent protests Mr Harding makes against that voice, defending himself by an imaginary performance on the cello, 'playing to himself some air fitted for so calamitous an occasion', or, to comfort himself and support his morale against bullying, 'create an ecstatic strain of perfect music, audible to himself and St Cecilia, and not without effect'.

The theme is illustrated by the finely detailed social comedy and its highlights represented by a few set pieces which repay analysis. The first such is the scene when the Archdeacon insists on publicly addressing the rebellious bedesmen in their hospital courtyard. Here we see that Trollope has been obliged to abandon the surface reflection of daily life for a symbolic representation of his deeper meaning. The Archdeacon becomes a statue representing the Established Church, in which its worldly and nineteenth-century aspects, its being wholly opposed to the Gospel conception of Christianity, emerge with an effect both comical and painfully disconcerting.

As the Archdeacon stood up to make his speech, erect in the middle of that little square, he looked like an ecclesiastical statue placed there, as a fitting impersonation of the church militant here on earth; his shovel hat, large, new, and well-pronounced, a churchman's hat in every inch, declared the profession as plainly as does the Quaker's broad brim; his heavy eyebrows, large open eyes, and full mouth and chin expressed the solidity of his order; the broad chest, amply covered with fine cloth, told how well to do was its estate; one hand ensconced within his pocket, evinced the practical hold which our mother church keeps on her temporal possessions; and the other, loose for action, was ready to fight if need be in her defence; and, below these, the decorous breeches, and neat black gaiters showing so admirably that well-turned leg, betokened the stability, the decency, the outward beauty and grace of our church establishment.

Here is a masterly evocation of the contrasting Quaker (anti-ecclesiastical and Gospel Christian), the worldly success, and belief in it manifested by fine linen and imposing head-gear, the coarse physique of the highly fed, and the typical attitude with the money-grasping hand and the other ready for pugnacity, as far as possible from turning the other cheek and giving up all to the poor. The last sentence brings us back to the ridiculous paradox of the archdiaconal statue of a Church militant and Church establishment. This is borne out by his address to the broken old paupers that follows, with its brutality that lacerates the Warden's soul, an effect the Archdeacon is incapable of sensing.

The next such highlight is the set-piece figuring the lawyer Sir Abraham Haphazard, who specializes in ecclesiastical subjects, and is supported by subordinate lawyers of the Church. They illustrate the legalistic attitude to religion. Our first sight of Sir Abraham is of a man

deeply engaged in preparing a bill for the mortification of papists, to be called the 'Convent Custody Bill' . . . and as there were to be a hundred and thirty-seven clauses in the bill, each clause constituting a separate thorn for the side of the papist, and as it was known the bill would be fought inch by inch, by fifty maddened Irishmen, the due construction and adequate dovetailing of it did consume much of Sir Abraham's time. The bill had all its desired effect. Of course it never passed into law.

Here Trollope is satirizing the Ecclesiastical Titles Bill that an outraged John Bull demanded should be passed in response to the 'Papal Aggression' of 1849, a bill that the Prime Minister knew to be undesirable and in fact useless except in placating public opinion. Sir Abraham makes a legalistic hedge round the proposed action against Hiram's Hospital trust. This delights the Archdeacon but further dismays Mr Harding. He absolutely insists on going up to London and interviewing the great lawyer personally in defiance of convention, the Archdeacon and his own worldly interests, in order to find out whether he can keep his wardenship without violating Hiram's will and his own conscience. Sir Abraham, however, can only tell him that he has possession and is legally able to retain it. Their dialogue and an analysis of the famous lawyer occupies chapter 17. Mr Jaggers, the criminal lawyer, did not appear till 1861, so as well as being a parallel study of the function of the lawyer and his morality, in Victorian society, it is independent. Though Sir Abraham is witty, successful and with a wife and children, his work had 'given him the appearance of a machine with a mind. His face was full of intellect, but devoid of natural expression.' He cannot understand Mr Harding's position and despises him for his scruples. Mr Harding had intended to abandon his defence, but finding from the lawyer that the lawsuit has been withdrawn (Eleanor Harding having worked a change of heart in her lover), Mr Harding announces to the disgust of Sir Abraham that he, doubting that the income from the hospital is justly his, has decided to give it up and starve on his precentorship, in peace of mind at least. The dramatic scene follows in which he has to make the Archdeacon aware of his decision – in a London hotel room, where Mrs Grantly persists in knitting till midnight in order to see that her father is not bullied by her husband, and where the Archdeacon consults his own face 'in a dingy mirror' on finding he cannot alter his father-in-law's resolution, that has been arrived at in long hours of introspection passed in the gloom of Westminster Abbey, where Mr Harding hides himself for the day to escape the Grantlys. A preliminary light on the Grantly ethos had been given in chapter 8, 'Plumstead Episcopi', where the fact that no money has been spared to achieve an apparently intended effect of heaviness and inelegance is discussed and carried on to show the oppressive richness of the breakfast viands, which somehow all bring to the visitor's mind that 'The fact that man shall not live by bread alone seemed to be somewhat forgotten'. In its quiet and yet deeply felt method, Trollope has made a weapon of attack upon the Victorian Church's ideas of righteous living, which for all its use of comedy and satire must have been found disquieting rather than entertaining. The publisher's reader who advised acceptance of *The Warden* did so on the grounds that it would have a public of 'all Low Churchmen and dissenters' – Mr Grantly's enemies of the Church whom Trollope was to satirize in his next novel, *Barchester Towers*. Michael Sadleir wrote in 1927: 'If tabloid evidence were needed of the immense influence of religious forms over the ordinary life of England in the early fifties, that evidence this report supplies.' One could fill this in, by pointing also to Trollope's feeling it necessary to write in gratuitous pieces of contemporary religious satire, as his representation of the three Grantly boys as recognizable Bishops of the day, the rhetorical chapter about the editor of the *Jupiter* (*The Times*) being the Pope of England, the satiric piece already cited about the Papal Aggression campaign, among others, and the reliance they show on the public's being able to take these religious references and enjoy them as natural in a novel of the day.

Trollope, following the example of *Joseph Andrews*, returns after the intrigues are over to his deeper insights, which are the novel's justification as literary art. Like Parson Adams, the Rev. Septimus Harding is the author's conception of the degree of true Christianity possible in an age that he understands well to be deterrent to Christian practice and the life of the spirit. Mr Harding has never blamed his enemy, knowing he also acted on a good impulse, and blesses his daughter's marriage to him now that the Radical doctor has ruined his income and driven him out of his beloved home. No one is the better for that; on the contrary, the old men have lost their friend and comforts, the beautiful gardens fall into wilderness, Mr Harding lives a diminished life in rooms over a shop in the High Street while he continues to sustain the cathedral music. The only cheering thought is that the Archdeacon has had a shock, but he, naturally, soon rallies. The role Mr Harding has been created to fill is activated wherever required through the rest of the Barsetshire sequence until he dies after the worst crisis in the Archdeacon's family and social and public life, in *The Last Chronicle of Barset*. Sadly unable to play the cello in his old age or raise his voice as precentor, he is at last too feeble to attend daily service in the adjacent cathedral, and as he is then deprived of all he lived for, he gladly dies, and Barchester has lost something valuable to its spiritual tradition. Behind him is a line through the Vicar of Wakefield and Parson Adams and those characters of humility, diffidence and trust in truth whom Bunyan preferred to the proud, great and self-confident, as embodiments of the religion he supported. Thus Trollope discovered his possibilities as a novelist of manners and social criticism by drawing on existing tradition and adapting it (patchily in *The Warden*, it is true, but his novel was experimental) for his own age's edification, by adding the attitudes to the religious events of his time and the contemporary techniques for presenting them critically, which were already available and generally understood.

Howard Sturgis:
Belchamber

Even Howard Sturgis, an American expatriate (probably the original of Ralph Touchett), writing in the Edwardian age (1904) and isolated to a considerable extent at the time by confinement as an invalid to an Anglo-American intellectual circle of visitors to his house at Windsor, a circle that included Henry James and Edith Wharton – even such an unlikely type for the purpose felt it necessary to account for the downfall of the aristocratic family and the future ruin forecast for their great house, Belchamber, by showing that it was the narrow Evangelicalism of their Victorian mother that was responsible for her crippled eldest son Sainty (who can't consummate his marriage) and the dissipated younger Arthur (whom she drives into marrying his mistress, a *passée poule-de-luxe* in the theatrical profession). In doing so Sturgis is perhaps taking over from literature and hearsay rather than personal experience a by then conventional anti-Evangelical case or stereotype; for, as we've seen, there were living testimonials then in High Life that an Evangelical upbringing could be admirable, as in the case of the Hamilton family where the Duke and Duchess of Abercorn, convinced and consistent Evangelicals, had successfully brought up their fourteen children with a horror of gambling, betting and irresponsibility generally but without unfitting them for a happy married life and a useful career. Sturgis takes over also from the Victorian novelists whom he had evidently studied (including especially Disraeli and Thackeray – *Belchamber* is a much more adult and artistically satisfying novel in the Thackeray tradition than Thackeray ever wrote himself and is witty in the manner of Disraeli) their assumption, so natural then, that English social life in the Victorian Age, including its hangover in the early twentieth century, was necessarily to be defined in its attitudes to nineteenth-century forms of religious theory. The Calvinistic Evangelicals are especially his target, but he is fair enough to note that as a reaction against the old Regency rakes and their wives (poor Sainty's grandfather, the previous Marquis, had ruined the estate and his heir's constitution, and both were salvaged temporarily by Sainty's Scotch mother) the Evangelical virtues were desirable though the narrowness that gave them their drive was liable, it is shown, to be self-frustrating in the long run. Sainty's mother Lady Charmington is the prime mover of the story. A dour, plain woman at twenty-seven, she has married the dissipated young heir to a historic house and title mainly because he awakens her missionary zeal, while he had fallen in line with her because she was 'the woman most unlike his mother he had ever met'. A few years later she is a widow with two little boys, a domineering woman with many problems on her hands that she tackles with complete assurance. Training her sons from infancy in the introspective process required by her religion, she is too successful in planting in the elder 'a morbid conscience', while driving the younger into deceit and rebellion, and by her inflexibility causes his social, moral, financial and physical ruin. The failure of the elder son's marriage – contrived by her as desirable, but which lands him with a depraved wife, whose child (his cousin's) he willy-nilly but with pangs of conscience accepts as his heir, dies in infancy – leaves the estate to be inherited by the spendthrift brother and his sons who 'take after' their mother's vulgar family. So the dishonour which originally caused the rise of the Chambers family and the financial ruin brought on it by typical successive heirs in the eighteenth and nineteenth centuries are both repeated in the new century in spite, or because of, the Evangelical interlude, and they are back where they were and would have been without her intervention. The plot is not merely neat, but convincingly and movingly tragic, for Sainty's mother meant well and Sainty does well but is trapped in his dilemma due to the depravity of his wife, cousin and brother and the self-righteousness of his mother.

The religious-sectarian attitudes and their consequences permeate the whole novel. The little boys' governess is the local Rector's daughter but though she is devoted to her

charges and her employer, Lady Charmington is uneasy
about her, as also the subsequent tutor, in case they have
High Church tendencies. The introduction to betting and in
due course a cast mistress of his cousin's, which set Arthur on
the road to ruin, and the seduction ultimately of Sainty's
wife, are the work of a deplorable cousin whom Lady
Charmington takes into her home and sends to Eton because
as her husband's nephew was brought up in France 'in an
atmosphere of papistry or atheism' – the two words meant
much the same to Lady Charmington – she is desirous of
'snatching a brand from the burning'. There is a scene of high
comedy when she has her sister-in-law to stay: she is scandalized by, among other signs of vice, that lady's reading of
French novels, since she herself 'read few novels in any
language; it does not seem to me very profitable. I was once
recommended Feuillet's *Histoire de Sybille* as quite unobjec-
tionable, but I found it very papistical', and she fears the
seductions of the Roman Church for both her nephew and his
mother. In due course Sainty, a studious lad, is sent by her to
Cambridge because of her 'curious lingering dread of
Puseyism' at Oxford, but there he meets the contemporary
Cambridge type of don, a Puseyite but a caricature of the
Broad Church position, who holds that because the old
creeds are 'outworn' there should be 'evolution in belief as in
other things; and he had dreams of a universal Church freed
from strangling dogmas, in which all sincere seekers after
truth should meet in a common brotherhood'; and he
encourages Sainty in his private rejection of conventional
Christian belief. At Sainty's coming-of-age house party at
Belchamber there is a great deal of trouble about the varying
religious practices of the guests:

At breakfast the question had arisen of which of the party would
attend the service at Great Charmington parish church . . . To Lord
Nonesuch, communion after breakfast was nothing short of sac-
rilege; he was a leading light in the High Church party, and this was
his first appearance at Belchamber since a memorable occasion
many years before, when he had said Lady Charmington was an
Erastian, and she had called him a Jesuit . . . The Dalsanies were
Roman Catholics . . . His [Lord Firth's] religion was of that comfortable, rational kind in which there is more state than church, and
which is first cousin to agnosticism, but infinitely more respect-

able. He took a great interest in the distribution of bishoprics and the proper conduct of the service, which, however, he rarely felt called on to attend, except in such cathedrals and college chapels as gratified his fastidious taste and fondness for sacred music.

From *Belchamber*, as from *Barchester Towers* or *Lothair* or *The Perpetual Curate* or *Helbeck of Bannisdale* or *Middlemarch* or *The Way of All Flesh* or *Villette*, a non-English reader could get a fair idea of the religious situation at each phase of Victorian England. In fact, no major novel or serious novelist then could afford to ignore the subject or even manage to avoid dealing with it, so fundamentally decisive were the attitudes set up in anyone then by his or her religious beliefs – or refusal to hold them, or loss of them.

After Sainty's marriage Lady Charmington goes up to London to stay with the newly-weds, in order to attend the Ladies' No Popery League, and there in crude scriptural terms denounces the sinful extravagance of the household and the loose conduct and appearance of her daughter-in-law. So the religious theme runs through the plot and indeed determines it. One of the less conventional strands in it is the appearance of a rich Jewish family, originally Isaacs but now de Lissac, of which, after the wife's death, the head allows himself and his daughters to be converted to please his second wife, the kind governess passed on to them by Lady Charmington. This is not only inspired by Trollope's *The Way We Live Now* (where there is a superior example of the Jewish financier, to offset the villainous one, no doubt, though grudgingly) and *Daniel Deronda*, but seems to be original and the fruit of observation or real-life report. It becomes part of the comedy of the book:

she was the means of leading a whole family after her into the fold, and it may be imagined the excitement she was to Lady Charmington under the circumstances. Mr de Lissac had not been a very fervent Jew, and he made a most unenthusiastic Christian; but he was nominally converted. Instead of not attending the synagogue, he now stayed away from church . . . Personally, his interest was in his work; he did not like the great people who had eaten his food and been rude to him. After a hard day in the city, he wanted his carpet slippers, a big strong cigar, and a volume of Schiller by the fire, or perhaps a sonata by Mozart or Beethoven.

He is almost the only genuinely cultivated person in the novel besides Sainty, so as well as the overt comic angle on Evangelical fervour for conversion his case provides, he registers a social change in the later Victorian era – the entrance into a Philistine society of the rich, cultivated Jewish businessman or financier, considered as a menace to conservative values by Trollope and his compatriots but seen by a French critic of English society in this age of the Prince of Wales and Edward VII as the beneficent means of intro- ducing aerating ideas, liveliness of mind, wit, social mobility and a genuine interest in the arts – music, painting, drama and intellectual literature. And at the end of the book we have the guileless de Lissacs involved in the disasters of the Chambers family, since the vicious cousin is about to marry Mr de Lissac's daughter for her money and go into parlia- ment through her father's influence, with consequences we may safely forecast. This engagement has also served the sinister Claude to free him from his now burdensome intrigue with Sainty's wife, who had been planning to leave her husband for Claude after the child's death, so Sainty is tied forever to her, her extravagance, her hatred and her scandalous goings-on which poison his home and his desire to lead a useful life. The novel is a legitimate – that is, inevitable, in the circumstances – tragedy, but the prime mover, Lady Charmington, is the mainspring of the action, just as religious differences are the cause of the tragedies of *Villette*, *Helbeck* and *A Simple Story* and *The Nowlans* (by Banim) and, less explicitly, of Gerald Griffin's *Tracy's Ambition*.

Literary values and the novel

In undertaking to talk to you about 'Literary Values and the Novel' I assumed that you had taken some thought on the subject already, since you are studying several major novelists and must have sampled many more. And as you are pretty sure to go on reading novels all your lives, the subject is likely to remain a concern with you. It also passed across my mind that it is the kind of subject useful to have to draw upon for Oxbridge entrance essays. I aim merely to help your own thinking by offering assistance in clearing up the area and providing some ammunition for you to make use of on your own and for me to use in demolishing some wrong attitudes to the novel. None of you is likely unthinkingly to hold fallacies such as that a purely 'aesthetic' approach to literature can be maintained. None of you is likely to be as unsophisticated about Art (with a capital 'A') as Tennyson, for instance, to whom a friend felt obliged to protest: 'but, Alfred, you can't *live* in a world of art' (or words to that effect). Even Cambridge graduates seem to have been rather innocent in those days, and it needed this, one would have thought self-evident, proposition to rouse Tennyson into realizing the dangers of his attitude to literature; and produced eventually his very diagnosable poem 'The Palace of Art', where he arrives at the conclusion that the aesthete is inevitably a *diseased* soul, and again in *The Lady of Shalott*, where for once an involvement in the real life of feeling destroys the artist in the ivory tower. And even Oscar Wilde, in his revealing novel *The Picture of Dorian Gray* leads us to the same conclusion, a surprisingly moral one, but borne out by his own case-history and those of the nineties artists in general, many of whom ended disastrously. The hero Dorian Gray, by shutting out the real world and making living an art, is not merely

self-indulgent: by rejecting human sympathies and responsibilities he becomes in the long run steeped in vice and
murder, and driven to suicide, though till his death he has
been able to preserve his delusion of moral nihilism and
social self-sufficiency by transferring the marks of experience
incurred in such a life as he leads to his portrait. But though
he locks away the portrait he cannot at last bear the humiliation its existence causes him, and by destroying it he completes the self-destruction his life has been. The parable and
symbolism are self-explanatory and give the novel its only
value. In it Wilde confessed his own dilemma and foresaw his
own fate.

But that this fallacy did not die with the nineties is a point
I think worth making. All admirers of Yeats will have seen in
the sequence of his poems, as well as in his prose autobiographies, how difficult he found it, bogged down from
youth in the aesthetic society of the nineties and Pre-
Raphaelite assumptions about what poetry is, to escape into
the real world – to 'endure', as he says, 'the timid sun', and to
cure himself of the idea that technical perfection is an end in
itself – for 'The fascination of what's difficult', he wrote, 'Has
dried the sap out of my veins and rent / Spontaneous joy and
natural content / Out of my heart.' And he had to devote himself painfully to discovering the function of the poet, the
relation of the poet to society; how, in the absence of a public
of ideal readers, to believe in writing poetry at all, and what
are the responsibilities of the creative artist. It is by doing so
that he became a great poet instead of remaining the artificer
of beautiful Pre-Raphaelite verses and Platonic love-poems.

But in our own age – or rather mine – the fallacy that the
creative artist can escape the responsibilities of life and
justify his solipsism by living the life of art in a moral void or
ivory tower of aesthetic self-indulgence has been repeated in
the world of Bloomsbury. I expect you have seen the reviews
– I hope you haven't wasted your time by reading the actual
books – of the recent biographical industry devoted to such
types of that age as Lytton Strachey, Virginia Woolf, Aldous
Huxley, Harold Nicolson, Vita Sackville-West, Bertrand
Russell, Lady Ottoline Morell, and so on, or such of their
journals, correspondence and autobiographies as have been
published by their relatives and executors milking the mar-

ket for scandal. The only thing of interest about these people
is how the climate Bloomsbury created destroyed talent and
made it necessary for a serious writer, an invulnerable genius
like D. H. Lawrence, to expend so much energy in exposing,
arguing with and resisting them. Another novelist who did so
successfully, though born into this world of privilege and
wealth, was L. H. Myers; though himself belonging to that
class by birth and education, he very creditably rejected it. I
want to quote him at some length in order to establish what
I believe to be the only tenable and profitable position for the
novelist and critic.

Myers despised and loathed Bloomsbury and his novels
are nearly all examinations of it indirectly. His main work, a
trilogy of novels published in one volume under the title *The
Root and the Flower*, has a most valuable preface. Writing just
forty years ago he stated in it his own profoundest belief as
a novelist. He starts by saying that his word is 'philosophic',
but 'only in the sense in which Molière's M. Jourdain talked
prose', for, says he,

There are few human beings who, when they think of themselves in
relation to the universe, are without a sense of curiosity, of wonder,
and even of awe; and in so far as this leads them into speculation,
they become philosophers . . . Overlook those needs, forget those
questions, and you are likely to become satisfied with art that is
petty, reasoning that is pedantic, and knowledge that is not bread
but a stone . . . When a novelist displays an attitude of aesthetic
detachment from the ordinary ethical and philosophical preoccupations of humanity, something in us protests – we charge him with
a kind of inverted cant, or of artistic snobbery. Proust, for instance,
by treating all sorts of sensibility as equal in importance, and all
manifestations of character as standing on the same plane of significance, adds nothing to his achievement, but only draws attention to himself as aiming at the exaltation of a rather petty form of
aestheticism.

For my part, I believe that a man serves himself better by showing
a respect for such moral taste as he may possess . . . While a great
deal is made of aesthetic sensibility and its refinements, we hear
very little about moral sensibility. It is ignored; and the deep-
seated spiritual vulgarity that lies at the heart of our civilization
commonly passes without notice. The arts have their connoisseurs,
but what of connoisseurs in character?

Myers's protest against the then prevailing climate of practice and opinion is made explicitly here, as implicitly in the novels that follow, against what he felt to be a menace to society in that it was a denial of integrity in life and was the enemy of serious art. And of course he was quite right in claiming that aestheticism is as art petty – it therefore becomes, as in Proust, boring – and that the subject-matter for the novelist is living and its problems. All the novelists whose works remain of interest agree on this, as their practice shows. Even Henry James, who is often claimed to exemplify the perfection of the pure aesthete in novel composition, and who spent so much of his prefaces in explaining the 'doing' of his novels (he wrote them long after the novels in his old age); even George Eliot, a tremendous intellectual and high-brow, who thought and wrote a good deal about the art of the novelist; even Jane Austen, a highly skilled practitioner whose 'art' is so much admired that readers have been diverted by it from seeing what her novels are about; and even Conrad, who most certainly believed in the art of the novel – can all be seen to agree with Myers. They all exemplify the argument that a great novelist is one who has an impelling theme, arising originally inside himself, spring-ing from his own deepest experience and the pressures of his own life; and though starting from his own experience not limited to picturing it but extending to embrace the quality and nature of life in his time, the life characteristic of his time, in which concern for the individual is inseparable from concern for humanity. What Arnold wrote of poetry applies even more literally to the novel, that it is inevitably a criti-cism of life. Hence the justice of L. H. Myers's demand that the novelist must be 'a connoisseur of character'. The novelist's driving force is his concern for society and humanity, but his means is his sensitiveness to and ability to compare and criticize individuals. When we think of great practitioners of the art of the novel like Jane Austen, Tolstoy, Dickens or George Eliot, we think of them as connoisseurs of character – they create characters to express value-judgements of life.

While the novelist starts with his own experience and with examining its nature, this can't remain merely personal if it is to produce a major novel. Pieces of purely personal experi-ence like Constant's famous *conte Adolphe*, Tolstoy's tale 'The

Kreutzer Sonata' and 'Family Happiness' and Kafka's tales and novels for instance, are confessions, reliefs to their writers as to their unassimilated and to them incomprehensible sufferings from life. Such works – significantly they are always *contes* – are short and formless, or like Kafka's novels unfinished because unfinishable, or like *The Story of an African Farm* which falls away into incoherence – are very limited in their literary value even, because they are *not* impersonal. They have little value except as illustrations of a helpless predicament, or to act as an awful warning: characteristically *they* arouse the response that Professor Quiller-Couch described to my husband as his reaction to Meredith's sonnet-sequence, *Modern Love*, which tells the story of Meredith's own unhappy marriage: 'Yes, yes', said Q, 'I'm awfully sorry for the poor chap – but oh, where did I leave my hat?' One only wants to get away and never hear any more of their harrowing story. This is not the effect of works of art. We feel, I think, that here was the raw material but from lack of wisdom, the ability of a mature artist to distance and evolve his material, his experience of life, and see it in perspective, it remains only of interest to the professional psychologist. Whereas a novel like Conrad's *Victory*, which embodies the tragedy of one Axel Heist, a sensitive and unhappy man who has been emotionally starved and cut off from life, from wholesome immersion in social life and from the comforts of human contacts, owing to the philosophic position inculcated by his father who indoctrinated him in youth on principle with 'an infernal mistrust of life' – this novel is a great deal more than a mere case-history. Axel Heist is not Conrad but Conrad had in common with him the experience of social isolation (as a Pole living in England), and Heist's tragedy might have been his own, which indeed in a phase of evident despair Conrad very feelingly symbolized in one of his finest tales, 'Amy Foster'. The immense pains the *novelist* Conrad took to embody Heist's history, in a setting and a series of dramatic actions that engage our interest and move our sympathies, are an aesthetic activity, but the outcome of the book is that the crisis inevitably evokes a moral and spiritual conclusion, though Heist can only escape from the disaster of his life by suicide, since he has lost everything that he had at last found made life worth living. Our admiration for the doing, the aesthetic form, of the novel is submerged, though the form was necessary to achieve the effect. The conclusion is paradoxically achieved by Heist's declaration after all he has recently learned of the possibilities of life has been snatched from him. Though he then kills himself, it is an affirmation to give us hope, for he declares: 'Woe to the man whose heart has not learned while young to hope, to love – and to put its trust in life!' I'll draw your attention to Martin Zabel's intelligent introduction to the Portable Conrad (a substantial selection of Conrad's work published by the Viking Press well worth owning), where Zabel wrote:

Though early enlised by his first literary friends in the search for 'form' and the *mot juste*, Conrad had an extreme aversion to the specialized theories that were encouraging the novel of arbitrary limits and schematized content. He considered aestheticism as much 'a treacherous ideal' as James did.

The term 'treacherous ideal' applied to aestheticism is James's.

Conrad wrote: 'Art itself may be defined as a single-minded attempt to render the highest kind of justice to the visible universe.' Far from thinking of the artist (the general term covering the novelist in the late nineteenth century) as an aesthetic practitioner, he likens him to the thinker (that is, philosopher) and the scientist, in his search for what he calls the truth of existence. But, he says, unlike the thinker and scientist, who speak to our commonsense and our intelligence, the one through ideas and the other through facts, the artist, in contrast, 'descends within *himself* and in that lonely region of stress and strife he finds the terms of his appeal'. In a letter written when he was over fifty he wrote: 'I have always approached my task in a spirit of love for mankind.' We may remember Lawrence's declaration: 'I write for the race.' Both express the major novelist's sense of the responsibility of the artist. Their art is not frivolous or petty. And George Eliot's various sayings about her practice as a novelist are in striking consonance. She wrote at various times in her letters and journals: 'If art does not enlarge men's sympathies, it does nothing morally', and again, paralleling Conrad's comparison between the philosopher, the scientist and the creative artist she wrote remonstrating with a friend:

Consider what the human mind *en masse* would have been if there had been no such combination of elements in it as has produced poets. All the philosophers and *savants* would not have sufficed to supply that deficiency. And how can the life of nations be understood without the inward life of poetry – that is, of emotion blending with thought?

She habitually wrote and thought of the novelist as a variety of poet, as indeed did Charlotte Brontë. These novelists support the position which I had better formally declare as my own, that there are no such things as 'literary values'; the values of great literature, I believe, can only be those of life itself, and the term 'aesthetics', whatever use it may be to the connoisseur of sculpture and painting, is only misleading, and can have no function for the literary critic.

George Eliot, whom many – even Henry James – have thought and written of as an excessively intellectual novelist, in fact gives us the clearest evidence of what I have described as the essential condition of true literary creation, that the work must be rooted in the novelist's experience, not written deliberately about an outside subject arbitrarily chosen for treatment (the cause of the failure of the Naturalist School in fiction both in France and in England). And yet so rooted, it must achieve impersonality – so that, as Conrad wrote to an admirer, stressing the impersonality of the true work of art (also showing the tone of the artist's humility): 'I feel grateful to you for the recognition of the *work*, not the *man*. Once the last page is written the man does not count. He is nowhere.' George Eliot at different times wrote of how her novels came into being in these terms: 'My stories *grow* in me like plants, and this [she was writing *The Mill on the Floss*] is only in the leaf-bud. I have faith that *the flower* will come.' And of *Silas Marner*: 'It is a story of old-fashioned village life, which has unfolded itself from the merest millet-seed of thought.'

Later still she wrote: 'My books are deeply serious things to me, and come out of all the painful disciplines, like the most hardly learnt lessons of my past life.' And finally:

The difficulties . . . press upon me, who have gone through again and again the severe effort of trying to make certain ideas thoroughly incarnate, as if they had revealed themselves to me first in the flesh and not in the spirit. I think aesthetic teaching is the highest of all teaching, because it deals with life in its highest complexity. When a subject has begun to grow in me, I suffer terribly until it has *wrought itself* out – become a complete organism; and then it seems to take wing and go away from me. *That* thing is not to be done again – that life has been lived.

You see, she always insists on the organic nature of artistic creation. It is not willed, like Flaubert's and Zola's and Arnold Bennett's and Galsworthy's. All the metaphors she instinctively uses to describe the process of composing a novel are those of natural growth in which the artist is the soil and nourishes the work of art out of his own past and present life. Even Jane Austen, whom one thinks of as a vastly different kind of creative artist, wrote of her first novel to her sister, when *Sense and Sensibility* was in the press: 'I can no more forget it, than a mother can her suckling child' – a simile that may strike us as surprising in a genteel spinster, but then spinsters, of whatever class, were not then cut off from life in the least. The novelist has to discover (by trial and error and instinctive tact), in fact evolve, that form which can alone embody the experience of life that each particular novel consequently is. Moreover, she makes the point that each true work of art is unique – '*That* thing is not to be done again' – and therefore requires its own form, as distinct from the repetitiveness of the little fiction writer, who in effect writes the same book over and over again, to a formula – as you can see in the case of Iris Murdoch, for instance. This is what Lawrence meant when he defended himself against Arnold Bennett's complaint of his changing the rules of construction.

Tell Arnold Bennett that all rules of construction hold good only for novels which are copies of other novels. A book which is not a copy of other books has its own construction, and what he calls faults, he being an old imitator, I call characteristics.

Look at the case-history of George Eliot's novel *Middlemarch*, which has been with justice considered the greatest novel in the English language and which fertilized Henry James, as you can see from his *Portrait of a Lady* and other works. She had great difficulty in writing it, though she had kept for years a notebook which she called 'Quarry for

Middlemarch'. Here she had jotted down in preparation for the actual writing suitable material and characters to exemplify her idea of exhibiting the provincial culture of a countryside centred on a manufacturing town, Middlemarch, in the early nineteenth century. But it proved fruitless – it was too mechanical a way of going to work, like Zola's. Then she left it to start writing something else which, she said, 'is a subject which has been recorded among my possible themes ever since I began to write fiction, but will probably take new shapes in the development'. This story she had always thought of as 'Miss Brooke'. Miss Brooke (Dorothea Brooke) was *herself* in her girlish Evangelical days – as she now, an emancipated woman, saw herself, her early self, with a mixture of pity and amusement – a girl Puritanical by upbringing and education, afraid of love and art, attempting to arrange her life on high-minded but impracticable principles that led her into constant pitfalls and ultimately a disastrous marriage, a subject very much inside George Eliot as to essentials (though she adapted some of the details and the marriage from a friend's history). But now, thanks to the passage of time, she was capable of projecting the subject outside herself for dispassionate examination in the light of her maturity and achieved wisdom, and instead, by being personal, it became a case-history of the English disease of the Puritanical anaemia of feeling and the self-deceiving high-mindedness of Evangelicalism. 'Miss Brooke' became the first section of the novel *Middlemarch* and the subject central to the fiction about Middlemarch, the country town now rooted in the individual's experience. George Eliot thus had a truly representative subject with which she herself was involved by sympathy and experience. She could in it deal with some of her deepest concerns, problems of living and of the necessity to reconcile ideals with practice (this problem is shown as that of all the leading characters – Bulstrode, Lydgate and Ladislaw as well as Dorothea). We can understand why George Eliot said of her creative writing that 'It gives value to my life', and wrote of 'the high responsibilities of literature that undertakes to represent life' and that 'My books are written out of my deepest belief as well as I can, for the great public.'

The origin of *Silas Marner* is even more interesting than that of *Middlemarch*. George Eliot had long been trying to write *Romola*, an uninspired story set in the Italian Renaissance requiring learning and immense research, which could only result, as it did, in a plodding, pedantic historical novel. Compiling the material for it depressed her, and no wonder. Suddenly she was impelled to abandon *Romola* and write a wholly different novel which, she wrote in her journal, 'has *thrust* itself between me and the other book I was meditating', 'a story [she wrote to her publisher later] which came *across* my other plans by a sudden inspiration'. Clearly, unlike *Romola*, a contrived work of purely intellectual origin which she subconsciously felt to be futile, *Silas Marner* demanded to be written. It forced itself on her because it provided a framework within which she could consider the problems that pressed on her, problems that her life up till now had presented her with and that she had had to solve or manage to deal with, problems more than personal since they were typical of her time. So *Marner* was a creative work of necessity, and it is of course highly concentrated; it was written straight off with hardly a correction; yet its appearance of simplicity is deceptive, for there are layers and layers of meaning in it, and it makes use of all the resources of art.

I can now advance for your consideration several propositions. The first is, that if the novel comes only direct from the raw material of a novelist's own life it is unsatisfactory because it isn't enough of a work of art, that is, it has no real form, no objectivity, no general application, and cannot offer value-judgements. In fact it isn't a novel, only a piece of autobiography like John Stuart Mill's. Dickens started to write his autobiography at one point to purge himself of his youthful sufferings, the meaning of which tormented him so, but he dropped it, preferring, being a true creative artist, to merge his own experience into the typical case-history of David Copperfield, and he wrote the novel instead. If on the other hand the novel is wholly outside the author it remains a sterile exercise, however much material has been amassed for it or however much 'art' and agony of searching for the *mot juste* the writer has put into its composition. The novel must be about and contain felt *life*, and, as George Eliot said, 'life in all its highest complexity'. If we are to take the novel seriously, if it's to be of lasting value, it must be neither a day-dream (like a bestseller), nor an aesthetic diagram, nor an argument with a *parti-pris* and only minimally flashed over, like *Jude the Obscure* (which is an unacceptable because fallacious argument, at that). And we can now see why we often find a comparatively artless novel, perhaps the novelist's very first or even only novel, or the early novel of a hardened professional novelist, more valuable than later, more ambitious and more accomplished fictions by the same writer.

Somerset Maugham often complained, feeling it as a slight to his status as a professional writer, that people were always saying that his first novel, *Of Human Bondage*, was so much better than anything he wrote afterwards, whereas *he* could see it was raw and faulty, while his later novels were works of art and why couldn't people see that? But one sees what these people meant – *Of Human Bondage* is more like a novel than any of the hard-bitten professional pieces of fiction, whether long or short, that Maugham contrived subsequently (even its suggestive title sets it apart). It has life in it (his own painful youth) and doesn't merely leave a nasty taste in the reader's mouth like his writings, formed in imitation of Maupassant and his school of cynical denigration of life. The preference for an early artless novel over a later artful or arty work by the same author is not therefore unreasonable. Arnold Bennett's first sustained novel, *Anna of the Five Towns*, in spite of flaws of composition anyone can easily spot, is the best thing he ever did, much more impressive and profound than the over-praised massive, ambitious *Old Wives' Tale*, which was motivated by his ambition to go one better than Maupassant's *Une Vie*.

Another pair you could well read together for this purpose is Mrs Gaskell's first novel *Mary Barton* and her later novel on exactly the same subject and material, *North and South*; but George Eliot's *Adam Bede* bears the same relation to her later grander and more sophisticated (in every sense) fictional works and in her own age it was generally considered her best, as well as being her most popular novel. After a successful career as translator, editor, intellectual journalist and literary critic George Eliot took to fiction not as a profession, or merely to make money, but to recapture the experience of her childhood in the rural Midlands and express her sense of its values. In the smoke and crowded streets and anonymous populace of Victorian London she yearned for the meaningful life of the countryside, the village community, the farmhouse and the cottage with the rectory and the Great House overall, the satisfying world she had been happy in before the Victorian era, and had heard tell of in its more primitive eighteenth-century form by her parents and relatives when she was a little child, something with an imaginative hold on her that she could find no substitute for in her intellectual society in London. So she wrote as an experiment first the tales, *Scenes of Clerical Life*, and then, with encouragement from her husband, she tried her hand at a novel. It is this recreation of meaningful felt life, and not her intellectual attainments, that gave *Adam Bede*, *Silas Marner* and *Middlemarch* their unique character and value. But there is very little 'art of the novel' in *Adam Bede*. It has only an emotional and nostalgic unity; in form it is nearly as incoherent and artless as *Mary Barton* and both are held together only by the class theme of seduction. George Eliot so much admired *Mary Barton* that I believe it helped 'precipitate' and shape *Adam Bede*, for George Eliot actually wrote to Mrs Gaskell, 'when I was writing *Adam Bede* I read over and over again those earlier chapters of *Mary Barton*'. Now the form of both these novels is a peculiarly feminine one. It is an organization that comes naturally to women, allowing the greatest scope for the kind of concern with life a woman has as distinct from a man. (Dickens had no difficulty in deciding that this work by an unknown writer with a man's name was by a woman.) And *Mary Barton* at once achieved European fame, especially in Russia where I believe it is still a current classic (though no doubt for the wrong reasons). A very artless work technically, its force and interest lie in its sincere recreation of the contemporary life of Manchester, a society of bitterly opposed starving millhands, and callous millowners, as Mrs Gaskell saw it, she being a gently bred country lady and by marriage to a Unitarian minister in Manchester experiencing as a bride the early industrial scene for the first time. She had never thought to write about it though till her husband launched her on the novel as a cure for her grief at the loss of her only boy. He saw that writing about the sufferings of others would distract her from her own, and the consequent novel, obviously the work of a novice, loosely constructed, with melodramatic effects, an implausible death-bed confession and forgiveness, a stock plot and so on moves the reader because of its emotional unity and the virtue of its compassionate insight into the nature of working-class life then. Later, in response to criticism from the millowners, she rethought the subject and treated it dispassionately and fairly, handling the theme in a rational way and carefully laying out the novel (*North and South*) methodically and with considerable technical ability, for Mrs Gaskell had now some experience as a novelist. But just as the value of *Mary Barton* is independent of its technical ('aesthetic') faults, so the later novel, with its temperate action and scrupulous fairness, that conditioned the balanced argument and exacted a schematic structure, is not therefore a greater novel, though still an interesting one.

But though *Adam Bede* and *Mary Barton* are specifically feminine novels and emanate strong personal and womanly feeling, they are not egocentric but *selfless* – the author intrudes on the reader no more than in a novel of Jane Austen's, because, like Jane Austen's novels, they too contain within themselves the values by which we are to judge the actors and action, without the novelist *telling* us in her own person and voice what we are to think. Painful as such novels as *Mary Barton* and *Adam Bede* are, in their various ways, they don't leave us depressed, as *Jude the Obscure*, for instance, does, because their effect, as that of Jane Austen's work, is to alert us to the nature of life and brace us to cope with it, not to oblige us to despair.

Another instance of the origin of a novelist's creativity is to be found in Edith Wharton's autobiography and prefaces. The daughter of the best-dressed lady in New York of the time, she was married off very young to a society man interested in nothing but sport and amusement. Being a naturally serious girl and a great reader, an admirer of Henry James, she soon found herself deeply dissatisfied and gradually realized that the reason lay in the nature of the society – the closed society of wealthy New York and New England that she was reared in. She took to writing to express her feelings about it, but it is significant that she did not write the easy satire, the *roman-à-clef*, of the Aldous Huxley or Bloomsbury school, with its self-protective irony. Her first successful novel, *The House of Mirth*, is a really mature, witty but responsible analysis of the destructive force of that society, which gave her a tragic theme. She thought at first that the triviality of this society made it unusable, but she saw, as she wrote, that 'such groups always rest on an underpinning of wasted human possibilities, and it seemed to me that the fate of the persons embodying *these possibilities* ought to redeem my subject from insignificance'. In an Introduction written a generation later, to the World's Classics reprint of this novel she says: 'When there is anything whatever below the surface in the novelist's art, that something can be only the social function on which the fable is built.' She was, instinctively, not content to be autobiographical or to be personal at all, in her novels – you notice she speaks of a *fable* – and she reached down and about for the sources that would account for her dissatisfactions with her world and thus to understand them, and enable others, not gifted with a novelist's insight, to understand and cope with theirs too. She wrote a line of such novels, and very valuable they are, as well as very good reading, with their wit and irony in the Austen tradition.

In Edith Wharton's and Henry James's time (they were close friends), as before in America right back to Hawthorne's work – and that began very early in the nineteenth century indeed – there had always been major American novelists. Poetry and painting did not notably come out of America in the nineteenth and early twentieth century, but the United States had a flourishing and valuable tradition of the novel of its own then. Yet by the middle of the twentieth century we find Randall Jarrell, in his important novel *Pictures from an Institution*, taking as his subject the failure of America now to produce creative art, and choosing to embody the failure in a typical American practitioner of the novels and a woman at that. Gertrude Johnson, of course, teaches Creative Writing in an American university – one of Jarrell's points is that the United States, vast and rich as it is, can't provide a public to support a creative artist; the creative artists have to teach art, music, poetry or fiction-writing in a university to make a living. That there is no educated public in America – no public that respects the creative mind and talent – is part of his case. European countries so much smaller in population and so much poorer have always produced artists richly, spontaneously and without taking thought and recognized them. What, he asks, is the matter with America that it doesn't and can't? He asked in despair, being a creative mind himself, and suffering from intolerable isolation in America far worse than Conrad's, who, as a mere alien in England, had plenty of congenial literary society and the respect and admiration of his peers. Jarrell sees that the failure has two aspects, which his novel illustrates very wittily and convincingly. One is the American theory of education and its commercially orientated society, with the nature of that society and social life thus engendered, and its consequent incomprehending attitude to the arts and artists; the other is that talent in such a world is perverted, made not creative but self-destructive. The talent has been fostered by love, sympathy, tenderness. The kind of man of letters it produces, he shows, is the stupid self-promoter, Mr Daudier; the university, which should have a healthfully critical effect on society, has abrogated its function in America, is represented by its president 'who was so well adjusted to his environment that sometimes you could not tell which was the environment and which was President Rollins'; literature is considered and taught as a therapeutic activity for the students by the last representative of the genteel tradition, Miss Butterson, who does not know what it is for or about, and so on – all placed for us by being seen through the eyes of a sophisticated European couple, professional musicians there resident. But the main case centres on Gertrude Johnson, so intellectual and well-informed, so articulate and witty, as a practised novelist, so confident, and so barren. As an Irishman says of her novels (of which there are seven to date) they are 'a Barmecide feast given by a fireworks company'. This accurately describes a whole line of novels since Aldous Huxley burst on the world with *Chrome Yellow*, and a line of biographies too since Lytton Strachey invented the modern substitute for biography with his *Eminent Victorians* – a school of biography which had undoubtedly influenced that school of novelists. The Lytton Strachey kind of biography hates its subject and has no respect for it (a recent example is John Carey's book on Dickens), it is motivated by animus and the desire to assert the critic's superiority by denigrating his subject. These are the qualities and attitudes Jarrell diagnoses in the typical modern American novelist – we all know that Gertrude Johnson is typical without dredging up actual names (and they need not be only female ones). And Jarrell truly saw that when a nation makes *this* of its literary talent, ruins and perverts its artists – which is even worse than starving them, for their works survived for posterity – there is no hope for it. Once upon a time a spoiled genius like Swift's was a rare case that could be accounted for by a disastrous personal history. But the Gertrude Johnsons *all* write with Swift's maniacal conceit and contempt for mankind, and morbid disgust with life, a turning of life against itself. Gertrude's books were not really novels at all; Jarrell sees her technical expertise is to the fore with nothing live behind it – 'The books were crushed down into method: as I read I was so conscious of what was being done that I scarcely noticed or cared what it was being done to.' We have all experienced this, I imagine, at some time in our novel-reading and it aligns this modern type of novelist with the aesthetic devotee of the nineties and the Edwardian Age. Her impulse in writing was 'to mock, lament and execrate – to condemn utterly' and to do this she got up all the necessary facts, and more. But she did not know, or care, how people *felt*, which is the novelist's true concern, and Jarrell says this fault 'was more radical than all the rest' in a writer.

'Gertrude pointed at the world and said "You see, you see!" But as you looked along that stretched shaking finger you didn't *see*, you *saw through*.' And Jarrell goes on to tell of her admiration for Swift. Like him 'she saw the worst: it was indeed her only principle of explanation. Consequently she seemed to most people a writer of extraordinary penetration – she appealed to the original La Rochefoucauld in everybody'. She had a style, says Jarrell, in which you could not tell the truth if you tried.

'So', Jarrell continues,

because of all this – of all this, and so much more – even the best of Gertrude's books were habitat groups in a Museum of Natural History: topography, correct; meteorological information, correct; condition of skins, good; mounting of horns, correct . . . Inside there were old newspapers, papiermâché, clockwork. And yet, *mirabile dictu!* the animals moved, a little stiffly, and gave the calls of their species, a little thinly – was it not a world?

It was a fairly popular world, even. Gertrude's readers did not understand things, and were injured by them; now for a few hours they injured and understood – and understanding was somehow the most satisfactory injury of all. They did for a while all that fear and pity and ordinary human feeling kept them from doing ordinarily, and they were grateful for it: if Gertrude had had sweep and sex (her method was microscopic, her sex statistical) she might have been considered a Great American Novelist. As it was, she was always called 'the most brilliant of our younger novelists'. *Brilliant!* People had called Gertrude brilliant before she could talk; she had been called brilliant so much that, five seconds after you said it, she couldn't remember whether you had said that or hello. It seemed to Gertrude that she had been writing for several centuries: weren't people *ever* going to stop calling her a younger novelist? But enough raw woman survived in her for her to be pleased in spite of herself with the word *younger*.

We recognize the novel of Aldous Huxley, C. P. Snow, Iris Murdoch, Mary McCarthy – the typical 'modern novelist'.

Another defect attributed to Gertrude Johnson is that though she'd had three husbands she had no children, she disliked children, she couldn't talk to them and they made her feel depressed. Our author says 'she had not had as much childhood as most people, and could remember almost none of what she had had'. This is a defect characteristic of all such anti-novelists. Think of what use to novelists the child and their own childhood has been. It is essential for a true novelist to remember what it was like to be a child, the stage when feelings are most passionate and unartificial and experience most intensely registered, when judgement is spontaneous: even childless women novelists like Jane Austen, George Eliot and Virginia Woolf have managed this. Even an outstandingly intellectual woman like George Eliot shows that she had kept taproots into her early life and understood its importance. Even Jane Austen, in general so critically aloof from her personae, shows in Fanny Price's childhood that she can recapture the child's sufferings and bewilderment in the alien adult world and, like Dickens, through a child's innocence and instinctively right values conveys a criticism of the adult society. The novel of Virginia

Woolf's most likely to last is *To the Lighthouse*, a recreation of her own childhood in order to examine the Victorian family in its relationships of mother and child, father and child, man and wife, and thereby the society that fixed these characters, a piece of psychological insight and an imaginative achievement through which the Leslie Stephen family becomes representative.

Gertrude Johnson's novels on the other hand were purely *rational* and her sentences were like a series of philosophic propositions, and, you may remember, she thought poets are only makers of stone axes – why make them *now*? The organic form comes (or did come) naturally to women, it allowed most scope for the kind of concern with life women have (or should have, if the human race is to continue). Only novelists can make us feel what the historians and sociologists notably fail to do, what it was like to live then and there.

'Yet', Jarrell says, 'underneath everything there must have been in Gertrude some uneasiness about her books. Her life looked chilly in the mirror that it held up to itself, and saw that it was full of quotations, of data and analysis and epigrams, of naked and shameful truths, of *facts*: it saw that it was a novel by Gertrude Johnson.' Of course a valid novel can't be made of such material, it leaves out life.

But there is one distinction between life and art that we are likely to have assumed without question. I can explain it most easily by an anecdote. When my eldest child reached the age when I thought he could appreciate Jane Austen I launched him on *Pride and Prejudice* (with some difficulty as it was by a woman and about *girls*) and he enjoyed it so much that I then moved him on to *Emma*. But he soon gave it up. He saw he could not bear Mr Woodhouse, Emma's selfish valetudinarian father. I suggested that there was this difference between life and art, that whereas in real life we might feel murderous towards Mr Woodhouse, in a novel, it being a work of art, we can enjoy him. My son replied: 'It may be a work of art, but I *still* want to smother him.'

On reflection, I think my son was right, in the sense that we do apply, can't help applying, to Mr Woodhouse the same judgement as if he were a near relative of our own, and this is surely because Jane Austen *wants* us to. Her point seems to be that while social decorum and personal affection and habit too make it unthinkable for Emma to treat and think of her father with anything but respect and forbearance, yet we as readers are not to accept the then current theory of parent–child relationship and duty due from a daughter, because in practice the test-case shows it to be a faulty theory. Emma is always saying to herself something like this: 'Whatever mistakes I have made, however badly I may have behaved to others, at least I do my duty at home, I am a *good daughter*', and this is true. But *we* can't help feeling with Emma that Mr Woodhouse is not a good father, and that when the duty and obligation have failed on one side they cannot be demanded on the other. In an apparently amiable way Mr Woodhouse is so selfish as to be heartless, and tries to prevent his daughters and dependants from marrying and leaving him for a life of their own. The subject had been broached in the earlier *Pride and Prejudice*, where we are given an opportunity to question the conventional parent–child relationship of the age in the instance of Mrs Bennett, the very trying and silly mother, who exacts deference and obedience all the time from her daughters. So in fact we are obliged to apply in the novel the values of life, and the 'literary' idea of belletrists, that Mr Woodhouse is formed to give us delicious entertainment, is in fact shallow and impercipient. He is meant to exasperate us on Emma's behalf.

This applies even in the realms of the fiction of entertainment strictly so-called. Take three writers who perhaps seem to some of you equally of this class – P. G. Wodehouse, Ian Fleming and Damon Runyon – I believe some of you young men have recently been initiated into the work of Damon Runyon and as I was responsible for it I'd like to end by saying something relevant about him.

The level of appeal of P. G. Wodehouse's humour is prep school; his stories take place in a Never-Never-land of silly asses and japes, unchanging stock characters and the situations of stage farce. They are harmless, except if they prevent a reader from moving on to something that is demanding and can yield dividends – Wodehouse seems to have stuck at the prep-school age himself. Ian Fleming's James Bond books are not harmless and cannot be read, as is sometimes claimed, for pure entertainment, for they are vicious and nasty and their inevitable effect is to oblige the reader to identify with their appalling hero, who always emerges triumphant and represents success. These tales are all too evidently the fantasies of a sadistic, snobbish and callous pornographer. We remember Yeats's wise lines: 'We have fed the heart on fantasies; the heart's grown brutal from the fare.'

But while Runyon's tales are about gangsters and criminals and are frequently – though not always, and rarely altogether – funny, they do not endorse vice or crime and they are not the products of a heated imagination but of a realist. Runyon was a sensitive, intelligent and responsible adult who lived in the New York of the Prohibition era when crime became organized, and was corrupting the police, the judiciary, doctors and lawyers. As a journalist he had to live in this very real world and report its goings on. But *his* tales – a voluntary side-line for him, drawing on actualities – reflect his opinion of this world and his insight into its effects on society and the individual; for between the lines they quite subtly expose its nastiness, and the futility of the lives of its participants. His skilful use of the gangster idiom conveys inescapably the dehumanizing effects of a life of crime. Runyon had no weakness for professional criminals (he had seen too many close up), though he evidently relished the contradictions of character and the piquant situations which the gangster world incidentally produced. He notes that the American respect for riches is a social weakness and is compassionate in his treatment of the wives and girls who are ill-used by their men, and many of his Broadway tales are grim and blood-chilling. If you read his tales with the care they deserve, you will see that their effect is to deglamorize crime and violence, and that what Wordsworth said in defending his admiration of Burns's less decorous poems is true also of Runyon's tales: that though they have no moral *intention*, they have, Wordsworth said, a moral *effect*. This I believe to be true of all good literature, for no artist can shut out from his work the values he lives by. What Henry James said is profoundly true, that the value of a work of art is determined by the quality of the mind of the writer.

Leslie Stephen: Cambridge critic

The reputation of Leslie Stephen as literary critic seems to have been at its lowest ebb when Mr Desmond MacCarthy in his lecture, *Leslie Stephen* (being the Leslie Stephen lecture for 1937) nailed down the coffin. No contrary demonstration was provoked among the audience or the press. However, some of us may feel that the last word has not yet been said, on our side, and on the other – the corpse's – that these bones can still live. Those of us who can remember the barren state of English literary criticism before *The Sacred Wood* reached the common reader and before *The Problem of Style* and *Principles of Literary Criticism* appeared remember also their debt to Leslie Stephen: for after Johnson, Coleridge and Arnold who was there who was any help? (Certainly not Pater or Symons or Saintsbury or . . .) We were grateful to Leslie Stephen not so much for what he wrote – though that was considerable – as for what he stood for, implied and pointed to. He seemed to us to be in the direct line of the best tradition of our literary criticism, to exemplify the principal virtues of a literary critic, and to exhibit a tone, a discipline and an attitude that were desirable models to form oneself on. This, to us, would have seemed the obvious starting point for any contemporary littérateur speaking on that subject. Mr MacCarthy, however, was entirely apologetic and deprecatory. This – he said, as it were – is what Leslie Stephen was, these were his scraps of abilities (and a poor showing they make, I grant you), of course he had none of the essential qualifications for a literary critic (we know what they are) and he had all these disabilities, but still there it is and I've done my duty by him.

I think it owing to Leslie Stephen to scrutinize Mr MacCarthy's critical values and to state, in greater detail than I have done above, what Leslie Stephen stands for and what his criticism consisted of. For, apart from Mr MacCarthy's unfortunate testimonial and the chatty informal *Life and Letters* by Maitland, there is nothing; except Stephen's own *Some Early Impressions*, which even in Cambridge no one seems to read. On the other hand, everyone has read *To the Lighthouse*; and the portrait-piece of Mr Ramsay by Leslie Stephen's gifted daughter elicited immediate recognition from the oldest generation. Yes, that's Leslie Stephen, the word went round; and that brilliant study in the Lytton Strachey manner of a slightly ludicrous, slightly bogus, Victorian philosopher somehow served to discredit Leslie Stephen's literary work. But it is obvious to any student of it that that work could not have been produced by Mr Ramsay. However, Stephen seems fated to be known only as the original editor of the D.N.B.

Mr MacCarthy starts by informing us that Leslie Stephen is 'the least aesthetic of noteworthy critics' – meaning, it appears, that Stephen was thereby at a disadvantage. His unfavourable criticism of Sterne, for instance, is due to his inability to enjoy what Mr MacCarthy called Sterne's 'elegant ambiguity' and he does not appreciate that 'Sterne's attitude towards all emotions was playful'. Actually Stephen's last word on Sterne was this: 'Sterne has been called the English Rabelais . . . We know that, on clearing away the vast masses of buffoonery and ribaldry under which Rabelais was forced, or chose, to hide himself we come to the profound thinker and powerful satirist. Sterne represents a comparatively shallow vein of thought . . . He is too systematic a trifler to be reckoned with any plausibility amongst the spiritual leaders of any intellectual movement.' Mr MacCarthy does not like this kind of criticism, and he consistently but not I think deliberately misrepresents it; you suspect that he finds it uncongenial because it represents a threat to his own existence as a critic. He notes with discomfort Stephen's seriousness, his refusal to compromise or to scale down his standards, and he complains that Stephen's strong sense of character affected his discussion of an author's work. That is, Mr MacCarthy deplores a moral sense in the critic. What he demands instead is easily discovered: 'Stephen was deficient in the power of transmitting the emotions he had derived himself from literature; he sel-

dom, if ever, attempted to record a thrill'. 'As a practising
critic he limited himself as far as he could to that aspect of his
subject which it was possible to argue.' Criticism, we are
further told, is the adventures of the soul among masterpieces, and the soul of Cambridge, he suggests, had no qualifications for embarking on such adventures 'in a region
where reason is at a disadvantage compared with intuition'.

Mr MacCarthy is placing not Leslie Stephen but himself
(he might be a vulgarized echo of Arthur Symons). Delivered
at Cambridge in 1937 his can only be described as an insolent
performance. For if the humanistic side of Cambridge
studies has any justification for existing it is in standing in
the eyes of the great world – as it does – for a critical position
descended from Leslie Stephen's and antagonistic to Mr
MacCarthy. Some part at least of Mr MacCarthy's audience
must not have been affected as he expected by his recital of
Stephen's limitations or failings – that Stephen seemed to
think that on the whole books ought not to be written unless
they are first-rate of their kind, that mediocrity in poetry is
unforgivable, that his studies 'might seem grudging, owing to
the number of reservations they contain, until the reader has
grasped that praise from Leslie Stephen, which he always
strove to make precise, meant a very great deal'. And so on.
Actually, I suppose the more intelligent section of Mr
MacCarthy's audience held these qualities, this outlook, that
mode of expression, to be indispensable to the practice of
literary criticism. 'I often think that the value of second-rate
literature is not small, but simply zero,' Stephen wrote. He
was not a Sunday reviewer, we perceive. And unless you are
one, or a minor poet, you can hardly be devoted to literature
without having reached the same conclusions as Leslie
Stephen independently. Again Mr MacCarthy cannot see the
point of Stephen's painstaking examination of Defoe's minor
novels (though his essay has the merit of destroying in anticipation the Woolf–Forster claim that Defoe is a literary *artist*)
and his similar pieces of critical analysis; he opines that criticisms of this kind (with which 'Leslie Stephen's critical
essays are crammed'), while they may 'increase our interest
when we think over an author's works', yet 'Of course, they
do not help us to decide whether the fiction in question is
good or bad.' When it comes to judgement, he says, 'the test

which Leslie Stephen applied was the relation of a work to life, the extent to which it ministered, in one way or another, to all human good'. This is not the best way of explaining Stephen's critical values, but we can gather the force of Mr MacCarthy's objections. Those of us who do not choose to linger in the aesthetic vacuum of the nineties can afford the courage of asserting that we agree with Leslie Stephen and not with Mr MacCarthy. Mr MacCarthy's critical position is revealed as the last heritage of the nineties (not the Cambridge nineties). It is a position which we might well have supposed not merely outmoded but abolished for ever, though I suppose its last recognizable sign of life was as recent as Mr Clive Bell's theory of Significant Form.

Let us recapitulate the grounds of dispute between Mr MacCarthy and Leslie Stephen. Stephen, misguided man, thought the critic should confine himself to what is discussible about a work of art instead of recording his thrill at experiencing it; the youngest hand will have the answer ready that it is the critic's business to advance the profitable discussion of literature, substitute-creation ('transmitting the emotions derived from literature') being indefensible egotism. His detailed analyses of writings, focussing on the writer's idiom and technical devices, do not help us to decide whether the work is good or bad, says Mr MacCarthy; we on the contrary who believe that literary criticism can be demonstrated and so argued about find Stephen's procedure – starting from the surface and working inwards to radical criticism – obviously right and convincing. We believe with Stephen that literary criticism is not a mystic rapture but a process of the intelligence. No doubt the environment of Clerk Maxwell and Henry Sidgwick was peculiarly favourable to the development of such an attitude to literature, but we recollect that Arnold and Coleridge also practised this method when they were most effectual. His feeling that the character of an author was a factor in his art to be reckoned with was, we are assured, a demerit in a critic, it interfered with his judgement of a piece of literature. We reply that Stephen had evidently a finer critical sense than Bloomsbury; if we mean by art something more profound than an 'aesthetic' theory can explain, we have to agree with Henry James, that in the last event the value of a work of art

depends on the quality of the writer's make-up. Art is not
amoral and everything is not as valuable as everything else.
Stephen did not apply a moral touchstone naively. In practice the question at issue is, can we or can we not diagnose
Sterne's limitations and George Eliot's only partial success
as artists in terms of these writers' make-up? Stephen
thought he could and we think he did. The position we share
with Leslie Stephen has been admirably stated by Mr L. H.
Myers in the Preface to *The Root and the Flower*, where he says
that 'Proust, for instance, by treating all sorts of sensibility as
equal in importance, and all manifestations of character as
standing on the same plane of significance, adds nothing to
his achievement, but only draws attention to himself as aiming at the exaltation of a rather petty form of aestheticism.
For my part, I believe that a man serves himself better by
showing a respect for such moral taste as he may possess.'
Unless we adopt this position, says Mr Myers, we 'are likely
to be satisfied with art that is petty'. Stephen had no use for
art that is petty; Mr MacCarthy wants to be allowed to rebuke
him for describing Sterne as 'a systematic trifler' representing 'a shallow vein'. Of course the academic attitude to literature is much the same as Mr MacCarthy's. 'It appears that
you prefer some authors to others, Mr Graves' is the classic
rebuke of authority to criticism. Stephen was not academic –
it is only one of his virtues but it is the fundamental one for a
critic – he was not conventional, timid or respectable in his
findings. 'It is tempting to try to clear away some of the
stupendous rubbish-heaps of eulogy which accumulate over
the great men when admiration has become obligatory on
pain of literary renunciation,' he wrote. And again on
Johnson's criticism of Milton:

His independent judgments are interesting even when erroneous.
His unlucky assault upon *Lycidas* is generally dismissed with a pitying shrug of the shoulders . . . Of course every tyro in criticism has
his answer ready . . . The same writer who will tell us all this, and
doubtless with perfect truth, would probably have adopted Pope or
Johnson's theory with equal confidence if he had lived in the last
century, *Lycidas* repelled Johnson by incongruities, which, from his
point of view, were certainly offensive. Most modern readers, I will
venture to suggest, feel the same annoyances, though they have not
the courage to avow them freely . . . Every critic is in effect criticiz-

ing himself as well as his author; and I confess that to my mind an obviously sincere record of impressions, however onesided they may be, is infinitely refreshing, as revealing at least the honesty of the writer. The ordinary run of criticism generally implies nothing but the extreme desire of the author to show that he is open to the very last new literary fashion . . . If Johnson's blunder in this case implied sheer stupidity, one can only say that honest stupidity is a much better thing than clever insincerity or fluent repetition of second-hand dogmas . . . He had the rare courage – for, even then, Milton was one of the tabooed poets – to say what he thought as forcibly as he could say it; and he has suffered the natural punishment of plain speaking.

Mr MacCarthy evidently thinks that the Cambridge ethos, which everyone including Stephen agrees was the decisive influence in shaping his character, was very inferior intellectually to old Bloomsbury. What sort of environment was it in fact? The best account of it is in *Some Early Impressions*, where Stephen himself records his debt. Stephen was born in 1832. His family was what he called 'the second generation from the Clapham Sect' (it is interesting to note that Macaulay's was the first generation from it and Virginia Woolf and Vanessa Bell's the third). Stephen did not react against the Clapham inheritance. His admiration for 'the essential Puritan' was derived from his early impressions. He naturally found the Evangelical leaning of Cambridge in 1850 congenial.

Cambridge has for the last three centuries inclined to the less romantic side of things . . . We could boast of no Newman, nor of men who, like Froude and Pattison, submitted for a time to the fascination of his genius and only broke from it with a wrench which permanently affected his mental equilibrium. 'I have never known a Cambridge man', as a reverent disciple of the prophet said to me, 'who could appreciate Newman.' Our version of the remark was slightly different. We held that our common sense enabled us to appreciate him only too thoroughly by the dry light of reason and to resist the illusions of romantic sentiment.

It was one of the advantages of Cambridge, he felt, that there was no such spiritual leader as Carlyle or Newman in the place. His mind was formed first by his mathematical tutor Isaac Todhunter, whose character impressed him as much as his attainments, by the great Whewell (who had no personal charm, and whose character, intellect and influence were markedly opposite to those of Jowett, for whom Stephen felt great distaste) and finally by the pervading influence of John Stuart Mill. 'Pure, passionless reason' was embodied in his works – which was all his disciples knew of him at the time. Stephen speaks of 'that shrewd, hard-headed, North-country type which was so conspicuous at Cambridge' and notes 'our favourite antipathy was the "imposter" – that is, the man given to allowing his feelings to override his common sense.' At Cambridge he found a conspicuous absence of interest in the struggle of Church parties then proceeding ('We left such matters to Oxford'), 'the religion of all sensible men' being generally the wear. This Stephen after some years as a don and tutor found dropping away from him painlessly, and he became and remained an agnostic. What Cambridge had to offer him is most clearly seen if we consider the contrasting experience of Mark Pattison, a natural Cantab as it were, who, as Stephen noted, 'fretting under the oppressive spirit of the old Oxford atmosphere' and feeling that Newman represented mere obscurantism, wore himself out in his efforts at educational reform in the university, thwarted by the insufferable Jowett. Stephen left Cambridge without loss of esteem on either side and entered journalism, the higher journalism that was then available to offer a career to talent without degradation. 'I joined the great army of literature because I was forced into the ranks', he wrote in afterlife, 'but also with no little pride in my being accepted as a recruit'. The *Saturday Review* succeeded Cambridge and stamped him afresh. He notes that, turning over the files many years afterwards to look for his own contributions, he was startled to discover that he could rarely distinguish them by internal evidence. It seems to have been a congenial extension of the Cambridge ethos; he speaks of the 'strong realistic common sense of the Johnson variety' that was practised. The last factor in shaping him as a critic seems to have been the D.N.B., whose editorship he accepted in 1882. There he 'learnt to think that the whole art of writing consists in making one word suffice where other ordinary men use two'. It also assisted him to perfect his dry, unobtrusive irony, thanks to which the dictionary is, as Maitland said, 'strewn with mantraps'. That impersonal but caustic wit, expressing an out-

look characteristically devoid of easy enthusiasm, is most
evident in the George Eliot volume he contributed to the
English Men of Letters series (of the others – Hobbes, Pope,
Johnson and Swift – the two last are admirable). It is a
decidedly unsympathetic study though admirers of George
Eliot find to their annoyance that he has said practically all in
her favour that there is to say; his critical appraisal of her
weaknesses remains an uncomfortable obstacle which they
cannot afford to neglect and which is not easily dealt with.

His belief in reason (as opposed to 'intuition'), deplored by
Mr MacCarthy, did not lead to crass blindness. He was not
ignorant of the fact that a work of art has its own internal
logic; but he did not consider that this exempted the author
or poet from intellectual scrutiny. He expected a poet who
deployed philosophic views to have sound ones, and he
realized, in spite of his great 'intuitive' admiration for
Wordsworth, that Wordsworth's were not always sound. For
Shelley's intellectual lights he had the greatest disrespect,
and was able to make a corresponding case against Shelley's
poetry – he protests to J. A. Symonds that he cannot agree
with his praise of Shelley in the Men of Letters volume, there
is 'a certain hollowness' about the *Prometheus*, an 'insubstan-
tial mist' in much of Shelley's most admired poems. His use
of 'reason' is in the Johnson tradition. Since it led him to
explode Lamb's sophistical defence of Restoration Comedy
and Hazlitt's of Wycherley, it was evidently a useful critical
technique. His cautious examination of what a writer has to
offer will seem to many of us, in spite of Mr MacCarthy,
worth more than a cartload of records of thrills. Do we or do
we not find the following kind of criticism more helpful than
transmission of the emotions derived from literature?

There are parasitical writers who, in the old phrase, have 'formed
their style' by the imitation of accepted models, and who have,
therefore, possessed it only by right of appropriation. Boswell has
a discussion as to the writers who may have served Johnson in this
capacity. But in fact Johnson, like all other men of strong idiosyn-
crasy, formed his style as he formed his legs ... Johnsonese was, as
far as we can judge, a genuine product. Macaulay says that it is
more offensive than the mannerism of Milton or Burke, because it
is a mannerism adopted on principle and sustained by constant
effort. Facts do not confirm this theory. Milton's prose style seems

to be the result of a conscious effort to run English into classical moulds. Burke's mannerism does not appear in his early writings, and we can trace its development from the imitation of Bolingbroke to the last declamation against the Revolution. But Johnson seems to have written Johnsonese from his cradle.

What Swift has really done [in *Gulliver*] is to provide for the man who despises his species a number of exceedingly effective symbols for the utterance of his contempt.

His style was no doubt precipitated by the conditions of working as journalist, editor and biographer, but it is a genuine expression of personality and an effective weapon. Aspects of it were registered in the contemporary mots: 'No flowers by request' and 'Stephen's ink was never watery' (or purple, it might have been added). He had the right to come down on Arnold for his rhetoric about the dreaming spires and to object to his mannerisms. Stephen was the type of critic who makes no parade of personality, has no studied attitudes, whose manner consists of an absence of manner but is felt as the presence of a mature personality. He himself described his style modestly as 'short-winded and provokingly argumentative', and says that whereas X 'can keep up a flow of eloquence' he himself cannot keep on the rhetorical level because he 'must always have some tangible remark to make'. Unlike his contemporaries we cannot consider this in any way unfortunate. His habitual tone and style are represented by this from the essay on Jowett:

To a distinct view of the importance of some solution he seems to have joined the profound conviction that no conceivable solution would hold water. 'He stood', says one of his pupils, in a rather different sense, 'at the parting of many ways', and he wrote, one must add, 'No thoroughfare' upon them all.

As a critic he stood for outspoken criticism all round: 'I like his [Huxley's] pugnacity – a quality I always admire. The more hard-hitting goes on in the world, the better I am pleased – meaning always hard-hitting in the spiritual sense.' His critical credo is constantly implied in the essays *Hours in a Library* (three volumes), *Studies of a Biographer* (four volumes) and the fragmentary *English Literature and Society in the Eighteenth Century*. It corresponds generally to the position that we hold to-day.

After all, though criticism cannot boast of being a science, it ought
to aim at something like a scientific basis, or at least to proceed in
a scientific spirit. The critic, therefore, before abandoning himself
to the oratorical impulse, should endeavour to classify the
phenomena with which he is dealing as calmly as if he were ticket-
ing a fossil in a museum. The most glowing eulogy, the most bitter
denunciation, have their proper place; but they belong to the art of
persuasion, and form no part of scientific method . . . Our faith in
an author must, in the first instance, be the product of instinctive
sympathy, instead of deliberate reason. But when we are seeking to
justify our emotions, we must endeavour to get for the time into the
position of an independent spectator, applying with rigid impartiality such methods as are best calculated to free us from the influence of personal bias . . .

Coleridge's specific merit was not, I think, that he laid down any
scientific theory. He was something almost unique in this as in his
poetry, first because his criticism was the criticism of a man who
combined the first simple impulse of admiration with the power of
explaining why he admired; and secondly, and as a result, because
he placed himself at the right point of view; because, to put it
briefly, he was the first great writer who criticized poetry as poetry,
and not as science . . .

Nothing is easier than to put the proper label on a poet – to call him
'romantic' or 'classical', and so forth; and then if he has a predecessor of like principles, to explain him by the likeness, and if he
represents a change of principles, to make the change explain itself
by calling it a reaction. The method is delightfully simple, and I can
use the words as easily as my neighbours. The only thing I find difficult is to look wise when I use them, or to fancy that I give an
explanation because I have adopted a classification . . .

The phrase 'criticism of life' gave great offence, and was much
ridiculed by some writers, who were apparently unable to distinguish between an epigram and a philosophical dogma. To them,
indeed, Arnold's whole position was naturally abhorrent. For it is
not uncommon now to hear denunciations of all attempts to con-
nect art with morality and philosophy. It is wicked, we are told, for
a poet, or a novelist, or a painter, to take any moral consideration
into account; and therefore to talk of poetry as destined to do for us
much that philosophy and religion used to do is, of course, mani-
festly absurd. I will not argue the point at length . . . Meanwhile, it
is my belief that nobody is the better in any department of life or
literature for being a fool or a brute: and least of all in poetry. I cannot think that a man is disqualified for poetry either by thinking

more deeply than others or by having a keener perception of (I hope I may join the two words) moral beauty . . . When Arnold called poetry a criticism of life, he only meant to express what seems to me an undeniable truth . . .

Critics in an earlier day conceived their function to be judicial. They were administering a fixed code of laws applicable in all times and places . . . There are undoubtedly some principles of universal application; and the old critics often expounded them with admirable commonsense and force. But like general tenets of morality, they are apt to be commonplaces, whose specific application requires knowledge of concrete facts . . . Criticism must become thoroughly inductive . . . Briefly, in talking of literary changes, I shall have, first, to take note of the main intellectual characteristics of the period; and secondly, what changes took place in the audience to which men of letters addressed themselves, and how the gradual extension of the reading class affected the development of the literature addressed to them.

I hope I have made it plain not only what Leslie Stephen's strength as a literary critic was, but why I have chosen to describe him as a Cambridge critic. His is not (unfortunately) the invariable kind of criticism practised at Cambridge or by Cambridge products, but it is what the world of journalism and *belles-lettres* means when it refers with respect or malice to 'Cambridge Criticism'. His style, his tone, his mental attributes, his outlook are what are considered the most admirable, or objectionable, or at any rate, whatever your opinion of it, the most characteristic features of the Cambridge school. Cambridge has not by any means produced only Leslie Stephens; it is sufficient to name Rupert Brooke and Housman as evidence that dug-outs exist as refuges from the prevailing wind, that east wind which Elton, I think, says might have done Pater so much good if he had been placed in the other university. In contemporary Cambridge where one section still holds literary criticism to be a charming parasite and sends its soul, with Mr MacCarthy's approval, adventuring among masterpieces, while another holds semasiology to have superseded literary criticism along with philosophy and the rest – it is high time for those who look back with respect to Leslie Stephen as the exemplar of a sound position and a profitable practice to put it on record why they honour his memory.

Professor Chadwick
and English studies

It is a pity Chadwick did not live to read the acknowledgement to his work by the younger generation in the last
number of *Scrutiny* [VI], and I am tempted by the inadequacy
of the obituary notices I've seen to try and put on record, in
more detail, just what he did do for English studies, and how
his work and personality affected his pupils. Particularly as a
lot of nonsense has been put about suggesting that he *harmed*
Anglo-Saxon studies by his peculiar views.

I see he started his career as a double-First Classic – what
a native endowment he must have had to survive that plaster-
of-Paris regime! But the first thing about him one noticed was
how unacademic he was, the refreshing absence of that aura
of anecdotes, social values and lack of real interest which is so
discouraging to the young. His kindly eyes looked at once
innocent and shrewd, he retained his Yorkshire accent, and
always wore a Norfolk jacket and bicycling breeches costume. When I came up he was one of the very few educational
influences a student of English was likely to encounter. It was
before the two all-literature English Triposes were invented,
and you took one comprehensive Eng. Lit. tripos ('English
A') and some other tripos; if you liked, the section of the
Archaeology and Anthropology Tripos created by Chadwick,
then called 'English B'.

Its conception and the way it was carried out were characteristic of the man. You can read his own account in his
invaluable little book, *The Study of Anglo-Saxon* (Heffer, 1941).
It's full of good things, written with the disinterestedness,
good sense and intelligent insight he brought to bear on all
subjects, but it's particularly the last chapter, 'The Future of
Anglo-Saxon Studies', which is important for the English
student. Here you can see why he so annoyed orthodox

academics; starting from observation and his experience as a teacher, he explains with shocking candour that, since few students have any gift for philology, compulsory philology and history-of-language courses are 'futile'. This came with peculiar force from the man who had started his academic career as a classical philologist. He goes on to argue that philology is 'a great hindrance to Anglo-Saxon studies':

The subject appeals to a very small proportion of the students, according to my experience. They should have the opportunity of taking it, at least as a subject for post-graduate study – for which it is best suited. But it is unreasonable to force it upon every student. It is no more necessary for the study of Anglo-Saxon than it is for that of Latin or Greek or a modern foreign language . . . The connection with (later) English studies has led to a very great increase in the number of people who have at least some knowledge of Anglo-Saxon. English literature is now one of the most popular subjects in our Universities; and in most of them Anglo-Saxon is, or has been, a more or less compulsory element of the course. As to the value of this connection for either subject, my own experience has been that, when Anglo-Saxon is compulsory, it is disliked, and the students gain little or nothing from it. On the other hand, when it is optional, the number who take it is very small – not more than one in ten – but these usually rather like it, if philology is eliminated, and most of them gain something thereby. To force it upon a larger number of students is, in my experience, a mere waste of time for both student and teacher. Most of the students regard it as a nuisance.

Worse, he goes on to argue 'in the interests of Anglo-Saxon studies' that

There are serious objections, however, to any scheme which involves an exclusive or even primary connection of Anglo-Saxon with English studies. The latter do not afford a good training for the former; and in Universities where this connection has ceased it is found that the majority of our best students come from other subjects than English. For Anglo-Saxon studies some inclination for the acquisition of languages and a wider historical outlook are desirable; English studies are too limited in their scope. Indeed, the two subjects appeal to different kinds of mind.

It is all too true, in fact indisputable, but how unprofessional to admit, even to notice, anything of the sort, in what bad taste to announce it from the house-tops! Compulsory

Anglo-Saxon, philology and history-of-language courses attached to the popular English Literature degree studies make jobs for specialists, provide subjects that can be *taught*, lectured and examined on mechanically (no nonsense about education, but just that 'factual matter' which somehow provides 'discipline') – surely that is all the justification needed. But Chadwick was perverse enough to uphold the interests not of professionals but of Anglo-Saxon studies – of which he, after all, held the Chair. He insisted that Anglo-Saxon should be studied in his university in its proper context, in association with the early history and antiquities of the country and in comparison with early Scandinavian studies similarly organized – that is, he made it a study of early civilizations. He wanted to do for our own early culture something comparable to what the Classical Tripos does for the early history of Greece and Rome, to provide a unified study which should be truly educational.

The number of students who will take such a course as this [he writes] will doubtless be small – at least until the importance of our early history is more generally recognized. At present the only way of getting a large number of students to learn Anglo-Saxon is by making it a more or less compulsory subject in a popular course – e.g., by making it impossible to obtain a degree in English without it. I have had experience of both systems, and have no hesitation in expressing my preference for the one which will secure a few keen students, who choose the course of their own free will, and will in all probability derive real benefit from it.

Well, a lot of 'English' students did opt for Chadwick's scheme nevertheless, and, as he says, got real benefit from it. His tripos opened for us the doors into archaeology, anthropology, sociology, prehistory, early architecture – all beginnings for future self-education, and he saw to it that these subjects, studied with reference to Scandinavia and England, should also extend to the Celtic and Mediterranean areas, opening fresh vistas. The interest and profit were inexhaustible. We didn't, under him and his colleagues, go through the philological grind ('an exercise of memory and faith' as he contemptuously describes it) and we didn't 'get up' Anglo-Saxon as a meaningless adjunct to medieval and modern English literature. Nor did we have to study *Beowulf* under the hypocritical pretence that it is great poetry; we used it as an interesting document. Anglo-Saxon literature, studies in connection with Old Norse literature in particular and other early literatures in general, gave us an insight into the origins of literature (his own three-volume work on this subject, *The Growth of Literature*, shows the breadth of his base). And this was only part of the larger scheme, in which the early literatures of Northern Europe and Great Britain were studied, not snatched out of their context as literatures nearly always are, but as part of their inseparable background, the cultures that produced them. This meant that anyone working under Chadwick had to study the history, archaeology, literature, arts, social life and so forth of Northern Europe from the Beaker period to the Norman Conquest; in fact, Northern Europe from the end of the Stone Age to the end of the Dark Ages was conceived and treated as a continuous cultural study. Of course this was a lot even for two years, but it was assumed that the student had special aptitudes. Most students grumbled and groaned when they were launched on two new languages at once, plus a terrifying syllabus which included the entire literatures of Anglo-Saxon and Old Norse, but all retracted later, for Chadwick's method made one take the merely memory work in one's stride – it was not going to be examined on for its own sake – and he was a remarkable teacher as well as a great scholar: the true original mind that can organize knowledge. He got together a good team too, which included Dame Bertha Philpotts, the authority on the Viking Age. Many look back on the two years they spent with him as the most valuable and formative period of their intellectual life. The effect of such a boldly conceived course of study was evident in the rapid maturing of the students. His system was the opposite of the spoon-feeding method that the modern universities adopt towards their students.

He and his tripos were wonderfully stimulating. There were drawbacks, of course. He was himself a linguistic genius, and, as his students used to complain, he apparently thought that everyone is born with a knowledge of runes, Celtic languages and Old High German; but when his attention was drawn to this misunderstanding, he was always very patient and considerate. He was not a theoretical educationist but he could see what is educational and what is not. Nor was he a writer on his special studies who could give them wide appeal, like W. P. Ker. He was simply a teacher and scholar who had hatched an educational idea and felt its value enough to be stubborn about preserving it. Obviously a strain of the publicist in his composition would have helped to promote his ends, and would have made him able to place his discovery and his methods before the educational world in a more persuasive light. He was too single-minded to be able or willing to grapple with academic politics. He complains: 'An unfortunate feature of University life to-day is that the time and energy which should go to teaching and research has to be spent in committee rooms.' But it is the academic with no vocation for teaching – with nothing to teach – who enjoys the power that can be exercised in committee rooms.

To sum up his achievement: he provided a course of study in itself highly educational. He showed how literary and linguistic studies could be made most profitable, by successfully correlating them with their social background – a very different matter from the scrappy 'Life and Thought' courses which are the inadequate gestures the English Tripos makes in a half-hearted effort to provide a similar organization for medieval and modern literature. (Just as his system of comparative study of early literature differs from the oddments of Italian and French set-book that the English Faculty Board piously hopes, one supposes, will do the trick for English literature.) After taking Chadwick's 'English B', those who proceeded to 'English A' realized what an opportunity was lost in the handling – or rather, lack of handling – of Medieval Literature and 'Life and Thought', even though the English School enjoyed the services of Dr Coulton. Moreover, Chadwick certainly showed how literary studies could be linked up with that school of sociological studies which Cambridge so notoriously lacks. In addition, he of course very considerably furthered Anglo-Saxon studies by getting texts edited and books written, by his pupils and friends as well as by himself, and by getting them considered in the larger and more fruitful light he brought to bear on them.

But the professor of Anglo-Saxon – who had given evidence before a Board of Education committee that 'It cannot be too clearly recognized that compulsory philology is the natural and mortal enemy of humanistic studies' and that the literary interest of Anglo-Saxon is 'not so great as to repay students of modern literature for the time they will have to spend in acquiring a sufficient mastery of the language to appreciate it'[1] – had to pay the penalty for his disinterestedness. He had insisted on taking his subject seriously and his position as an educationist responsibly, instead of accepting both conventionally, and he was always aware of official opposition. It was true he already had, and so was secure in, the Chair. But an obscure movement, of which we shall never know the exact history, seemed to him to threaten his life-work all along, and it has taken on fresh vigour since his retirement in 1940. In his book on *The Study of Anglo-Saxon* he refers to 'authorities responsible for English' who 'wish to acquire control over Anglo-Saxon studies' and that such a scheme as his is likely to meet

with much opposition. The teaching staff may be unanimous in its favour, and the students may be well satisfied and keen, but opposition or interference may come from persons or committees who have no knowledge of Anglo-Saxon studies, but who may think that interests of the studies for which they are responsible may be affected in some way by such a scheme.

Presumably some not very creditable episode of academic history led Chadwick twenty years ago to remove his studies and himself from the English Faculty to the School of Archaeology and Anthropology, which in the person of Dr A. C. Haddon received him with open arms. That great man and he were two of a kind. Haddon must have been a fertilizing influence for him as well as a congenial presence and an ally. One knew what the academic 'English' attitude to Chadwick's scheme was, from the tone in which it was mentioned: resentment. The desire to undo Chadwick's work is one sign of that hatred of life which academic history illustrates in so many ways. For Chadwick was a rare instance of what is supposed to be typical academic disinterestedness but what the academic milieu is instinctively hostile to. No doubt, under the plea of 'getting Anglo-Saxon back into the English Tripos' his work on the other side, as to which he was equally firm, that of freeing English students from compulsory linguistic and philological cram, will be undone, and, in his own words, 'the herding of masses of students along familiar lines, some of which are barren and useless enough' will be resumed some day – in whose interest? Not the students', assuredly, as Chadwick has shown, at any rate.

Reviews

Charlotte Yonge and 'Christian discrimination'

Charlotte Yonge, by Georgina Battiscombe (Constable)
Christian Discrimination, by Bro. George Every, S.S.M.
    (Christian News-Letter Books)
The Literary Outlook, by S. L. Bethell (Christian News-Letter
    Books)
Man and Literature, by Norman Nicholson (S.C.M. Press)

There has long been an Amanda Ros vogue of Charlotte
Yonge's writings and this biography is chiefly a product of
that vogue. Miss Battiscombe has made an attractive book in
which information about the life is interspersed with some
just comments on the novels and illuminating bits of
background. It is perhaps the only kind of book on Charlotte
Yonge for which a wide public could be expected now, the
popular Lytton Strachey treatment suiting well enough the
period and the Amanda Ros aspect of the subject. But to be
amused merely by Charlotte Yonge is not the most profitable
reaction. Miss Battiscombe wobbles between amusement
and a desire to claim literary status of some kind for some of
Miss Yonge's novels that she enjoys in some way she can't
explain. To see these novels taken at their own and the contemporary valuation we must turn to *Theology* and some
recent related publications, where claims for this writer as a
serious artist and a very valuable Christian novelist have
been made. Evidently these ought to be investigated before
the canon of English Literature finds itself permanently
burdened with one of the prolific fiction writers whom time
alone has already expelled.

It seems incredible that Charlotte Yonge's novels could be

taken seriously as literature except by those of her own way of thinking, and the claims I have referred to seem in fact to be based on the asserted value of her fictions as religious myths. Charlotte Yonge was a day-dreamer with a writing itch that compensated her for a peculiarly starved life. What was pushed out of her is interesting to us not for what it enunciates but for what it reveals and only in so far as a critical apparatus is brought to bear on it. The profitable book on her would be a contribution to the sociological history of literature: an illuminating contrast to Bunyan and a comparison with Jane Austen suggest themselves at once as revealing something about the cultural conditions which nourish a writer or otherwise, the kind of religious outlook that can produce a humane art and the kind that can't. This author had no medium at her command for conveying through literature such moral perceptions as she had, for unlike Bunyan she had no popular inherited art of literary expression to draw on, and the personal sensibility of the writer which creates its own artistic language she decidedly had not. Jane Austen, in contrast, shows what the spinster of the previous generation gained by enjoying a real social life of the family and community, the life fed by adult conversation, free play of the mind and character, observation of all sorts and varieties of life and attitudes to it at different social and moral levels appreciated by standards that had arisen out of life itself instead of, like Charlotte Yonge, living only in the ignorant idealization projected by an inhuman theory.

As a moralist she is on a par with pulpit denouncers of short hair and slacks for women – that is, she couldn't distinguish between social conventions and morals of a less superficial quality, and having no sense of proportion she gave as much attention and censure in her novels to the former as to Dissipation and Doubt, the blanket concepts which she used for sin (not being acquainted with any more concrete expression of it). A person for whom evil consists of impropriety and some things she has vaguely heard tell of would seem to be disqualified as a framer of religious myths. And correspondingly she lacked (unlike the fanatic Bunyan or the spinsters Miss Austen and Miss Edgeworth) any sympathy for and even recognition of the natural sources of healthy life. The innocence of the dove is itself hardly an adequate equipment for a novelist, but even the race of doves would have died out soon after the Creation if as lacking as Charlotte Yonge in the instincts that make for survival. This brings us back to her attitude to life, that seems to have determined the interpretation she gave to the Anglican faith imparted to her by Keble. The Church seems to have been less an illumination of life for her than a substitute for living, so we see her selecting the anti-Life elements in Christianity for stress and idealization. The resulting picture of human action is not only impracticable but morbid. Consider the typical pattern of her novels. There is a permanent invalid who is a hero or heroine; tubercular invalids are peculiarly saintly and frequently an idiot is idealized; the most blessed marriages are those in which one party is diseased or physically incapable; the most blessed betrothals are those where the death of one party prevents marriage at all; the most blessed life for a man is to give up the natural field for his abilities in order to become a South Seas missionary, and for a woman to renounce a possible husband in order to devote herself to her relatives, even if they are only imbecile grandparents, or on the mere wish of a parent – self-sacrifice is an end in itself. She makes much play with symbolism but as was inevitable in so poorly nourished an imagination (the arts meant nothing to her and life gave her no more pregnant experience than the death of a parent, no greater stimulus than a missionary meeting), her symbolism is schoolgirlish. Comparison with any novel where symbols are deployed by an original mind in vital connection with life would illustrate this – *Jude the Obscure*, *Moby Dick*, *Hard Times*, Conrad's *Victory*, one of Hawthorne's or T. F. Powys's works. It is her unconscious symbolism that is more interesting – for example, the type of admirable wife who is no wife because of an accident to her lower limbs or spine, the saintly clergyman who has either gone blind or developed consumption, the passionate relation between brother and sister in a picture of life where the idea of sex is prohibited. It is understandable that some should find this vision of the good society congenial but that will not convince the majority that it is literature that makes for any kind of health or can offer anything to the mature.

We are entitled to press home this kind of criticism because it has a demonstrable bearing on the failure of

Charlotte Yonge's fictions to be of literary value. We are not concerned with her qualifications as a Christian but as a novelist. The lack of roots in first-hand experience for her imagination, of substance for her moral passion, prevent her most cherished effects from conveying what she evidently thought they would. It would have required a genius like Kafka's or Bunyan's, with that imaginative pressure which gives body to allegory and that artistic genius for expressing it, to make as literature anything of the new-born infant's baptism and the deferred confirmation scenes she so often stages. Art is a realm where the will can never be taken for the deed, and readers may be forgiven for smiling at places where the utmost solemnity of response is confidently expected by Miss Yonge. Even compared with writers of her own age and class she was deficient in this respect: she had none of that capacity for fable which enabled Kingsley to create in the gist of *The Water Babies* a Christian myth which children readily feel even before they understand it. 'The essence of moral energy is to survey the whole field', wrote Henry James in his study of the novelist's function. It is certainly something required of the novelist whose claims to our attention are that she staked everything on presenting religious values. But Miss Yonge is so timid and inexperienced morally that her effects are in fact trivial. Religious small-change is handed us on every possible occasion; if, for instance, anyone is disappointed in some trifling matter, mamma or elder sister is sure to remark: 'I dare say it is very good for us not to have our ambition gratified. There are so many troubles worse than these failures, that it only shows how happy we are that we should take them so much to heart.' Surely such inflation lowers the value of the moral currency? The limitations that produced moral triteness are paralleled by her worldly ignorance that cripples her fictions: meeting the mass of humanity only as Sunday scholars – she never set foot in a cottage – she yet undertook, with the bestseller's confidence, to treat the largest social and ethical questions in a China-to-Peru setting of real life, so that 'there is a bad Chartist spirit among the colliers' is the only recognition of something wrong that she makes in a novel explicitly dealing with the social problem.

The Yonge type of moral fervour impresses one as amounting to nothing more than a refusal to allow anyone else moral or spiritual privacy or freedom. She has therefore no basis for the moral drama essential to the novelist's art. We think in contrast of Richardson, who subscribed like her to the antediluvian theory of parental control of a daughter's hand and the submission of the daughter as a religious duty. In *Clarissa*, where this theory is the mainspring of the action, it is checked by the novelist's deeper feeling that if we look at the particular instance the theory won't do because it outrages human sympathies. The interplay between the theory (accepted as morally right) and the test-case (appealing to another source of values) produces the tragedy: Clarissa can act only as she does, in duty to herself, but from the moment she violates the theory by taking the only means of escape in her power – accepting Lovelace's offer of assistance – she is doomed; yet after suffering every form of degradation she commands respect and triumphs. Richardson's conviction of the importance of his theme informs with power the smallest details of his setting. There is no such drama in Miss Yonge's novels because she was incapable of perceiving that moral theory may require revision or reinterpretation in the light of experience or in consequence of a change in the sensibility of a society. In her fictions a moral lesson is deduced from theory as mechanically as in a Sunday-School story of the last century. Apart from the ideal of Christian living described, as to the desirability of which there can evidently be more than one opinion, she has nothing to present but a moral ethos where everybody's first duty is to give up everything for everybody else and where no one can enjoy anything without feeling guilty and obliged to justify himself at a moral bar, where every impulse is suspect and made to seem sinful, and where the only sanctionable activities unconnected with religion are parlour games and a form of lively conversation where humour is restricted to thoroughly harmless puns. As representing a religious culture these novels are not impressive and it cannot do the Anglican cause a service to resurrect her fictions as propaganda.

It remains to ask, why should anyone want to resurrect them? Charlotte Yonge was logical as only a simple-minded fanatic can be, pressing her theory to its extreme conclusions. Thus she held, and bases the action of novels upon

the argument, that there can be no secular art (not by
inclusion but by rejection – no secular music should exist,
only Victorian Sacred Music), she objected to any higher
education for women because only by being in a religious
order could they justify it, and so on. She shows, says a contributor to the current number of *Theology*, how far a clearly
conceived dogmatic outlook will carry a writer. And it is on
these grounds that she is put forward as a valuable author by
the critics of a new school who seem to derive, as they
acknowledge inspiration, from Mr T. S. Eliot's *After Strange
Gods*, where 'the standard of orthodoxy' was explicitly
brought to bear on literature. This school of Anglican
criticism has already produced its text-books, its poetry, its
drama, and has in *Theology* its organ. It therefore calls for consideration here, like the Marxist literary movement of the
thirties which we discussed at the time and which it in many
respects resembles. It offers to perform two critical functions. First, to improve the orthodox by opening up access for
them to the literature of the age, in which we have only to
offer them our best wishes for success. Second, there is a very
evident assertion that what Bro. George Every calls
'Christian Discrimination' has a superior light by which literary criticism should be directed, which can by innate virtue
short-circuit literary criticism.

We have to insist, as we did with the Marxists, that the
essential thing in undertaking literary criticism is that you
should be a literary critic, concerned, with complete disinterestedness, to demonstrate by the methods of literary
criticism exactly what it is that a piece of literary art is doing.
This is often quite different from what it alleges it is doing or
undertakes to do, and we have to repeat to the dogmatic
Christian discriminator the warning we gave to the Marxist
critic, that before certifying a work on the grounds of content
or apparent orthodoxy it is as well to be sure that its actual
'message', what it inevitably and essentially communicates,
is what you thought it was. By not applying the method of
literary criticism to Charlotte Yonge's novels the Christian
discriminator has undertaken to endorse something that
many Christians of all kinds would agree, one imagines, to
deplore and disown. Miss Dorothy Sayers provided a similar
test in her novels and drama, and we see the principle at work

exposed in *Blackfriars*, where an ecclesiastic recently declared that her literary productions are valuable art *because* she is orthodox. The avowedly Christian critic would have to be a saint indeed to be capable of the disinterestedness necessary to expose the writings of a pillar of his orthodoxy as bad art. (Catholic critics have before now incurred animus in their own community by suggesting that Chesterton and Belloc, for instance, were not only not good poets but have an undesirable aspect.) Though Bro. George Every does allow that a Christian artist is not necessarily always better than a freethinking one, he is nevertheless generally seen in the position of the Evangelical preacher who condemned Maria Edgeworth's novels because they insidiously showed perfect happiness and virtue without religion; thus he values highly Charlotte Yonge's novels because she shows that you cannot be good and have no right to be happy unless you are a High Anglican. Similarly we see Mr Bethell concerned in his book not to be a literary critic but to make an appearance of literary criticism for his own purposes – to prove that he may enjoy best-sellers and detective stories and the rest without any loss of face as a Christian soul, that his tastes in fiction and poetry, those of *l'homme moyen sensuel*, are not inconsistent with alleged possession of the finest perceptions in life and art and the realm of the spirit (thus contradicting one of Bro. George Every's avowed arguments in his book in the same series). If the Christian critic of literature is not a literary critic he is nothing, and having become one he will hardly be content to cease to be one, to exercise some 'standard of orthodoxy' or to indulge in special pleading. For in examining a piece of literature as a literary critic he is inevitably appraising it, and the appraisal is a process much more subtle than the application of any standard of orthodoxy or the extraction of any moral lesson or the discovery of some panacea for a situation producing works of art that don't answer to his doctrinal specifications. Grant a position of privilege to the Christian as a literary critic and we must admit the equivalent claims of the Marxist, the agnostic, and the sub-divisions of Christian critics, each with his own standard of orthodoxy and each concerned to push the claims of his equivalents of Miss Sayers and Miss Yonge and his sect's Georgian poets (and to denounce the other parties' literary productions). Sectarian literary criticism would lead to a variety of subjective criticism where little if any common agreement as to value would be possible. At present we have, the inheritance from a long tradition, a centre of merely literary critics whose disinterested evaluations have made possible some recognition of poets and novelists who subscribe to no orthodoxy, that is, nearly all creative artists of the last two centuries; this centre moreover provides an atmosphere and milieu where value-judgements can be discussed with some freedom. When Bro. George Every published a piece in *Theology* some years ago mentioning the work of *Scrutiny* in this field, Mr C. S. Lewis promptly wrote up invoking anathema on him and *Scrutiny*, and when Mr Turnell eight years ago founded *Arena* as a focus for Catholic discrimination and argued (at a very much more impressive critical level than the Anglican critics) that Catholics lost something by cutting themselves off from the live tradition of contemporary literature, *The Tablet* made a response similar to Mr Lewis's. The violence and narrowness of Marxist dogmatism are too generally known to need illustration. Perhaps what a work of literature has to offer us is not best discovered in an atmosphere in which the spirit of theology is given play, in which (as in *After Strange Gods*) the direct inspiration of the Devil is imputed to any artist who runs counter to our prejudices, in which access to the one source of absolute truth is confidently claimed by the critic, and anathema invoked on dissentients.

The method of literary criticism, as repeatedly defined in these pages, is to secure the maximum general agreement for evaluation by starting with something demonstrable – the surface of the work – and through practical criticism to proceed inwards to a deeper and wider kind of criticism commanding assent (or giving an opening for disagreement and discussion) at every step. It may well be shocking to the mere literary critic that Christians and even professional maintainers of standards of orthodoxy should be unable to read what is in front of them, should be unable, for example, to discover for themselves, even if they cannot point to the evidence in the texture of her writings, that Miss Sayers unconsciously incarnates a very inferior set of attitudes and values, or (conversely) cannot because of theological differences see that *The Pilgrim's Progress* is great art. It seems to follow that a specialist non-theological training is necessary to make sure what it is we are discussing when what we want to discuss a poem or a novel. Bro. George Every looks forward (in *Theology*, Sept. 1940) to a company of Christian critics who, being trained in theology as well as what he calls our grammar and rhetoric, will be able to provide literary criticism that he has no doubt, he says, will be better than the criticism of *Scrutiny*.[1] This seems too sanguine. There is no reason to suppose that those trained in theology, or philosophy for that matter, are likely to possess, what is essential to the practice of literary criticism, that 'sensitiveness of intelligence' described by Matthew Arnold as equivalent to conscience in moral matters. A theological training seems to have a disabling effect and has subsequently to be struggled against when literary criticism is the concern. And there are other dangers. When theology is made a substitute for literary criticism or is tacked on to bad criticism the result is disastrous. In *Man and Literature* Mr Norman Nicholson, following up *After Strange Gods*, is seen at work, armed with a few theological themes, on all kinds of recent authors. Though no doubt of interest to those of his own outlook who cannot begin to read for themselves, the results are quite useless for any other purpose, one would have thought, for this writer has no fineness of perception and no corresponding critical idiom and method. The chapter on D. H. Lawrence is particularly gross and therefore misrepresenting. (The assumption that they are all addressing a W.E.A. kind of audience would account for the crudeness of Mr Bethell's and Bro. George Every's arguments too, but the tone of Christian knowingness they all employ does not improve matters, nor add grace to their pillaging of other writers without acknowledgement.) It was in the palmy days of *The Criterion* that theology became the latest *chic* in the fashionable intellectual's outfit, and we can observe in some members of the *Theology* group the point where the Christian discriminator and the Bloomsbury exhibitionist do not merely meet but overlap; if theology is going to be aired for those purposes the gravest suspicions of its value to literary criticism will be confirmed. The method of *After Strange Gods* is temptingly easy, and particularly adapted to further individual and group complacency, it is evident.

The line for a Christian apologist for literature to take is surely that in the work of considerable poets and novelists – few of whom were or remained churchmen, and we may well ask why this is so – the finest and keenest perceptions of an age show themselves, communicated in the language by which we live as social beings; and that to deprive oneself of them, in the name of religious orthodoxy or anything else, is to deprive oneself of full life and real understanding of the world we are part of. The tendency of orthodoxy is to repress these perceptions for its own convenience and cause a moral cramp in the developing consciousness – an effect very obvious in Charlotte Yonge's novels so that these might justly be described as undesirable literature.[2] The spontaneous explosive reaction of artists to this kind of pressure is as inevitable as a drowning man's struggle for air: Blake, Samuel Butler, the early Shaw and Lawrence among others bear violent witness to the force of a repressive moral environment and the waste of energy exerted to lever it off. When Lawrence wrote:

It is the way our sympathy flows and recoils that really determines our lives. And here lies the importance of the novel properly handled. It can inform and lead into new places the flow of our sympathetic consciousness, and it can lead our sympathy away in recoil from things gone dead.

he indicates the most important part of the novelist's function, and suggests how much more delicate and complex that is than the work of the moralist or theologian, enjoying his clearly conceived dogmatic outlook and ordering his final judgements by the 'standard of orthodoxy', can be. The novelist, unlike the theologian, works in terms of concrete particularity.

If Christian discriminators wish to gain a respectful hearing they must jettison their Charlotte Yonges instead of trying to thrust them on us, and show themselves in opposition to that tendency of all orthodoxies for which some phrase needs coining to express the converse of what Arnold called 'the dissidence of Dissent'. They must possess a finer sensibility in their own province as well as in ours. 'Brother Every, discriminating Christianly', as Mr Bethell puts it, states dogmatically of the maintenance of standards and work of the literary critic, that this 'capacity is certainly a matter of intelligence and not virtue' and therefore inessential for a Christian (though possibly an added grace); Mr C. S. Lewis made a similar statement even more vehemently in the attack in *Theology* cited above. The virtue that does not include this kind of intelligence, we reply, can be only a very qualified variety and contains an element of danger to itself. When Charlotte Brontë in *Villette* records the recoil of a Protestant conscience from a professedly Christian society which seemed to her to have 'gone dead'; when Stendhal diagnoses the seminary world of the day in *Le Rouge et le Noir*, when Henry James and Edith Wharton examine the values by which a society lived, they are doing in a sharp local way what all good novelists are doing, the work of the critic and maintainers of standards; and Bro. George Every's idea that if only general education could be stopped (and he hopes it may)[3] the need for literature and criticism would disappear shows how shallow his recognition of the uses of literature must be. If the Christian discriminators singled out for recognition the art of the Stendhals and Conrads and Tolstoys and showed they could understand and utilize such novels as *Nostromo*, *Middlemarch*, *Anna Karenina*, *Darkness at Noon*, *The Portrait of a Lady*, *The Root and the Flower*, instead of deploring George Eliot, claiming Jane Austen as a 'Christian novelist' because they know she was a clergyman's daughter, and displaying superiority on theological grounds to Thomas Hardy, their own intention would be advanced as well as the cause of literature. That they should desire to make literature 'the handmaid of theology', as Mr Bethell says, is natural, but when supported by so very poor a showing of first-hand literary criticism their efforts to prove that they can make it so, let alone that it should be so, are peculiarly unimpressive.

Hardy and criticism

Thomas Hardy (English Men of Letters), by Edmund Blunden
    (Macmillan)
Hardy the Novelist, by Lord David Cecil (Constable)
The Southern Review, Thomas Hardy centennial issue, Summer 1940

'No, I think I shall do much better to be allusive and charming and
rather subtle, you know the sort of thing, and tender. I think one
ought always to *see* a book before one starts it. Well, I see this rather
like a portrait by Van Dyck, with a good deal of atmosphere, you
know, and a certain gravity, and with a sort of aristocratic distinction. Do you know what I mean? About eighty thousand words.'

He was absorbed for a moment in the ecstasy of aesthetic con-
templation. In his mind's eye he saw a book, in royal octavo, slim
and light in the hand, printed with large margins on handsome
paper in a type that was both clear and comely, and I think he saw
a binding in smooth black cloth with a decoration in gold and gilt
lettering.

So the man of letters in Mr Somerset Maugham's little
masterpiece, *Cakes and Ale*, explains his intention of writing a
critical biography of that novelist whose works so curiously
resemble those of Thomas Hardy. And now (though of
course you can't have large margins in wartime) the thing has
been done, or at least one cannot avoid the suspicion that
when Lord David Cecil was invited to give the Clark Lectures
at Cambridge he started with very nearly that intention. No
one can suppose he was impelled by a sense of urgent critical
work to be done. Take a fair specimen:

Hardy's books do not always end thus on a crashing major chord.
He is also master of the dying fall, the Miltonic close in calm of
mind, all passion spent, the fading echoing music that, when soft
voices die, vibrates in the memory. *Under the Greenwood Tree* presents
us with an example.

This is the kind of prose in which much of *Hardy the Novelist* is
written. I should have thought that to anyone it was obviously a style in which literary criticism cannot be conveyed;
it is certainly a style which undergraduates are discouraged
from using in their first term at the university to which these
lectures were addressed. Yet the publisher informs us that
'The aim of this book is – while taking advantage of the

greater extent of modern knowledge – to return to the true critical path.' And besides its subtitle, 'An Essay in Criticism', there is an opening section explaining how all criticism is wrong which is not purely aesthetic. It is solely the critic's function, we are told, 'to illuminate our appreciation of them [books], to define the nature of the satisfaction they give, to analyse the circumstances conditioning their production and the arts by which they make their impression'. Lord David makes it clear that he intends this to be understood in the narrowest sense.

Those interested in the criticism of novels – or perhaps in this connection one should say of The Novel, for to the aesthete the Novel, the Epic, the Lyric, are profitable abstractions – will recollect that the doyen of this school of novel critics was Mr Percy Lubbock with his *Craft of Fiction*. I must say that I have never been able to see that the *Craft of Fiction* approach to novels ever justifies itself, and it seems a criticism of this method that it produces in all the instances I have seen only a succession of commonplace observations put across in fine writing at tiresome length, and that when the aesthetic critic tries to go further he dries up in a desert of meaningless phrases such as shallow modelling, narrative and visual art, and unreal distinctions between form and content, and even sets up such concepts as the Comic Spirit and tragic feeling to be permanent stumbling-blocks in the way of the young. It is not thus that criticism can come to grips with a work of art. In fact, the conclusions that the approach Lord David favours provides, seem to have little connection with the experience of the sensitive reader – e.g. he says '*Under the Greenwood Tree* is one of Hardy's most faultless works', whereas the facetious tone of the book and its being made entirely out of Hardy's comic-relief material without anything to be relieved, anything (that is) which comes from the deeper and more vital sources of his experiences and interests, must strike any critical reader, I should have thought, and mark it as the novel in the canon (excluding the hopeless failures such as *The Well-Beloved*) least likely ever to be noted for re-reading. Again, 'No one describes love more impressively than Hardy . . . ' I should have thought no one did less so in his novels, for it is a mere counter and convention in all Hardy's, being one of three stock varieties – either the grand-passion convention, or the faithful love of the worthy man or woman, or the philandering motions executed by the other sort. No, to be a critic it is necessary to bring more pressure to bear on the undertaking than the aesthete can; he is a lay fellow: without bothering to verify he slaps down his first impressions, and doesn't notice whether he is expressing conventional judgements or contradictions or other people's ideas misunderstood, or what mess of clichés, fine writing and empty phrases he is making on the paper. In so far as the method may have an incidental usefulness when properly practised, it is felt to be impertinent, for what can it do at best but point to the mechanism of a novel? – the part played by the characters in forwarding the plot and the part played by the plot in shaping the work of art, where is the author's viewpoint and mouthpiece, which parts of the narrative are dramatic and descriptive and why, and similar pieces of elementary surface observation, the kind of thing any intelligent reader can and should do for himself at second reading if he hasn't mechanically done so during the first. If he cannot do it for himself be cannot be said to read at all. I don't see how Lord David can think he has fulfilled a mission by telling a university audience:

The creative gift, the power to apprehend his material aesthetically, he possessed in the highest degree; but, for complete success a writer cannot rely on the aesthetic qualities alone. He must know how to present his imaginative conceptions to best advantage. Hardy was a great artist, but not a great craftsman.

I must repeat – Hardy's novels are visual novels. It is in his ability to make us 'see' that his greatest strength lies . . . Hardy's creative power also shows itself in his characters . . .

Lord David in short violates the first law of literary criticism, whether aesthetic or otherwise, which is, that when you haven't anything to say, don't say it.

As a revelation of the pretensions of the lecturer I should like to make one more quotation:

Indeed, it is the inevitable defect of a spontaneous genius like Hardy's that it is impervious to education. No amount of painstaking study got him within sight of achieving that intuitive good taste, that instinctive grasp of the laws of literature, which is the native heritage of one bred from childhood in the atmosphere of a high culture.

Hardy, we may justly reply, had a good Victorian education, was further equipped in the special arts and crafts of music and architecture, was generally well read and thoroughly understood what he read, as his notebooks show, had a remarkably acute grasp of literary theory and a most intelligent response to its practice;[4] that if his style was often bad in the sense of being gauche, pedantic and so on, it was at least his own style and succeeded in expressing something real and personal; and that he had a heritage more valuable than that of 'one bred from childhood in the atmosphere of a high culture' (whatever that may be, for the implication that Hardy's cultural milieu was a low one is preposterous).

I am not carping because I disagree with Lord David's valuation of Hardy the novelist, in fact it would be hard to do so because his book leaks all kinds of opinions and ideas that have been current about Hardy and his novels, without any attempt to distinguish critically or to formulate them incisively so that anyone else may. I am registering a protest against his critical theory and practice. When Mr Somerset Maugham (to whom we may turn to take the taste of elegant aestheticism out of our mouths) writes of his fictitious novelist:

He was for long thought to write very bad English, and indeed he gave you the impression of writing with the stub of a blunt pencil; his style was laboured, an uneasy mixture of the classical and the slangy, and his dialogue was such as could never have issued from the mouth of a human being . . . His prime belonged to a period when the purple patch was in vogue, and there are descriptive passages in his works that have found their way into all the anthologies of English prose . . . It should be a mortification to me that I cannot read them without discomfort . . . My own heart sank when he led me into the forecastle of a ship or the taproom of a public-house, and I knew I was in for half-a-dozen pages of facetious comment on life, ethics, and immortality. But, I admit, I have always thought the Shakespearean clowns tedious, and their innumerable progeny insupportable . . . His women hardly come to life. But here again I must add that this is only my own opinion; the world at large and the most eminent critics have agreed that they are very winsome types of English womanhood, spirited, gallant,

high-souled, and they have been often compared with the heroines
of Shakespeare. We know of course that women are habitually con-
stipated, but to represent them in fiction as being altogether devoid
of a back passage seems to me really an excess of chivalry. I am
surprised that they should care to see themselves thus limned.

(*Cakes and Ale*)

then, though as it stands it is not literary criticism (neither is
Lord David's),[5] yet it presents incisively a critical attitude,
and a response to certain elements in the work that cannot be
ignored by the critic, and is therefore useful, as good sense
and first-hand judgement always are. When one of the contributors to the Hardy centennial number of the *Southern
Review* writes:

Only the disenchanted sophomore can be deeply impressed by
Hardy's view of life. Although it was an outcome of the new scientific views, it now seems like a simple variant of supernaturalism
... And although Hardy properly objected to treating his fiction as
a 'scientific system of philosophy', the trouble is that he often wrote
as if it were. The scheme of his novels is typically all too rigid and
diagrammatic, their argument all too formal and explicit ... The
serious objection, at any rate, is not to his philosophy *per se*, the dis-
mal generalizations he illogically induces from the extraordinary
actions he invents. It is to his artistry, the inventions themselves.

then one sees that critical argument is being advanced by
someone with a central grasp of the subject. In this case, the
critic (Herbert J. Muller, 'The Novels of Hardy Today') is
actually citing the serious faults of his subject before dis-
posing of these objections by advancing his own account of
the greatness of Hardy the novelist. I mention this in order to
make it clear that I do not object to some people's criticism
of Hardy because I disagree with their verdict, like the supervisor who failed a paper I once produced on Shelley because
she admired the poet so fervently that no adverse criticism of
Prometheus Unbound, however plausibly argued and substan-
tially supported, could be allowed merit. I am merely
expressing a preference for criticism that comes from some
kind of a mind, instead of no kind.

Hardy criticism has even in our time passed through
several phases. To his contemporaries, as Mr Edmund

Blunden abundantly demonstrates in his volume on Hardy in the English Men of Letters series, he was just another Victorian novelist. They were not deep enough in the machine age to ecstasize over the glimpses of pastoral England his novels afford, and they had enough good models current in fiction to recognize how awkward his style was, how limited his conception of characterization, and (when they were not, as with the last novels, provoked by his moral unconventionality) the imperfect relation between the moral feeling and the fable he found for embodying it. One can sympathize with the Saturday Reviewer who complained of *Tess* that 'Few people would deny the terrible dreariness of the tale, which, except during a few hours spent with the cows, has not a gleam of sunshine anywhere.' One sees what he meant about the gratuitous nature of the tragic action, and is grateful for the degrading of the dairy-idyll passages to 'a few hours spent among the cows', when so much since has been written rapturously about the novel largely on the strength of those descriptions.

The next phase, recognizing Hardy both as a beautiful writer of descriptive passages about rural England and as a creator of Sophoclean tragedy, came about I suppose when the knowledge of writers like George Eliot and Richard Jefferies faded. With Meredith, the then current comparison, he could of course only be compared to his advantage in every respect. In *Thomas Hardy: A Critical Study* by Lascelles Abercrombie (1912) this very solemn acceptance of Hardy's novels is well expressed. If you want an analytic account of Hardy's novels in such terms, this remains the best work of the kind, unencumbered by other material (if you ignore the account of the poems and *The Dynasts*). Lionel Johnson's six essays, *The Art of Thomas Hardy* (1892) is in the same direction, but too pervaded by Lionel Johnson.

It was Hardy himself who claimed for his novels an Aeschylean intention and a Sophoclean unity and grandeur. But even examination papers have ceased on the whole to demand comparisons between *Tess* (and the other 'great' tragic novels) and Greek Tragedy. A more sober rate of admiration has been given to the Hardy novels since, for there have been exasperated debunking efforts by unsympathetic writers with quite other kinds of demands from fiction (such as Mr Somerset Maugham); and the growing acceptance of the greater art of Conrad and Henry James, who unlike Hardy are in no respect shown up by time as old-fashioned, has probably helped to put the Hardy novels in juster perspective.[6] It would be well if it were recognized that the novelist who can be most profitably employed for 'placing' Hardy is George Eliot, from whom he derives (Lord David couples him with Scott and the academic world with Meredith); a useful critical exercise is to recommend for reading *Silas Marner* after *Under the Greenwood Tree*.

George Eliot in her novels and stories (except *Romola*) shows a corresponding seriousness of outlook and purpose embodied in similar fictional forms, but, it seems to me, she excels Hardy in every respect. She is the finer artist with wider capacities, the sounder thinker in her account of the relation of man to environment, people to the community, and personalities to each other, the wiser moralist, the more efficient writer, and gives us a more interesting and sensitive apprehension of character. She is equally sincere without being so simple. She has a vein of wit whereas he has only rustic humour, and her irony is real where his is merely the tragic brand. And though she too is saddened she is not morbid. But Hardy's superior appeal has lain in something like morbidity combined with the overpoweringly dramatic impression left by his conceptions. It is a fact that his novels have for at least a generation provided something that no other body of work could or at any rate did. In spite of the critic whom I have quoted as saying that 'only the disenchanted sophomore can be deeply impressed by Hardy's view of life', there is always a generation of such readers, and few people can re-examine dispassionately writings which have impressed them deeply at so critical a stage in their emotional development. Mr E. L. Woodward the Oxford historian in his most interesting biography *Short Journey* (Faber, 1942) is representative when he writes:

During my last year at school and my first two years at Oxford, the poems and novels of Thomas Hardy influenced my mind far more than the work of any other English writer ... The book [*Tess*] moved me so deeply that I could not read more than a chapter at a time ... So I read on until I had come to the end of everything which Hardy had published. I have read these novels and poems over and over again. They are part of my life.

Whether some other novelist will ever replace Hardy for this purpose is a matter for speculation. But we need not speculate on the ultimate effect of reading Hardy at any phase of development. We can only be grateful for having a body of fiction that proceeds from so honest, worthy and compassionate a nature, so sensitive to human misery and so powerful to record its distresses at the spectacle of suffering, so disinterested, unworldly and unfailingly tender.

Mr Edmund Blunden's biography is an index of current judgement. He is extremely cautious of making high claims, confines himself in the critical field to countering adverse criticism of the less radical kind, and gives a surprising proportion of his book to extracts from the contemporary reviews. While conveying the peculiarities of Hardy's character as it appeared in old age, with some interesting reminiscences by men of letters of the impression his personality made on them, he does not give us the essential anecdotes and reminiscences about Hardy's youth which provide a clue to his morbid sensitiveness to suffering or even the appearance of it in nature (such as his weeping at seeing the leaves fall). Perhaps he wished to avoid overlapping with Mrs Hardy's *Early Life* and *Later Life of Thomas Hardy*, which remain indispensable, although written in the most unfortunate style of standard biography. Nobody tells us the facts, which are only vaguely known, about his emotional history and its reactions on his writings – for instance the estrangement from his first wife which produced the attacks on marriage and the marriage laws in his writings at that time (*Jude*, *The Woodlanders*). The really useful critical biography of Hardy has not yet been written. But, in a quiet way, and leaving the reader to read between the lines, Mr Blunden has gone some way towards producing it.

As a start there are some stimulating and constructive essays in Hardy criticism in the Hardy centenary issue of an American periodical I have referred to, nearly all by Americans. Some of the contributions are, inevitably, academic in the derogatory sense, but, to point out the live wood, I should like to specify Mr Zabel's 'Hardy in Defense of his Art: The Aesthetic of Incongruity' (perhaps I am biassed by his specifying the *Scrutiny* evaluation of Hardy in June 1934 as still one of the best essays written on the novels); the valuable analysis of '*Jude the Obscure* as a Tragedy' by Arthur Mizener – such a really fundamental analysis of one novel done with intelligence and critical method, and by someone in possession of a great deal of parallel information about Hardy's mentality and outlook, is more illuminating than a library of 'aesthetic' flounderings; and the final essay on 'The Novels of Hardy Today' by Herbert J. Muller. These really are essays in criticism which it would be enlightening instead of insulting to present to a university audience. One is glad too to have a spirited, able and critically demolishing essay by the distinguished short-story writer Miss Katherine Anne Porter, 'Notes on a Criticism of Thomas Hardy', in reply to the outrageous account of Hardy's work in *After Strange Gods*. One understands why Henry James in a letter about *Tess* permits himself to refer to Hardy the novelist as 'the good little Thomas Hardy' – he was in a position to employ the patronizing 'little', though we aren't, and the attribution of innocence and moral worth in the combined adjectives is just right in contrast to Mr Eliot's criticism of the novelist, which could hardly be more wrong in tone, intention and expression. There are also a number of essays on Hardy's poems in the memorial number of this periodical, but I have been concerned here with the criticism of Hardy's fiction. What really warms one's heart is the complete absence of the belletristic approach or of any aesthetic posturing, in this collective enterprise. Could one believe that any similar undertaking on this side of the Atlantic, even before the War, would have been so profitable or even harmless? It is certainly the most helpful critical work on Hardy I know, and since the best essays in it are by tough-minded critics with a corresponding tightness of argument and idiom, who raise many debatable critical problems, it could be recommended for teething purposes at the university. Unfortunately the *Southern Review* has become a war fatality, and back numbers are probably unobtainable.

Lives and works of Richard Jefferies

Jefferies' England – Nature Essays, by Richard Jefferies, Edited
    with an Introduction by S. J. Looker (Constable)
*Richard Jefferies, Selections of his Work, with Details of his Life and
    Circumstance, his Death and Immortality*, by Henry
    Williamson (Faber and Faber)
Hodge and his Masters, by Richard Jefferies, Revised by Henry
    Williamson (Methuen)

Mention Richard Jefferies to anyone under thirty-five and he
or she will almost certainly say 'Do you mean *The Story of My
Heart* man? I never read it'; and they may recollect having
read *Bevis* when young. An uninviting title and a boys' classic
seem to be all that remains for the majority of a once considerable reputation. It is excellent therefore that selections
from his works should be issued now to bring him before a
new public, calling attention to the variety of his genius, with
critical essays by the editors enouncing its nature. Unfortunately these selections have been undertaken by the wrong
people or in the wrong spirit. It is not true, as some of the
reviewers alleged, that they have chosen almost identical
extracts – only two pieces are in fact duplicated – but neither
book is likely to do Jefferies much good in the way of inducing
the intelligentsia to give his entire *oeuvre* a trial. Mr Williamson's selection is much the more attractive and more just in
its representative variety, but unhappily so strongly does the
editor's personality interleave the pages and so possessive is
his attitude to his victim ('My Jefferies' he calls him, and
apostrophizes and converses with him with complacent
impertinence)[7] that many readers who will decide or have
long ago decided that they can't stomach the author of *The
Village Book* will not realize that Jefferies is quite another kind
of writer on rural themes. It would be a pity if Jefferies should
become the property of Mr Williamson, as Cobbett became
the property of G. K. Chesterton.

Jefferies was one of those comprehensive geniuses from
whose work you can take what you are inclined to find. Mr
Looker selects to sell us a noble Victorian Jefferies (the
mystic, the nature-philosopher, etc.) and not unintentionally: 'It is the purpose of this book to show the real Jefferies

... It celebrates the author of *The Story of My Heart* ... [where] Knowledge has given place to Wisdom'. This is scarcely an aspect that will appeal to the contemporary public, and reviewers indeed found Mr Looker's Jefferies dull. From the other selection, which while keeping the same principle (of chronological representation) might have been made far more intelligently, you would conclude that Jefferies had written a much larger proportion of weak, ephemeral or eccentric stuff than is the case, and you are deprived of most of his strongest, finest and characteristic things.[8]

Disinterested campaigning for Jefferies would rather ask Messrs Hutchinson to reprint Edward Thomas's *Richard Jefferies, His Life and Work* (1908) (preferably in the cheap pocket edition); since second-hand booksellers ask a guinea for this Life there must be a long-felt want. This book should be recognized as a classic in critical biography, to stand with Lockhart's Scott and Mrs Gaskell's Brontë in point of intrinsic interest and containing better literary criticism than many critical works. The well-known fact that Thomas did hack-work for publishers has probably prevented recognition of this book, which he did voluntarily and evidently took much trouble to perfect. Since subsequent writers on Jefferies take all their facts from him as well as his careful bibliography, generally without acknowledgement, and since there is nothing more to be found out about Jefferies (the old inhabitants who knew him having passed away and Thomas anyhow observing, 'Of the man himself we know, and apparently can know, very little'), to reprint Thomas's work would automatically render further book-making unnecessary. His is a model biography. The author is recognized as being present only by the sympathy that informs the narrative and the intelligence that directs the criticism and determines the selections. The selections from Jefferies's works there are so abundant and well-chosen that Thomas's Life of itself will send the reader to their sources. Another good piece of Jefferies criticism is an introduction to one of the novels, *Amaryllis at the Fair*, by Edward Garnett, prefixed to the New Readers Library edition.[9] Garnett exposes the silliness of the Saintsbury kind of critique of Jefferies and declares, with a supporting argument that is at least as necessary now as it was then, that 'in his judgment *Amaryllis* is one of the very few later-day novels of English country life that are worth putting on one's shelf, and that to make room for it he would turn out certain highly praised novels by Hardy which the critics and the public, with touching unanimity, have voted to be of high rank'.

In fact Jefferies was a many-sided and comprehensive genius, not merely a peculiarly English genius but one whose interests, ideas, and temperament associate him with other peculiarly English geniuses: he recalls or embodies now Cobbett, now D. H. Lawrence, now Dickens, now Edward Thomas himself, and he had a sensuous nature akin to but more robust than Keats's; he has too a strikingly contemporary aspect as social satirist, and he is in the central and most important tradition of English prose style. No selection can do him justice that does not present and even stress these aspects of a writer who has been too generally represented merely as a word-painter of natural beauties, a sort of early Keats in prose.

Perhaps a few quotations from a mass of similar material will illustrate his characteristic vein of vigorous feeling.

Up in the north they say there is a district where the labourers spend their idle hours in cutting out and sticking together fiddles. I do not care twopence for a fiddle as a fiddle; but still I think if a labouring man coming home from plough, and exposure to rough wind, and living on coarse fare, can still have spirit enough left to sit down and patiently carve out bits of maple wood and fit them together into a complete and tunable fiddle, then he must have within him some of the true idea of art, and that fiddle is in itself a work of art.   [*The Dewy Morn*]

He minded when that sharp old Miss — was always coming round with tracts and blankets, like taking some straw to a lot of pigs, and lecturing his missis about economy. What a fuss she made, and scolded his wife as if she was a thief for having her fifteenth boy! His missis turned on her at last and said: 'Lor' miss, that's all the pleasure me an' my old man got'.   [*The Toilers of the Field*]

In this book some notes have been made of the former state of things before it passes away entirely. But I would not have it therefore thought that I wish it to continue or return. My sympathies and hopes are with the light of the future, only I should like it to come from nature. The clock should be read by the sunshine, not the sun timed by the clock. The latter is indeed impossible, for though all

the clocks in the world should declare the hour of dawn to be midnight, the sun will presently rise just the same.

[*Round About a Great Estate*]

As himself of noble birth, Felix had hitherto seen things only from
the point of view of his own class. Now he associated with grooms,
he began to see society from their point of view, and recognized
how feebly it was held together by brute force, intrigue, cord and
axe, and woman's flattery. But a push seemed needed to overthrow
it.

[*After London*]

To me it seems the most curious thing possible that well-to-do
people should expect the poor to be delighted with their condition.
I hope they never will be.

[*Field and Hedgerow*]

There were parsons then, as now, in every rural parish preaching
and teaching something they called the Gospel. Why did they not
rise as one man and denounce this ghastly iniquity [hanging for
steep-stealing], and demand its abolition? They did nothing of the
sort; they enjoyed their pipes and grog very comfortably . . . The
gallows at the cross-roads is gone, but the workhouse stands . . .
that blot on our civilization, the workhouse.

[*Field and Hedgerow*]

Then to unlearn the first ideas of history of science, of social institutions, to unlearn one's own life and purpose; to unlearn the old
mode of thought and way of arriving at things; to take off peel after
peel, and so get by degrees slowly towards the truth – thus writing,
as it were, a sort of floating book in the mind, almost remaking the
soul. It seems as if the chief value of books is to give us something
to unlearn. Sometimes I feel indignant at the false views that were
instilled into me in early days, and then again I see that that very
indignation gives me a moral life.

[*Field and Hedgerow*]

And even from *Bevis*, which its editors tell you is an idealization of his boyhood:

Loo said they were all hungry, but Samson was most hungry. He
cried almost all day and all night, and woke himself up crying in the
morning. Very often she left him, and went a long way down the
hedge because she did not like to hear him.

'But,' objected Bevis, 'my Governor pays your father money, and
I'm sure my mamma sends you things' . . . Bevis became much agi-
tated, he said he would tell the Governor, he would tell dear
mamma, Samson should not cry any more. Now Bevis had always
been in contact almost with these folk, but yet he had never seen;
you and I live in the midst of things, but never look beneath the surface. His face became quite white; he was thoroughly upset. It was

his first glance at the hard roadside of life. He said he would do all sorts of things; Loo listened pleased but dimly doubtful, she could not have explained herself, but she nevertheless knew that it was beyond Bevis's power to alter these circumstances.

In his own time interest was drawn off at his death in disputations about 'Did Richard Jefferies die a Christian?'[9] and when such questions ceased to burn Jefferies was practically relegated with them to limbo. There has always been a garden-suburb cult of *The Story of my Heart* which has assisted in discrediting him. It is an unfortunate title, and the book itself unless read in its place with the whole body of his writings will do him no good. Jefferies was not a 'thinker' whose thinking is of any use to us without the recreation of the experience that occasioned it, and his 'message' is more successfully conveyed in such relations, not in the prose poem which he attempted. The other factor that pushed Jefferies out of sight for the post-war generation was the Bloomsbury cult of W. H. Hudson. The impression left was that Hudson did everything Jefferies did, only much better because he was an artist, a great stylist, and the other a clumsy amateur who wrote journalism. It is hard now to understand how anyone could have had patience with the precious style Hudson affected or have been interested in his Victorian Utopias. We did not venture to disagree openly with Mrs Woolf and Mr Herbert Read and Mr Murry and the *Athenaeum*, but we privately found Hudson a bore and, in his sentimentalization of human life, embarrassing. No one had the strength of mind of the child in 'The Emperor's New Clothes', and by the time Hudson had ceased to be read Jefferies had dropped back out of sight. It took the red blood of Mr A. G. Street and the happy ingenuousness of Mr Adrian Bell to get country life back into the circulating library. It is generally difficult to persuade people to persevere with *A Shepherd's Life*, the best of Hudson's country books, so discouraging are the first two chapters, yet it is well worth reading: but how strained, how literary, how unconvincing compared with the mounting life that informs *Round About a Great Estate*, to take only one out of a pile of Jefferies's good things. And how Hudson dates! while his predecessor is still a modern.

To secure Jefferies his right to be read, several points could
be made. One is the intrinsic value as literature of the rural
life of much of his work. The large public that enjoyed
Farmer's Glory and *Corduroy* would equally enjoy *The Amateur
Poacher*, *Wild Life in a Southern County* and *Round About a Great
Estate* (one of the most delightful books in the English
language). Those who have found *Change in the Village* and
Change in the Farm relevant to their interest in social history
will be glad that *Hodge and His Masters* is again in print and will
be impelled by that to search Jefferies for more documentation; since three of the least useful chapters have been
chosen for the Faber anthology the reprint will be even more
welcome. It is characteristic of Jefferies that he expressed
regret that Gilbert White 'did not leave a natural history of
the people of his day'. The element in Jefferies's writings
represented by the interest that Gilbert White lacked is the
decisive one; some of his best work can be described as such
a natural history – for instance 'The Country Sunday' among
other essays in *Field and Hedgerow*, and pieces throughout his
other volumes of collected essays, *Nature Near London*, *The Life
of the Fields*, *The Toilers of the Field*. But it also led him to collect
folklore, rustic idiom and dialect words, and to note dying
crafts and changing ways of living at a time when these subjects were little considered. To a far larger section of the
intelligentsia an impressive case could be made for bringing
Jefferies to their notice as an approved social thinker. His
case-history would make useful propaganda; one of those
Left journalists who turn out biographies showing that
writers like Dickens were really just the same kind of writer as
Mr Alec Brown ought to be instructed to do Jefferies. Starting
as a member of the yeoman-farmer class with all its Conservative prejudices and habits of social conformism he
emancipated himself by nothing but the force of daily experience and sensitive reflection to a position of daring freedom
from the ideas of his class, his age and his country (he died in
1887).

It would be noted in such a Life that he planned to write
(and may even have written but never published) works
called 'The New Pilgrim's Progress; or, A Christian's Painful
Progress from the Town of Middle Class to the Golden City'
and 'The Proletariate: The Power of the Future'; that he

hated the Church as an oppressor, calling it 'a huge octopus' and noting with pleasure that 'the pickaxe is already laid to the foundations of the Church tower'; that he wrote of 'laws made by the rich for the rich' – 'Most certainly the laws ought to be altered and must be altered'; that he protested in reference to projects for the cultural elevation of the villagers, 'For the enjoyment of art it is first of all necessary to have a full belly'; that he never had the smallest hankering after the Merrie Englande past[10] but wanted the latest mechanism for agriculture and 'the light railway to call at the farmyard gate' and protested that the village had church and chapel but no cottage hospital, library, or lecture system to put the country folk in touch with the mental life of the time – villages should own themselves and have the right by Act of Parliament, like the railways, to buy land back from the landowners at a reasonable price – 'in the course of time, as the people take possession of the earth on which they stand . . . ' he writes; that he never idyllicized country life or rested for long content with the sensuous beauties of nature – 'I am simply describing the realities of rural life behind the scenes', he says in 'One of the New Voters' and it might often serve as his epigraph; that he was acutely conscious of the class war and the monetary basis of modern society – *After London; or, Wild England*, which is always written of as though it were of the *News from Nowhere* or *A Crystal Age* type of pretty day-dream impresses as contemporary not with Morris or Hudson but with *The Wild Goose Chase* (it seems to me to be a consistent satire on the system Jefferies found himself living under and to be in great part autobiographical).[11] Jefferies hated the class distinctions which exacted servility from tenants and farm-hands, kept a hold over the morals of the cottager and strangled his independence, and the fierce attacks on this aspect of rural life should make *The Dewy Morn*,[12] his most considerable novel, a Left Book. I have quoted a significant passage from *Bevis*, and even *Wood Magic*, a storybook for little children, has every claim to be admitted to the socialist nursery. Edward Thomas notes that although Jefferies was aloof and 'not a talker', yet he 'talked with ease and vigour on his own subjects, most eagerly on the Labour Question'.[13] These notes, which might be multiplied if space allowed, could feed a new biography which would make Jefferies appear alive and congenial to our younger generation as neither Mr Looker's lofty thinker nor Mr Williamson's alter ego can be. And it would have the merit of being nearer to the truth – the truth of Jefferies' character, that core of his varied writings that unites them and gives them significance. But of course as an account of his work and its importance for posterity it would be ludicrously inadequate, for these facts and quotations only impress when given prominence by extraction and accumulation. Jefferies' 'message' is so much more complex and deep-rooted that the total impression made by anything he wrote is not of this simple order. For instance, his instinctive humanity and indignant expression of it are controlled by a characteristic irony – that irony of Jefferies' which is so disconcerting that Mr Looker preferred to ignore it. Nor has *After London* any trace of the crude propaganding and spiritual vulgarity of *The Wild Goose Chase* with which I have suggested a comparison.

For Jefferies was an artist, though not of the Hudson genre. His writing never reaches after effect and seems unconscious of achieving any; he is therefore the best possible model and for this reason alone should be in common possession, as Addison once was. He might indeed, if a judicious selection were made, supersede *The Coverley Papers* (which have got to be a bore in schools), not to speak of those positively vicious models of Style and The Essay children's taste is officially formed on. Thomas's account of his prose cannot be improved:

These words call no attention to themselves. There is not an uncommon word, nor a word in an uncommon sense, all through Jefferies' books. There are styles which are noticeable for their very lucidity and naturalness; Jefferies is not noticeable even to this extent . . . His style was not a garment in which he clothed everything indiscriminately . . . He did not make great phrases, and hardly a single sentence would prove him a master . . . Though he had read much, it was without having played the sedulous ape that he found himself in the great tradition.

He did not make great phrases. Anyone in Bloomsbury can make a phrase, but Jefferies' effects are cumulative. They express a play of character and an original outlook, so that in their context the simplest groups of words are pregnant, as when he writes in 'Bevis's Zodiac': 'The sparkle of Orion's stars brought to him a remnant of the immense vigour of the young world' or, to take something widely different, in 'The Country Sunday', when describing the villagers going to chapel in their best clothes 'all out of drawing, and without a touch that could be construed into a national costume – the cheap shoddy shop in the country lane'. The curious anticipations of D. H. Lawrence here are widespread in his mature work and suggest both how original his outlook was and what direction his gifts might have taken had he lived (he died at thirty-eight). Nothing came to him through literature, he is as unliterary as Cobbett though of greater personal cultivation and finer native sensibility; a contemporary suggested, says Thomas, that he avoided literary society deliberately in order to preserve his native endowments. And he is an artist in another sense, that compared with his works his life has little interest – all of him that holds value for us exists complete in his writings. He left no revealing letters, he did not mix in any kind of society, his domestic life was happy and normal.

Why he has not got into the literary histories (Elton does not mention him, Saintsbury is fatuous, subsequent historians have followed one or the other) and the university courses in literature is a mystery, but reason seems to have no hand in deciding these things. Yet as a source of evidence for 'background' courses he is surely more reliable as well as more original than the novelists, as an essayist he has surely more claim to be studied as literature than all these Lambs and Paters, and as a novelist himself he cannot be ignored where Hardy is studied (unless on quantitative grounds). Jefferies wrote four novels of permanent worth as well as some negligible ones. I have mentioned *After London*, which is written in Jefferies' mature style – the superb opening describing 'The Relapse into Barbarism' as the wild supplanted the cities should be a well-known piece. *Greene Ferne Farm* is the best of his early novels, comparable with the Hardy of *Under the Greenwood Tree*, while the most ambitious and novel-like of his later attempts, *The Dewy Morn*, reaches out towards D. H. Lawrence. The contrast between the maturity and originality of the content and Jefferies' clumsiness in manipulating the devices of the novel form is striking and may put off many readers. But the clumsiness is merely indifference, and when in *Amaryllis at the Fair* (another unfortunate title) he found a form that could convey all he was interested in treating without obliging him to satisfy the conventional demands on the novelist, he produced a masterpiece. But both *Greene Ferne Farm* and *The Dewy Morn* are too good to be let stay out of print. The Victorian features of these novels bulk at least as largely in Hardy's novels, but it is only in Jefferies' that the vitality and genuineness of the rest makes that conventional idiom appear ludicrous; most people seem able to read *The Return of the Native* with its 'Do you brave me, madam's?' without any feeling of incongruity between the melodrama of the parts and the total 'tragic' effect. But in Jefferies' novels the best parts are better and more mature than the best parts of most of Hardy's. The portrayer of rustic life who notes the village woman telling the welfare-worker who scolds her fecundity: 'That's all the pleasure me an' my old man got' and describes (in *Greene Ferne Farm*) old Andrew Fisher with his *Wuthering Heights* past receiving the clerical suitor for his granddaughter's hand thus:

'Jim! Bill! Jock!' shouted the old man, starting out of his chair, purple in the face. 'Drow this veller out! Douse un in th'hog vault! Thee nimity-pimity odd-me-dod! I warn thee'd like my money! Drot thee and thee wench!'

is not a novelist who could conventionalize his villagers for purposes of humorous relief as Hardy does. In *The Dewy Morn* he goes further than any Victorian novelist towards the modern novel – I mean the novel that seems to have significance for us other than as a mirror of manners and morals; I should describe it as one of the few real novels between *Wuthering Heights* and *Sons and Lovers*. The final justification for asking the twentieth century to read Jefferies is, in Edward Thomas's fine words, that 'His own character, and the characters of his men and women, fortify us in our intention to live.' And we are more in need of fortification now than when those words were written.

We are now waiting for some sensible publisher to launch the Wiltshire Edition of Jefferies' Collected Works – Jefferies must be more or less out of copyright now – with Jefferies' wood-anemone-leaf signature stamped on the covers. It should lead off with Thomas's Life, follow with *Greene Ferne Farm* and *Amaryllis* in one volume, third *The Dewy Morn*, then the other out-of-prints (*Toilers of the Field*, *Red Deer*, *The Hills and the Vale*), then those not available in cheap editions (*Hodge*, *Field and Hedgerow*), then all the rest. Those essays that have never been reprinted might be dug up from the nineteenth-century magazines he wrote for, and collected for us, perhaps by Mr Adrian Bell. Mr Williamson is not to be allowed, as two publishers have here allowed him, to print his barn-owl device with Jefferies' wood anemone on the title-pages (though he says 'I know you won't mind [Jefferies]'); he or anyone else is to have no finger in it. Jefferies needs no editor to stand between us and him and to interpret him by the light of petty egotism, he needs only to be available entire in a cheap and attractive form together with Edward Thomas's book. I am sure this publisher would not lose his money.

Gissing and the English novel

Stories and Sketches, by George Gissing (Michael Joseph)

These stories, which mistaken piety must have induced Mr A. C. Gissing to publish, will unfortunately persuade no one to read George Gissing who is not already interested in him. They exhibit chiefly his weaknesses and give no indication of his virtues. This is nothing like as interesting a volume of stories as the better of his other two collections, *The House of Cobwebs*, which ought by now to have been put into one of the pocket libraries, together with the interesting long 'Introductory Survey' Thomas Seccombe wrote for the 1906 edition. But if this new volume had persuaded reviewers to look up Gissing's novels, re-estimate his achievement, and demand for *New Grub Street* recognition as a classic, its publication would have been justified. There have been no such signs of a reviewer's conscience. It is odd that the Gissing vogue – subsequent to the Meredith vogue and much less widespread – has faded even out of literary history.

This is discouraging, but let us disinter Gissing nevertheless. He wrote twenty-two long novels but only one that posterity would want to read, two books of reminiscence (one the extremely popular *Private Papers of Henry Ryecroft*), two (now three) volumes of short stories, and the best existing critical introduction to Dickens, in twenty-six years of authorship (he died in 1903, aged only forty-six). He has already received adequate biographical and critical attention in *George Gissing: A Critical Study* by Frank Swinnerton, a capital piece of work which looks like remaining the last profitable word on Gissing as a man and a writer. (Nevertheless academic theses have since been excogitated on the same subject in English, German and American.)

Gissing's life and temperament, with the problems that they raise, are the key to both his many failures and his single success as an artist. He made a false start in life, it is true (a blasted academic career, a spell in prison, a spell in America, an impossible marriage), but on the literary side his sending a copy of his first novel (*Workers of the Dawn*, 1880) to Frederick Harrison resulted much like Crabbe's application to Burke. Harrison recommended Gissing to Lord Morley, then editor of *The Pall Mall Gazette*, and engaged Gissing as classical tutor to his two elder sons, also helping him to get other pupils. He was thus, with the *entrée* to the *PMG* and as many pupils as he could teach, provided for congenially enough for any other man of letters. But his unfortunate idea of what was suitable for the possessor of literary genius interfered with Harrison's benevolent arrangements. He refused to write more than one sketch for the *PMG* on the grounds that journalism was degrading work for an artist, and though Mr Austin Harrison says that from 1882 onwards Gissing had a living income from teaching which he could increase at will, he continued to live, if not actually in cellars and garrets on one meal a day as before, at least in near poverty, because, says Mr H. G. Wells, 'he grudged every moment taken by teaching from his literary purpose, and so taught as little as he could'. The interesting point here is not Gissing's romantic conception of what is due to genius, but that he continued to describe himself as the starving and unrecognized martyr of letters; he was for long neither well-to-do nor famous, but Mr Austin Harrison characterizes his accounts of his 'continued struggles with abject poverty' as 'fiction of fiction'. Gissing apparently needed that fiction to support his self-esteem, his belief in his own genius, for actually he must have been well aware, like his wretched Edwin Reardon, that he had written mostly what was unworthy of his best abilities. He had to explain his failure by blaming material circumstances; and though his output was really enormous we find him in *Ryecroft*, in the year of his death, picturing himself as the writer obliged to earn his living uncongenially so that he could allow himself, ah but how rarely, the luxury of writing a novel at intervals of many years, and thus was his genius blighted. The facts, as we have seen, were otherwise.

It was not lack of time or means that hampered him, nor yet his unhappy temperament. The latter was perhaps his chief asset, since it produced an absolutely personal way of responding to life and his fellow-men, and when a measure of ultimate success came to (as they say) 'mellow' him the results of his work, as seen in *Ryecroft*, were deplorable. It is instructive to compare the benevolent portrait in *Ryecroft* of the writer N, the successful author and good mixer, with the earlier study of the same type, Jasper Milvain, in *New Grub Street* (when any nineteenth-century novelist names a character Jasper I think we may safely conclude that the character is intended to be the villain). Apart from his temperament all the other qualities he brought to his novels – his scholarship, his bookishness, his enlightened interest in all the leading topics of his day (religious reform, politics, education, emancipation of woman, ethics, science, sociology . . .) – bear witness to his being an exceptionally cultivated man and exceptionally alive in his age, yet apart from *New Grub Street* how those novels date, how unreadable they now are! (It is thus that I seem to hear the literary critic of *Scrutiny*, vol. L, describing the novels of Mr Aldous Huxley, whom Gissing in some respects resembles.) But there was no interaction between his subject-matter and his sensibility, so the exhibition of life he gives us seems arbitrarily blighted by a novelist always functioning below par as it were; Mr Swinnerton, to account for his unpopularity, says 'he was condemned by novel-readers as a writer who whimpered at life'. But when he took as the subject of a novel his most vital interest – the problem of how to live as a man of letters, the literary world being what it is,[14] without sacrificing your integrity of purpose – he produced his one permanent contribution to the English novel. I think it can be shown to be a major contribution. The subject was both inside and outside him. The best way to suggest his achievement is to say that put beside the other best treatments of the same subject – Maugham's *Cakes and Ale* and the many fine short stories on aspects of the literary life by Henry James which should be read as a whole – Gissing's *New Grub Street* is quite different, equally serious and equally successful as a piece of art.

The Gissing temperament suitably colours the book, which, like *Cakes and Ale*, is consistently written in one tone, here an irony weighted with disgust. This strikes one as being the right outlook on the literary world ('such things were enough to make all literature appear a morbid excrescence upon human life', the heroine reflects at one point), if less suited to life in general. However, life in general is here seen from the point of view of the slenderly talented Reardon who wants to support his family by his pen and yet at the same time write only novels and essays worthy of himself. We see him go under, weighed down by a wife who thinks social and material success the due of her beauty, by his lack of influential friends, most of all by his choosing to abide by the values of Dr Johnson in an age where the policy of Alroy Kear had become requisite for success. We see his acquaintance Jasper Milvain deliberately choosing literature as a profitable field for his unliterary talents and ending up more successful than even he had dared expect, his marriage with Reardon's widow (become an heiress) symbolically ending the story. Delicacy and fineness, the strongly noble and the devotedly disinterested elements in human nature, are not ignored or denied, they are presented with complete success – this is a measure of Gissing's total success here – in the persons of Marian Yule, whom Milvain jilts and leaves to wretchedness, and Reardon's friend Biffen, who is driven to remove himself from a world that has no use for his devoted labours. Such are shown doomed to misery and failure. The old-style man of letters, part hack and part stiff-necked enthusiast, is skilfully contrasted (Alfred Yule) with the new-style man of straw (Whelpdale), successful because pliant in his complete lack of any literary conscience. There are many masterly studies of the emotions and conduct peculiar to those who live by literature and journalism, and in spite of a certain stiffness of style from which Gissing was never for

long free the smallest touches are effective. The subject
seems likely to remain of permanent interest and Gissing has
raised crucial problems. The central problem, one ultimately
of values, is put by Reardon to his wife thus:

A year after I have published my last book, I shall be practically forgotten . . . And yet, of course, it isn't only for the sake of reputation
that one tries to do uncommon work. There's the shrinking from
conscious insincerity of workmanship which most of the writers
nowadays seem never to feel. 'It's good enough for the market'; that
satisfies them. And perhaps they are justified. I can't pretend that I
rule my life by absolute ideals; I admit that everything is relative.
There is no such thing as goodness or badness, in the absolute
sense, of course. Perhaps I am absurdly inconsistent when – though
knowing my work can't be first-rate – I strive to make it as good as
possible. I don't say this in irony, Amy; I really meant it. It may very
well be that I am just as foolish as the people I ridicule for moral
and religious superstition. This habit of mine is superstitious. How
well I can imagine the answer of some popular novelist if he heard
me speak scornfully of his books. 'My dear fellow', he might say, 'do
you suppose I am not aware that my books are rubbish? I know it
just as well as you do. But my vocation is to live comfortably. I have
a luxurious house, a wife and children who are happy and grateful
to me for their happiness. If you choose to live in a garret, and,
what's worse, make your wife and children share it with you, that's
your concern.'

Whether Milvain could have existed at that or any time has,
by way of objection, been doubted, but Seccombe, who was in
a position to speak with authority, says 'Jasper Milvain is, to
my thinking, a perfectly fair portrait of an ambitious publicist
or journalist of the day – destined by determination, skill,
energy and social ambition to become an editor of a successful journal or review, and to lead the life of central London.

    The original temper that the novel manifests is notable in
every detail, for example:

Alfred Yule had made a recognizable name among the critical
writers of the day; seeing him in the title-lists of a periodical, most
people knew what to expect, but not a few forbore the cutting
open of the pages he occupied.

They had had three children; all were happily buried.

'but I was never snobbish. I care very little about titles; what I look
to is intellectual distinction.'

'Combined with financial success.'
'Why, that is what distinction means.'

Amy now looked her years to the full, but her type of beauty, as you
know, was independent of youthfulness. You saw that at forty, at
fifty, she would be one of the stateliest of dames. When she bent her
head towards the person with whom she spoke, it was an act of
queenly favour. Her words were uttered with just enough deliber-
ation to give them the value of an opinion; she smiled with a
delicious shade of irony; her glance intimated that nothing could
be too subtle for her understanding.

The last example is strikingly in the modern manner, and
Gissing's best work, *New Grub Street* almost entirely, seems
contemporary with us rather than with Meredith.

As a general thing, the same outlook characterizes
Gissing's other novels, but elsewhere it seems merely
depressed and therefore depressing. Poor Gissing was
sliding down the hill which Dickens and his robust contemporaries had climbed in such high spirits. Seccombe explains
it well:

In the old race, of which Dickens and Thackeray were representative, a successful determination to rise upon the broad back of
popularity coincided with a growing conviction that evil in the real
world was steadily diminishing . . . In Gissing the misery inherent
in the sharp contrasts of modern life was a far more deeply
ingrained conviction. He cared little for the remedial aspect of the
question. His idea was to analyse this misery as an artist and to
express it to the world. One of the most impressive elements in the
resulting novels is the witness they bear to prolonged and intense
suffering, the suffering of a proud, reserved and oversensitive mind
brought into constant contact with the coarse and brutal facts of
life. The creator of Mr Biffen suffers all the torture of the fastidious,
the delicately honourable, the scrupulously high-minded in daily
contact with persons of blunt feelings, low ideals, and base
instincts.

Outside *New Grub Street*, however, you too often feel that the
provocation is inadequate to the suffering. Gissing's suscep-
tibilities are not all equally respectable and in some cases he
seems only a querulous old maid, too easily provoked on
such subjects as bad cooking, slovenly lodgings, ungenteel
personal habits and lack of secondary school education. But
in *New Grub Street*, just as what is elsewhere mainly bookish-

ness becomes transfused into a passionate concern for the state of literature, so his other minor feelings have turned into positive values, and he produced the one important novel in his long list. It occurs less than half-way down, so its unique success is not a matter of maturity or technical development.

The difference between its technical efficiency and the incompetence of the rest is startling too. It might have been written by a Frenchman rather than an Englishman of those days, and Gissing's interest in and admiration for the nineteenth-century Russian and French novelists is significant. He was never able to make use of them as consistently as did Henry James or Conrad, but he was conscious that the English novel tradition he had inherited would not do and he was groping for help where it seemed to offer. (He later met Meredith and must have studied *The Egoist* with a certain degree of profit. Literary historians ought to inspect *Our Friend the Charlatan* (1901) which obviously was conceived and treated in the spirit of *The Egoist* though without ceasing to be Gissing's.) Gissing is an example of how disastrous it may be for a writer whose talent is not of the first order to be born into a bad tradition. A score and more of novels painfully sweated out of his system, the exceptional system of an exceptionally intelligent and well-educated and devoted writer, and only one that amounted to something. The absence of what now enables anyone in Bloomsbury to write a readable novel made Gissing's efforts mostly futile. Mr Swinnerton justly talks of 'the wreckage of the Victorian tradition by which it [Gissing's best work] is now encumbered'. But in *New Grub Street* Gissing not only solved, if only temporarily, his own problems, he helped all later writers to solve theirs, and the recognition this novel at one time received from literary men is significant. It is probably an ancestor of the novel of our time.

It is an important link in the line of novels from Jane Austen's to the present, which an adult can read at his utmost stretch – as attentively, that is, as good poetry demands to be read – instead of having to make allowances for its being only a novel or written for a certain public or a certain purpose. In the nineteenth century, to take the highlights, Jane Austen, *Wuthering Heights*, *Middlemarch*, *The Egoist*, *New Grub Street* con-nect the best eighteenth-century tradition with the serious twentieth-century tradition that Henry James, Conrad, Lawrence, Forster, Joyce, and Mrs Woolf have built up. There are inferior novels (for instance *The Way of All Flesh*) in this tradition as well as good ones, and very minor successes (like Howard Sturgis's *Belchamber*) as well as major contributions, but they are all immediately recognizable as novels, distinct from what we may more usefully call fiction. It is time the history of the English novel was rewritten from the point of view of the twentieth century (it is always seen from the point of view of the mid-nineteenth), just as has been done for the history of English poetry. The student would undoubtedly be glad to be allowed to reorganize his approach and revise the list of novels he has to accept as worth attention; it would be a matter chiefly of leaving out but also of substitution, for the list consists only of conventional values. I don't know who will dare touch off the first charge to blow up those academic values. Mr Forster once made an attempt on Scott and the response in the academic world was most interesting; the subsequent Scott centenary was a rally of the good men and true to batten down the hatches on Mr Forster's wholesome efforts to have that reputation reconsidered. What is commonly accepted as the central tradition is most easily examined in the middling practitioner – such as Trollope or Charles Reade. *The Cloister and the Hearth* is a puerile example of what *Esmond* is a highly accomplished form of, but both are undeserving of serious attention and both are on the educational syllabus, at different ends; though I never knew anyone but the old-fashioned kind of schoolmaster who could bear the former, and the latter's ventriloquial waxworks in period costume (prick them and do they not bleed red paint) are a direct ancestor of Sir Hugh Walpole's own great trilogy which will in time, who can doubt, get on the list too. It is time also that we sorted out the novels which form or enrich the real tradition of the English novel from those which (like Trollope's and Wells's) are rather contributions to the literary history of their time and to be read as material for the sociologist; from those which (like Scott's and R.L.S.'s and George Moore's) perpetrate or perpetuate bogus traditions; from those which (like Charlotte Brontë's) are the ill-used vehicles for expressing a point of view or, as in other novelists' hands (Aldous Huxley's), ideas; and from all the other kinds. As one step towards this desirable scheme I suggest that *New Grub Street* be made generally available by reissuing it in Everyman or The World's Classics editions. Sir Humphrey Milford has already ventured to make some surprising additions to the world's classic novels on his own responsibility (Constance Holme for instance) and Messrs Dent have similarly helped Galsworthy and Priestley to get on everyman's list of great novels, so they might do something for Gissing whose best novel will soon be due for a half-centenary.

George Gissing: *Born in Exile*

It's a novel of Gissing's experience in the fullest sense of the intellectual tone of his own age. Born in 1857, he was in time to register the after-effects of the Victorian revaluation of Christianity, democracy, idealism and the class-structure: effects that he personally experienced. It is entirely of its age in making the questions of orthodox belief in Christianity – whether it was any longer possible, even if desirable – the central consideration. It belongs with the novels of religious emancipation but not happily so, for its tone is poignant and its outcome harrowing. But its seriousness and complexity in handling its problems make it more rewarding, even if depressing, than the cheerfully shallow treatments of the same themes in a novel like *The Way of All Flesh*, or the arid treatment in a schematic and theoretic novel like *Jude the Obscure*.

The intellectual world here is seen discomfited by and retreating before science: that is, German scholarship applied to disintegrate the inspiration of the Bible plus the unsettling effects of the discoveries of geology and evolution and the comparable philosophic movements such as Schopenhauer's pessimism about the nature of life and society and woman. But, and this is a basic paradox employed for irony, the clergyman is socially still high in esteem – an eligible *parti*, whatever his own birth, for a young lady of good family, particularly when his career offered substantial rewards such as a deanery or a bishopric if he was able and astute in suiting his views to the taste of his time. This dichotomy in the later Victorian world provided an uncomfortable intellectual and dissatisfied human being like Gissing with a brilliant theme for a novel, and one with which he could largely identify himself. This is a requisite in making a truly successful English novel instead of a merely Flaubertian 'work of art'.

The protagonist is Godwin Peak, a symbolic name, the first part chosen by his ambitious but defeated father after the author of *Political Justice*. Blighted by his distasteful social circumstances and frustrated by poverty, Godwin has impressive intellectual energy and drive and a bent towards science. After scholarships to a local college (Owens College, Manchester, where Gissing himself had a broken education), desperate self-education and a year at the School of Mines in London, he secures a post in a chemical works at Rotherhithe, the only career open to him failing a university degree, which he couldn't afford. But unlike Hardy's Jude he is no defeatist. Gissing does not attempt to make him winning to the reader, but to express and obtain sympathy with his plight: he is (like Gissing) intellectually arrogant and inclined to be generally contemptuous, but this is explicable in a talented man who has no personal life, and is made touching by his recognition of what he lacks, though he is unwilling to admit that what other men strive for is worth having.

After ten years as what he calls 'a hopeless slave in a vile manufactory' and living alone in lodgings over a shop – and too fastidious for vulgar dissipation – he has formed himself deliberately on the model of the remembered speech and manners of his college teachers and his better schoolfellows (who had been able to afford to go on to the universities and so had been lost to him). On a holiday in Devon he meets one of them again, who introduces Godwin into his own father's country house, being kindly and now embarked on a career in Radical politics. Thanks to his self-grooming and a good tailor, and his knowledge of geology, the Warricombe father's hobby, Godwin makes a temporary footing for himself in the family. He is enchanted, poor starving creature, with the whole ambience – the handsome intelligent sons and daughters and the good old father who is a serious amateur geologist, the comfort that wealth traditionally employed provides, the personal refinement and the good taste of the household. He forms for the first time in his life a daydream of happiness, of marrying the eldest daughter, Sidwell, a cultivated, intelligent, lovely woman, and thus achieving a personal life of feeling, family ties, and a place in the social world.

But the father and mother, though not the children, are conventionally religious, and Godwin Peak as a believer in science has always been an arrogant contemner of accepted religion. By an irresistible temptation, and without planning it, he declares himself about to study for ordination and actually withdraws from his chemical post to live in Exeter on his savings while preparing to take orders, the object being a successful career and acceptance by the Warricombes as a suitor for their favourite daughter. His footing with them thus secured, he is making an impression on Sidwell, but her mother is antagonistic and the eldest son suspicious of his old acquaintance's good faith, though Peak conciliates the father by disingenuous arguments to support the old gentleman's desire to believe that science could be reconciled with orthodox Christian beliefs.

In London Peak had frequented a circle of congenial bachelor friends – Bohemian intellectuals in journalism, science and politics – who know he shares their general scepticism of democracy and idealism and their contempt for the Church and churchmen. For in their world it is an axiom that religion is an exploded fallacy and in their view a man who becomes a parson is either a fool or a knave. It is essential for Peak to conceal from them where he is and what is his new mode of life. But he had previously placed through one of them a destructive major article attacking a leading book that attempted to reconcile scientific discoveries and the Bible, and its delayed appearance threatens his present and future. Though he had published anonymously, the magazine, a leading intellectual organ, is inevitably seen by the Warricombes, and accidental contact between the elder son and some of Peak's London circle (not a coincidence, for it was bound to happen some time) reveals the authorship and also that they know Peak to be a scoffer like themselves. Armed with this evidence of duplicity, Buckland Warri-

combe goes home to blow up Peak's life. The irony is that the
son had always been in conflict, if amiably, with his father
over religious orthodoxy, but he has always been open about
his views and despises all dishonesty. He is angry that Peak
has deceived them all but – a profound insight on the
author's part – what really makes him relentless is that Peak
has employed hypocrisy to insinuate himself into a class
otherwise out of his social reach (scratch a gentleman
Radical and you find a class-consciousness below the level of
political opinions, Gissing is suggesting, and that Buckland
too is dishonest even if unconsciously so). Buckland is
furious at the possibility that his sister has an attachment to
Peak and makes the disastrous revelation at home after
honourably warning Peak in advance.

A further irony is now made apparent. Sidwell, under
Peak's influence, has had her orthodoxy softened and her
mind opened (and perplexed) till she has come to believe
that it is only the spiritual truths of Christianity that must be
retained. But fearing that the decay of religious belief will
undermine morality, she feels that *some* forms there must be:
a general feeling of sensitive intelligent people of the age
(anticipated by George Eliot's own attitude to religion). The
characters are surrounded by excellently rendered varieties
of period types and most notably a caricature of the new
Broad Church clergyman (post-Dr Arnold) of the new scientific era, who, while believing in nothing but the name of
Christianity, and able to say so in an acceptable form to Mrs
Warricombe, enjoys social prestige and apparently may
hope, through a high society marriage, to end a Bishop.[15] He
is enthusiastic for 'science', saying confidently that 'scientific discovery has done more for religion than all the ages of
pious imagination' and, confusing Sidwell insensibly in her
alienation from all accepted forms of religious faith (for she,
unlike her stupid mother, despises the Rev. Bruce Chilvers),
drives her closer to Peak. Unlike the examples in Peak's
London circle of the modern 'advanced' woman he had
despised as much as he does the commonplace girls or the
dull conventional matrons like Mrs Warricombe, Sidwell is
really suited to make his life worth living. But the final irony
is that though, when enlightened by jealousy she recognizes
her love for Peak, and can understand and even sympathize

with, and so forgive, his imposture or concocted change of front, and though she would not now expect him to become a clergyman, she finally admits to herself that she has not the moral courage to break with her family and social class and marry him. A legacy from an 'advanced' woman who had vainly courted Peak would now enable him to live in moderate comfort away from Rotherhithe or St Helen's, to which his technological qualifications had doomed him.

Peak accepts defeat after a struggle with her, and goes abroad to travel and forget, but also to seek now only the free, intellectual people – men who have done with the old conceptions – though he had found in the past that such a life was arid. He soon dies of fever in Vienna, 'miserably alone', he wrote, after 'all these years' savage striving to knit myself into the social fabric' and, as his confidant reflects, 'dead, too, in exile', as he was born – the bleakest reflection we have of the intellectual in later Victorian England.

E. M. Forster: *Abinger Harvest*

Apart from the Clarke Lectures, reprinted as *Aspects of the Novel*, and the memoir of Lowes Dickinson, this is the only book Mr Forster's eager public has been given since *A Passage to India*, and it is a disappointing book. It is composed of reprinted essays, reviews, articles, etc., divided into sections: one is of literary criticism, another about the East, another on aspects of contemporary England, and one of essays mostly in the popular historical manner (née Strachey) on figures of the Past. The publisher tells us 'the range of outlook is even wider' here than in Mr Forster's previous work, but even his greatest admirers will hardly find anything more than a casual restatement of Mr Forster's outlook, split up as it were under a spectroscope. *Abinger Harvest* ought to be an occasion for some critic to make a revaluation of the novels too. However, we must be content here with summarizing what this volume alone shows.

It is a mixture of autobiography and criticism. What it chiefly does is to furnish a key to Mr Forster's peculiar poise, that poise which constitutes the individuality of his novels and from which his characteristic irony springs. Under the spectroscope it is seen to be a balance between a critical and a charming stance. He is gifted with impulses in both directions, and, hovering as he necessarily does between the serious and the playful, this makes him unduly concerned to be whimsical. He is often here merely playful and then he tends to become a bore (e.g. last half of the group of sketches called 'Our Diversions'), or personal in the worst sense. His weakness, felt in the novels as an uneasy wobble in some of the ironic effects, is here revealed as a frequent inability to decide which he wants to be – critical or charming. You get the impression that he is positively unable to resist following out a whimsical train of thought, whatever the business in hand. 'My Wood' is an instance of turning this habit to profit by the use of a serious overtone, but it stands almost alone on this level. Generally his poise in these essays is unstable; he seems, as so rarely in the novels, to be uncertain what he intends to convey or where he means to alight (hence perhaps his liking for Ronald Firbank, who will remain a tiresome fribble to most of us). 'A Flood in the Office' shows a characteristic surrender to the easier current; it starts from a dispute between two eminent engineers about the irrigation of Egypt and continues, at a tangent, about Father Nile. Mr Forster sees from the corner of his eye the real significance of the dispute – the eternal antipathy between the disinterested intelligent man and stupidity allied with vested interests – but it is not the spectacle of integrity struggling to make its voice heard that arrests his imagination: it is the whimsical fancies suggested by 'the unique mass of water.' Of course it makes a more amusing essay this way. The objection is that the consistently whimsical outlook has the effect of making any other appear priggish – exactly as *Punch* does, which Mr Forster very feelingly denounces on other grounds. And you do get the impression that Mr Forster is disinclined to risk being thought too serious, he takes so much care to elicit the 'How amusing' response.

The literary criticism carries us a step further in our analysis. The intuitions are good, there are striking flashes of discernment (some of the critical stuff, such as the essay on Sinclair Lewis, is better than anything in *Aspects of the Novel*), but he doesn't seem to know how to consolidate. As in that book, it is amateur criticism; there is some kind of mental habit that prohibits discipline and sustained effort. The amiably whimsical–personal approach is not made to seem justified as a profitable mode of literary criticism: essays like that on T. S. Eliot are so inadequate that it is surprising that Mr Forster should have thought them worth reprinting. The brief note on Conrad makes the radical criticism of this novelist who has been written and lectured about with so little profit:

This isn't an aesthetic criticism, nor a moral one. Just a suggestion that our difficulties with Mr Conrad may proceed in part from difficulties of his own. What is so elusive about him is that he is always promising to make some general philosophic statement about the universe, and then refraining with a gruff disclaimer . . . These essays [*Notes on Life and Letters*] do suggest that he is misty in the middle as well as at the edges, that the secret casket of his genius contains a vapour rather than a jewel . . .

And again on Ibsen, how acute, how just:

Although he is not a teacher he has the air of being one, there is something in his method that implies a message, though the message really rested on passing irritabilities, and not on any permanent view of conduct or the universe . . . Moral ugliness trespasses into the aesthetic . . . Poetry might perhaps be achieved if Ibsen's indignation was of the straight-hitting sort, like Dante's. But for all its sincerity there is something automatic about it, he reminds us too often of father at the breakfast table after a bad night, sensitive to the defects of society as revealed by a chance glance at the newspaper, and apt to blame all parties for them indiscriminately. Now it is the position of women that upsets father, now the lies people tell, now their inability to lie, now the drains, now the newspaper itself, which he crumples up, but his helpers and servers have to retrieve it, for bad as are all political parties he must really see who got in at Rosmerholm.

Yet you feel he is not wholly aware of the force of his criticisms, for he always proceeds to shy away from the point he has made so convincingly and go back on himself – generally out of benevolence.

You go on to conclude that Mr Forster is not so adequate a critic as he might be – as he ought to be, judging by his natural endowments. His blind spots are particularly instructive; they seem to be created by a social environment whose influence would repay investigation. There is the section of essays on The Past. They have none of Lytton Strachey's hateful qualities – the cheap irony, the vulgar prose effects, the assumption of superiority to his historical puppets – but it is significant that he should be sufficiently an admirer of Strachey's to try his hand at this genre, and sad that he should have been encouraged to think the attempts worth republishing. (But no doubt many will find them delicious.) In these circumstances his personal touch deserts him. 'Presently the old mistress [Hannah More] will ring a bell, Louisa will fail to answer it, there will be horror, dis-illusionment, flight, the Industrial Revolution, Tolstoy, Walt Whitman, Mr and Mrs Sidney Webb.' This, along with *The Common Reader* 2nd Series from which it might have come, shows the unfortunate meeting-ground of three writers. It is distressing to see so distinguished a writer sinking to this. From this volume posterity will do some deducing about Mr Forster's background: he feels amiably towards the sub-merged layers below him ('Me, Them and You', and there are other indications of a desire, creditable rather than effective, to gear in with the great world); and is critical of those aspects of his economic class which his circle have agreed to consider targets (e.g., 'It is different for me'), but his most successful achievements here are in a very small way (e.g., 'The Doll Souse' and 'The Scallies'). There isn't much appearance of sharply felt first-hand criticism. Everything points to an uncritical taking-over of group-values. For instance, he boldly confesses to being one of the highbrow minority who can 'make fun' of Wembley, while the next essay displays him revelling in the deliciousness of Mickey Mouse and Co.; anyone who has observed a highbrow film audience relaxing from the effort required to appreciate Russian or surrealist films and preparing to really enjoy themselves when the Walt Disney turn follows must feel this a worthier subject for an ironical pen. A satirist, to command our respect, ought to be aware of his blinkers as well as of his tether. Thus it seems at least somewhat arbitrary to assume that the British Empire is ridiculous whereas Mr Clive Bell isn't; posterity's Bloomsbury (not very long hence) may judge otherwise.

Where suitable subjects occur, when his critical abilities

are able to function on important topics that are also congenial, Mr Forster produces his best work. The best section
in this volume is that on The East, and the best essay in it on
'The Mind of the Native Indian State'. This is not merely
whimsical, merely charmingly witty, but witty to a serious
purpose; it is responsible:

The Princes have studied our wonderful British Constitution at the
Chiefs' Colleges, and some of them have visited England and seen
the Houses of Parliament. But they are personal rulers themselves,
often possessing powers of life and death, and they find it difficult
to realize that the King Emperor, their overlord, is not equally
powerful. If they can exalt and depress their own subjects at will,
regard the State revenue as their private property, promulgate a
constitution one day and ignore it the next, surely the monarch of
Westminster can do as much or more. This belief colours all their
intercourse with the Government of India. They want to get
through or behind it to King George and lay their troubles at his
feet, because he is a king and a mighty one, and will understand. In
the past some of them nourished private schemes, but to-day their
loyalty to the Crown is sincere and passionate, and they welcomed
the Prince of Wales, although his measured constitutionalisms
puzzled and chilled them. Why did he not take his liegemen aside
and ask, in his father's name, for the head of Gandhi upon a
charger? It could have been managed so easily. The intelligent
Princes would not argue thus, but all would have the feeling, and so
would the reader if he derived extensive powers under a feudal
system and then discovered that it was not working properly in its
upper reaches. 'His Majesty the King-Emperor has great difficulties in these days': so much they grasp, but they regard the
difficulties as abnormal and expect that a turn of the wheel will
shake them off. However cleverly they may discuss democratic
Europe or revolutionary Russia with a visitor, they do not in their
heart of hearts regard anything but Royalty as permanent, or the
movements against it as more than domestic mutinies. They cannot understand, because they cannot experience, the modern
world.

It concludes with a sample of Mr Forster's personal brand of
wisdom – a deprecating refusal to be easily wise. The same
note is struck elsewhere, as in the capital little sketches
'Advance, India' and 'The Suppliant', which might both have
come from *A Passage to India*. It is sustained in the most
impressive thing in the book, the courageous and useful

address, delivered last year at the International Congress of
Writers at Paris, on 'Liberty in England', which contains
passages that every civilized person will be grateful to Mr
Forster for. (This recalls Mr Forster's valuable report of that
congress in *The New Statesman and Nation*, 6 July 1935.) Along
with this goes 'A Note on the Way', which is personal in the
best sense. You conclude that Mr Forster's courage – and
courage is readily felt to be an important part of this writer's
make-up – is not associated with his irony so much as with his
delicate emotional machinery. Certainly it is something in
the nature of courage which provides the mainspring:
courage to assert the virtue of the finer feelings. Compared
with the other major novelists of this century Mr Forster
exhibits a lack both of personal vigour and of that intellectual
strength which impresses as the best source of vitality; you
can't imagine him making the kind of personal judgements
that Lawrence made nor has his irony anything in common
with the refreshing sardonic quality of Lawrence's. Nor has
he shown a capacity for such an ironical achievement as *Cakes
and Ale*, which, side by side with a sardonic criticism of the
writer's environment, exhibits positive values convincingly
incarnated. Niceness has its drawbacks apparently, in letters
if not in life; Mr Forster in *Abinger Harvest* shows himself to be
the nicest kind of person, but so nice as to be somewhat tame
perhaps – or else what accounts for the disappointment the
book leaves? Though his public work (for example, formerly
as president of the Society for Cultural Relations with Soviet
Russia and till recently as president of the National Council
for Civil Liberties) is a reminder that it is not necessarily his
most ponderable side that is presented to the reader.

Dorothy Richardson: *Clear Horizon*

This is the eleventh and latest, but not last, volume of the
novel-cycle *Pilgrimage*, the first, *Pointed Roofs*, having appeared
in 1915, when it fell like a rock from a height into the literary
waters. Since then each succeeding volume has made less of
a splash, and the latest is likely to part the surface with
scarcely a ripple. Reading the extravagant praises that were
heaped on the early volumes by distinguished littérateurs it
is hard now to understand how they could have aroused so

much excitement and enthusiasm. But her contemporary reputation was not a bogus one, like Stephen Phillips's, nor did it spring from a genuine perennial bad taste, like Rupert Brooke's. Her volumes were certainly important at the time of their first appearance, though it looks now as though (if these metaphorical liberties may be allowed) they were less a torrent in themselves than straws showing the course of a current. *Pilgrimage* has evidently less intrinsic than historical value; the third generation from Dr Oliver Elton will have its author docketted for literary-history purposes as a 'precursor'. Miss Richardson was plainly an early if not very inspired employer of the 'stream of consciousness' method, and she was undoubtedly an influence of sorts on at least one far greater novelist. In the earlier work of Virginia Woolf before her mature style crystallized out, amid signs of incomplete assimilation of Joyce and Meredith, there are occasionally to be found sentences that might have been written by Miss Richardson; certainly it looks as though the latter might have provided the matrix for the characteristic 'feminine' sentence which Mrs Woolf claims to have been consciously trying to evolve as the unit of her medium.

The intrinsic interest of *Pilgrimage* is slight and best sampled in the first volume, which remains the strongest of the series. Thereafter it will be found to become increasingly small beer. For posterity, or such of it as studies literature for degrees, there will have to be an abridged edition like those of Miss Richardson's namesake for the same purpose. For the 'stream of consciousness' method, like any other method, is dependent finally on the quality of the sensibility behind it, and to use successfully this particular method, which excludes implicit criticism and the variety afforded by the play of mind from the outside on to the subject-matter, it is indispensable that it should be backed by a distinguished, rich and profound personality. That Miss Richardson's is not so has become painfully apparent by now, without of course in any degree lessening the historical value of her achievement. Her outlook is narrowly limited by class and sex factors, as indeed Charlotte Brontë's, among others, was, but lacks the force and vitality which can make such limitations interesting. For instance, her preoccupations date already as being those of a period when Woman – as distinct from individual women – was a matter for defiant assertion of interest; she seems by way of being nothing more than an expansion of the weaker side of Mrs Woolf, and the impression one accordingly gets is one of a failure to mature. In Mrs Woolf this weakness seems to be kept out of her best work, and never manifests itself at all in her novels as crudely as it does in *A Room of One's Own*, for example, while in the early *Night and Day* it actually flowers into a valuable kind of sensitiveness. In Miss Richardson however it is a pervasive weakness, the feminine self-consciousness that has to find an outlet in some form of assertion or demand; at that time it was for the right to vote, and now seems to have found its level in the right to love (Marie Stopes) and the right to lead an uninhibited life (Ethel Mannin) at which level and temperature it may well be left. The demand for mass rights can only be a source of embarrassment to intelligent women, who can be counted on to prefer being considered as persons rather than as a kind, just as they will wish to work out individual solutions to their problems, if they have any; nor are they likely to have more sympathy with the implicit appeal to 'We women' than intelligent men have for the equivalent appeal to 'We men'. But apart from this kind of obsession, which demands a forbearance on historical grounds that it will take all the reader's patience to maintain, Miss Richardson's consciousness has little to offer. But she will be a gift to the research student of the two-thousands.

The literary life respectable

I EDWIN MUIR

The Story and the Fable, by Edwin Muir (Harrap)

I was born before the Industrial Revolution, and am now about two hundred years old. But I have skipped a hundred and fifty of them. I was really born in 1737, and till I was fourteen no time-accidents happened to me. Then in 1751 I set out from Orkney for Glasgow. When I arrived I found that it was not 1751, but 1901 . . . I was brought up in the midst of a life which was still co-operative, which had still the medieval communal feeling. We had heard and read of something called 'competition', but it never came into our experience. Our life was an order. Since the Industrial Revolution there has not really been an order except in a few remote places . . . To be born outside your age and have to catch up with it and fit into it is a strain. Yet I would not for any price have missed my knowledge of that first pre-industrial order; for it taught me something which is inherent in every good order.

This is the conclusion of Mr Muir's autobiography. It explains why the author is important for us: he not merely *is* that but he knows it. It is a wise book, it contains a good deal that is incidentally interesting and fruitful, but there is likely to be a general complaint: it is not the kind of book we expected. If written with another object, we may lament, it would have been an important document. However, Mr Muir can hardly be blamed for writing his own book and not the one we wanted. For of course when his autobiography was announced we looked forward to having that much needed section of literary history, that invaluable account of the central literary world in the formative post-war years, the era of *The Calendar of Modern Letters* and *The Athenaeum*, Eliot's poetry and the early Virginia Woolf and all the rest, which hardly anyone but Mr Muir is qualified to describe at once from the inside and yet outside the feuds and partisanships and social relations. The author of *Transition*, contributor to Orage's *New Age*, Murry's *Athenaeum* and *The Calendar*, Mr Muir was the best critic at that time of that phase of our literature; and his reputation since in every branch of letters – as the translator of Kafka, the critic of Scottish literature, incidentally poet and novelist, always, even when reviewing fiction for the BBC, notable for his integrity and his grasp of standards – has encouraged us to expect from his autobiography a contribution to literary history, something like an English equivalent to Malcolm Cowley's *Exile's Return* only much less ephemeral. But apart from an account of Orage there is scarcely an indication that the author has played a part in literature. It is not so much that Mr Muir is unnaturally modest (though he does seem to be) as that he has chosen to conceal what is for most people their public and utterable life and reveal what is commonly the private and hidden existence; he gives us instead of his intellectual career an account of his semi-conscious and psychoanalytic experience. Disappointing for most of us.

There remains the account of his Orkney childhood, of
that 'virtually self-supporting life' with its roots in the soil
and its peculiarly expressive speech-idiom based on 'syntac-
tical feeling' – a fine start for a writer. At fourteen he
accompanied his family to Glasgow, which meant being
'plunged out of order into chaos', 'a meaningless waste of
inherited virtue'. After that he drifted from one horrible
Glasgow clerkship to another. He was converted to Socialism
and extended his reading, then suddenly it is let fall that he
decided to marry. Neither of them having a job they went to
London, and, we are simply told, met Orage, whereupon Mr
Muir got simultaneously a post on *The New Age* and work for
The Scotsman and *The Athenaeum* (it can hardly have been as
simple as that and we should like to have been told how it was
done); and then just when the prologue seems to be over,
down comes the curtain on his literary life. We have only
what he has published elsewhere to go by. No doubt the life
of a man of letters is his printed work. We can draw some conclusions in spite of Mr Muir's reticence. We can compare his
achievements with those of literary men apparently more
favoured in their origins.

Mr Muir was born outside his age. What of those who are
born very much inside it, at the social centre, and who
instead of having to strain to catch up and fit in like Mr Muir
are effortlessly borne on the tide, who are by virtue of their
environment convinced of their right to take the centre of the
stage on which the arts exhibit (to give a choice of images,
though perhaps the most felicitous is one culled years ago
from Mr Maurice Baring's autobiography: 'I have a seat
under the dome' – Mr Baring, the type of those born with a
prescriptive right to literary success)? A good point of depar-
ture for such a comparison and contrast would be the Julian
Bell memorial volume (Hogarth Press), backed by such culturally related works as Cyril Connolly's *Enemies of Promise*,[16]
Mrs Woolf's *Roger Fry*, Lowes Dickinson's *McTaggart*, E. M.
Forster's *Lowes Dickinson* (and we can expect to have richer
documentation available in due course when another of the
group gives us a *Forster*, when the David Garnett reminiscences appear, and when Lord David Cecil produces a
biography of Mr Desmond MacCarthy). It can hardly escape
observation that the virtues of Old Bloomsbury – though

even in their original incarnations, such as Lowes Dickinson, Forster and Lytton Strachey, dangerous weaknesses are apparent – were endangered from the beginning by being set in a social context. The 'centre' that Mrs Woolf describes Roger Fry desiderating for the arts and letters in London seems to have soon produced a little world in which social life made the exercise of critical judgement bad taste; every member accruing to the group became entitled to eminence at it were.[17] To be born outside any such group and to have to make his way by hard work and native endowment has its own reward for the man of letters – Mr Connolly drops a hint: 'Critics in England . . . discover one day that in a sense their whole life is an accepted bribe, a fabric of compromise based on personal relationships.' One can see the kind of pressure to which *The Criterion* succumbed early on in its career and why the literary side of *The New Statesman* was foredoomed. Mr Muir's merits are precisely that he sprang (like Lawrence and Hardy) from another kind of society. His literary criticism is distinguished by good sense, decent impartiality and personal judgement (not the glib currency of a social group), and impresses one with an integrity that comes from *not* being committed to compromises based, etc. The moral seems to be that the literary life respectable can nowadays only be lived outside the centre. To be a man of letters of any worth you must be a man of character too, in the sense that Hardy and Lawrence were. It was not after all 'a waste of inherited virtue' when Mr Muir left the Orkneys for the twentieth-century city, the inherited virtue was translated.

What is all this fuss about, I may be asked, what has the man added to English Literature that can be pointed to as of the first importance? Like Leslie Stephen and various other men of letters his value lies in what he stands for as much as in what he has done. I do not myself think much of Mr Muir's fiction or of his recent book on *The Present Age*. But if you were to challenge me: Do I think Mr Muir has contributed more to English letters than Mr Desmond MacCarthy, Mr Raymond Mortimer, Mr George Rylands, Mr David Garnett, the late Julian Bell, Mr Clive Bell, or Lord David Cecil? I should unhesitatingly reply Yes, and more than all of them put together.

2 GEORGE ORWELL

Inside the Whale (Gollancz)

Mr Orwell unlike Mr Muir belongs by birth and education to 'the right Left people', the nucleus of the literary world who christian-name each other and are in honour bound to advance each other's literary career; he figures indeed in Connolly's autobiography as a schoolfellow. This is probably why he has received indulgent treatment in the literary press. He differs from them in having grown up. He sees them accordingly from outside, having emancipated himself, at any rate in part, by the force of a remarkable character. His varied writings bear an unvarying stamp: they are responsible, adult and decent – compare *The Road to Wigan Pier* with Spender's *Forward from Liberalism*, which is a comparison between the testament of an honest man and a helping of flapdoodle.

Mr Orwell has not hitherto appeared as a literary critic, except incidentally, but as a novelist, a social thinker and a critic-participator in the Spanish War. Now he has published three literary essays which, promisingly, are all quite different. One is an examination of Dickens, another an analysis on not altogether original lines of boys' school stories, and the third a piece of contemporary criticism. From his other books we could deduce that he was potentially a good critic. For instance, he takes his own political line – starting from an inside knowledge of the working class, painfully acquired, he can see through the Marxist theory, and being innately decent (he displays and approves of bourgeois morality) he is disgusted with the callous theorizing inhumanity of the pro-Marxists. His explanation (see pp. 168–72 of *Inside the Whale*) of the conversion to Russian Communism of the young writers of the thirties is something that needed doing and could hardly have been done better. And he drives home his point with a piece of literary criticism, an analysis of a stanza of Auden's *Spain*. Again, he has lived an active life among all classes and in several countries, he isn't the usual parlour-Bolshevik seeing literature through political glasses; nor is he a literary gangster, his literary criticism is first-hand. These are exceptional qualifications nowadays. Without having scholarship or an academic background he yet gives the impression of knowing a surprising amount about books and authors – because what he knows is live information, not card-index rubbish, his knowledge functions. A wide field of reference (provided it is not gratuitous), outside as well as inside literature proper, is a sure sign of an alert intelligence. While Mr Orwell's criticism is discursive his pages are not cluttered up with academic 'scholarship' nor disfigured with the rash of the exhibitionist imposters who displayed in *The Criterion*. His writings are not elegant, mannered or polite, or petty either; his style is refreshing, that of the man whose first aim is to say something which he has quite clear in his head – like the pamphleteering Shaw without the irresponsibility (which produced the paradoxes and the cheap effects). He really knows the stuff he is writing about (for instance, Dickens) and has not got it up in a hurry for the occasion (like Spender on Henry James in *The Destructive Element*).

This is his most encouraging book so far, because while his previously successful books have been *The Road to Wigan Pier* and *Homage to Catalonia*, not only timely but valuable in themselves, they had not seemed to lead anywhere. Mr Orwell must have wasted a lot of energy trying to be a novelist – I think I must have read three or four novels by him, and the only impression those dreary books left on me is that nature didn't intend him to be a novelist. Yet his equivalent works in non-fiction are stimulating. It is the more evident because his novels are drawn from his own experience (*Burmese Days* is based on his five years in the Indian Imperial Police Service in Burma, others on his experiences as a down-and-out and so on). Yet these novels not only lack the brutal effectiveness of B. Traven's for instance, they might almost have been written by Mr Alec Brown. You see what I mean. He has even managed to write a dull novel about a literary man, which is a feat – an attempt to do *New Grub Street* up-to-date, but Gissing was an artist and Mr Orwell isn't. What an impressive book Mr Orwell made out of his experiences in the Spanish War (*Homage to Catalonia*), but that isn't a novel; in spite of its patches of spleen and illogicality, what insight, good feeling and practical thinking are revealed in *The Road to Wigan Pier* (for sponsoring which the Left Book Club earned one of its few good marks), but if it had been a novel one can't believe it would have been as stimulating and convincing. It looks as though if he would give up trying to be a novelist Mr Orwell might find his *métier* in literary criticism, in a special line of it peculiar to himself and which is particularly needed now. He is evidently a live mind working through literature, life and ideas. He knows what he is interested in and has something original to say about it. His criticism is convincing because his local criticisms are sound (always a test), and though his is not primarily a literary approach he is that rare thing, a non-literary writer who is also sensitive to literature. Thus his criticism of Dickens, while a lot of it is beside the point from *Scrutiny*'s point of view, contains nuggets of literary criticism (for example, p. 81), and you can see his superior literary sensibility on the one hand to the Marxist critics of Dickens (pro or con) and on the other to the Hugh Kingsmill type. He is not sufficiently disciplined to be a considerable literary critic: he is and probably always will be a critic of literature who, while not a Communist, has nevertheless corresponding preoccupations, but the great thing is, he has a special kind of honesty, he corrects any astigmatic tendency in himself because in literature as in politics he has taken up a stand which gives him freedom. He can say just the right things about Comrade Mirsky's nasty book on *The Intelligentsia of Great Britain*, he can tick off MacNeice in a characteristic attitude, expose Upward's puerile theorizing, diagnose Auden and Co., and 'place' the school of Catholic-convert apologists. Even his enthusiasms – another test – turn out to be sound criticism. Thus, you may think that the only thing wrong with the title-essay of this book is that he seems to think Henry Miller a great novelist, but it turns out after all that he doesn't. He claims for *Tropic of Cancer* no more than that it is an example of the only kind of tolerably good novel that can be written now ('a completely negative, unconstructive, amoral writer, a passive accepter of evil') – and expects, as you and I do, that Miller will 'descend into unintelligibility, or into charlatanism' next.

Whether he will come to anything as a literary critic will probably depend on whether he can keep clear of the atmosphere of Bloomsbury and the literary racket. And there are other dangers. He reminds one of Mr Robert Graves in his promising period in the twenties, and Mr Graves's history

since, from the standpoint of literary criticism, has been
rather a sad one. Probably the best thing for him and the best
thing for us would be to export him to interpret English
Literature to the foreign student, instead of the yes-men who
generally land the Chairs of English abroad. Everyone would
benefit; though one doesn't see him accepting such an offer.
But one thing above all there is to his credit. If the revolution
here were to happen that he wants and prophesies, the
advent of real Socialism, he would be the only man of letters
we have whom we can imagine surviving the flood
undisturbed.

Academic case-history

Haddon the Head Hunter, by A. H. Quiggin (C.U.P.)

Everyone knows that A. C. Haddon established the study of
Anthropology at Cambridge. How he managed to do so is
less common knowledge, so it is fortunate that the biography
we have been given is frank about the subject. The facts are
recorded with some appropriate though subdued indignation, and it is well that the facts should be put on record,
instead of the usual humbug which whitewashes an institution at the expense of the victim. Chapters 5 and 6, called
'Cambridge and Anthropology', provide instructive documentation about how an institution, endowed to promote
learning and light, behaves when it is offered the services of
a uniquely qualified specialist and teacher who is concerned
to break new ground.

Haddon after leaving Cambridge became a zoologist, but
an expedition he undertook to Torres Straits in 1889 convinced him that while zoology could wait, the materials for
the study of Anthropology must be collected at once before it
was too late. Cecil Sharp made a similar discovery about
English Folksong and Dance, but as his materials lay at his
back-door, so to speak, he was able to collect them and
support himself concurrently. Haddon was in a more
awkward position – his data existed in Oceania. He was
urged to devote his remarkable talents to Anthropology by
such eminent pioneers as Frazer and Huxley, and in 1893
Haddon moved from Dublin, where he was professor of

Zoology, to Cambridge, in hopes of getting endowment. In 1898, after scraping together funds, he conducted a famous anthropological expedition, the first of its kind, having enlisted the services of W. H. Rivers, McDougall, Seligman and C. S. Myers, whom he made recruits to the new science. This expedition achieved so much that Frazer and Ridgeway in 1899 sponsored a Memorial urging the university to provide instruction in Ethnology by creating a post for Haddon, pointing out not only his eminent fitness for the post but that 'he has already laid the University and science under great obligations by teaching Anthropology in the University without a salary for three years' and laying stress on his genius as a teacher. Alas, though the universities were originated by great teachers and are only kept alive by them (not only spiritually but in a very material sense, since it is they who attract students to the schools), yet to arouse enthusiasm as a teacher is not the way to become *persona grata* in the academic world; and though it was well known that the university had resources, and the Memorial was supported by many Heads of Houses and Departments, and by eight professors, all that could be got for Haddon and Anthropology was a lectureship of £50 a year, in 1900. The strength of the opposition behind the scenes may be gauged by the force of the supporting party.

In 1901 Haddon was elected to a fellowship at his own college, and with this nucleus of an income and no facilities except those provided by the generosity of other departments, he settled down to establishing a school of Anthropology. For most of his life he had to make out an income by reviewing, writing and lecturing up and down the country in addition to his university work, and he mostly had to finance from this the equipment, materials and books he needed. In a speech on his seventieth birthday, Haddon observed: 'Our University sometimes seems to behave more like the traditional step-mother than Alma Mater – the Nourishing Mother'. There was indeed a considerable period of his life when the motto of his university must have seemed to him a bitter joke. He had, however, his work, his teaching and his enthusiastic students, and, as time went on, his grateful old pupils all over the world; and he had the support of appreciative scientists everywhere; he was sustained too by the belief that if he 'held on in Cambridge' he might get Anthropology permanently endowed there. As his biographer says, 'he had no selfish aims'; to money and status for their own sake he was perfectly indifferent. The real burden fell on his wife, who had to raise a family under the most difficult conditions of financial and psychological strain.

In 1904, in face of opposition, the Board of Anthropological Studies was officially recognized and Anthropology appeared on the Lecture List, though for ten years longer he had to depend on the goodwill of other departments even for the use of a room for lecturing or teaching. He fought the battle of Anthropology more successfully than his own, for by 1907 future Colonial administrators were being given courses at Cambridge in General Anthropology to suit their particular needs – a scheme Haddon had long urged in various quarters – and the next year a Diploma in Anthropology was established. But it was not till 1909 that Haddon's friends and admirers felt in a position to address a Memorandum to the General Board of Studies recommending that 'Dr Haddon, an enthusiastic and inspiring teacher and an anthropologist of world-wide reputation' should be appointed Reader in Ethnology. This was successful; £200 a year was actually wrung out of the university for the purpose and Haddon appointed (though insulting opposition 'enlivened the discussion in the Senate', where the proposal was described as 'the most reckless and culpable waste of money that could possibly be imagined'). He held this princely readership till he was over seventy, resigning in 1925, 'having borne the whole burden of teaching in the Department for nearly a quarter of a century'. The chair which he had so richly earned was not established until he was technically too old to be eligible, in 1933.

He died in 1940, in his eighty-fifth year. In spite of everything, or rather everybody, he had achieved much of what he had wanted and more than could possibly have been expected in the circumstances; his life was not tragic for he was happy and successful according to any real code of values, and he had all along the recognition of his peers. But why did it have to be 'in spite of'? Haddon was in an innocent sense a good mixer, and had connections and friends in the right places, he was even 'a regular churchgoer' and had the gift of making Anthropology acceptable to Bishops and missionaries: he was not the sort of man who is described in the academic world as 'dangerous'. For this reason no doubt no campaign of personal calumny and social ostracism was undertaken against him, as is usual in similar cases, and no hostility to his project of establishing the new study was exhibited, as might have been expected, by the contiguous schools of Archaeology, Geology, etc. The general public might well ask, who, if not professors and Heads of Departments and Houses, supported by the testimony of pupils and outside authorities – who if not these can take action, who in fact runs our universities anyway? It almost looks as though there must be some basis for the belief I have heard expressed, that at the older universities everything is managed by committees and all those committees by a few wicked old men. This is perhaps an extreme statement; at least, the practice of intrigue is not the prerogative of the old. The answer does seem to be that the academic world, like other worlds, is run by the politicians, and sensitively scrupulous people tend to leave politics to other people, while people with genuine work to do certainly have no time as well as no taste for committee-rigging and the associated techniques. (Haddon ignored University politics and was surprised to find that 'what to him was a matter of opinion' would be to some important person 'a matter of offence' – this gives perfectly the temperature of academic life.) And then of course there are the forces of native stupidity reinforced by that blind hostility to criticism, reform, new ideas, and superior ability which is human as well as academic nature.[18] These forces are always present to be directed for their own ends by academic politicians, but perhaps they can be trusted to defeat themselves in time. Though material triumph may be lacking, a Haddon comes out on top in the end because it is he and not they who gets results and reputation, and the cause of Anthropology is eventually won. To be sure, he will incur in the process all the malice, thwarting and jealous misrepresentation which the jungle of academic society can produce. It is not surprising that the academic world should be so much like a small town, since human nature is essentially the same in both places; the grounds for indignation are that a university is supposed to be a place where different values reign, and different objects are pursued, than in the outside world. And it is true that in the realm of the sciences there is a tradition of impartial appointment and generous recognition, because in science there are objective standards to appeal to. Haddon was fortunate in having this disinterested world of science behind him; without its backing he could not have found a party to press his claims on the university and would have been wholly frustrated in his work. The real tragedies lie elsewhere.

When Haddon consulted his wife about giving up Dublin and Zoology for Cambridge and Anthropology she replied: 'You might as well starve as an anthropologist as a zoologist.' But there is the specialist of genius who cannot even starve in his own way. There was Haddon's linguistic expert, S. H. Ray, who was the only English authority on Melanesian languages available for the 1898 Expedition. 'Haddon never felt quite happy about Ray. The other members of the Expedition all rose high in the world, and he could feel that their work with him had not been unrewarded. But Ray who had sacrificed more, had no earthly reward; he remained an assistant elementary schoolmaster to the end of his days. The file of correspondence shows the efforts Haddon made to obtain recognition for him, but all in vain, and this man of genius, one of the world's greatest authorities on Oceanic languages, was compelled to earn his living for forty years by teaching elementary arithmetic to large classes of little East-End London boys, snatching what odd hours he could spare for his linguistic work.' It was impossible to get Ray, with all his qualifications, a foothold in the academic world. He had no college to give him a tardy fellowship. For him not even a lectureship of £50 a year could be secured. All that Haddon could get for him from the academic world was an honorary M.A. degree at Cambridge. When one thinks how much money there was to dispose of in the universities, where comfortable livings seem to have been available for so many insignificant scholars and posts for so many without vocation, where young men have so freely been elected into fellowships on promissory notes that have not by any means invariably been honoured, and where, in short, the most casual glance round would reveal a number of people who seem to have no reason for being supported with income and status except their strong sense of their right to be – the tragedy of a Ray seems unnecessary.

Haddon's case, even more than Ray's, has the importance of being representative, and it represents a problem which neither Royal nor Statutory Commissions can favourably affect nor any reform that can conceivably follow on the War. If there had not been some elasticity in the departmental system at that time, Haddon could never have established himself (and Anthropology); in those days anyone within the university could give lectures and classes, having extracted some kind of permission, and collect the fees, if he could attract enough of an audience to make it worth while and some kind of living for himself. This is what Haddon did. (It is through this loophole that Dr Richards, for example, was able while in the moral sciences school to give lectures to English students and make his career as a new kind of specialist by publishing the results – *Principles of Literary Criticism.*) Thus even with less than no encouragement from a department an innovator or otherwise obnoxious character has been known to hold on until in the course of time it became apparent that he was in fact a great man and must be admitted, however reluctantly, into the fold, if only to avert scandal. I once heard the late W. E. Johnson, who had taught all the Cambridge philosophers from Russell on, observe that he remembered when some of the most distinguished minds and most influential teachers in Cambridge were free-lances who supported themselves, without fellowships or faculty posts, in this independent way, but that with the tightening-up of things effected by the introduction of the faculty system such a state of affairs had become impossible.[19] He considered this unfortunate. And it is easy to see that without such a means of bucking the party machine, so to speak, a Haddon can never again force his way into the stronghold of vested interests that faculties inevitably become. While this makes things more comfortable for the politicians and deadheads, it is not so good for the under-graduates, or for the humanities and sciences, or for the intel-lectual life of the universities in general, or for the prestige of a school in the outside world. But this brings us to the ques-tion, for whose benefit are the universities run? and at this dangerous point we must call a halt to speculation.

Aldous Huxley: *Eyeless in Gaza*

Mr Peter Quennell recently wrote (in a book reviewed in the last number of *Scrutiny* [vol. IV]): 'Huxley, supremely intelligent, appears to suffer from the very complexity of his apparatus.' This, as one might expect, is an echo of the stock Bloomsbury account of Huxley. His 'intelligence' is popularly considered to be so great that it inhibits his other powers as novelist, particularly his ability to 'feel'; this account is supposed to explain what it is that even Mr Quennell feels to be wrong with Mr Huxley's novels. But supreme intelligence in other literary artists – Shakespeare, Blake, for instance – is not a handicap or disability: on the contrary, it is the condition of their outstanding achievement. It is obvious that 'intelligence' here needs examining. There must be different kinds of intelligence and Mr Huxley's is an inferior and inherently defective kind.

The generally accepted explanation of Huxley's fatally supreme intelligence originates, it is of interest to note, with Mr Huxley himself. What he had hinted earlier and made explicit in *Point Counter Point* (in the character of Philip the novelist-protagonist) is repeated in his new novel, though Anthony, the new hero, is only writing an amateur literary *Elements of Sociology*; nevertheless we read again of 'the temperamental divorce between the passions and the intellect,' etc., and we are repeatedly given to understand that though the feeling powers are admittedly weak the intellect is first-class. There is an instructive instance in Chapter 6 of *Point Counter Point* of the way Mr Huxley's intellect functions and the value the reader is instructed to place upon it. There is only space to quote the conclusion:

A poor starved pariah dog had its back broken under the wheels and the incident evoked from Philip a selection from the vital statistics of Sicily, a speculation about the relativity of morals, a brilliant psychological generalization. It was amusing, it was unexpected, it was wonderfully interesting; but oh! she almost wanted to scream.

Philip's wife wanted to scream because her husband's mental processes struck her as being inhuman, but some readers may with more justice object that the product is not brilliant, nor wonderfully interesting, and that Mr Huxley's *procédé* is not even amusing for very long. In a novelist it is a form of laziness: a Henry James, a Stendhal or a Flaubert dissolves his general ideas into his particular material – their novels are saturated solutions, whereas Mr Huxley's are a preposterous mixture like the White Knight's pudding. This extract also betrays our novelist's overestimate of his own bright ideas – for of course Philip's intellect, like Mr Huxley's, works by stringing together in a rapid conversational way dubious generalizations from other people's printed conclusions. *Il prend son bien où il le trouve*, and he doesn't risk looking the *trouvaille* in the mouth. On inspection his learning is found to be painlessly acquired like his information from such obvious sources as encyclopaedias, the scientific best-sellers, the current popular sociological, psychological, anthropological works, the more expensive and less well-known equivalents of Benn's sixpenny series (if, on reading *Eyeless in Gaza*, you notice that he has been using *Patterns of Culture* as a source book, you will equally reflect that it is just the sort of book he finds useful and congenial); nor does he discriminate between one borrowed theory and another, all grist. He remarks himself (*Eyeless in Gaza*, p. 171) that this is a form of laziness and self-indulgence, and continues, characteristically, to include in this charge all 'Higher Lifers': scholars, philosophers, and men of science – all are rather contemptible escapists. He asserts that all intellectual efforts are identical in kind with his own undisciplined and slipshod filching of other people's labours. Of course it is impossible to tell how far this too may be merely an irresponsible bright idea. But 'sincerity' at this level can mean nothing; it doesn't signify.

Mr Huxley's intelligence looks like being merely a matter of a great deal of reading and a great deal of note-taking (significant that all the novelists in his books take copious notes of ideas and extracts to be worked up into their texts), combined of course with a natural flair for picking up superficially impressive ideas. This goes along with his flair for embodying the *Zeitgeist*, and it is cheering to see how the naughty nasty short-story writer of the twenties has become the earnest essayist of the thirties. The serious element in

Eyeless in Gaza is represented by a crusade for an academic kind of pacifism based on the Shelleyan or *Prometheus Unbound* perfectionism (see pp. 170–1). However, we are not here concerned with this but with the novel to whose tail it is very clumsily and perfunctorily tied. As a piece of fiction it reveals the death-throes of a novelist. Mr Huxley is so bored with it that the characterization and bits of experience are for the most part merely repetitions of those used in previous novels of Mr Huxley and other people; they don't even come out of a new note-book. This sterility of invention is the nemesis of the novelist who has chosen to resort to books instead of to life for his raw material. It is the logical result of the boredom with and contempt for humanity so evident in *Beyond the Mexique Bay*, and of course to a lesser degree in his previous novels and stories. The novelist who is bored is also, inevitably, boring.

Mr Huxley's defects of intelligence are seen to be the source of his defects as novelist (thus contradicting the orthodox account of his make-up). There is no relation between his bright ideas (his 'intelligence') and his sensibility, so his technique accordingly remains a matter of bright ideas too. His 'technique' in the text-book sense was always a matter of lifting dodges from Gide and Proust and applying them from outside; in the present novel the by no means new device of the time-shift is used quite arbitrarily and in practice merely to the reader's confusion. As for technique in the important sense, the incompetence here is pronounced. For instance, if the social drama part of the new fiction and of *Point Counter Point* serves any end, it must be to expose the futility of the lives of the pleasure-chasing members of the opulent classes; any novelist who takes so many words to achieve so simple an effect ought to read the novels of Mr Evelyn Waugh and blush for himself. At showing the middlebrow fear in a handful of dust Mr Waugh outclasses Mr Huxley every time. And Mr Huxley's radical defect as a novelist, his lack of interest in the novelist's raw material, is responsible for his insensitiveness to speech and emotional idiom; his characters are identifiable if at all by gross verbal mannerisms, and Mr Wyndham Lewis, in a pamphlet *Have With You To Great Queen Street*, reproducing the first page of

Point Counter Point, remarked with justice that it might nearly all come from a penny novelette.

The one hopeful sign in *Eyeless in Gaza* is that Mr Huxley represents his hero Anthony as turning, if only on theoretical grounds, from the *Antic Hay* attitude to his fellows – the attitude of would-be scientific contempt ('My original conception was of a vast *Bouvard et Pécuchet*, constructed of historical facts. A picture of futility, apparently objective, scientific, but composed, I realize, in order to justify my own way of life. If men had always behaved either like half-wits or baboons, if they couldn't behave otherwise, then I was justified in sitting comfortably in the stalls with my opera-glasses. Whereas if there were something to be done, if the behaviour could be modified . . . ') – to a use of 'his raw material of life, thought, knowledge' as a means, apparently, in the service of humanity. The writer who has taken up for so many years the stalls-and-opera-glasses position can hardly be outstandingly intelligent, nor equipped with the understanding and courage that are the accompaniments of real intelligence in an artist. The inability to follow up any line of thought, to resolve his bright ideas beyond the elementary stage of indiscriminate acquisition, has produced Mr Huxley's notable distaste for committing himself to any position. His characters, it is generally recognized, mostly represent positions Mr Huxley has liked to see himself in, was afraid of seeing himself in, or was trying himself out in. It is interesting to see how he protects himself against the possible charge of taking seriously any serious position he is advancing by loading the mouthpiece with some ridiculous characteristic (for example, Brian Foxe's stammer). Mr Quennell's distinction between thinking and feeling doesn't look very sensible.

Brave New World and some of the less pretentious essays are so much better than the ponderous novels because Mr Huxley has had there, by the nature of the undertaking, to commit himself to a line and take serious thought in advance about where he was coming out. As literary critics it is our business to assess merely Mr Huxley's possibilities as a man of letters. And it seems evident that Mr Huxley's talents are not those of a novelist but of a popularizer of ideas: this, if we had the reasonably serious large reading public we have a right to expect after nearly seventy years of compulsory education, would be a function needing several hundred middlemen of Mr Huxley's calibre, nor would the crop be difficult to raise. But in fact the market for such writers disappeared with the old heavy reviews. There remains the public Mr Huxley has secured; with that his success depends on keeping up with the intellectual fashions and getting his wares early to market, for it is a public that is always looking for tips.

The case of Miss Dorothy Sayers

Gaudy Night (Gollancz)
Busman's Honeymoon (Gollancz)

With the above two novels Miss Sayers stepped out of the ranks of detective writers into that of the best-seller novelists, and into some esteem as a literary figure among the educated reading public. Only D. H. Lawrence (see *Phoenix*) could have reviewed these novels adequately. I confine myself to some incidental observations.

Miss Sayers belongs with Naomi Mitchison and Rosamond Lehmann and some others who are representative of the new kind of best-seller, the *educated* popular novelist. Like the Ouidas and Marie Corellis and Baron Corvos of the past they are really subjects for other kinds of specialist than the literary critic, but unlike those writers these are to some extent undoubtedly conscious of what they are doing (and so are able to practise more adroitly on their readers). Thus, for instance, the heroine of *Gaudy Night* is a Harriet Vane who writes detective stories, merely for a living and in all modesty, for was she not an Oxford Scholar and a first-class in English? But returning to her Shrewsbury College after many years for an Old Students' celebration, she finds, with what grateful surprise, that not only her coevals but all the best dons clear up to the Warden (Philosophy) are 'fervent admirers' and 'devotees' (in their own words) of her writings. Miss Sayers can hardly be as artless as all that, and it is not surprising that the world has taken her tip and proceeded to talk obediently about her

'artistry' and 'scholarly English'. The hero is of course
Harriet's suitor and ultimate husband, and here again I think
Miss Sayers has overstepped the limits of what even a best-
seller's public can be expected to swallow without suspicion.
Lord Peter is not only of ducal stock and all that a Ouida hero
was plus modern sophistication and modern accomplish-
ments – such as being adored by his men during the Great
War and able to talk like a P. G. Wodehouse moron – he is
also a distinguished scholar in history, a celebrated cricketer,
an authority on antiques, a musician, a brilliant wit, a dip-
lomat on whom the F.O. leans during international crises, a
wide and deep reader and no doubt some other things I've
overlooked. Whatever he does he does better than anyone
else and he is one of those universal geniuses like Leonardo.
Women naturally find him irresistible. Miss Sayers only
omits to add like Ouida that 'He has the seat of the English
Guards.' He does say however to his bride, 'In the course of
a misspent life I have learnt that it is a gentleman's first duty
to remember in the morning who it was he took to bed with
him' and Miss Sayers does actually write of him (thus going
one better than Ouida, who was a lady), 'He remembered
that it had once been said of "ce blond cadet de famille
ducale anglaise" – said too, by a lady who had every opportunity of judging – that "il tenait son lit en Grand Monarque
et s'y démenait en Grand Turc." '

I will not comment further on the large part played in these
novels by passages such as I have quoted, Miss Sayers being
(unlike Mr James Joyce and the late D. H. Lawrence, of whom
reviewers could say what they liked with impunity) in such
good standing with the respectable. But there is no harm in
saying, since it is demonstrably true, that these two passages
are fair samples of what Miss Sayers thinks on the one hand
witty and on the other daringly outspoken; and we are
accordingly in a position to draw some conclusions about the
taste of the public which likes such stuff and recommends it
with conviction not merely as entertainment but as Good
Stuff. For it is not, as you might have thought, as a successor
to Marie Corelli and Ouida that Miss Sayers is valued.

This odd conviction that she is in a different class from
Edgar Wallace or Ethel M. Dell apparently depends on four
factors in these novels. They have an appearance of literari-

ness; they profess to treat profound emotions and to be concerned with values; they generally or incidentally affect to deal in large issues and general problems (e.g. *Gaudy Night*, in so far as it is anything but a bundle of best-selling old clothes, is supposed to answer the question whether academic life produces abnormality in women); and they appear to give an inside view of some modes of life that share the appeal of the unknown for many readers, particularly the life of the older universities.

Literature gets heavily drawn upon in Miss Sayers's writings, and her attitude to it is revealing. She displays knowingness about literature without any sensitiveness to it or any feeling for quality – that is, she has an academic literary taste over and above having no general taste at all (there can hardly be any reader of Donne beside Miss Sayers who could wish to have his poetry associated with Lord Peter's feelings). Impressive literary excerpts, generally seventeenth century (a period far off, whose prose ran to a pleasing quaintness and whose literature and thought are notoriously now in fashion) head each chapter. She – I should say Harriet Vane – proudly admits to having 'the novelist's habit of thinking of everything in terms of literary allusion'. What a give-away! It is a habit that gets people like Harriet Vane firsts in English examinations no doubt, but no novelist with such a parasitic, stale, adulterated way of feeling and living could ever amount to anything. And Miss Sayers's fiction, when it isn't mere detective story of an unimpressive kind, is exactly that: stale, second-hand, hollow. Her wit consists in literary references. Her deliberate indecency is not shocking or amusing, it is odious merely as so much Restoration Comedy is, because the breath of life was never in it and it is only the emanation of a 'social' mind wanting to raise a snigger; you sense behind it a sort of female smoking-room (see the girlish dedication to *Busman's Honeymoon*), convinced that this is to be emancipated. (How right, you feel, Jane Austen was not to attempt male conversation unless ladies are present.)

The patter about value and the business of delving into emotional deeps seems to me more nauseating than anything else in the productions of this kind of novelist, not because anything much is said but because such clumsy fumblings stir up mud in the channels of life that heaven knows, we all know, it is hard enough to keep clear anyway. And in the matter of ideas, subject, theme, problems raised, she similarly performs the best-seller's function of giving the impression of intellectual activity to readers who would very much dislike that kind of exercise if it were actually presented to them; but of course it is all shadow-boxing. With what an air of unconventionality and play of analysis Miss Sayers handles her topics, but what relief her readers must feel – it is part no doubt of her success – that they are let off with a reassurance that everything is really all right and appearances are what really matter. You may be as immoral and disillusioned as Lord Peter, and in fact immorality, etc., are rather fetching qualities and humorous too, but you MUST go to Church and be married in it, and whether you are intellectual, nudist or hard-up your frock MUST be well-cut – this seems to be the moral burden of these books. It would be unkind to boil Miss Sayers's wisdom down to this and label it What Oxford Has Meant to Me, but evidently Miss Sayers's spiritual nature, like Harriet Vane's, depends for its repose, refreshment and sustenance on the academic world, the ideal conception that is of our older universities – or let us say a rationalized nostalgia for her student days.

I think indeed that the real draw of *Gaudy Night* was its offering the general public a peepshow of the senior university world, especially of the women's college, which has been less worked at by novelists than undergraduate life and has the appeal of novelty. (*Dusty Answer* made a similar hit.) It is a vicious presentation because it is popular and romantic while pretending to realism. Miss Sayers produces for our admiration an academic world which is the antithesis of the great world of bustle and Big Business that her readers know. Whereas in their world, she says, everything is 'unsound, unscholarly, insincere' – the implication being that the academic world is sound and sincere because it is scholarly – you have here invulnerable standards of taste charging the charmed atmosphere. ('Thank Heaven, it's extremely difficult to be cheap in Oxford', says Lord Peter.) If such a world ever existed, and I should be surprised to hear as much, it does no longer, and to give substance to a lie or to perpetuate a dead myth is to do no one any service really. It is time that

a realistic account of the older universities was put into circulation. Unfortunately for Miss Sayers's thesis the universities
are not the spiritually admirable places she alleges. People in
the academic world who earn their livings by scholarly
specialities are not as a general thing wiser, better, finer,
decenter or in any way more estimable than those of the same
social class outside. The academic world offers scope for personal aggrandizement much as the business world does, with
the results you might expect. No one who has had occasion to
observe how people get a footing in the academic world, how
they rise in it, how appointments are obtained, how the social
life is conducted, what are its standards, interests and
assumptions, could accept Miss Sayers's romanticizing and
extravagant claims (' "There's something about this place",
said Peter, "that alters all one's values." ') In fact the more
one investigates the academic world the more striking
appears its resemblance to the business world (I recently met
someone who had collected a lot of data showing this; he was
distressed). Here too to be disinterested or unconventional is
to be eccentric and dangerous, here too to be materially successful you must be a good herd member, here too the trade
union and the club spirit obtain. Even assuming that the
intellectual virtues Miss Sayers postulates are required by
the scholar for his studies, it does not follow that these are
carried over into his daily living; in point of fact it is a commonplace of experience that they rarely are. Perhaps we need
not call in the psychologist to account for this anomaly. And
the academic is even more liable alas to be bogus as a
specialist or scholar. Of course this is not surprising really, it
would perhaps be more surprising if it were otherwise – only
best-seller novelists could have such illusions about human
nature – but the actual state of affairs everyone must feel to
be unseemly, and in fact the accepted pretence is that things
are as Miss Sayers relates. Perhaps this accounts for much of
her success among the academics themselves; certainly one
would rather account for it like this than in any other way.
Yet it would surely be healthier from every point of view if the
critical winds of the outside world could be let blow through
these grimy edifices, and perhaps they would if the facts ever
leaked out and left a loophole for criticism to get in by. But
popular novelists like Miss Sayers are busy shoring up these

hallowed fragments against their ruin; if Miss Sayers were more intelligent you could call it the latest case of *Trahison des Clercs*, but you suspect her of being a victim of propaganda herself.

But Miss Sayers is after all a product of Shrewsbury College as well as its producer. Who is responsible for this combination of literary glibness and spiritual illiteracy? Are her vices unique and personal? We all know they are not, experience confirms what her style of writing suggests, that she is representative. That inane wit, that unflagging sense of humour, those epigrams, that affectation of unconventionality, that determined sociality, what a familiar chord they strike. 'Are the women at S— College really like that?' someone says she enquired, after reading *Gaudy Night*, of someone on the spot. 'My dear, they are *much worse*!' At any rate Miss Sayers's fictions are clearly the product of a sympathetic milieu somewhere and one that pretty evidently had a university education. What is to be said for the female smoking-room that has set its approval on Miss Sayers? How far is Harriet Vane reliable when she reports her dons devoted to her novels? Some of the conversation of the oldest generation of women dons sounds convincing – Miss Sayers has caught the authentic acid note in personal intercourse and the genuine intellectual passion that distinguished them from the succeeding generations – and I don't think they would have had any use for Harriet's lucubrations; but if the younger generation read her novels with pleasure as she alleges then the higher education of women is in a sadder way than any feminist could bear to contemplate.

What does seem indisputable is that Miss Sayers as a writer has been a vast success in the senior academic world everywhere. The young report that their elders recommend *Gaudy Night* to them, Miss Sayers has the *entrée* to literary societies which would never have opened their doors to Edgar Wallace, she is canonized as a stylist by English lecturers already, and so on; after all, her reputation as a literary figure must have been made in such quarters. Speculation naturally turns on how anyone can devote himself to the study and teaching of the humanities (we will let off the scientists, in spite of their living in a place that alters all one's values) and yet not be able to place a Dorothy Sayers's novel on inspection if it comes his way. Well it does seem queer, but such a lapse is not without precedent. Run your eyes over enough academic bookshelves – not those housing shop but those where they keep what they really choose to read – and you get accustomed to a certain association of authors representing an average taste which is at best negative: Edward Lear and Ernest Bramah's *Kai Lung* (delicious humour), Charles Morgan and C. E. Montague (stylists), Rupert Brooke (or Humbert Wolfe or some equivalent) ... we can all supplement. Dorothy Sayers can take her place alongside without raising any blushes; these or their kind are the writers she admires herself. But doesn't it raise some awkward questions? What is the value of this scholarly life Miss Sayers hymns if it doesn't refine the perceptions of those leading it? If your work was of any value to you would you want, would you be able to relax on Edgar Wallace (much less on Dorothy Sayers)? Miss Sayers innocently presents her typical admirable scholar, an English don, engaged on her life's work of what but a History of English Prosody (an all too plausible undertaking). Apart from the fact that the lady was engaged in perpetrating a sort of public nuisance, think of the effect on the teaching of English in her college of that attitude to the study of poetry. No education could take place there; studying English Prosody will not show anyone why Miss Sayers isn't a good novelist. That kind of scholarship never gears in with life. But is there any other kind? Miss Sayers however finds it wholly admirable. By this code, she says, the only unpardonable thing is to be unscholarly; evil consists in producing a popular life of Carlyle without any research. But which is really worse, to be unscholarly or to pass writers like Miss Sayers? Mistakes about Carlyle are not a menace to civilization.

I once conversed on these or similar lines with a Professor of Classics, a man of genuine but diffident literary tastes. He remarked that it seemed unaccountable to him that the writings of a fellow-classic were so highly esteemed by his colleagues. He himself, he said modestly, had an unconquerable aversion to them, they seemed to him empty, the man's 'style' cheap and his wit puerile, but none of his friends agreed with him; it was so discouraging and he felt he must be in the wrong. I said Not at all, his colleagues' insensitive-

ness to their native literature seemed to me an illustration of
the evident fact that you could spend a lifetime in the study
of any language ancient or modern, or any branch of the
humanities, without acquiring the rudiments of literary taste
or any apparatus for forming a just estimate of a piece of
writing. And I added, no doubt brutally, 'What's the good of
classics, what justification for a classical training can there
be if it doesn't form a decent taste?' My friend was taken
aback. But he was a conscientious professor and he tried to
find an answer. After a bit he brought out hopefully, 'Well,
some people are interested in philology.'

I have always tried to bear that maxim in mind. After all
philology is as legitimate a study as mathematics, and every
branch of the humanities has its philological aspect so to
speak. I recommend anyone at a loss before the spectacle of
the scholar's bedside reading to adopt the above explanation. Miss Sayers, who might evidently have been an
academic herself, is probably quite sound on the philological
side.

'Femina vie-heureuse' please note

I'm Not Complaining, by Ruth Adam (Chapman and Hall)

It is pleasant to be able to recommend a novel by a woman
novelist in strong terms. Though Mrs Woolf has declared it
to be a popular fallacy, the Jane Austen–Emily Brontë–
George Eliot circle still defies addition. These women
novelists represent female triumph in the realm of character
at least as much as of art – I mean the author's character. It
is in terms of deficiency in character that Mrs Woolf's
degeneration and Katharine Mansfield's deficiency as artists
are to be explained. The Feminist movement ought to have
helped things, you feel, but looking before and after you cannot help noticing that, to take two women of about the same
kind of ability, a feminine Mrs Gaskell has the advantage of
a feminist Winifred Holtby and not conversely. What the
Feminist movement seems to have done in the literary camp
is to set up an ideal, an ideal of the brilliant emancipated
woman of wit, intellect and literary genius. No doubt it was
inspired by George Meredith's novels. As commonly found,

incarnated in a Rebecca West (not Ibsen's) or an Ethel Mannin, it seems it must be an inherently trashy ideal. But there is another kind of feminism, represented by Charlotte Brontë most notably. She was considerably more gifted in character than literary ability, and the abiding interest her novels have is the outlook – the peculiar angle on life and the personal sense of values – of the author's mouthpiece, Lucy Snow or Jane Eyre.

Miss Adam is evidently such another, though she is as evidently a feminist too in the other way – she conveys powerfully an impression that a man is generally a pitiful object. *I'm Not Complaining* ought to get a literary prize, though you can be sure it won't; it has not the qualities that appeal to prize-awarding committees. It is about the Elementary school in a depressed district (no doubt typical enough in these hard times), presented through the personality of a mistress in a Junior and Infant school. The facts are convincing in themselves as they are narrated, though anyone with a friend or two in the profession, or who has been through an Elementary school not too long ago, is likely to be familiar with most of them already. Miss Adam's feat is not merely to convey these facts convincingly and unforgettably, but to have made them into the material of art. The nits in the children's hair, the rude words chalked on the walls, the perpetual petty thieving, the troublesome milk bottles, the eternal registers, are used not as facts to elicit laughter or political action but collectively to build up the atmosphere of a complete culture. Being art it does not demand any such simple response as indignation. Contributors to *New Writing* might profitably study Miss Adam's method, and admirers of the *New Writing* reportage might be stimulated by *I'm Not Complaining* to realize that the *New Writing* stories are almost uniformly uninteresting, not literature, and in their lack of literary ability not even convincing as fact. Miss Adam is steeped in the details of her culture and her novel yields more at every reading.

She has a talent for writing, unlike poor Charlotte. Without any gestures or pretensions she rolls up her sleeves and gets right down to it with the opening sentence. Everyone I have shown the novel to has agreed that you only have to read the first page to realize that here is a unique good thing. Miss

Adam has a style characterized not only by condensation, simplicity and objectivity, but by a tone which like Charlotte's is not sympathetic. It is even a bit grim, for underlying it is always an implied criticism. It is the attitude of an uncompromisingly intelligent woman, contemptuous of the unreal – sentimentality, idealism and any kind of emotional silliness. Here is the headmistress: 'She believed that most coughs and all sniffs could be controlled by the child with a full sense of responsibility towards the school and towards its fellow-scholars.' What she despises most is sentimentality applied to education. For instance, there is the literature professor's wife who greets her (this is really so true to life as to be hardly bearable) with 'You mustn't mind us. We're very unconventional', and presently we get:

I asked where their child was, and she said he was at school. It was a very enlightened co-educational boarding-school, she hastened to add, where there was no nonsense about segregating the sexes and thus putting impure thoughts into the children's minds. I said that we didn't have any nonsense about segregating the sexes at our school either, but that, so far as we could judge, the impure thoughts were in their minds all ready-made.

In its context, following the picture of children who have not come from sheltered homes, this doesn't read like the *Punch* or E. M. Delafield humour it may here suggest. It conveys a commonsense criticism of impractical theory from someone qualified to hold an opinion because she spends her best energies trying to impose the elements of civilization on children to many of whom, because of their home environment, theft and lies and immorality come as naturally as dirty heads and malnutrition. On fifty-six children at once. Homer Lane worked in an isolated community I believe, and even our expensive advanced boarding-schools are said to complain that their children show a relapse after every vacation. Miss Adam is able in the same style to treat finer and subtler issues, which is a proof that there is nothing superficial about her attitudes. For example:

After dinner she came in very shyly and looking very scared and laid a note on my desk ... They always have a pathetic belief, that nothing will shake, that an actual letter, written by a parent's hand, has a world-compelling power over any dictum of authority from the laws of the Education Committee downwards. Sometimes they even infect parents with their dazzling faith. Often, between the lines of the ill-written and usually threatening scraps, you can see a mental picture of the unhappy child, creeping into the fancied security of its home, out of the merciless machine of the State, begging for help – so sure that Father or Mother has only to put stubby pencil to dirty paper for God himself to climb down off His perch and let Tommy or Betty go to the lavatory when they want, if you don't mind, teacher . . .

I have tended to talk about the book as though Miss Adam were voicing it. Actually these are the sentiments of Madge Brigson, who is carefully built up as a character and a personality; and the novel anyway is too well constructed for us to forget that we are reading a piece of art and not a pamphlet. Nevertheless Miss Adam must be credited with sponsoring her views, though it is sometimes hazardous to decide which way the irony is meant to cut. For an irony calling so little attention to itself that it might often be overlooked is a characteristic of Miss Adam's method ('She was one of our very few respectable children. Her father was a warder in the local jail'). No novelist has wrung more drama out of the richest scenes in history than Miss Adam elicits from Inspectors' visits, abusive parents, undisciplined Night School, demonstrations of unemployed, dishonest caretakers and staff conflicts.

To the creations of art Madge Brigson is an impressive contribution. She makes feminism respectable if not interesting. Her character is of high calibre, like Jane Eyre's. She listens to the training-college professor mouthing conventional enlightenment and reflects devastatingly, 'He was a silly man,' to the religion-bitten social reformer and says, 'I thought he was a sentimental old fool' to the Left reporter who babbles, 'I think school ought to be such a happy place that they don't need any Attendance Officer to dragoon them into going'; and comments, 'I had talked that sort of stuff myself at college, but I thought he ought to have got over it at his age . . . we soon disposed of him.' You believe her.

The environment in which traffic accidents thin out the children already blighted by slums and too large families is artfully set off by a background of the County busy cherishing horses and cats, nursing the weakly puppy of the litter and marvelling how much dogs *know*. Animal non-lovers (not necessarily identical with child-lovers) will find Miss Brigson's sense of proportion cheering. Its importance for a wider category of people who cannot join up with any existing herd is that her enlightenment is apparently unattached to politics of any shade, her social criticism is not from a *parti pris*. She is careful to see that responsibility for the state of things she witnesses is not put in the wrong place: slum parents are merely incompetent not brutal, tenement dwellers who stand callously on nice points of morality will show Christian charity in other respects, and so on. No haphazard indignation, no cheap irony and no caricature of types or classes invites a stock response. Emotional scenes and situations are deflated and analysed as they occur. We are not allowed any easy outlet for the blend of distress, disgust and exasperation that her themes elicit. Miss Adam, that is, has both an artistic and a moral conscience, whereas what is called a social conscience is nowadays made an excuse for the absence in writers of either. Yet I cannot see that anything but a social conscience could have prompted her to undertake her novel, and it affects me as being likely to awaken a social conscience in people who would remain unmoved by all the recommendations of the Left Book Club. What does Miss Adam want us to blame? There is of course the Government, and Madge Brigson reflects that better management of depressed districts would obviously be desirable. But she cannot help looking deeper:

Squalor did not frighten me. When you live so close to it, and are paid to fight it, it is not terrifying – merely a tiresome and tireless adversary. But somewhere beneath it all was a live, burning thread that ran through these human miseries that was not just mismanagement, nor stupidity, nor a faulty social system, but something living, primitive, terrible – something I dare not look in the face. A hundred nauseating images seemed to rise up in my mind – all somehow connected . . .

Hence her lack of enthusiasm for her young communist colleague – 'extremely earnest. She was given to causes.' Madge Brigson distrusts the effect of causes on people. She knows that only a part of what she is fighting can be altered by legislation or doctrinaire revolution, though you gather she is willing to try anything that offers in those lines. Commonsense often seems to sensitive people no more than the most complacent form of stupidity, but Miss Adam's variety of commonsense is the means of exposing some of the more plausible and pernicious kinds of stupidity.

Apart from Dickens's admirable satires on the old system in *Hard Times* and *Our Mutual Friend*, the only account of the modern state school in literature comparable with Miss Adam's is a chapter ('The Man's World') in *The Rainbow*. We may be sure that Lawrence would have liked her book. It is to his essay *Education of the People* that we may profitably turn on laying down *I'm Not Complaining*.

The background of twentieth-century letters

A Number of People, by Sir Edward Marsh (Heinemann)
Unforgotten Years, by Logan Pearsall Smith (Constable)
Enemies of Promise, by Cyril Connolly (Routledge)
Modern Poetry, by Louis MacNeice (Oxford)

Sir Edward Marsh was the patron of the Georgian poets, Mr Connolly is the co-mate of the post-war literary gang, Mr MacNeice is a contributor to the contemporary poetic renaissance. Each has recently published a book about his circle. We have the socio-literary history of three phases for inspection, and may take the opportunity to draw some conclusions about the literary *milieu* of our age, the background of twentieth-century letters. If you are inclined to think this a norm read the history of the same period in American letters, as recorded by Malcolm Cowley in *Exile's Return*, and Lincoln Steffens in his autobiography. Sir Edward Marsh's picture has nothing in common with Steffens's, MacNeice's case-history of self and partners in no way resembles Cowley's. No one could deny that the American history represents a healthy development, an evolution out of chaos and futility to a general recognition of standards and an agreement as to abiding values, in literary criticism. The 'critical' sections of the two later English books are depressing reading. Mr Connolly's list of who's who in modern literature, his choice of the hopes for English literature and those whom he thinks are reviving imaginative writing, has to be read to be believed, and Mr Connolly is an exceptionally able and bright-minded member of our higher journalism. However, the third section of his book, 'A Georgian Boyhood', should be read carefully by literary critics as well as educationists: his account of the Eton education and its effects on taste and character – Eton standing for the English public-school system generally – offers a comprehensive answer to the questions raised by a comparison of these books with their American equivalents. The information he unconsciously gives about the relation between knowing the right people and getting accepted in advance of production as a literary value is even more useful than the analysis he consciously makes of the stultifying effects of an exclusively classical education conducted in an exclusively upper-class and male establishment.

Sir Edward Marsh's book raises all the questions. He is a beautiful specimen, a perfect litmus paper without, as a literary critic, any individuality, personal taste or character. A Classic at Westminster, he passed second in the Civil Service examination and thereafter, mixing as intensively as possible with the best people, he became an innocent blotting-paper to all literary aspirants he met in the right company, particularly good-looking young men with fetching manners. He was overwhelmed by Rupert Brooke, and after meeting Ivor Novello he became so impressed with the talents of the author of *Keep the Home Fires Burning* that he even took a passionate interest in musical comedy. It was his representative quality that enabled him to produce in the Georgian Poetry Books something that went like hot cakes (the second volume sold 19,000). And as his classical education gave him an unshakable conception of what poetry ought to be, so his environment gave him no occasion to doubt his rightness of judgement. He still believes that 'Rupert Brooke is destined to remain as a considerable figure in English Literature', that Gordon Bottomley's and Lascelles Abercrombie's poetic dramas are great poetry, that Georgian poetry will soon be rehabilitated, and is confident of his own place beside Tottel (predicted by Gosse) for anthologizing it. He still feels how right he was to refuse in 1925 to have anything to do with the 'new directions' of English poetry (the only reference to Eliot's poetry is a silly joke), and it never occurs to him, any

more than to Mr Connolly, to question Mr Desmond
McCarthy's right to refuse anyone else the right to criticize
Milton – for both of them it is enough that he is an Etonian.

The same complacency, an inability to apply purely literary criticism to literature because of an unconscious acceptance of social values in this as in all other fields, is visible in
Connolly almost equally, even though he sets out to account
for his feeling that something is wrong somewhere. *The Waves*
is a supreme work of art, Isherwood and Orwell are the
coming great writers, 'The prose of Spender is also unusual,
and in his critical book *The Destructive Element* he makes a
study of that great Mandarin, Henry James, which must
affect the values of any contemporary who reads it.' I suppose
it is because instead of knowing Mr Spender personally I
have been reading Henry James's novels for fifteen years that
the only way in which his study affected me was as a
botched-up piece of journalism by someone who had not only
no capacity for examining James's novels critically but who
had not even read them with ordinary care and intelligence.
Though Mr Connolly attacks the classical culture of Eton as
'by nature sterile' and though he protests against the College
literary values of his time – the Victorian Romantic and the
facetious in verse, Pre-Raphaelite prose – he does not think of
questioning the social foundation of the world of letters. He
ends his case-history:

Since I was unable to write in any living language when I left Eton
I was already on the way to becoming a critic. My ambition was to
be a poet, but I could not succeed when poetry was immersed in the
Georgian or Neo-Tennysonian tradition . . . I was however well
grounded enough to become a critic, and drifted into it through
unemployability.

He does not apparently think this a criticism of the state of
our literary journalism. But this does explain what has
always puzzled some of us. Contemplating the literary
reviewing we cannot help wondering how it is that these
reviewers, who know all the literary figures of their world,
have had the most expensive education, and are not so over-
worked that they have no time to think if they wanted to, are
not only unable to make first-hand judgements but are also
completely ignorant of informed opinion. Where did Mr A

get his reputation for brilliant wit, how is it that B's stuff is
counted devastating satire, why does Miss C get respectful
reviews, on what grounds could anyone assert Mrs D's latest
novel is worth serious attention? are questions that regularly
recur to many readers of our literary weeklies, monthlies and
even quarterlies. Mr Connolly early in his book observed:
'Critics in England do not accept bribes, but they discover
one day that in a sense their whole life is an accepted bribe,
a fabric of compromises based on personal relationships.' Sir
Edward Marsh is incapable of such a reflection, but even as
aware a man as Mr Connolly does not seem able to see its full
implications for literary criticism. He tells us how when he
and his Eton set were faced with leaving College for the university the prospect seemed 'exhilarating and cosy, for, subject to a little permutation, the sentimental friendships from
College continued unabated with undergraduates from other
schools forming an audience, who, at a pinch, would con-
tribute new blood to the cast'. A parable of the structure of
our little world of letters. Skip a step and you see how it is that
these elegant unemployables get into the higher journalism,
and even the academic world, and how reputations are made
– you have only to get the right people, whom you already
know or can get introductions to, to write the right kind of
thing about you in the right places. The odious spoilt little
boys of Mr Connolly's and so many other writers' schooldays
– their education surely no less strange than that of the Nazi
aristocracy as described by Erika Mann in *School for Barbarians*
– move in a body up to the universities to become innane
pretentious young men, and, still essentially unchanged,
from there move into the literary quarters vacated by the last
batch of their kind. Rupert Brooke in 1906 at Cambridge 'was
in the set which filled the place that mine had held when I was
"up",' writes Sir Edward. Mr Connolly and his set expected
to succeed Rupert Brooke's, and are now seeing to it that the
literary preserves are kept exclusively for their friends. We
who are in the habit of asking how such evidently unqualified
reviewers as fill the literary weeklies ever got into the profession need ask no longer. They turn out to have been 'the
most fashionable boy in the school', or to have had a feline
charm or a sensual mouth and long eyelashes. And in the
creative field the same process is seen at work. The Oxford

group moved naturally into the place left by Sir Edward's Georgians, to create the latest poetic renaissance, almost straight from school and, having no critical standards to reckon with as we have seen, they have remained what they were at school. Hence Mr MacNeice's account of his friends and their work reads like a book written by a schoolboy for schoolboys.

Going to Germany soon after leaving Oxford, Auden took readily to post-War Germany's intellectual curiosity and spirit of heroic or idyllic Kameradschaft. He admires the cinema's unrivalled capacity for rapportage; Auden has always believed that a good writer must be first a good reporter. His poetry is obviously conditioned by his background and experiences, and also by his not unfriendly contempt for the female sex, whom he regards as still precluded from civilization by circumstances.

It is no use looking for growth or development or any addition to literature in such an adolescent hot-house. The one literary artist of serious performance, vitality and worth in the period covered by Sir Edward and Mr Connolly was D. H. Lawrence. He imports the only jarring note into the former's memoirs, otherwise so happily studded with affectionate anecdotes of the best people in society and the arts. Lawrence is reported to have said that Eddie Marsh ought to have his bottom kicked (for his impudence in telling Lawrence that his poetry didn't scan – see the Lawrence *Letters*). Eddie records it serenely, for Lawrence was an outsider. The tone taken by the literary reviews at the time Lawrence required obituary notices is a testimonial to the success of the public school–university hold over literary criticism. No one who ever read Lord David Cecil, for instance, on Lawrence can fail to appreciate that the achieved reputation of an outsider was felt as a personal insult by the people who run our literary world. Order is revealed among a chaotic puzzle of memories: we read in the paper that two young men are the likely candidates for the something literary prize or poetry medal, one being sponsored by Sir Edward Marsh and one by some other bigwig – neither would be sponsored by the literary critic; we could never before account for Mr Connolly's write-up of Naomi Mitchison's embarrassing bestseller *We Have Been Warned*; Sir

Edward himself tells us how he was asked by the authorities whether Henry James ought to be given the Order of Merit, and instructed to find out whether Joyce ought to be given a Civil List Grant. Henry James got his OM on his death-bed after some trouble, but suppose it had been Lawrence (D. H.) or someone as unconventional and society-shunning as Walt Whitman? The gulf between disinterested opinion on contemporary literature and fashionable esteem is for a variety of reasons deplorable.

Mention of Walt Whitman brings us to the other book listed here, the memoirs of Logan Pearsall Smith. Mr Smith was an American Quaker in the distant days before he settled down to become an English littérateur. Unlike Henry James and Mr T. S. Eliot he sold his birthright for a mess of pottage, or more precisely the Paterian tradition of fine writing and the English social tradition of letters. The earlier parts of his book are good reading, for his origin provided him with a point of view and a fruitful background. His reminiscence of Walt Whitman is something that no one else in this gallery could have been capable of setting down, and his criticism of the Balliol ethos of his time is correspondingly refreshing. But that was long ago. He is now as convinced as Eddie Marsh that modern poetry and modern prose are no good, and as sure as Rupert Brooke that style means decoration and stilts. 'This draught of Shakespeare's brewing – the potent wine that came to fill the great jewelled cup of words he fashioned', he writes and even in unimpassioned argument: 'There are two main methods of attaining excellence in writing, two ways of attempting to reach the peaks of Parnassus.' Responsibility for failure to develop his initial endowment must lie with the company he kept, which though it has always reviewed with extravagant praise his literary criticism and his creative efforts will never convince posterity that the *Trivia* are not boring or the monograph on Shakespeare not empty fine writing. The advantages Americans enjoy in having no public school system, no ancient universities and no tradition of a closed literary society run on Civil Service lines can hardly be exaggerated.

Lady novelists and the lower orders

These books should be read by the workers because they find a different
point of view and how we are thought of by the other class.

Mrs Scott, *Life As We Have Known It*

Mrs Mitchison's new novel, *We Have Been Warned* (Constable),
naturally recalls *To Tell the Truth* by Mrs Williams-Ellis published two years ago. These novels seem to demand attention
here less for the reasons for which they are read and praised
than for what they reveal about the outlook of their authors.
Both are attempts, more or less direct, to arouse revolutionary feeling on behalf of the workers of England. By mating an
aristocratic Highland female with an Oxford don who is
Labour candidate for an industrial area and sending them
both on a trip to Russia Mrs Mitchison has contrived a
setting in which anything she wants to talk about can be
plausibly dramatized. By sending a suspicious Komsomol to
England in search of the truth about the condition of the
workers under capitalism Mrs Williams-Ellis has tacked
together a light structure from which to make a Voltairean
survey of our society. The first embodies nearly as uncritical
an enthusiasm as the second for what they assert are the aims
and values of Soviet Russia, and both spring from the same
innocently bourgeois background; to the reader whose class-
feeling derives from a less advantageous social origin there is
something peculiarly irritating about the implicit assumption of authority that is apparent in these writers – an
assumption grounded, it would appear, on nothing but class.
Both give the same impression of having had to go out, notebook in hand, to examine proletarian homes and their
inmates to equip themselves for writing about what their
literary ancestors would undoubtedly have called the lower
class. Much of both novels is intended to serve as social
propaganda of a desirable and familiar kind – abolish slums,
provide better housing, abolish the Means Test, cure
unemployment, provide easy access to information about
contraception for all, etc., etc. In so far as they do this few of
their readers are likely to disagree, or be much enlightened;
the creation of such an elementary social consciousness I
should have thought could be done more convincingly by

popular factual booklets such as Hutt's *Condition of the Working Class in Britain* and more vividly by other methods – for example, simple illustrated articles such as *The Listener* has run in the past. But one readily agrees that this work is never finished: there can hardly be too much repetition and insistence.

It is a small matter that first provokes criticism. Mrs Mitchison's novel shows spasmodic doubts about, and Mrs Williams-Ellis's positive animus against, any intellectual worker engaged in almost any other activity than demonstrating the evils of back-to-back houses and the Means Test; the exceptions allowed seem to be the hierarchy of useful scientist, heroic engineer and that modern idol the mathematician. This position is evidently open to objections, and in any case it seems too easily assumed by advanced political thinkers – and Communism is fashionable now – that such other activities necessarily go along with absence of a social conscience and are unprofitable to the community, while you may retain your leisure, servants, holidays and cocktail parties with an even enhanced complacency provided only you learn the Russian alphabet and take a trip to the USSR, and say very loudly all the time that back-to-back houses are disgusting and the Means Test inhuman. You thus enjoy the luxury of having it both ways *and* the pleasure of feeling superior to those who haven't. Thus a new snobbery seems to have been created (amusingly illustrated by the dedication to *We Have Been Warned* – unfortunately too long to reproduce here). There is a complacency of enlightenment no less undesirable than the complacency of conservatism.

Thus aroused, one constantly discovers further material for uneasiness. Isn't it odd that a genuine concern for the emancipation of the workers and an immersion in working-class society should not have produced at least freshness of perception and some response to the peculiar quality of life dealt with – should not, in sum, have resulted in technical originality and locally authentic writing? One remembers the vitality and spontaneity of much of *The Forty-Second Parallel* and its sequel. Mrs Williams-Ellis would probably agree to a description of *To Tell the Truth* as simple propaganda in the form of a pleasing fiction; objections must be that the propaganda is not merely simple but simple-minded and that the fiction is irritating in the shallowness of that bright complacency which takes itself for Voltairean irony, while the discussion of ideas is puerile.

We Have Been Warned is more ambitious. It does not deliberately set out to simplify as Mrs Williams-Ellis has done; all kinds of social and personal problems come up for discussion and the worlds of Oxford, Bloomsbury, an industrial centre, the Highlands, Moscow and others provide juicy material for description of the gossip-column order. In fact, apart from, or in spite of, its political views and general intellectual pretensions, *We Have Been Warned* is just another best-seller. To be more particular, passages from throughout the book could be mixed up with passages from the fictions of Mr Gilbert Frankau and perhaps no one but their authors would be able to re-sort them correctly. The style, when occasions for imitating *The Waves*, *Mrs Dalloway*, James Joyce, the moderns in general, and Mrs Mitchison herself in her former manner as a novelist of ancient history, do not obviously determine it, is just that of the average magazine story ('Dione, her hands behind her head, and looking definitely rather pretty, added . . . ' is about the staple). The general competence of the writer is thus dubious. What confidence can be placed in the political 'thought' of a writer who visualizes in terms of magazine-story situations, whose perceptions can be embodied in *pastiches* and clichés and whose emotional equipment is no more refined than that of the best-seller of the corrupt bourgeois public? As an intellectual (and she is self-consciously one) this novelist seems to be no better equipped. Her opinions and values are not personal, they are those of a 'set', fashionable not intelligent – accepted without any suspicion of criticism as 'modern'. Take the following characteristic example from the passage where the heroine (whom in a general way – apart, that is, from incident – the reader is invited to identify with the authoress) is expressing what England means to her: 'She was proud of Dunbar and Shakespeare and Donne; she was proud of Virginia Woolf and Lawrence and Shaw and Wyndham Lewis and Aldous Huxley.' This is Mrs Mitchison's conception of the English literary tradition. Dunbar is a concession to the heroine's northern birth, Shakespeare goes without saying, Donne 'came in' some time ago, Mrs Woolf has long been a *chic* value and Lawrence notoriously 'advanced'; no irony seems to lurk in the inclusion of the last three names: they have been taken over in the same uncritical fashion as currency values, though so ill-assorted (in *To Tell the Truth* also Shaw is a value). Similarly she knows that Browning has gone out but that Tennyson is coming in again, that Eddington is not an authentic great thinker, that your ideas to command respect must be coloured with science or given an anthropological note, and so on. Her ability to appreciate Lawrence may be determined by her bright idea that he might have written that typical Lord Leighton Academy piece 'Now sleeps the crimson petal, now the white'. Apart from the matters of social amelioration on which all decent people agree, her enlightenment seems to amount to nothing more than knowing what are the right, that is to say the fashionable, views on an assortment of topics, and campaigning on behalf of contraception, the free use of the more respectable improper words, the necessity for dealing with 'sexual repressions', and moral and physical nudism for all.

I have thought it worth going into these points in some detail because such an equipment is the usual one nowadays for such a writer. It amounts to a major disability. Its effects are most obvious when Mrs Mitchison tries to describe the sufferings and worthiness of the English working class and when she tries to conjure up an alluring Utopia for us to strive to bring about, a Utopia that, like Mrs Williams-Ellis, she sees being achieved in Soviet Russia. In the section 'Under the Red Flag' we are shown a society for whom the machine is an absolute value. The women, who are the heroic figures in it, are engineers, technicians, radio specialists (compare Mrs Williams-Ellis's Candide who is also an engineer); these occupations, we are to assume, have intrinsic value, for there are contemptuous references to the 'typical petty bourgeois' life in which the married woman makes a profession of home-keeping and child-rearing instead of, like the heroic Marfa, working in a factory all day and locking up her child in her absence. The further superiority of the women of this society consists in willingness to sleep casually with any party member and to share or exchange lovers as convenience dictates. Mrs Williams-Ellis presents us with a similar picture of an admirable society. Neither thinks of questioning the ends which radio, for example, serves, or feels any doubts about machine-tending as the good life. Neither has any use for the sensitiveness that would find such a Utopia repulsive. Perhaps that is why they fail so notably in their dealings with the English workers. No amount of reporting of trivial conversations, and no amount of observation of the district-visiting kind, however conscientious and however creditable to the industry and heart of the novelist, will produce a convincing substitute for adequate response to the quality of the working-class life.

The easiest way to make this point is by referring the reader to an American novel, Grace Lumpkin's *To Make My Bread*, which won the Gorky Prize for Proletarian Literature for 1933. Its immense superiority to the English novels is not due to this authoress's greater concern for artistry; she is less concerned for it, and this novel only misses greatness, it seems to me, because of a lack of craftsmanship. Its superiority lies in the fineness and percipience of the author's make-up. There is no obtrusion of the author's personality – no novel could be more impersonal; she is so genuinely concerned for the people she writes about that she does not make her concern an excuse for asserting superiority; she does not have to offer us a worker's paradise of emancipated machine-tending because simply by reflecting the quality of the lives of the Southern mill-hands she leaves the reader convinced that such a people, given economic freedom, could live to exemplify the best possibilities of humanity (which I suppose is what everyone would agree a society should do if a revolution is to be justified). Miss Lumpkin's novel is better literature as well as better propaganda, and it is better propaganda because it is better literature.[20]

For instance, Miss Lumpkin has perceived that simple people living at the lowest economic level are not necessarily incapacitated for delicacy and refinement of feeling, and perhaps are the less likely to acquire an inadequate set of values – one for instance in which, as Mrs Mitchison seems to think, having only a 13/11d Co-op frock for best would be a major distress and attending a Bloomsbury studio party would be a major satisfaction. You cannot in fact unless you are yourself capable of perceiving fineness in others and valuing it duly, convincingly attribute an outlook demanding admiration to those whose cause you may have most at heart. If your own conception of pleasure is trivial then you have no criterion of seriousness to measure by. Consider the example of desirable high-level amusement Mrs Mitchison offers – and she gives it some prominence: it is one of the positives of the novel, like the Russian section. The heroine is taken to a studio party that is alleged to be the equivalent of the 'good parties' of the Athenians and the kind of amusement that everyone will rejoice in at the millennium. It turns out to be the vulgarest idea of a good time – dancing to the gramophone, too much alcohol, and universal petting – with the added thrill of rubbing shoulders with artists (presented in the persons of 'a very eminent painter [who] asked her to be his mistress, and she was very proud of that till she heard him ask someone else the same thing in exactly the same words ten minutes afterwards' and a recently undergraduate New Poet who 'sees civilization working up for a new religion' and 'dances very well and he kisses one's neck while dancing, which is so clever of him'). The arts are additionally represented by someone singing carols and a folksong and Campion. There is also pseudo-intellectual conversation of an incredible inanity. 'Yet there's nothing wrong with this party except that it isn't actively getting on with the revolution'; and the fact that the working class are not present is also a drawback but she thinks they might be got to fit in.

So Mrs Mitchison and Mrs Williams-Ellis do not do justice to their subject. They even do the workers' cause a positive disservice. A key passage in each of their novels is worth examining. This is the summing-up of the Candide of *To Tell the Truth* on the cultural situation generally:

He had tried to show Mr Hake how it had once been true that it was difficult for the workers to have enough of anything. Because of the struggle with nature, they had no time to have culture. So works of art and science were made only by the bourgeoisie, and paid for so heavily by the workers that it made the more sensitive bourgeois doubt if they were worth having. But now, he explained, with electrification, there was no excuse for this exploitation of the workers, and the mass of the people could have culture . . . 'But now all that needs to be done can be done without exploiting anyone, and, because of machines, all the work of the world can be accomplished in peace and justice. And what is that splendid glorious fact except this very thing – Progress? So now we must have a classless society everywhere, not only in Russia, and then soon we can have all we need, Isotto Hispanas, for example, without exploitation. Technics! Technics coming after Science sets free the world.'

The above piece of theory may profitably be compared with the conclusions implicit in the following piece of direct observation (the meaning ascribed to 'culture' by each writer deserves especial note):

The present inhabitants of the Laurel Country are the direct descendants of the original settlers who were emigrants from England and, I suspect, the lowlands of Scotland . . . It is fairly safe, I think, to conclude that the present-day residents of this section of the mountains are the descendants of those who left the shores of Britain some time in the eighteenth century.

The region is from its inaccessibility a very secluded one . . . the inhabitants have for a hundred years or more been completely isolated and shut off from all traffic with the rest of the world. Their speech is English, not American, and, from the number of expressions they use which have long been obsolete elsewhere, and the old-fashioned way in which they pronounce many of their words, it is clear that they are talking the language of a past day.

Economically they are independent. As there are practically no available markets, little or no surplus is grown, each family extracting from its holding just what is needed to support life, and no more . . . Many set the standard of bodily and material comfort perilously low, in order, presumably, that they may have the more leisure and so extract the maximum enjoyment out of life . . . They are a leisurely, cheery people in their quiet way, in whom the social instinct is very highly developed . . . They know their Bible intimately and subscribe to an austere creed, charged with Calvinism and the unrelenting doctrines of determinism or fatalism . . . They have an easy unaffected bearing and the unselfconscious manners of the well-bred . . . A few of those we met were able to read and write, but the majority were illiterate. They are, however, good talkers, using an abundant vocabulary racily and often picturesquely. Although uneducated, in the sense in which that term is usually understood, they possess that elemental wisdom, abundant knowledge, and intuitive understanding which those only who live in constant touch with Nature and face to face with reality seem able to acquire . . .

That the illiterate may nevertheless reach a high level of culture

will surprise those only who imagine that education and cultivation
are convertible terms. The reason, I take it, why these mountain
people, albeit unlettered, have acquired so many of the essentials
of culture, is partly to be attributed to the large amount of leisure
they enjoy, without which, of course, no cultural development is
possible, but chiefly to the fact that they have one and all entered
at birth into the full enjoyment of their racial heritage. Their
language, wisdom, manners, and the many graces of life that are
theirs, are merely racial attributes which have been gradually
acquired and accumulated in past centuries and handed down
generation by generation, each generation adding its quotum to
that which it received . . .
That culture is primarily a matter of inheritance and not of education is, perhaps, a mere truism . . . Of the supreme cultural value
of an inherited tradition, even when unenforced by any formal
school education, our mountain community in the Southern Highlands is an outstanding example.[21]

The most obvious criticism to make of the first passage is
that Mrs Williams-Ellis can really know nothing about the
cultural history of the working class of her own country, however well up she may be in that of Russia. The assertions that
'Culture', even if it be so preposterously narrowed down to a
mere equation with 'works of art and science', is something
that the workers never enjoyed until 'electrification' and
Soviet Russia have brought it within their reach, and that
access to this Culture was impossible for those without the
leisure which the new mechanization is producing, are
simply ignorant nonsense; and such ignorance of the social
history of the English working class looks odd in one so
devoted to their cause. No one would of course suggest that
all the English workers, or the whole of any other class in any
country, are or have been at any period 'cultured'; but it can
be reasonably asserted that there has existed in this country
a working-class 'culture' in Cecil Sharp's sense – indeed, as
he points out, his Laurel Country community is only an
isolated example of the old English rural culture – and it can
also be shown that working-class men could have access if
they chose to seek it (and many did) to the best 'Culture' (in
Mrs Williams-Ellis's sense) of their time and nation, until
this generation.
We have abundant evidence to this effect. Is it possible

that Mrs Williams-Ellis has not even read the well-known Chartist document *The Life and Struggles of William Lovett in his Pursuit of Bread, Knowledge and Freedom*,[22] a document so completely representative that, happening to have followed up an interest in this question of working-class culture, I could cite a large number of close parallels covering over a century and a half in time and most of England and Lowland Scotland in space.

Their implications in sum form an indisputable case against Mrs Williams-Ellis. They could mostly say with J. D. Burn (born 1820): 'Like a large number of my own class I was born in poverty, nursed in sorrow, and reared in difficulties, hardships and privations', but neither that, nor the dawn-to-dusk working hours nor the generally miserable wages could check their tremendous vitality of spirit. Here is a significant passage from Lovett's autobiography:

That which first stimulated me to intellectual inquiry, and which laid the foundation of what little knowledge I possess, was my being introduced to a small literary association entitled 'The Liberals', which met in Gerard Street, Newport Market. It was composed chiefly of working men, who paid a small weekly subscription towards the formation of a select library of books for circulation among one another. They met together, if I remember rightly, on two evenings in the week, on one of which occasions they had generally some question for discussion, either literary, political or metaphysical . . . Seeing that their library contained the works of Paley and other authors that I had often heard cited from the pulpit as the great champions of Christianity, I felt an ardent wish to read and study them . . . I now became seized with an enthusiastic desire to read and treasure up all I could meet with on the subject of Christianity . . . and often have I sat up till morning dawned reading and preparing myself with arguments in support of its principles. Political questions being also often discussed in our association caused me to turn my attention to political works, and eventually to take a great interest in the parliamentary debates and questions of the day. In short, my mind seemed to be awakened to a new mental existence; new feelings, hopes and aspirations sprang up within me, and every spare moment was devoted to the acquisition of some kind of useful knowledge. I now joined several other associations in its pursuit, and for a number of years seldom took a meal without a book of some description beside me . . . I commenced also about this time the collection of a small library of my own, the shelves of which were often supplied by cheating the stomach with bread and cheese dinners.

This surely sounds like a civilized version of the barren 'educational' course pursued by the Russian factory workers of *We Have Been Warned* and regarded respectfully by Mrs Mitchison ('Maria showed them proudly her pile of books, an algebra book with the page doubled down at the beginning of quadratic equations, one on elementary physics, several copy-books half-full of what might have been essays, and three text-books of economics or Marxist history').

There is not merely the widespread autobiographical evidence of this kind and biographical evidence such as that collected for example by the maligned Samuel Smiles in his *Lives of the Engineers, Industrial Biographies*, etc. There is the tremendous surge of working-class aspiration[23] of which the Mechanics Institutes and working men's societies for 'self-elevation', 'self-improvement', etc., in the earlier half of the nineteenth century were only surface indications. The minutes of evidence taken before the Select Committee on Public Libraries in 1849, with reference to the whole country, are highly suggestive of the extent of the political consciousness and serious reading common to the poorest of what was then called 'the industrious class'. Chartism was a wave of cultural as well as political aspiration (for the way in which Chartist meetings and activities inextricably mingled political with literary enthusiasm see, for instance, *The Life of Thomas Cooper. Written by Himself*); and that progress from an awakening through religious (or atheistic) enthusiasm to political consciousness and general self-culture which is illustrated from Lovett above, is a pattern that can be traced in the lives of large numbers of the articulate members of the working class long before Chartism was thought of. It occurs equally among the agricultural and the industrial workers, and it is completely independent of formal instruction. (A useful survey of some of the facts of this matter is contained in A. E. Dobb's *Education and Social Movements* (1919).)

I do not see how you can avoid the conclusion that these people got their personal culture from each other (each case-history of course implies a whole background or *milieu*) – that is, from a common stock which constituted a traditional culture and which had the important virtue of including that 'culture' dependent on 'works of art and science' which is conceived by Mrs Williams-Ellis as possible only to the leisured class.[24]

This traditional culture has, moreover, profoundly affected the culture that is expressed in literature, indeed it would be truer to say that the latter has always depended largely on the former. It is not merely that we have such solitary monoliths as *Pilgrim's Progress*, for instance, standing up here and there throughout our literary history; there is the English language itself, the most powerful testimony poss-ible to the existence of that culture rooted in the lives of the workers, and perpetually renewed from them.[25]

This traditional culture is not easy to define or even describe briefly – it needs at least an anthology to illustrate it – but summarily it can be said to consist of two elements, participation in the national culture (chiefly through Shake-speare, Bunyan, the Authorised Version, and later on Dickens) and another participation that is manifested as a quality of character. The second point brings up another question, a betraying passage from *We Have Been Warned* (the heroine is talking with her husband):

> 'Mrs Grove is dead. In childbirth.'
> 'Oh, lord. Is he fearfully cut up about it, poor chap?'
> 'I don't know. They're all so matter of fact. They make me feel as if I was another race, full of elaborate hot-house, high-brow feel-ings. Are we as bad as that?'
> 'The Two Worlds. People like you have been bothered about that for the last hundred years. Yes, a lot of our fine feelings are just a very unimportant by-product of too much money. That's why I can't stand all these novels and poems about them.'

Far from being highbrow, this recalls a familiar lowbrow attitude (compare Warwick Deeping and 'Sapper'). How-ever, we may take it that in spite of a confused desire to have it both ways Mrs Mitchison wishes to assert that the working class lack the 'finer' feelings of her own class and that this is a mark of superiority because it comes from closer contact with reality, that (a) workers cannot afford to have 'fine' feel-ings and (b) therefore a system of values which excludes 'fine' feelings is the most desirable. Her account of the Soviet state is a logical conclusion from this argument; such a day-dream must occur inevitably to writers in this position so that though it corresponds with Mrs Williams-Ellis's account of Russia one would not be surprised to learn that it has no more basis in actuality than the Noble Savage convention of a previous age.

But to anyone with first-hand knowledge it will seem that Mrs Mitchison is doing a gross injustice to the respectable poor of her country. There is fortunately more convincing evidence to this effect than one's personal observation. Such a collection as that published by the Hogarth Press in 1931 under the title *Life As We Have Known It* shows the uneducated worker to be capable of no less subtle and perhaps more impressive kinds of feeling than some authors of propaganda on their behalf. These letters from Co-operative working women to a General Secretary of the Co-operative Guild are the better evidence for not having been written for publication (punctuation and spelling have presumably been regularized). The impression left by these women is very different from that left on one by the workers, selected to secure sympathy, in the novels under discussion. The quality of the working-class character is conveyed in concrete instances, so that Mrs Woolf, in an acute and sensitive introductory letter, rightly characterizes it as 'stimulating', 'not downtrodden, envious and exhausted; they are humorous and vigorous and strongly independent'. So George Sturt noticed in his cottage neighbours a remarkable spiritual temper:

To some extent doubtless it rests on Christian teaching, although perhaps not much on the Christian teaching of the present day. Present-day religion, indeed, must often seem to the cottagers a tiresome hobby reserved to the well-to-do; but from distant generations there seems to have come down, in many a cottage family, a rather lofty religious sentiment which fosters honesty, patience, resignation, courage. Much of the gravity, much of the tranquillity of soul of the more sedate villagers must be ascribed to this traditional influence, whose effects are attractive enough, in the character and outlook of many an old cottage man and woman . . . It is not a negative quality . . . in the main the force which bears them on is a traditional outlook . . . in the little cottages the people, from earliest infancy, were accustomed to hear all things – persons and manners, houses and gardens, and the day's work – appraised by an ancient standard of the countryside.[26]

Absence of such sensitive reaction to the character of their material is responsible to a great extent for the failure of these novels as propaganda. Raw facts are invariably more moving than when similar situations are worked up into their fictions. Here for example is the fiction:

The guide led them along the corridor to the great hall, with the benches and flags and the dais with the picture above it. This was rather magnificent, Dione thought, beginning to wake up more thoroughly, this light, this white and scarlet and unpainted wood, and the great low-brow picture of Lenin! . . . Dione found herself pressed against Donald, and he was whispering: 'He was here, Lenin was here; oh, Dione, we were not here helping him!'

[*We Have Been Warned*]

Here is the fact:

Occasionally working men in distant parts of the country who had heard Crooks speak or watched his public work would send in their mite, generally anonymous. One such contribution sent during the Woolwich by-election, consisted of four penny stamps, stuck on a torn piece of dirty paper, on which were written the words:

Will you please except four stamps towards the expens of will Crooks election and may god bless him in being successful in winning the seat for Labour.

from a working man.

[*From Workhouse to Westminster. The Life Story of Will Crooks, M.P.*, by George Haw, 1911]

This is fiction:

She paid a visit to ex-Councillor Finch's elder daughter Dorothy, who was married and living down there – and on the Means Test. She was a jolly, intelligent girl, with a young baby. When Dione came in she apologised for the smell – Dione had always hoped you didn't notice it if you lived there – saying it usedn't to be so bad, but they'd had to sell the lino off the floor and now there was nothing but the bare quarries, much worn from earlier tenants. 'I scrub and scrub', the girl said, 'but I can't seem to get the smell away. The suds go down the cracks between the quarries, Mrs Galton; they aren't properly mortared in, and there isn't any foundations, like. And there's always a draught under the door, and they're that cold to walk on. And now there's the beetles. If we'd known how it would be, Bill and me wouldn't never have got married, but he thought he'd got a steady job – he'd been four years at the Synthex works – and now there's the baby and I don't know how ever I shall manage!'

She began to cry bitterly, seeing it all as she said it, and Dione sat beside her and petted her, and by and by asked a few leading questions. There was one practical thing to be done: the next day she and Dorothy went over to the Sallington birth-control clinic ...

[*We Have Been Warned*]

This is fact:

When I got better, I went to work at Christie's Hat Works in a lovely room, six stories up, with big windows and a splendid view of the hills. We had to be at work by 7 a.m., and you could see the day break over the hills, and they are always such a comfort and help ... We were working hard all day, bringing work home and working until eight or nine o'clock at nights for 13/- or 15/- per week, so I left and went to work at Lees and Hatconk's. I wish you could have seen that workroom. It had been built for a warehouse, thick glass windows and a tank of water on the roof which leaked. The room was low, and when the lights were lit it was awful, damp streaming down the walls. Still we had some good times. I worked with a Conservative, an Irish girl, and some Radicals and Socialists, and we used to have full-dress debates. When we began someone would call 'Parliament is now sitting' (this is thirty years ago), and we would discuss everything. I remember once, after I was married, the Irish girl came one Monday and said: 'Nellie, the priest said last night all married people who had no children would go to hell', and I retorted: 'I should think I deserved to go to hell if I had brought some of the children into the world I have seen' ... I always remember going down a street lined with great mills on either side and hoping I should never have to bring a child into the world if it was condemned to that life, for I reasoned: If I were asked to work in one of these mills (for I hate machinery) I should hate it, and I have no right to bring anyone else if this is all we can offer it, because I should love it too much to give it such a life.

[*Life As We Have Known It*, 'A Felt Hat Worker']

Such comparisons might be multiplied. It is not merely that these novelists evidently have no first-hand experience of the kind of life and the kind of feelings they are trying to reproduce; it is often the artist's business to communicate what he may have experienced in imagination only. There is

of course the absence of that knowledge which forms the
basis of imaginative insight, so that when Mrs Williams-Ellis
wishes for instance to present a well-known type of working-
class housewife she has to do so in such poor terms as 'Mum's
keen on the Co-op', leaving it to the reader to provide for
himself such a background as:

The house we lived in during our early married life was 5/- per
week. In those days I made 18/6 per week, and kept the house going
after my rent was deducted. I had my family quickly, and my
dividend helped me over these times, and paid the doctor's bill. In
fact I do not know how I could have managed without it, as I have
always been determined to keep free of debt

and:

I attended the Guild Annual Meeting, which was a revelation. I had
longings and aspirations and a vague idea of power within myself
which had never had an opportunity of realisation. At the close of
the Meetings I felt as I imagine a War Horse must feel when he
hears the beat of the drums.
    [*Life As We Have Known It*, Extracts from Guildswomen's Letters]

What seems really disabling to the impartial reader, who
may have left-wing sympathies to begin with, is the attitude
of these novelists to their material, and it is the accent with
which they write that sounds so fatally wrong in one's ear. I
do not mean merely that Mrs Mitchison, for instance, as is
obvious from the extracts above, smears everything she
handles with a nauseating brand of sentimentality, so that
Revolutionary feeling is for her bound up with an incessant
kissing and pawing between and among the sexes (her
Utopia is open to the objection that Saintsbury or someone
made to Browning's idea of Heaven, that it is a place where
everyone sits on everyone else's lap). There is something far
more radically wrong. In neither of these novelists can one
find any trace of humility. To most of us, it may be assumed,
a woman who has brought up several children decently and
kept a family sound and united on anything less than sixty
shillings a week is an object of profound respect – for a variety
of reasons, such as that her life represents a daily triumph
over harsh circumstances and that she shares the quality
common to a class, a quality to which Mrs Woolf, an artist,
reacted readily. To Mrs Williams-Ellis, however, she seems

to be no more than a symbol of capitalist exploitation, while to Mrs Mitchison she only means reflections of the 'How horrible to have to live in such poky little rooms . . . Silly of her not to have found out about contraception' type. To both, as to *Punch*, she is a member of an alien order whose speech requires the forbearance of a conventional spelling or idiom and is lacking in the finer articulateness of the public-school class. Mrs Woolf, at the Congress of the Women's Co-operative Guild, was moved to reflect, 'How many words must lurk in those women's vocabularies that have faded from ours! What images and saws and proverbial sayings must still be current with them that have never reached the surface of print, and very likely they still keep the power which we have lost of making new ones.' The power of D. H. Lawrence's writings is not merely that of genius; or, rather, the individual genius drew power from a rich environment – from that culture which Mrs Williams-Ellis denies the English worker to have possessed. Neither Mrs Mitchison nor Mrs Williams-Ellis has taken the trouble to acquaint herself with this aspect of working-class culture and character.

But if left-wing novelists do not concern themselves fundamentally with the nature of the working-class culture, they can do no more for their cause than the statistician; and if, in obedience to the ideology of a political party, they deny that such a culture has ever existed, they are helping to deprive the English workers of the cultural heritage which their ancestors heroically earned. Because, thanks to such disruptive forces as the loudspeaker, the cinema and the Press, that culture is threatened with extinction; it is chiefly among the older generation that the tradition survives. It is not yet true, as Mrs Williams-Ellis asserts, that the English worker is culturally in the position of the Russian worker at the time of the Revolution, it will not be true until the memory of that tradition dies out, and it is therefore important that the memory should be kept alive. That is why it seems to some of us that such novelists are, as I have said, not doing the workers a service. When you look back at this working-class tradition and bear in mind Cecil Sharp's observation about the 'supreme cultural value of an inherited tradition', it seems a pity to throw that away on the chance of something more satisfactory emerging from such a social order and such

values as are implicit in Mrs Mitchison's 'Under the Red
Flag'. The English working-class culture was based upon the
family and transmitted by it; in the community desiderated
by these novelists the interests of the adults are monopolized
by machine-tending and machine-designing: the young are
handed over to the State as soon after birth as practicable.

To deny the workers values as civilized as those you yourself possess is a preliminary to thrusting your own upon
them. So Mrs Mitchison wants for them the joys of the
Bloomsbury studio party and Mrs Williams-Ellis wants them
to have high-powered cars and both want for them the right
to be promiscuous without inhibitions. Whether these and
what they symbolize are the kind of satisfactions the solider
element of the English working class have wanted up till now
is another matter. Even Mrs Mitchison confesses to some dis-
couragement in this respect:

Every now and then she would come up sharply against something
very trying, most often among the women – a kind of idea that the
new millennium would mean more and better Co-ops, everyone
with a five-roomed house and vegetable garden of their own and
earning £5 a week. She went round one evening and talked to
Reuben Goldberg about it. He was gloomy: 'There's not ten per
cent of the Labour Party here who're class-conscious', he said. 'I
don't mind telling you I had a look at the I.L.P., but half of them are
no better.'   [*We Have Been Warned*, p. 390]

Put like this however it does not perhaps impress as the
utterly contemptible and unworthy aspiration that Mrs
Mitchison implies:

At the time my fifth boy was born, my husband was having 26/6 a
week to keep us all, and no children at work. I have seen the day
when my white tablecloth and clean empty pots were waiting for
father to bring his wages, before we could have something to eat, for
I would not go to a little shop as I got better value for my money at
the Co-operative Society, and there was something at the end of the
quarter for clothes. I was feeling myself after my eldest boy began
to work for 5/- per week. When the next came to work for another
5/-, and the next went out with newspapers, while the fourth boy,
only young, delivered milk, I began to get on my feet, and with
making all their clothes it was a great help. It was then I determined
to let them have music lessons in their turn. I am glad to think now

that we did our best for our children. I have gone without my dinner
for their sakes, and just had a cup of tea and bread and butter.

Our idea for our children was to give them the best education,
a trade and music, that we could afford, so that they would grow up
to be clean, honest and truthful, and to go straight in life and
become good citizens. Each boy as he became 14 years of age, was
put to a trade of his own choosing. Between the father and the five
boys we had almost every musical instrument there was, excelling
in trombone, piano and violin. Reggie was an excellent violinist,
having passed many exams . . . There was the Women's Co-
operative Guild, to which I owe a great deal for my education . . . I
joined the Suffrage, because having had such a hard and difficult
life myself, I thought I would do all I could to relieve the sufferings
of others.   [*Life As We Have Known It*, 'A Plate-Layer's Wife']

It may be that the kind of family life implied in the second
of these extracts will have to go and even that it is desirable
that it should go; certainly I wish to make it clear that I am
not trying to justify, on the ground that they thus made possible something admirable, the economic conditions which
have made the lives of a large section of the community a
bitter struggle. I only wish to suggest that the spiritual
temper of the second extract is so much finer than that of the
first that it exposes the 'advanced' writer's attitude, in its
obtuseness and uncomprehending ignorance, as impertinent. The ideals and beliefs of a whole group of people with
extreme left-wing opinions seem to lay themselves open to
this charge, nor do they appear to have anything more worthy
to offer in place of what they are so complacently ready to
sweep away.

From this point of view the attitude of such writers to the
working class is seen to be in effect that of Hannah More,
even though her 'Stories for Persons in the Middle Ranks'
and 'Tales for the Common People' were written with an
opposite intention. The workers received decidedly more
intelligent treatment at the hands of Mrs Gaskell, and one
can perhaps see why by inspecting the second chapter of her
Life of Charlotte Brontë; that character of the people of Haworth
is a remarkable document to have emanated from the pen of a
lady. It looks as though being a lady was not always and
necessarily disabling. Nor being a gentleman; the exact
antithesis of the attitude to the working class that I have been

considering is provided by Cecil Sharp. With no political or even cultural axe to grind, starting only from the musician's respect for the quality of the folksongs he devoted his leisure to collecting, he was led to extend his respect to the folk-singers and all that they stood for. The process is recorded in his *English Folk-Song: Some Conclusions* (1907). He was eventually able to produce evidence of a whole popular culture that but for him would have disappeared from the life of England without leaving traces by which even the archaeologist could piece it together. His virtues seem to have been threefold: he was completely unsentimental, he was intelligent enough to perceive that all cultural questions involve complex issues, and, as his singers are known to have observed, he was 'so common'.

Notes

'That great controversy': the novel of religious controversy

1 Margaret Mary Maison, in a monograph, *Search Your Soul, Eustace* (1961), published by Sheed and Ward and long out of print, gave a brief survey of the field, but scarcely touched on the major achievements, writing in a spirit of lighthearted journalism.

2 Addison had early deplored 'enthusiasm' in *The Spectator* as potentially dangerous, and Lord Chesterfield later advised his godson that religion should not be discussed in company but left to specialists in private: 'Therefore never mingle yourself in it any further than to express an universal toleration and indulgence to all errors in it, if conscientiously entertained: for, every man has as good a right to think as he does, as you have to think as you do; nay, in truth, he cannot help it.' Chesterfield was of course a Whig, and tolerance was their party line; but no one can deny that the reasons he gives his godson for the principle of toleration in religion is rightly and indeed nobly expressed, and was the only means of keeping the social peace, then or since. But it became an impossibility for Victorians, and indeed they in general rejected such an ideal. (John Stuart Mill was the product of a pre-Victorian ethos.) Even apparent toleration was not systematic or on principle – for example, Dr Arnold and Pusey, though in favour of Catholic Emancipation, were hotly opposed to 'removing' Jewish disabilities; Lord Shaftesbury, in many ways a noble character, showed shocking animus and lack of principle (other than Evangelical *parti pris*) in other respects.

3 This was at least true enough for Cardinals Wiseman and Manning to think it necessary to prevent Catholics from going to English universities long after they had been opened to Catholics.

4 Dissenters and Evangelicals had so much in common that one stereotype generally served for both in novels of entertainment.

5 *Thatched With Gold, the Memoirs of Mabell, Countess of Airlie.*

6 Nothing adverse can really be deduced from this. Many Anglican memoirs show the author in Victorian childhood (even Thomas Hardy) dressing-up to act parson taking service and giving an extemporized

sermon, as voluntary play, and the large family of W. G. Ward, brought
up on the assumption that the boys of the family would be priests and
the girls nuns, were so conditioned that

> The imitative instinct which leads many boys and girls to play at
> being soldiers, or sailors, or gypsies, or fairies, led us to play at
> being priests and nuns, and this most elaborately and systemati-
> cally. It was so systematic that it was hardly 'playing' and had in
> it an element of seriousness. There was nothing histrionic in all
> this and there was hardly ever an outsider present. It was all
> undertaken with the lively encouragement of Fr Herbert
> Vaughan and of my mother.
>
> (Wilfred Ward, *Reminiscences, 1856–1867*)

7 The Rev. Sydney Smith, formed in pre-Evangelical days, after visiting
an Evangelical family, said he had tried in vain to give them 'more
cheerful ideas of religion', 'to teach them that God is best served by a
regular tenour of good actions – not by eternal apprehensions'. 'Cheerfulness' in religion was the first casualty of Evangelical zeal as a general
thing. Yet Shaftesbury's young relatives testified to the jollity of his
home.

8 By G. I. T. Machin, in *The Catholic Question in English Politics 1820 to 1830*
(1964). 'The Catholic question', wrote the Bishop of Oxford to Peel in
1827, 'is mixed up with everything we eat or drink or say or think',
which might have been repeated by any English bishop at the date, less
than twenty years later, when Newman seceded to Rome and started a
landslide.

9 It was a regular Victorian practice to choose a suitable historical period
or situation onto which the problems of his own day that the novelist
wished to treat could be projected; making a fallacious parallel with the
present, and allowing the novelist to express views he could not comfortably state as criticism of his contemporaries. Bulwer Lytton seems
to have been early in the field employing this technique: *The Last of the
Barons* (1843) and *Harold, or The Last of the Saxon Kings* (1848), the best of
his 'historical' novels, are really about the political parties and situations of his own time. Cf. also Kingsley's *Hypatia* and *Westward Ho!*
(blows struck against Catholicism and monks), and the Oxford Movement threw out some ephemeral examples of the *genre*. *Esmond* may be
said to belong in this category too.

10 Mrs H. Ward, in her autobiography *A Writer's Recollections*, says her
mother's family had a tradition that they were French Huguenots
expelled in 1685 and had settled in England, and that

> one of its original elements which certainly survived in her
> temperament and tradition was of great importance both for her

own life and for her children's. This was the Protestant – the
French Protestant element; which no doubt represented in the
family from which she came, a history of long suffering at the
hands of Catholicism [and a tradition of an ancestor who had]
abandoned his country and kinsfolk, in the search for religious
liberty.

11 Including Mark Twain in *A Tramp Abroad*, and Mr Gladstone, who had
at Naples seen 'the religious and Catholic conception of government',
which historians tell us left him for life with a humour that produced in
him his later hatred of ultramontanism.

12 Richard Whately was a power at Oxford in his day for good, both anti-
Evangelical and anti-Catholic. To his credit he supported Catholic
Emancipation, however, and also the claim of the Jews to exemption
from the parliamentary oath. The friend of Hampden, whom he had
recommended for the chair of divinity, he was necessarily opposed to
Newman, the rival candidate, on this as well as all other grounds; he
supported Graham by publishing a paper attacking the High Church
view of baptism, and he considered Apostolic succession an undesirable assumption; in fact he was Protestant in the best sense, and was a
stout ally of those opposing the divisive Catholicizing tendencies of
Oxford and all other extremes, such as Calvinism. He was of course,
being born in 1787, pre-Victorian in his formative period, hence his
un-Victorian virtues.

13 Gwen Raverat, *Period Piece* (1954).

14 *Some Early Impressions* (1924).

15 Trollope, who had of course noticed this English disease, thought it a
joke. In *Doctor Thorne* the enthusiastically High Church young parson is
described as 'delighting in all the paraphernalia of Anglican formalities
which have given such offence to those of our brethren who live in daily
fear of the Scarlet Lady. Many of his friends declared that Mr Oriel
would sooner or later deliver himself over body and soul to that lady.
But Mr Oriel remained in the arms of the Church of England'. Though
the Oxford Movement caused so many conversions, yet the new
Anglicanism acted in many cases as vaccination against Rome. Mrs
Oliphant in *The Perpetual Curate* (1863–4) noted with amusement a new
type of High Churchman, her hero, who 'was as near Rome as a strong
and lofty conviction of the really superior catholicity of the Anglican
church would permit him to be.' Though his brother the Rev. Gerald
Wentworth converts to Rome after agonies of torment, the Perpetual
Curate has no difficulty in rejecting his brother's arguments and
equally resists his Evangelical aunt's pressure in the direction of an
inflamed Protestantism.

16 Built by funds provided secretly by Pusey and whose clergy he had

chosen himself. The first vicar, the Rev. Richard Ward, had previously gone over to Rome.

17 Hence Spooner's witticism when someone said he had heard there was a secret passage under St Giles, leading from the Jesuit house (Campion Hill) to Pusey House; 'Spooner answered, "There may be, but *it leads the other way*." ' E. L. Woodward, *Short Journey: An Auto-biography* (1942).

18 *The Perpetual Curate* (1864).

19 Sydney Smith drew the line at Methodist missionaries in the East for their interference with the natives; and in later days referred with scorn to 'Newmania', while Puseyism and ritualism he described as 'posture and imposture'. But these are the imperfect sympathies inevitable in one who had what Greville thought 'the true religion'. His tongue was perhaps too sharp for a good Christian, as when he said: 'I must believe in Apostolic Succession, there being no other way of accounting for the descent of the Bishop of Exeter from Judas Iscariot.' It was owing to such remarks, as well as to his outspoken liberalism, that he never rose higher than to be Canon of St Paul's, the Whig government not daring to make him a bishop in Victorian England.

20 The battling Bishop of Exeter had had public rows with his dean and chapter, though not on the same grounds as those at 'Barchester'.

21 Mary Paley Marshall, *What I Remember* (1947).

22 Carleton's *Traits and Stories of the Irish Peasantry*.

23 Disraeli in 1844 said: 'A starving people, an alien church, and an absentee aristocracy is the Irish question.' He wished, like Sydney Smith, that the Roman Catholic Church should be established in Ireland as a solution. Pusey held that the state could not be allowed to interfere with the Church of Ireland by reducing the number of bishoprics and diverting their funds to the support of Catholic education and the priesthood, and he campaigned against such reform.

24 The Tithe War, which features in many Irish novels, was over by Victoria's reign, as it lasted from 1830–7, but it formed part of the Irish anti-English history and frustrations.

25 Cf. the Irishman 'who will recant the errors of Popery, and embrace those of Protestantism'.

The Anglo-Irish novel

1 Mark D. Hawthorne, *John and Michael Banim (the O'Hara Brothers): A Study of the Early Development of the Anglo-Irish Novel*, Salzburg, 1975.

2 Originally published in the *National Magazine*, 1831.

Mrs Oliphant

1 Chatto and Windus, 1969.
2 He does of course figure in *Framley Parsonage* (1861) but oddly enough he is always described there as the incumbent of Hogglestock Parsonage and never as the perpetual curate, which he is throughout the later novel, *The Last Chronicle of Barset*.
3 *Autobiography and Letters*, Leicester University Press, 1974.
4 E.g. a derogatory account of Mrs Oliphant and her novels, explicitly derived from *The Equivocal Virtue*, is confidently given by Gordon S. Haight in his life of George Eliot.
5 This book tells us a good deal about her career that is not in the *Autobiography* and should be consulted accordingly.

Professor Chadwick and English studies

1 *The Teaching of English in England*, H.M. Stationery Office, 1921.

Reviews

1 It seems that in self-protection we should point out that *Scrutiny* critics come from all kinds of social and religious backgrounds, and that we have repeatedly published contributions from at least four Roman Catholic critics. It would be interesting to know whether these could be picked out on internal evidence alone, and if Bro. George Every could indicate exactly in what way he thinks their criticism of, say, *Le Misanthrope*, *As You Like It* and other Shakespeare plays could be improved by the addition in some way of theology.
2 There is a quotable instance, in one of her most esteemed novels, that localizes the general effect described above. A small child decorating the room with holly has climbed on a chair by the fire, forgetting this was forbidden, and a moral and emotional scene at the child's expense is staged on the subject of transgression, ending with the curate's reporting with emotion:

> Wilmet recommended not taking the prize prayer-book to church [as punishment], and she acquiesced with tears in her eyes. A good child's repentance is a beautiful thing –
>
> O happy in repentance' school
> So early taught and tried.   (*The Pillars of the House*)

The determination of the educated that a secular school system should take children out of the clutches of the religious is understandable.
3 *Theology*, September 1940.

4 E.g. in 1883 he remarked of Mark Twain 'Why don't people understand that Mark Twain is not merely a great humourist? He's a very remarkable fellow in a very different way' and specified *Life on the Mississippi*. His notebooks, quoted by Florence Hardy in the two volumes of her husband's life, show a constant preoccupation with the theory and practice of novel-writing, and a very critical response to reviews of his works.

5 I should perhaps in fairness add that the *Times Literary Supplement* however describes *Hardy the Novelist* as 'criticism of the first rank', 'a wise and gracious book'.

6 One contributor to the *Southern Review* remarks that he wouldn't have known Hardy to be a great novelist if he hadn't been told.

7 Someone ought to register a protest against this kind of vulgarity, from which no dead writer seems to be safe. Posterity will think the twentieth-century *literati* had no spiritual manners. Jefferies has been one of the worst sufferers – cf. Guy N. Pocock's introduction to the Everyman *Bevis* and the last life, an indefensible piece of book-making by Reginald Arkell, *Richard Jefferies* (Rich and Cowan, 1933).

8 Though not all – there are two good long selections from *Amaryllis at the Fair* which ought to send people to the novel.

9 See Thomas's Life and Bibliography.

10 'Dearly as I love the open air, I cannot regret the mediaeval days. I do not wish them back again, I would sooner fight in the foremost ranks of Time.' – 'Outside London'.

11 No selection from it is given in either anthology but it is fortunately still in print in the New Readers Library and should make a popular classroom text.

12 Nothing from it is given by either editor. Jefferies requested the publisher not to give the MS. to a Tory reader, who would be certain to reject it. Jefferies refused help from the Royal Literary Fund, which might have prolonged his life, because 'he believed that the fund was maintained by dukes and marquises instead of authors and journalists.'

13 Here is an interesting passage from the posthumous 'Thoughts on the Labour Question': 'Then, for Heaven's sake, let us all have a fair chance: do not make its possession dependent upon morality, virtue, genius, personal stature, nobility of mind, self-sacrifice, or such rubbish.'

14 It seems to have begun to be as we know it in Gissing's time. Jasper Milvain differs from Alroy Kear (*Cakes and Ale*) only in being a simpler psychological study. Reviewing was much the same as now:

> The book met with rather severe treatment in critical columns; it could scarcely be ignored (the safest mode of attack when one's author has no expectant public) ...

> The struggle for existence among books is nowadays as severe as among men. If a writer has friends connected with the press, it is the plain duty of those friends to do their utmost to help him. What matter if they exaggerate, or even lie? The simple, sober truth has no chance whatever of being listened to, and it's only by volume of shouting that the ear of the public is held.

Conditions governing material success were taking modern shape:

> Literature nowadays is a trade. Putting aside men of genius, who may succeed by mere cosmic force, your successful man of letters is your skilful tradesman ... To have money is becoming of more and more importance in a literary career; principally because to have money is to have friends. Year by year, such influence grows of more account ... Men won't succeed in literature that they may get into society, but will get into society that they may succeed in literature.

15 Perhaps not merely a caricature, for we see in the *Life and Letters* of Dean Church that this is how he saw Arthur Stanley, of whom he wrote impatiently when Stanley had become Dean of Westminster: 'What is this nineteenth-century religion for which all things have been preparing, and to which all good things, past and present, are subservient and bear witness? ... He seems to me in the position of a prophet and leader, full of eagerness and enthusiasm and brilliant talent, all heightened by success – but without a creed to preach' and later, sadly, of his late friend's 'incapacity for the spiritual and unearthly side of religion' and his 'aversion to metaphysics and dogmatic statements' in a letter analysing Stanley after his death to the Warden of Keble in 1881. Stanley had married a Lady Augusta, achieved high position in the Church, influence with the royal family, and great social and popular esteem, without committing himself to Christianity as generally understood hitherto, and yet without cutting himself off from the conventional world. A more thoughtful and responsible type of cleric like the modest but devout Dean Church felt obliged to consider Stanley as the enemy in spite of an unbroken, if unenthusiastic, friendship with him. And as regards his view of science, the Rev. Bruce Chilvers seems to derive from the Rev. Charles Kingsley.

16 Reviewed in *Scrutiny*, vol. VIII, no. 1.

17 See the 'London Letter' by Raymond Mortimer in *The Dial*, March, 1928.

18 Cf. the experiences of an unimpeachable authority, the Oxford historian E. L. Woodward (Domestic Bursar of All Souls, History Tutor of New College, Proctor, etc.) in his recent autobiography, *Short Journey*: 'I thought of these things when the wife of an elderly don told my wife that it would be nice for me to learn "how the university was run". I am

bound to say that I thought it was not well run [c. 1930] and that I was
astonished at the incapacity of most of the members of the university
council and other bodies of administrative importance . . . The committee system was overdone', etc. He gives an instructive account of his
few attempts to effect reforms in University affairs. His chief failure
was an attempt to get a very obvious reform through – to persuade the
authorities to make suitable provision for a modern library instead of
the hopelessly congested and unsuitable Bodleian, which it was proposed to supplement by a mere bookstore in the heart of Oxford. He
found that all the powers were hostile, having been canvassed by the
old librarian, that he wasted a year of his time and energies in trying
unsuccessfully to interest likely people in the affair, and that all he and
his few supporters could achieve, beyond alienating all the elderly
scholars of his acquaintance and incurring a lot of ill will generally, was
a bad compromise (and even this was almost wrecked finally by the
efforts of the opposition and only saved by the Vice-Chancellor). 'We
might have planned, on an open site, with space for future expansion,
a building which would stand as a monument to our foresight and our
wisdom. And the whole business was botched, in the last resort,
because one obstinate old man had not given up his job as librarian at
the ordinary retiring age, and because no one had bothered to reform
the constitution of the board of curators of the library. *As for me, this
experience taught me a good deal about the lengths to which people will go merely to
keep things as they are* ' (my italics). It is hardly necessary to point out the
disastrous effects of such an environment on appointments committees, for example; or what rare courage and sense of duty must be
required in anyone who refuses to acquiesce in what is, however small
the occasion. Obviously such a state of affairs as that outlined in this
review can only exist if an innocent or cynical acquiescence in it by
everyone can be taken for granted; hence one of the resulting moral
obliquities is that it is not the existence of an undesirable situation, but
calling attention to it, which is considered offensive and earns censure
(to put these matters on record is the last crime, and in fact documents
like *Short Journey* and *Haddon the Head Hunter* don't often see the light). A
sociological expedition would have a fruitful yield if it undertook field-
research into the academic world. And it is a world – the other universities are very largely stocked from Oxford and Cambridge and moreover are closely connected with them by social filaments, so that to be
posted at one of these last is to be boycotted all round, the penalty of
the *mauvais sujet* which few dare risk incurring. Another relevant point
is that intellectual matters are hopelessly overlaid by social life; for
instance, the reasons for professorial and other appointments would
often repay investigation, as in general the extent to which intellectual
standards have in different places been stultified by social factors and

academic politics. Outside the sciences, careers founded solely on log-rolling and social contacts are not unknown, and keeping the right company is in many fields the best, if not the indispensable, means of advancement. There is a pretty general recognition that the further the subject is from being a science the less have real qualifications to do with appointments or influential position in the academic world of the humanities; this means that a great disparity commonly exists in such schools between what the body of academics recruited in this way has to offer, and the demands of their students, a situation producing dis-comfort or uglier manifestations of a sense of inferiority on the one side, and lasting resentment on the other. The sociology of the academic world is a sadly neglected subject.

19 Chiefly through the imposition of a substantial composition fee which entitles the undergraduate to attend a number of lecture courses authorized by the faculty. In practice it is levied on every under-graduate, even if he complains that the lectures in his subjects are unprofitable and he has not attended any of them (he still has the right to stay away at the older universities, though not at the modern ones). Thus he could hardly be expected to pay in addition separate fees for freelance courses of lectures. He must also attend and pay for tuition by a supervisor (Oxford, tutor) selected by his college; though his right to choose his supervisor would no doubt be theoretically granted if it occurred to him to claim it, to claim it often requires considerable moral courage, particularly if the college, when stimulated to the effect by a faculty representative, signifies disapproval of his choice. Thus as a supervisor also the freelance is debarred from competing with the regulars, so that anyone outside the ring can be starved out of the academic world. The composition fee means that the only real check of whether a lecture course is of value to those who pay for it – the size of the regular lecture-audience – can be disregarded; and that the good lecturers pay for the inadequate ones. It leads also to obvious abuses, such as repeating a course year after year, even if the substance has been published in book form or has been proved useless by non-attendance. These are real grievances which have been expressed by generations of undergraduates without effect. It is not unnatural that they should take more interest than the authorities in whether they are receiving value for their parents' money and their own time. In the last number of *Scrutiny* the review of Dr Löwe's book, *The Universities in Trans-formation*, quotes him as concluding: 'It may well be necessary first to educate a new generation of university teachers before real headway can be made [in the humanities]'. No doubt; and here and there perhaps they are being educated. The difficulty lies in getting them admitted into that closed circle where they should function; how does Dr Löwe propose to find them posts, since the system sketched here is

self-perpetuating and even the holes in it have now been blocked? Failing a holocaust of most of the existing personnel and radical alteration of the machinery in their hands, endowment seems the only hope. But Nuffields and Rockefellers endow only sciences.

20 The nearest thing to such a desirable kind of propaganda we have over here seems to be Storm Jameson's *The Mirror in Darkness*, of which the second and latest volume, *Love in Winter*, offers a marked contrast. *We Have Been Warned*. Miss Jameson too has set out to give a cross-section of contemporary society, and the comparison, most noticeable in such particular instances as their treatments of the election and the celebrities' party, is entirely in her favour. She shows how much can be done by observing and composing with nothing more showy than stubborn honesty, humility and sensitiveness that goes with solidity of character.

21 Cecil Sharp, *English Folk-Songs from the Southern Appalachians*. Introduction to the first edition, 1917.

22 1876, reprinted with an introduction by R. H. Tawney in 1920.

23 Typical of its period is the title page of *The Autobiography of an Artisan* (1847), which quotes 'More life and fuller 'tis we want', and bears a dedication 'To the Artisans and Labourers of England, Fellow-Workers in the Holy Cause of Self-Elevation, and the Friends of the Industry of England'.

24

... as foreigner observers recognized, the general intelligence of Englishmen was of a high standard. The speeches and writings of those whose business it was to make as direct an appeal as possible to the people are a proof. The shorthand version of the demagogue Thelwall's address to the famous Copenhagen Fields mob in 1795 is a straight-forward appeal to the understandings of his listeners. It is in vain to look in it for the foolish digressions, the cheap witticisms, the puerile anecdotes, with which a more modern orator would conciliate the impatience or pander to the ignorance of his audience. But the instance of Thelwell, who, experienced as he was in public speaking, could not make the people behave as he wished on this occasion, is not so good a one as that of Thomas Paine, who, although the prophet of a revolution which never took place, admittedly produced an enormous effect by his writings. His influence extended not only to the lowest grade of those able to read, but to large numbers who, although unable to read, were willing to listen to what was read to them. The last of his principal works, and the most influential, the *Rights of Man*, was far from being a revolutionary squib, filled with appeals to greed and class jealousy. It was a sober treatise upon the form of government best able to secure the persons and property of the people whom it represents.

A. F. Freemantle, *England in the Nineteenth Century, 1801–1805*

25 For illustration see Logan Pearsall Smith, 'Popular Speech' and 'English Idioms' in *Words and Idioms*.

26 George Bourne, *Change in the Village* (1912).